VOODOO WARRIORS

Dedication

Dedicated to all those who produced, flew and supported McDonnell Voodoo operations world-wide.

Any profits to the author will be donated to service charities.

VOODOO WARRIORS

The Story of the Voodoo McDonnell Fast-jets

Group Captain Nigel Walpole

OBE BA RAF

Pen & Sword

AVIATION

First published in Great Britain in 2007 by
PEN & SWORD AVIATION
an imprint of
Pen & Sword Books Limited
47 Church Street
Barnsley
S. Yorkshire
S70 2AS

ISBN 978 1 84415 414 2

A CIP catalogue record for this book
is available from the British Library.

Printed and bound in Singapore
By Kyodo Printing Co (Singapore) Pte Ltd

Pen & Sword Books Ltd incorporates the imprints of
Pen & Sword Aviation, Pen & Sword Maritime, Pen & Sword Military,
Wharncliffe Local History, Pen & Sword Select,
Pen & Sword Military Classics and Leo Cooper.

For a complete list of Pen & Sword titles please contact:
PEN & SWORD BOOKS LIMITED
47 Church Street, Barnsley, South Yorkshire, S70 2AS, England.
E-mail: enquiries@pen-and-sword.co.uk
Website: www.pen-and-sword.co.uk

CONTENTS

ACKNOWLEDGEMENTS

Voodoo Warriors could not have been written without many contributions in words and pictures from those who helped give birth to and nurture the aircraft, flew it and provided essential support on the ground throughout its life. Some were my friends, colleagues and acquaintances, others I have never met and sadly there are those who are no longer with us.

I offer special thanks to the McDonnell technical representatives and those in the public relations office, to Joseph D Caver and the staff of the United States Air Force Historical Research Agency at Maxwell AFB and to Robert F Dorr for helping with the facts, donating photographs and advising on their use. Then there were many others who also searched diligently for the facts or provided verification, adding anecdotes and photographs to humanise our story; they included Bob Archibald; Jack Bowland; Earl Butts; Doug Brittian; Al Brunstrom; Conrad Binyon; Steve 'Burgie' Burgeson; Bill Bernert; Kay Berry; Bill Baugh; Dick Campis; Brigadier General Robert Caudry; Jack & Mary Coghlan; Michael Cromie; Bob Case, John Clearwater; Brian Cluer, George Cowgill; Alan Curry; Howard Davis; Richard Doritty; Frank Dunn; Wilf Dobbin; Darryl Danner; Major General George Edwards; Don Elwood; Doug Gordon; Bob Gould; Evelyn Grubb; Dewey Hemphill; Dick Holm; Mike Hobbs; Major General Paul Hodges; Mike Hobbs; Norman Huggins; Jim Ifland; Don Karges; General Bill Kirk; Keith Kuester; Joe Kuhlmann; Martin Keenan; John Linihan; Chuck Lustig; Tish Lynn; Al Magazzine; David Mulinder; George Malton; Terry Mays; Jerry Miller; Mike Moore; Fred Muesegaes; Gene Morris; Larry Milberry; Jim Murphy; Howard Myli; Gordon Macadie; John Nevill; Chuck O'Connell; Joe O'Grady; Brigadier General Robin Olds; Carl Overstreet; Fred Paradie; Lou Picciano; Nick Pishvanov; Jules Plamondon; Marv Reed; Dick Reese; Harry Runge; John Roddick; Major General Jerry Rogers; Tom Saunders; Scotty Schoolfield; John Summers; Steve Pace; Ed Satterfield; Ray Scott; John Stants; Jim Tidwell; Ray Tiffault; Mike Tschida, 'Turbo' Tarling; John Turner; Dick Vaughters; Lister Vickrey; George Wehling; John Wheeler; Gwyn Williams; Burt Waltz; Joe Witt; Stuart Whalley; Don and Wynette Wolf; Dick Wood; Jimmy Wylie; Doug Yates. I do apologise if I have omitted others in this sincere appreciation.

Finally, I thank all those who commented so constructively on my drafts within their specialisations and, in particular, David Baron and my wife, Margreet, who waded through the final version in toto. This was indeed a team effort.

GLOSSARY

AAA	Anti-Aircraft Artillery		DMZ	Demilitarized Zone
AAM	Air-to-Air Missile		DO	Director of Operations
AAR	Air-to-Air Refuelling		DR	Dead Reckoning
AB	Air Base		ECCM	Electronic Counter Counter Measures
ABCCC	Airborne Battlefield Command & Control Centre		ECM	Electronic Countermeasures
AD	Air Division		EW	Electronic Warfare
ADC	Air Defence Command		FBS	Fighter Bomber Squadron
ADF	Automatic Direction Finder		FBW	Fighter Bomber Wing
ADIZ	Air Defence Identification Zone		FIS	Fighter Interceptor Squadron
ADVON	Advance Echelon		FITS	Fighter Interceptor Training Squadron
AFB	Air Force Base			
AFC	Air Force Cross		FOD	Foreign Object Damage
AFM	Air Force Manual		FOL	Forward Operating Location
AI	Aircraft Identification		'G'	Gravity (force)
AMC	Air Materiel Command		GCA	Ground Control Approach
AMS	Avionics Maintenance Squadron		GCI	Ground Control Interception
ANG	Air National Guard		GPI	Ground Position Indicator
ARDC	Aircraft Research & Development Centre		HE	High Explosive
			HF	High Frequency
ASOC	Air Support Operations Centre		HOJ	Home-on Jamming
AW	All Weather		ICC	International Control Commission
AW(F)	All Weather Fighter			
BDA	Bomb Damage Assessment		IFF	Identification, Friend or Foe
BOQ	Bachelor Officers Quarters		IFR	Instrument Flight Rules
BX	Base Exchange		IGB	Inner German Border
C3	Command, Control & Communications		IMC	Image Motion Compensation
			IP	Initial Point
CAF	Canadian Armed Forces		IPIR	Immediate Photo Interpretation Report
CAP	Combat Air Patrol			
CAS	Close Air Support		IR	Infra Red
CASF	Consolidated Air Strike Force		ITB	Invitation to Bid
CCTG	Combat Crew Training Group		JATO	Jet Assisted Take-off
CCTS	Combat Crew Training Squadron		JCS	Joint Chiefs of Staff
			KIA	Killed in Action
CF	Canadian Forces		LABS	Low Altitude Bombing System
CFB	Canadian Forces Base		LADD	Low Angle Drogue Delivery
CIA	Central Intelligence Agency		MACV	Military Assistance Command Vietnam
CINCPAC	C-in-C Pacific Air Command			
CRS	Consolidated Reconnaissance Squadron		MAG	Military Advisory Group
			MAGTHAI	Military Aid Group Thailand
CRU	Composite Reconnaissance Unit		MDC	McDonnell Aircraft Corporation
DEFCON	Defence Condition			
DFC	Distinguished Flying Cross		MIA	Missing in Action

MOB	Main Operating Base
MRBM	Medium Range Ballistic Missiles
NASA	National Aeronautics and Space Administration
NATO	North Atlantic Treaty Organisation
NBC	Nuclear, Bacteriological and Chemical
NORAD	North American Air Defense
NOTAM	Notification to Airmen
NVA	North Vietnamese Army
NVNAF	North Vietnamese Air Force
OMS	Organisational Maintenance Squadron
ORI	Operational Readiness Inspection
OTU	Operational Training Unit
PACAF	Pacific Air Forces
PCS	Permanent Change of Station
PDJ	Plain des Jars
PI	Photographic Interpreter
POL	Petrol, Oil and Lubricants
POW	Prisoner of War
PPC	Photographic Processing Cell
PPIF	Photo Processing, Printing & Interpretation Facility
PRF	Pulse Recurrence Frequency
QRA	Quick Reaction Alert
R & R	Rest and Recuperation
RCAF	Royal Canadian Air Force
RHAW	Radar Homing and Warning Receiver
RITS	Reconnaissance Intelligence Training Squadron
RO	Radar Observer
RP	Route Pack
RTAF	Royal Thai Air Force
RTS	Reconnaissance Technical Squadron
RWR	Radar Warning Receiver
SAC	Strategic Air Command
SAGE	Semi Automatic Ground Environment
SAM	Surface to Air Missile
SEA	South East Asia

SEATO	South East Asia Treaty Organisation
SFW	Strategic Fighter Wing
TAC	Tactical Air Command
TACAN	Tactical Air Navigation
TACEVAL	Tactical Evaluation
TARC	Tactical Air Reconnaissance Center
TDY	Temporary Duty
TEWTS	Tactical Electronic Warfare Training Squadron
TFW	Tactical Fighter Wing
TOT	Time Over Target
TRS	Tactical Reconnaissance Squadron
TRTS	Tactical Reconnaissance Training Squadron
TRW	Tactical Reconnaissance Wing
UHF	Ultra High Frequency
USAAF	United States Army Air Force
USAFE	USAF Europe
USMAG	US Military Advisory Group
VFR	Visual Flight Rules
VNAF	Vietnamese Air Force
VOQ	Visiting Officers Quarters

FOREWORD

BY MAJOR GENERAL PAUL H HODGES USAF RET'D

I was serving in an RF-84F Thunderflash tactical reconnaissance squadron at Sembach Air Base, Germany, when the mighty RF-101 Voodoo entered the NATO arena in Europe in 1958. Supersonic fighters were not new to us there but this was an aircraft with enormous power and great range, primarily for use in daytime photo reconnaissance. The Voodoo, contrary to popular belief, was not a difficult aircraft to fly and the pitch-up regime was easily avoided. Our transition into the aircraft went so well that within months we were taking part in the international reconnaissance competition, Royal Flush. The F-101 nuclear delivery fighter bomber and F-101B interceptor were versions coming on line in a similar timeframe, and they are not neglected in this book.

Perhaps it was on the virtual battleground of Royal Flush, or unwittingly in the skies above Europe that I first met Nigel Walpole but it was not until 1961, when we served together as instructors on the 4414th Combat Crew Training Squadron, at Shaw Air Force Base, South Carolina, that I got to know him, and we have remained in touch ever since.

I know that he took up the challenge of writing this history of the Voodoo only after a great deal of soul-searching, feeling at first that he was underqualified as a chronicler of another Air Force, with too little knowledge of the aircraft and its operations from his one tour with the USAF and no involvement with it in South East Asia. However, with his extensive background in tactical reconnaissance and other high performance jet aircraft, his understanding of the needs and means (he also served for six years as a battle manager in NATO), and assiduous research, he was well equipped for the balanced account written here and in his previous books on similar subjects.

Although many of the facts have been taken from official archives, there may be those in the Voodoo fraternity who have different versions of events which happened some forty years ago

Brigadier General Paul H Hodges, Joint Chiefs of Staff Reconnaissance Operations Centre, Washington DC, 1981.

and some used by the author in good faith may have been embellished a little in the retelling. War stories, like fish tales, tend to alter over time, and in this the author is sometimes helpless. Where primary evidence has been in conflict the author has had the unenviable task of arbitration so we should not be too pedantic over detail.

In sum, this is a factual and anecdotal story of the Voodoo warriors. It is an enjoyable recap of the aircraft in its several incarnations and the men involved, in both war and peace. It covers the whole of the Voodoo era, from the initially indecisive and then heady days of the 1950s and early 1960s, to the very dramatic times in South East Asia from the mid-1960s. I believe it is a valuable chronicle of our heritage.

PREFACE

My primary motivation for writing 'Voodoo Warriors' is to pay tribute to all those involved with that family of McDonnell aircraft, in the air and on the ground, in peace and war. I had the privilege of flying the Voodoo in its early days and thereafter stayed in touch with its fraternity throughout the halcyon days of Cold War peace in America, Europe, the Pacific and the dreadful years of conflict in South East Asia (SEA). The more I heard from the Voodoo men, of their comfortable routine in peace to the spectacular and dangerous in war, so I became increasingly interested.

It is clear that through individual and collective enterprise, industry and determination, these men made their sometimes recalcitrant steed work effectively in roles, places and times for which it was not originally designed. In some cases they had to overturn inhibiting conventional wisdoms and habits of the past that proved no longer tenable. This was most obvious during the ultimate test in SEA, when silver aircraft were camouflaged, camera configurations changed and low level profiles no longer offered a panacea solution to survival, having in any event to succumb all too often to photographic demands. The pilots (some of whom had also flown in WW2 and Korea) then faced additional risks from the new, rapidly developing and proliferating anti-aircraft artillery (AAA) and surface-to-air missiles (SAMs), again bringing the pros and cons of flying in pairs or with escorts under scrutiny as the potential of electronic counter-measures (ECM) and airborne refuelling became increasingly clear. The men on the flight line came to know very quickly what was needed to bring air warfare up-to-date in these circumstances, the hierarchy sometimes less ready to be convinced. Political pressures often outweighed military imperatives and micro-management at the highest level became the order of the day, to the serious detriment of essential flexibility in mission planning and execution. All this led to unnecessary cost - with the fliers paying the highest price.

I offer this book in all humility, not as an expert on the aircraft or any of its roles, nor with personal knowledge of those very hostile skies over SEA to which the reconnaissance variant, the RF-101 was committed. Consequently, the framework for this book is based first on primary and secondary evidence drawn from official archives, then enlivened by personal testimony from those far better acquainted with the aircraft and its employment.

Having said that, I flew some 400 hours on the Voodoo in 1960/61, at Shaw Air Force Base (AFB), South Carolina, the home of USAF tactical reconnaissance, serving on an operational squadron and as an instructor pilot on the aircraft's conversion and role training squadron. In so doing, I gained some insight into the aircraft and its modus operandi then, and at our many reunions since I have learned how the Voodoo men went to war in the RF-101 in SEA. In the relatively relaxed days of the late 1950s and early 1960s few of us thought the unthinkable, that the Cold War would turn 'hot', although we convinced ourselves that had it done so we would have been able to acquit ourselves well in our respective aircraft, and we did not know then what the 'One-O-Wonders' would face in SEA. We simply enjoyed the great exhilaration of flying one of the new breed of 'century series' jets, of taking the best pictures we could with the RF-101's cameras, thereby hoping to win national and international recce competitions. There was much debate then and even now on how far these contests prepared us for the realities of any war or provided a definitive comparison between units as to their overall war fighting capability, and I will touch on this later.

I thought long and hard about my right to intrude into this close-knit family, into matters which some might now prefer to forget and with which I was not personally familiar. However, after a period of soul-searching reflection, encouragement from old friends and new acquaintances, I took up my pen with self-imposed caveats.

Many will be disappointed that I have not been more critical of the political determinates of the war in SEA, with all the associated constraints impacting on the strategies and military tactics that were imposed on those who came to risk their lives in order to do their duty. To that charge I am indeed guilty, but I consider it presumptuous for one who was not there on the ground or in the air to pass judgement on matters with which some felt very strongly at the time - and maybe more strongly now as they reflect on what they had to endure and the friends they lost. I have at least laid a trail of hints where I think, as others have, that things might have been done differently.

There will be other criticisms, perhaps that I have mentioned many good deeds but failed to do full justice to others, to record some awards and not others and to recall only some who perished. Again I am guilty, but space precludes more than a few examples picked almost at random from the facts and anecdotes provided by those who responded to my plea for contributions. Also, with the passage of time memories have become a little clouded and where several versions of some legendary tales have emerged I have had to be the final arbiter.

This could matter to, even distress some of those who were involved directly and if so I seek their forgiveness. The same is true where identical photographs have come to hand from different sources, and again I have had to make the final choice with the publisher selecting those best for reproduction. Some sections, typically that on the Royal Canadian Air Force/Canadian Armed Forces (RCAF/CAF), have been oversubscribed and personal favourites may have been omitted. Finally, with a file on source details inadvertently destroyed, and no success in tracing some donors, I may have some credits wrong. In all these cases I apologise.

Despite all its imperfections, I hope you will find this an acceptable résumé and a just tribute to the Voodoo warriors.

THE AUTHOR

Group Captain Nigel J. R. Walpole OBE BA RAF, passed out from the Royal Air Force College, Cranwell, in 1954. He flew Hunter day fighters and Swift fighter reconnaissance aircraft in Germany before an exchange tour with the USAF at Shaw Air Force Base, South Carolina, flying RF-101 Voodoos.

On promotion to squadron leader he commanded 234 Squadron (Hunter fighter/ground attack) and II (AC) Squadron (Hunter fighter reconnaissance), before being appointed Brigade Air Support Officer with 16 Parachute Brigade as a wing commander. He commanded No 12 Squadron (Buccaneer maritime strike/attack) and became Wing Commander Operations on the Jaguar Strike/Attack Wing in Germany. After a tour as Group Captain Operations at HQ RAF Germany, he completed his service career as Assistant Chief of Staff Offensive Operations, Second Allied Tactical Air Force. Following civilian employment as the air weapons advisor to British Aerospace, he and his wife retired to Suffolk. This is his fourth book on tactical air operations.

Flight Lieutenant Nigel J. R. Walpole, 4414th Combat Crew Training Squadron, Shaw Air Force Base, South Carolina, 1960.

CHAPTER ONE:
EVOLUTION

'Military history is filled with the record of military improvements that have been resisted by those who would have profited richly from them.'

B H Liddell Hart, 1944

Throughout the latter stages of WW2 the United States Army Air Force (USAAF) wrestled with the problem of replacing its venerable P-47 and P-51 long range escort fighters with aircraft capable of taking on the formidable new German jet fighters, the ME 163 and ME 262, on their terms. These war years bred the vision and imagination needed, and the jet engine added a new dimension.

The USAAF looked at the Bell XP-83 powered by two jet engines, and such innovations as the ConvairXP-81 with its nose-mounted turboprop and a jet engine at the rear, but both projects failed to meet expectations and were rejected. When the war ended, work was already in progress on the Bell P-59 (which turned out to be a disappointment), the Lockheed F/RF-80 (a better aircraft) and the Republic F-84. It was envisaged then that the F-84 would fulfil short term requirements and much of the impetus for developing more ambitious projects was lost.

That said, brave hearts continued to beaver away at new designs nurtured by sporadic official encouragement and a contract for the McDonnell Aircraft Corporation (MDC) of St Louis, Missouri, was received from the USAAF in late 1945 for two XP-85 'parasite' fighters. These would be small, single-seat, gun-armed jet aircraft which could be carried by B-36 heavy bombers, launched against any threat and 'caught' by a gantry of hooks and wires when recovering to the mother aircraft. This concept also proved unsatisfactory and the project was terminated in 1948, as were further parasite trials involving F-84s attached to B-29 or B-36 bombers.

However, the USAAF was adding another string to its bow. In August 1945 Air Materiel Command (AMC) issued an Invitation to Bid for a multi-role long-range bomber escort fighter for Strategic Air Command (SAC), which could double as a ground attack aircraft. The original concept envisaged an armed, two-engine, single-seat fighter with a maximum speed of 600 mph, a combat radius (fully loaded) of 900 statute miles and a service ceiling of 40,000 ft. These ideals would change as work progressed and eventually be greatly exceeded.

MDC rose to the occasion with its Model 36C Penetration Fighter Project, which centred on a large and heavy aircraft powered by two Westinghouse axial-flow J34 turbojets, this initiative being rewarded by a Letter of Contract in June 1946. A mock-up was required within two months, with the first of two aircraft (XP-88) to fly in April 1948 without afterburners, the second (XP-88A) with afterburners. Chief Project Engineer, Bud Flesh, and his team were given their head and gained a reputation for 'boldness with conservatism' which would serve them well. There emerged a low/mid wing design, with flying surfaces swept back 35 deg, the horizontal stabilizer set low on the fin and two engines housed centrally below a long and spacious fuselage. This aircraft, which could be adapted to several roles, would be renamed XF-88 when the USAF was formed in 1947, the prefix 'P' for Pursuit being changed to 'F' for Fighter.

MDC's Chief Test Pilot, Bob Edholm, flew XF-88 (designated 46-525) on its maiden sortie

on 20 October 1948, a little later than scheduled but still only 28 months after clearance to proceed. He found the aircraft quite manoeuvrable and easy to fly, some directional oscillations and yaw/roll coupling problems being overcome with dampers and speed brake buffet remedied by reducing the opening span and perforating the surfaces. True to the old adage, it looked right and flew right.

Edholm soon achieved Mach 1.175 with XF-88 in a dive from 41,000 ft, with no adverse effects in the transonic zone. However, with only 6400 lb of thrust from the two J34 engines the aircraft was badly underpowered and thrust augmentation was clearly required. Afterburners were the preferred solution but, with any extension to the tailpipes limited to 52 inches, to retain the necessary ground clearance, the engine manufacturers were unable or unwilling to meet the need and MDC produced its own afterburners for the XF-88s, well within the limit.

The second test vehicle, XF-88A, given the serial number 46-526, first flew on 26 April 1949, with a variable geometry stabilator (combined stabilizer and elevator) and six 20-mm cannon. In June 1949 it was the first of the two XF-88s to be retrofitted, initially with one and then two afterburners, which provided 34% more static thrust, a 9% increase in speed at sea level (to 700 mph) and a greatly improved rate of climb. Unfortunately, the price was a significant increase in specific fuel consumption and a commensurate reduction in endurance, already one of the critical shortcomings. XF-88A was immediately committed to an intensive test programme at Edwards AFB, which included brief trials in weapons carriage and delivery, and was selected to take

part in the Penetration Fighter Project 'fly-off' to be held in June and July 1950.

Soon after its arrival at Edwards, 6526 was damaged in a wheels-up landing and had to be replaced by 46-525, hastily re-engined with the afterburning J-34s to become the second XF-88A. The other two contenders in the competition were the Lockheed XF-90 'Super Star' and North American Aviation YF-93A 'Sabre Cat'. All three aircraft were found to suffer to a greater or lesser extent from similar problems; in particular, they were all underpowered. The YF-93A could achieve a similar top speed to that of the XF-88A (some 708 mph in level flight) with one Pratt and Whitney J48 (derived from the British Rolls Royce Tay engine) which produced 8,750 lb of thrust in afterburner, but it did not have the inherent 'get you home' advantage of a second engine. On the other hand, the XF-90, although generating similar thrust from two Westinghouse J34 in afterburners, could only reach some 667 mph. A consensus among the seven pilots involved was that the North American entry was the least attractive option

Value Added. XF-88A, 46-526, with the MAC afterburners gave more power but not enough. The 20-mm cannon and perforated airbrakes are also evident. USAF

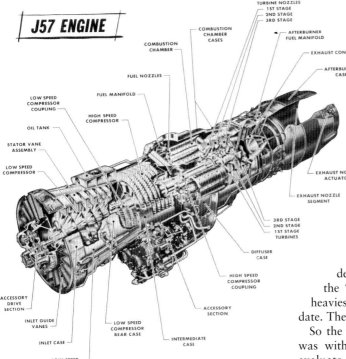

J57 ENGINE

TURBINE NOZZLES
1ST STAGE
2ND STAGE
3RD STAGE

COMBUSTION
CHAMBER
CASES

COMBUSTION
CHAMBER

AFTERBURNER
FUEL MANIFOLD

EXHAUST CONE

FUEL NOZZLES

AFTERBURNER
CASE

FUEL MANIFOLD

LOW SPEED
COMPRESSOR
COUPLING

HIGH SPEED
COMPRESSOR

OIL TANK

STATOR VANE
ASSEMBLY

EXHAUST NOZZLE
ACTUATOR

LOW SPEED
COMPRESSOR

EXHAUST NOZZLE
SEGMENT

3RD STAGE
2ND STAGE
1ST STAGE
TURBINES

DIFFUSER
CASE

HIGH SPEED
COMPRESSOR
COUPLING

ACCESSORY
DRIVE
SECTION

ACCESSORY
SECTION

INLET GUIDE
VANES

LOW SPEED
COMPRESSOR
REAR CASE

INLET CASE

INTERMEDIATE
CASE

LOW SPEED
COMPRESSOR

Voodoo Power. The two Pratt and Whitney J-57 engines, each generating 15,000 lb of thrust in afterburner, gave the Voodoo an edge over all its contemporaries, and remained the basic power plant throughout the aircraft's life. USAF

of the three. They were also unhappy with the Lockheed XF-90, despite its great structural strength its performance overall was poor.

So it was that MDC's entry won the day, but even this fell short of the specified requirements and no contract was issued. During the fly-off, anticipated budgetary cut-backs began to bite as funds were diverted to support other air force projects, specifically the B-47 nuclear bomber programme, and this resulted in the cancellation of the Penetration Fighter Project. As a consequence, both 46-525 and 46-526 went into storage but there would be resurrection.

MDC's foresight in continuing to make design changes and maintain the pressure on AMC to proceed with improved variants of their aircraft

eventually paid off. SAC had found the F-84 to be inadequate as a penetration fighter and still wanted the greater capability. Among the options offered by MDC was one equipped with the two very powerful Pratt and Whitney J-57 engines, each generating 10,000 lb of thrust (dry) and 15,000 lb in afterburner, making it very attractive to the USAF. In 1952, funds were made available to MDC to continue its work and the firm received an initial contract for what was now designated F-101, an early member of the 'century series', fast-jet club and the heaviest, most powerful single-seat fighter to date. The Voodoo was born.

So the trials resumed, during which 46-525 was withdrawn for NACA (later NASA) to evaluate several supersonic propeller permutations with an Allison turboprop engine added in the nose to create an XF-88B 'trimotor'. Modifications included the displacement of the nose leg to one side to make room for the turboprop and extending it to give the required propeller clearance; a fuel cell also had to be removed to stow test instrumentation. This aircraft first flew on 14 April 1953 and thereafter with NACA at Langley AFB.

McDonnell's Hybrid. Voodoo 46-525, fitted with an Allison XT-38 turboprop engine, the trimotor XF-88B, made its first flight at St Louis on 14 April 1953, the nose gear seen here offset to the right to make space for the turboprop engine. Robert F Dorr

First of Many. The first Voodoo F-101A, 53-2418, had its maiden flight from Muroc Dry Lake on 29 September 1954. USAF

Size is Everything. This side-by-side comparison with the XF-88 shows the much larger F-101A, 53-2418 needed to accommodate the bigger engines and more fuel. The photo also shows the latter's high tailplane and forward-hinged airbrakes. USAF

The first F-101A Voodoo 53-2418, made its maiden flight at Edwards AFB on 29 September 1954 with Robert Little at the controls. This was a very different aircraft from the XF-88, with a much larger fuselage to accommodate the two Pratt and Whitney J57-P-13 turbojets and the extra fuel necessary. The horizontal stabilizer had been moved to high on the fin, clear of the afterburner plume, and the speed brakes were now hinged forward. Little found everything about the flight 'spectacular'; he left the T-33 photo plane and F-100 chase aircraft far behind from take-off, climbing to 35,000 ft at Mach .92 in 'dry' power and going supersonic in a shallow descent (thought to be a 'first' on any initial test flight). Apart from failing to get the nose gear fully retracted quickly enough and suffering some disconcerting engine stalls, all went well, but there would be problems during the subsequent, more demanding trials. On his fourth flight Little had a double flame-out attributed to the failure of one fuel booster pump with the other being incorrectly wired, leaving him only gravity feed to the engine and an exploration of best gliding speed until a relight was achieved and a successful landing completed. It was on his seventh flight that 'all hell broke loose', both engines stalling violently at Mach 1.4 as Little tried to find out how fast the aircraft would fly. The problem continued with both throttles returned to idle, the speed brakes being used in earnest for the first time at supersonic speed until the speed reduced to Mach .8, after which the engines behaved normally and allowed another safe landing. In time all the major defects were overcome or minimised by modifying the engines or aircraft; engine stalls much reduced by correcting uneven pressures across the compressor with redesigned engine intakes and adding turning vanes. Other difficulties could be avoided by adhering to prescribed handling procedures.

Then there were the undercarriage (landing gear) problems, that of the 'hanging nose wheel' avoided by retracting the gear before

Wheel Dramas. Stories of 'hanging' nosewheels (left), collapsing main gear legs (right) and short tyre life abound throughout the life of the Voodoo, but all three had much to put up with the take-off and landing speeds of this heavy jet. USAF

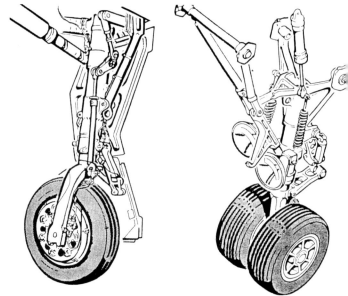

reaching 250 kts on take-off (sometimes rather easier said than done!). Generally, the main wheels took the heavy aircraft's high take-off and landing speeds well, but in less than ideal circumstances, particularly with severe side loads, the collapse of one or both main legs was not unusual. Tyre wear was very high. Of greater concern was the legendary pitch-up - a potentially disastrous occurrence. Over simplified, the wing would mask the tailplane from the airflow at high angles of attack, or deflect a down-flow on to the high-set stabilizer, causing a loss of control and nose-up pitching moment, often followed by a spin, from which recovery could be very difficult. At first, the aforementioned engine problems had priority but when these were largely resolved pitch-up became the major issue. Early Voodoo history is littered with horror stories of pitch-up, which seemed to presage the death knell of the aircraft, but MDC would have none of it. An exhaustive exploration into the phenomenon was included in the trials programme, but Captain John Dolan was killed in an F-101A on a routine test flight when he stayed with the aircraft trying to recover from an unintentional spin until it hit the desert, flat and with no forward airspeed. For spin trials a parachute was fitted to assist recovery but the operating switch was located next to that which activated the explosive cable-cutter to release it after use and in the drama of the moment one pilot selected the wrong switch - thus losing the all-important 'chute which he had intended to deploy. He ejected successfully at the last moment. In the flat spin evaluations demanded by the USAF, MDC lost two more aircraft, an F-101A and a two-seat F101B fighter, their very able and well-prepared test pilots again ejecting safely at the last moment.

In the end, concerted efforts by aerodynamicists, engineers and pilots came up with an amalgam of partial solutions. The inclination was to bring the horizontal stabilizer down into the afterburner blast, new technology now allowing this, but at this stage in production the cost and weight penalties were considered too great. Instead, the aircraft was equipped with an 'active inhibitor' which, if correctly calibrated, generated audio signals to warn of an impending pitch-up and a 'stick-pusher' to emphasise the urgency of recovery action. Clear guidance was also issued on the conditions conducive to pitch-up, the earliest and subsequent signs of its onset and development, and the immediate actions required at each stage to avoid a full-blown pitch-up or spin. Ultimately, if the aircraft was not under control by 15,000 ft, pilots were advised to eject. In peacetime training it might be reasonable to expect the warning devices to suffice, given adherence to the guidance available, but again this was easier said than done in certain flight conditions and infinitely more difficult in combat. A full understanding of the phenomenon and the application of appropriate flying skills remained the key to avoidance and recovery, the risks deemed to be acceptable for the rewards offered by the aircraft, but the risk of pitch-up would remain throughout the Voodoo's life.

There was also the need to measure precisely and if necessary enhance the structural integrity of the aircraft, this again concentrating great minds at MDC in a cautious flight test programme which sometimes generated some alarming film. Bob Little was involved and recalls camera footage of the tailplane 'bending over almost 20 deg during severe rolling pullouts', but no aircraft came to grief during trials which eventually led to a much increased threshold of 7.33 'G'.

The experience of pitch-up may have contributed to a growing belief in the early 1950s that the Voodoo would be more suited to roles which capitalised on its great acceleration

Testing Times. F-101A, 53-2431, a nose probe fitted, undergoing trials at Edwards AFB in March 1956. USAF

and high maximum speed rather than one which required the agility and manoeuvrability implicit in that of SAC bomber escort. This, together with random problems which caused the delivery of the first F-101As to the USAF to be postponed, and as changes were introduced in SAC's modus operandi, heralded the demise of the original concept for the aircraft. So it was that the two-seat F-101B missile-carrying interceptor, deep penetration reconnaissance and fighter bomber variants were conceived and developed, roles which would indeed make the best use of the Voodoo's inherent attributes, and in which pitch-up might be of less concern. For all these incarnations exhaustive flight trials continued unabated.

Senior Master Sergeant Edgar M Mays encountered the Voodoo first when assigned to the Aircraft Research and Development Command (ARDC) at Eglin AFB, where much of the USAF's operational equipment was evaluated and developed. He recalls:

Trials and Development. F-101C, 54-1486, undergoing acceptance trials, while F-101A, 53-2426, carries out engine development tests with two J-57-P-55 turbojets. This aircraft would go on to break the world's absolute speed record in Operation Fire Wall (Chapter Two). USAF

'The squadron to which I was assigned comprised some 1,100 personnel to look after 72 aircraft of all types, including RF-101 Voodoos involved in photographic cartridge trials. These particular tests caused some consternation among the locals when drive-in movies were interrupted, the screens going blank when these cartridges lit up the night sky in the vicinity. Inevitably in work of this kind, there were many dramatic incidents in the air and on the ground, some involving Voodoos. On one occasion, when people from our squadron and the collocated Aircraft Test Centre had gathered outside to see what was expected to be an interesting take-off, the highly respected Major Lonnie Moore (an 'ace' pilot from the Korean War) gave them more than he and they had bargained for. The RF-101 took off too steeply, pitched up at about 150 ft from the ground, snapped rolled to the right and crashed back to the ground inverted, killing Moore on impact.'

This incident added to the Voodoo's initial bad reputation for poor handling in certain flight configurations, even among the elite pilots serving at Eglin. To build up much needed confidence in the aircraft and to show that it could be operated safely within the specified criteria, McDonnell sent their chief test pilot to Eglin. He demonstrated the correct take-off and landing technique published in the aircraft's Dash One and even showed that pilots could, within certain limits, get away with that which had led to the sad loss of Lonnie Moore. In fact, he did everything except make the '101' talk! Convinced, the Eglin pilots continued trials flying with the Voodoo - if with sensible caution.

With the introduction of the 'century series' fighters the 1950s were of course exciting years for the USAF's fighter/fighter bomber fraternity. Pride among those who operated each of the new aircraft abounded - as did competition - and no less among the Voodoo men evaluating the aircraft at Eglin. This led to a 'one-v-one' contest between two very able fighter pilots, one flying an F-101 the other a new F-102, Delta Dagger (from another Eglin Unit commanded by Colonel Paul Tibbets, the pilot of B-29 'Enola Gay' which dropped the first atom bomb). The two pilots were good friends who had flown in combat together in the Korean war, and there would be no holds

Ready to Go. F-101A, 54-1471, ready for the front line. George Cowgill Collection

barred that day. Edgar Mays was among the many watching from the ramp, again hardly expecting the events which followed. Having run up their engines together at the runway threshold the F-102 rolled first, dramatically losing several 'turkey feathers' (exhaust flaps which regulated engine thrust/exhaust gas temperatures) as it became airborne. This resulted in a loss of control causing the aircraft to slam back to the ground beside the runway; the fuel-filled wings exploding in a major inferno. Miraculously, a vacuum in the cockpit saved the pilot, who survived with back injuries. The Voodoo pilot, who believed that his friend had perished, taxied back in a state of shock and had to be brought back to his senses with a liberal dose of aircrew 'combat medicine' when he and his aircraft reached dispersal! (The RF-101 and F-102 used the same J-57 engines but with different afterburners).

Other incidents were less spectacular. One Voodoo pilot came back from the weapons range seriously concerned about a jet of hot air

Still to Come. A second batch F-101A, 54-1471, joined by F-101B, 56-233 (lead) and RF-101A, 54-1501, in August 1957. George Cowgill Collection

In Business. Part of the second batch of 49 F-101As, 54-1461, began active service with the 524th TFS, 27th TFW, Bergstrom AFB, in June 1957. Robbie Robinson Collection

blowing up his flight suit legs. A defective G-suit valve was quickly and correctly diagnosed by the crew chief, who then resorted to a temporary expedient (involving masking tape) which enabled flying to proceed until a replacement valve became available. All this was part of a fast learning curve which ultimately led to a growing confidence in the Voodoo, provided it was properly prepared for flight and flown as prescribed, essentially in a team effort.

Later, in rather more sinister trials held above the Bikini and Eniwetok Atolls in the Pacific, an F-101A would be used to evaluate the effects of nuclear weapons detonations on aircraft, Major John Apple the pilot in the combined USAF/MDC team in 'Project Redwing'. Little was known then of the potential effects of nuclear explosions, the sole safety measures of goggles for the pilot and a 'radiation hood' for the Voodoo being very rudimentary by today's standards. On many flights through the 'mushroom clouds', some supersonic, surfaces within the cockpit smouldered and smoked with very visible but largely superficial damage to external surfaces, the Voodoo surviving it all. Inter alia, tests confirmed that the aircraft was capable of carrying and delivering the small nuclear weapons, a prophetic conclusion.

On 2 May 1957, the first F-101A (the 41st off the production line underlining the extent of the trials programme) was accepted by the USAF and flown to SAC's 27th Strategic Fighter Wing (SFW) at Bergstrom AFB, Texas. The Voodoo had truly arrived, and there would be many more to come.

The End of the Beginning. An ignominious end for XF-88A, 46-526, on the scrap heap at Langley AFB, Virginia in 1959, XF-88B, 46-525, suffering the same fate - but read on. Robert F Dorr

CHAPTER TWO
THE GLOBE TROTTERS OF TACTICAL AIR COMMAND

'Aptitude for war is aptitude for movement'

Napoleon

Nineteen fifty-seven was the first big year for the Voodoo, beginning with the F-101's turbulent introduction into service at Bergstrom AFB as a strategic fighter with SAC's 27th SFW, this unit redesignated the 27th Fighter Bomber Wing (FBW) in July and later renamed the 27th Tactical Fighter Wing (TFW), Tactical Air Command (TAC). Built up over the next year with a mix of 77 F-101As and 47 F 101Cs, the Wing comprised the 522nd, 523rd and 524th TFS, differentiated by their star-studded fins in red, yellow and blue respectively.

TAC immediately set about proving the aircraft's capability and its world-wide mobility; the Wing's primary mission was to deliver a single weapon, with the secondary option of ground attack with its four 20-mm cannon. Perhaps it was not until 12 December 1957 that the Voodoo hit the headlines, when Major Adrian Drew captured the World Speed Record from the British in Operation Fire Wall, with an average speed of 1,207.6 mph over two runs in F-101A 53-2426, at a height of 39,000 ft over Edwards AFB. This aircraft had been employed in trials with uprated engines giving 12% more power. More

ground-breaking flights followed in 1958, among them two F-101Cs averaged 480 mph over a 5,600 mile circuit with Air-to-Air Refuelling (AAR) in May, while in June four F-101Cs flew non-stop with AAR from Andrews AFB Maryland, to Liege, Belgium in 6 hours 12 minutes. The F-101s also went across the

Major J Dunn, 522nd FBS, 1957.

Robbie Robinson Collection

524th TFS, 1957. Robbie Robinson Collection

522nd TFS, RAF Bentwaters,1958.

Robbie Robinson Collection

522nd FBS, Kadena
AB, Okinawa, 1958.
Robbie Robinson Collection

Out With the Old - In With the New. Veteran
RF-84Fs nearing the end of their time with
the 363rd TRW but showing with this loop
that they still had life left in them!
Bob Sweet and Shaw AFB

Operation Fire Wall. Major Adrian Drew
flew this pre-production
F-101A, 53-2426, into the record books at
Edwards AFB on 12 December 1957.
USAF & George Cowgill Collection

Pacific when tension rose over the waters between the Chinese mainland and the Nationalist held Formosa (Taiwan), but they saw no action there. In August the first of the 27th TFW Voodoos were transferred to the 81st TFW, United States Air Force Europe (USAFE) at RAF Bentwaters/Woodbridge (Chapter Six), as the 27th TFW began its transition to F-100Ds.

Meanwhile, the 363rd Tactical Reconnaissance Wing (TRW), 837th Air Division (AD), 9th Air Force, at Shaw AFB, South Carolina, was receiving its RF-101s, in a quantum performance jump from the RF-80s and RF-84Fs in the tactical reconnaissance (tac recon) role. For more than the next decade the predominantly day recce Voodoos would share the base with variants of the B-66 Destroyer which were also able to conduct high level, night, weather and electronic reconnaissance. Shaw would remain the 'home' of the USAF's tactical reconnaissance until 1989.

Four years earlier SAC had identified the need for a limited number of fast jet recce aircraft and a contract had been placed for two

Above & below; The RB-26s and RB-47s made way at Shaw for the RB-66s and RF-101s.
Bob Sweet & Shaw AFB

Voodoo Home. Shaw AFB - lifetime home to the RF-101s. Shaw AFB

First of Many. YRF-101A, 54-149, flew its maiden flight from the McDonnell base at St Louis on 30 June 1955. George Cowgill Collection

prototypes. A mock up of the reconnaissance variant was accepted in 1954 and McDonnell took the 16th and 17th aircraft from the F-101A production line for the necessary modifications. The first of two YRF-101As, 54-149, flew on its maiden flight from St Louis on 30 June 1955, and a year later three production RF-101As were accepted, not for SAC (which had lost interest in the Voodoo) but for TAC, which recognised a potential to meet its needs. Thirty-five RF-101As, all of which were limited to 6.33 'G' and some fitted with additional 90-gall fuel tanks in each wing, had arrived in TAC by October 1957. These were followed by 166 RF-101Cs, all stressed to 7.33 'G', deliveries to USAF complete by March 1959.

Modifications to the fighter included the removal of the four guns and ammunition boxes and installation of an elegant, lengthened nose to house the cameras. Initially, the all-

Operational Fit. Early RF-101s were equipped with these 6-inch KA-2 oblique and KA-1 36-inch split vertical cameras.
John Nevill Collection

important role equipment consisted of a Fairchild KA-1 forward-facing camera, KA-2 cameras in the vertical and two oblique stations, and a KA-18 strip camera, but camera configurations would change continuously throughout the RF-101's service life, most significantly with the incorporation of KA-1, 36-inch split vertical cameras in the rear station. Camera ancillaries included mechanically driven intervalometers and count limiters to set trip rates and intervals between exposures, shutter speeds and exposure apertures, which on previous systems had to be selected on the ground. These innovations had the virtue of simplicity but still failed to capitalise on the high-speed, low level capabilities and flexibility inherent in the Voodoo. Then came the Simplified Universal Camera Control System, incorporating solid state electronics and reduced in size from that used in the RB-47, which included Image Motion Compensation (IMC). During the film's exposure, IMC enabled the film magazine itself to be moved bodily along the aircraft's heading, according to a pre-determined relationship with automatic inputs of height and speed, thus enhancing image quality at higher speeds and lower levels. Later, some RF-101s would be modified to give them a limited night photography capability.

Three RF-84F pilots from the 17th Tactical Reconnaissance Squadron (TRS) at Shaw AFB, Captains 'Barney' Barnard, Bob Smith and Bob Sweet, went to the McDonnell factory in St Louis in May 1957 to check out on the RF-101 with the help of the firm's test pilots; Barney Barnard being the first of the three to fly the aircraft. The first RF-101 (54-1503) destined for the 17th TRS reached the front line at Shaw on 6 May 1957. The excitement this caused was palpable, with a huge crowd on hand to get an early glimpse of the aircraft many of them would fly or tend for the next decade or so. Compared with its forerunners, the RF-51, RF-

Three Pioneers. Captains Robert L Smith, Martin J Barnard and Robert M Sweet , 17th TRS, the first to convert to the RF-101 at McDonnell's plant, St Louis, in 1957. Bob Gould

80 and RF-84F, this was a huge aircraft; 69 ft long, it matched the length of the DC-3 Dakota and the power it exuded was awesome - giving it the capability to fly supersonic straight and level.

The 363rd TRW Wing Commander, Brigadier General Stephen B Mack, commandeered one the of the first RF-101As (54-1515) as his personal mount, he and selected pilots from the 17th TRS being the first to fly the new aircraft. Captain Bob Gould was among these privileged few; he recalls that his briefing from their 'expert' Barney Barnard terminated with the comment: *"He'll probably kill himself but you have to take chances once in a while!"* This had the desired effect of achieving quite the opposite, earning Bob the comment from his mentor, *"That was the best take-off and landing yet"* - and this new boy went on to fly the aircraft with distinction in all its theatres of operation.

More RF-101s flew into Shaw in the following weeks to complete the replacement of RF-84Fs on the 17th, 18th, 20th and 29th TRS. Despite initial shortages in photographic equipment, the Voodoo men were soon hard at

Commander's Privilege. One of the first RF-101As at Shaw, 54-1515, became the personal aircraft of the commander, 363rd TRW, Brigadier General Stephen B Mack. Shaw AFB

Proud Emblems. The 17th TRS was the first to receive the RF-101 on 6 May 1957, quickly followed by the 18th TRS (designed by Andy Capp), the 20th TRS and the 29th TRS.
Robbie Robinson

to George AFB, California, in early November 1957 to begin their training in earnest. The key to success was rapid rendezvous and 'hook-ups' with the newly commissioned KC-135 tankers which were capable of using both probe and boom systems for AAR seven miles above the earth. As could be expected, these rehearsals were not without incident; Gus Klatt had to make an emergency landing at a private airstrip in the South West, theoretically too small for the Voodoo, but with great skill he brought the aircraft to a stop undamaged. There he was fêted royally by local admirers until his aircraft was ready for more and he got it safely off the short strip. Thanks to intensive training, the efficiency of the radar controllers and expertise of the pilots and tanker crews, the join-ups and refuelling during the operation were largely faultless with the results speaking for themselves.

work, the pilots learning fast how to handle the aircraft and the maintenance men how to keep them in the air. They would soon be thrust into the limelight.

In the autumn of 1957, 9th Air Force was ordered to establish international air speed records across the USA, east to west coast, west to east coast, and for the round trip non-stop, in Operation Sun Run. Shaw-based RF-101s would be air refuelled by KC-135 tankers and the record attempts made between 2 November and 31 December 1957. Intensive planning brought TAC, SAC (tankers), Air Defence Command (radar), MDC and many supporting agencies together, as six RF-101s were prepared. With Lieutenant Colonel William Nelson as the Project Officer, six carefully selected Voodoo pilots from Shaw: Captains Burkhart, Hawkins, Kilpatrick, Sweet, Schrecengost and Lieutenant Klatt, flew their aircraft (brightly coloured to aid identification)

Chosen Men. Four of the six RF-101 pilots selected for Operation 'Sun Run'. (L to R) Captains Robert Kilpatrick, Gustav Klatt, Robert Sweet and Ray Schrecengost. Shaw AFB

The Best of Birds. Sun Run RF-101, 60164, being prepared for the Sun Run at the McDonnell factory, St Louis, Missouri.
Robert F Dorr Collection

Boom Time. A Sun Run pilot about to take fuel from a KC-135. George Cowgill Collection

Record Team. Captain Bob Sweet, record winner, with his crew chief. Bob Sweet

All expectations were fulfilled; Bob Sweet established a non-stop Los Angeles - New York - Los Angeles record of 6 hours 46 minutes and a New York to Los Angeles record of 3 hours 36 minutes, while Gus Klatt set up a Los Angeles to New York record of 3 hours 7 minutes. Ray Schrecengost and Bob Kilpatrick also broke existing records. Bob Burkhart and Donald Hawkins, in the spare aircraft, were not needed. With its great speed and range, the Voodoo was probably the only aircraft at the time capable of achieving such successes and everyone involved was given great credit for a job well done.

At this time, TAC was fighting for its survival, pinning its hopes on demonstrating an ability to respond to any 'brush fire' anywhere in the world at a moment's notice. Mobile Zebra, an exercise requiring F-100s, RF-101s and RB-66s to cross the Pacific with AAR using KB-50 tankers in an itinerary which would take them to Hawaii, Japan, Okinawa, Taiwan and the Philippines, was planned to this end. It was an ambitious beginning to a long string of similar deployments to prove a global capability, particularly given the Voodoos' initial failure on occasions to take on a full fuel load in the air and calculations revealed that even with full tanks they could not complete the leg to Hickam AB, Hawaii, with safe reserves. However, these problems were overcome by replacing defective fuel transfer valves and activating the two internal wing tanks which had been isolated because of random leaks (now remedied), thereby giving 1,000 lb more fuel.

The flight positioned itself at George AFB and set off for the long sea crossing on 15 November 1957, with Bob Gould detailed to fly one of the spare aircraft. On all the rehearsals he had been needed to replace someone, but on this occasion it was he who aborted on start-up. Thanks to meticulous planning and execution the flight arrived intact in Hawaii, leaving Bob with a lonely trip home to Shaw. En route he encountered forecast thunderstorms over Mississippi, the sort which century series fighter pilots would normally avoid, but Bob believed he could climb above them. This was easier said than done; maximum (military) power took him to 47,000 ft where, at barely above stalling speed, the afterburners failed to light and give him that extra power he needed. Then an engine which had begun to surge, stall and overheat had to be shut down, and there was no alternative but to descend. As he hit what he called 'one of those boiling clouds', Bob was flipped into a loop, saw the airspeed indicator fall to zero and the artificial horizon (which was not supposed to 'tumble') spinning like crazy - as was the altimeter. Having obviously 'pitched-up', he took immediate recovery action by deploying the drag 'chute to bring the aircraft gradually under control and thereafter relying on the basic teaching of 'needle, ball and airspeed'. Suddenly, when straight and level, he 'popped into the clear at 17,000 ft, having lost 30,000 ft'. Here was a case of simulator drills paying off, Bob finding that he had even trimmed the aircraft out after the engine had been stop-cocked. He then re-started the engine, said; *"to hell with the regulations"*, smoked a cigarette, cancelled IFR (Instrument Flight Rules) and made his way gently back to Shaw under VFR (Visual Flight Rules).

Bob Gould was among many Voodoo pilots who were to learn the rules of the game the hard way; he admits that he might have been a little too anxious to get home, that he asked too much of the Voodoo to climb so high at that all-up weight and that he had underestimated 'mother nature'. On the plus side, he had proved that the drills worked with the correct recovery action, and he was one of few to recover from a pitch-up. He survived where others would not, and he would be the better for it.

In February 1958 the 837th AD incorporated the 363rd and the 432nd TRWs, but a year later all TAC RF-101 assets at Shaw were placed under the command and control of the 363rd TRW. More milestones lay ahead, with four aircraft from the 18th TRS completing the first non-stop crossing of the Atlantic by Shaw-based RF-101s on 16 May 1958, in 8 hours 35 minutes. Their arrival at Phalsbourg AFB, France was unusually spectacular when the flight leader was forced to eject as his aircraft went out of control in a steep climb over the airfield; he landed safely two miles away.

Flights across the Atlantic and Pacific would soon become regular practice for the TAC pilots, who had to be ready to go anywhere, at any time.

True to tradition the Voodoo squadrons at Shaw had their own identities, underlined with every opportunity. The 'Lonesome Polecats' of the 18th TRS revered their squadron insignia, designed by the cartoonist Andy Capp, complete with appropriate head dress, telescope and camera. One of their number, Captain 'Rich' Richardson, remembers a party in the Officers Club for which the squadron dressed as native Indians, their improvised wigwams strategically positioned so that any partygoer needing their restroom could be intercepted and have his or her forehead stamped with their mark.

The USAF tac recon force had become regular hosts to RAF exchange officers. Flight Lieutenant John West handing over to Flight Lieutenant 'Paddy' King at Shaw AFB in June 1957. Paddy flew the RF-84F before converting to the Voodoo later that year to fly much of his time at Shaw with the 29th TRS; he was an experienced recce pilot already, having flown Meteor and Swift aircraft on a fighter reconnaissance squadron in Germany and would play an almost full part in the Wing's activities. The 'almost' refers to an operational recall of all the squadron's personnel at 0500 hours on 15 July 1958, in anticipation of a commitment overseas during the developing crisis in Lebanon. Excitement was high, preparations were well in hand and Paddy was raring to go with his fellow warriors when his squadron commander disabused him with, *"your lot didn't let us go to Suez - so you're not coming with us to Lebanon!"* - and that was that.

Ray Schrecengost, who had recently left the 18th TRS to take up the prestigious appointment of Standardisation Officer on the 837th AD at Shaw, was also up early that morning; he had been selected to lead the six RF-101s, as part of the TAC Composite Air Strike Force (CASF), to Adana, Turkey, for Operation Blue Bat. The plan was to fly non-stop to Chaumont AB, France, with two air refuellings from KB-50 tankers, the six primary aircraft and two spares being flown by Ray, Captains Burkhart, Klatt and Yeager, Lieutenants Nelson, Richardson, Powell and Miller. Bob Gould went too, in the relative

Flight Leader. Captain Ray Schrecengost, 363rd TRW Standardisation Officer, led the Blue Bat RF-101 force to Lebanon in 1958.
Ray Schrecengost

comfort of a C-130 to take up Command Post duties as Day Recce Officer.

After several delays, with changes in routeing and alternate airfields, the flight got airborne from Shaw at 1700 hours that evening and headed east into the dark, a long day behind them and many more hours of hard work ahead. The success of the mission depended now on the pilots' dead-reckoning (DR) navigation skills, proficiency in air-to-air refuelling and general airmanship; it was a tall order, especially for the leader. Early in the flight, Klatt, Nelson and Powell aborted with technical problems but the five survivors pressed on despite three of them having defective external lighting. 'Mayday' calls from four F-100 pilots who had failed to refuel from their tankers and were trying to reach alternates did little for morale. (In fact, three of the 'Huns' did make it but one pilot had to eject). Things were now looking grim for the Voodoos too, with the four KB-50s flying at a relatively low altitude in the pitch black and heavy turbulence, between cloud layers and thunderstorms. However, with good DR and help from their ARA-25 direction-finding radios, the Voodoo pilots found their tankers just as they all reached 'Bingo'(minimum fuel

before diversion) and all 'hooked up' to take fuel successfully. Considering the circumstances, this had been no mean feat.

The Voodoos then climbed back into cloud, only breaking into clear air as they approached the Lajes refuelling area. DR and the ARA-25 again served them well, but they were then advised that no tankers would be available as planned and that they would have to land at Lajes. Normally, such news would not be unwelcome but the weather at Lajes AB was already down to minimums, with Ground Control Approach (GCA) mandatory, and the pilots had to call on all their skills to complete faultless instrument penetrations after a flight of nearly six hours, in a day already 17 hours old.

At Lajes the Voodoo men were told to turn their aircraft round at once and continue immediately to Chaumont, but Ray Schrecengost was having none of it and ordered the aircraft serviced properly for a daybreak departure. The 'Go' pills given the pilots before they left Shaw had the required effect for the final three hour flight direct to Chaumont, where GCAs were again the order of the day before there could be any rest. Another three hour flight on the following day took them to Wheelus AB Tripoli, where the legendary Colonel Robin Olds, commander designate of the 81st (F-101) TFW at Bentwaters, tried without success to get Ray to let him fly one of the RF-101s. The final leg to their destination and a highly successful if stressful trip was marred only by one of the Voodoos landing with a burst tyre at Incirlik, thereby blocking the runway temporarily on this very active deployment base. It was the Voodoo men themselves who managed to manoeuvre the aircraft out of the way sufficiently for operations there to resume, before a General Officer could carry out his threat to 'bulldoze it clear'.

Bob Gould arrived at Incirlik after a much less adventurous ride, Gus Klatt and Grayson Powell also joining the party with their Voodoos two days later and thus bringing the RF-101 force up to seven aircraft. In a detachment which lasted three months rather than the two weeks expected, the RF-101 pilots flew numerous 'training' sorties all over Lebanon, to be shot at occasionally and have one aircraft sustain minor damage. Ray, the detachment commander, flew 44 sorties from

On the Job. In the CASF Operation Blue Bat the RF-101s of the 363rd TRW flew continuously over Lebanon in their peacekeeping role. USAF

The British are Back! Flight Lieutenant Paddy King, RAF Exchange Officer, 17th TRS, 29th TRS and 4414th CCTS, his Voodoo bearing RAF Wings at Myrtle Beach AFB in 1958. Paddy King

Incirlik and all the Voodoo pilots deserved the Air Medals with which they were rewarded.

While he missed the Lebanon trip, Paddy King did make the most of other opportunities, typically accompanying the WW2 pilot Clyde East, who had flown with the RAF's Eagle Squadron as a flying officer in the Battle of Britain and was now a major, on a direct flight (with AAR) to Nouasseur, (Casablanca), in November 1958. There are no reliable accounts of their rest and recuperation they are reported to have enjoyed downtown Casablanca! Paddy became an instructor pilot, flight leader, flight clearing officer and flight test pilot, his personal Voodoo adorned with RAF Wings

With a new and demanding aircraft, accidents will happen. On 22 January 1959, Captain Robert L Smith, 17th TRS, was returning to Shaw at 36,000 ft after a successful test flight in RF-101C, 56-177 when the aircraft 'yawed violently, snapped over on to its back, pitched-up and became uncontrollable'. Smith took all the prescribed corrective action but could not recover the aircraft and ejected successfully at 3000 ft. This accident was attributed to a technical defect but others

Southern Snow. Paddy King braved a slippery Shaw AFB to photograph a snowy South in the 1958 cold spell which killed much of the orange crop deep into Florida. Paddy King

would be down to human errors. As always in the nature of military aviation, a number of Voodoo accidents and incidents were self-induced, whether by tempting providence, pressing on regardless or through a simple mistake. Some inherently very capable pilots seemed more susceptible than others, often escaping harm or censure against all the odds. There were also those within the force who defied the old adage that 'there are old pilots and bold pilots, but not many old and bold pilots'. Take the case of one spirited RF-101 pilot who took on a fighter and failed, impressed his admiring audience at an air display - but not as he would have wished - and who 'pressed on' but wished he hadn't. In the first incident this intrepid aviator from Shaw experienced a pitch-up in his frustration at losing out to an F-100F pilot from Myrtle Beach; only his skill, inbred recovery procedures and the drag 'chute saving the day. His adversary, on seeing these remarkable gyrations, is believed to have thought at first 'Sure wish I knew that manoeuvre' then on seeing the 'chute deciding 'No I don't!' Then there was the air display at Richards-Gebaur where the same individual decided to thrill the crowd with a dramatic take-off by selecting his gear and perhaps flaps 'up' before the wheels left the ground; the aircraft settled back on the runway as the gear folded beneath - a dramatic spectacle indeed! Nothing daunted, he pressed his luck again during his time with the Pacific Air Forces (PACAF) when leading a pair on take-off knowing that his wingman's radio transmitter was unserviceable. All would have been well had he locked his canopy or noticed the big red light warning him that he had not done so; his No 2 did see it but could not bring it to the attention of his leader. Inevitably, the canopy departed on take-off, leaving a very windswept pilot in the fresh air until he burned off enough fuel to land safely. He had got away with it again, where others might have perished.

At about the same time there were two other minor accidents. In the first, Lieutenant Cloves L Easter, 20th TRS, had a combined generator, drag 'chute and anti-skid failure on landing at Stewart AFB, Tennessee. The aircraft rolled into soft dirt some 50 ft beyond the runway, where the nose gear collapsed. Easter climbed from the aircraft unhurt. In the second, Lieutenant Merl Kimball had just lowered the gear

downwind in the traffic pattern when the canopy separated from the aircraft, but he was able to complete a normal landing. The canopy had unlocked due to a short circuit in the electrical system. There were also serious accidents. Tragically, Captain Donald Romans was fatally injured on 5 March 1959 when he crashed during a turn to finals at Shaw in poor visibility, but on 20 May 1959 two pilots were rescued after their Voodoos had collided and they had ejected safely into the sea off Bermuda.

As with most new aircraft, the RF-101s suffered technical defects. Shortages in role equipment had been largely resolved by 1959 but the aircraft were grounded periodically with undercarriage and hydraulic problems. Bob Gould had a hydraulic failure while on a cross-country to Hill AFB and a recurrence on the subsequent 'test hop', after which he returned to his unit by civilian aircraft. No sooner did the spate of hydraulic problems seem under control than corrosion caused cracks in the aircraft's skin; all of which required immediate remedial action. Other difficulties would follow but whatever they were the 'Voodoo Medicine Men' would find the cause and a solution (Chapter Twenty).

The Voodoo became front page news again in April 1959 when two RF-101s from Shaw were detached to Edwards AFB, California for Project View-Do, attempts to break the 100-km and 500-km air speed records. Colonel Ed Taylor led the team with Captain George Edwards earmarked initially as reserve pilot until he was withdrawn to fulfil other duties and his place taken by Captain Jim Murphy. The 1000-km route would take the Voodoo from Edwards AFB direct to San Francisco, then into the turn for a recovery to Edwards starting over Oaklands; the 500-km course took a triangular route over the mountains to the north-east of Edwards. On the day Colonel Taylor had a faultless flight in RF-101 60119, breaking the 1000-km record with an average speed of 700.047 mph. Jim Murphy, following as planned 15 minutes later, had fuel transfer failure and was forced to jettison his external tanks, thereby leaving him with insufficient fuel to complete the full course at supersonic speed, but even so his average speed was only slightly less than that of his leader. Not surprisingly, this epic flight did not go unnoticed on the ground, with local newspapers carrying puzzled

Project View-Do. RF-101C, 60119, one of two Voodoos from the 363rd TRW which established new 1000-km & 500-km air speed records from Edwards AFB in 1957. George Cowgill Collection

reports of mysterious bangs which shattered windows, cracked walls and triggered water sprinklers. At first, the sonic booms were blamed on US Navy fighters in the area and the Voodoo men sensibly laid low until the furore had died down. Only later did they make a formal admission that they might have been responsible.

There was a flurry of activity to repair the spare aircraft, but then Jim fell sick and George Edwards was called up from Shaw to lead an attempt on the 500-km record. Jim recovered in time to fly the back-up but again his aircraft had a fuel problem and could not be flown at the speeds planned. George Edwards broke this record, with a speed of 816.279 mph, and Jim again had the satisfaction of beating the previous record. In the celebrations which followed, Mr R H Charles, Executive Vice-President of the MDC, stated that the last Voodoo for TAC would depart from the firm's airfield at St Louis that day, the 2263rd Voodoo take-off from that airfield. Colonel Taylor responded by saying;

"*We in TAC and the 837th AD fly what we consider to be the Cadillac of aviation - the RF-101.*"

In 1959, the 17th and 18th TRS were transferred to the 66th TRW in Europe. Later, the 20th and 29th TRS, with the Voodoo's newly formed 4414th Combat Crew Training Squadron (CCTS), plus two RB-66 Destroyer squadrons, the 9th and 16th TRS and the Destroyer's 4415th CCTS, made up the flying components of the 363rd TRW. The

Shaw units were now being organised, equipped and trained to provide the 'eyes of TAC', supporting TAC's CASF whenever it was needed, world-wide, with minimum delay.

To demonstrate this capability TAC laid on an Operational Readiness exercise in November 1959, which called for 100 assorted aircraft, using the KB-50 tanker force for AAR, to be sent to Europe with little forewarning from their home bases in the United States, in Operation Spearhead. Captain Conrad Binyon, 29th TRS, was selected to fly one of two spare

Just Rewards. The pilots involved in Operation View-Do hosted at McDonnell, St Louis.
(L to R) Mr S N McDonnell, RF-101 Project manager, Colonel Edward H Taylor, Mr R H Charles, MDC, Captains George A Edwards and Jim Murphy. Jim Murphy

aircraft supporting the main force of eight RF-101s from the 363rd TRW. They were to fly the 770 miles direct to Kindley AFB, Bermuda, for refuelling and then continue to Laon AFB with two air refuellings on the 3100-mile route. All the aircraft were serviceable on landing at Kindley but on the subsequent take-off at 0130 hours the gear on Merl Kimball's aircraft failed to retract and Lieutenant Colonel Louis Benne, commander of the 29th TRS and overall flight leader, ordered Conrad to take Kimball's place as No 2 to Lieutenant Bill Kirk, an element leader. With a new moon the night was dark and the aircraft were visible in loose formation only by their position lights; this was no 'walk in the park' and some of the eight pilots may have viewed the AAR to come with some trepidation. As Conrad Binyon said:

> *"Take it from me, there's no better feeling when you're hooked up and maintaining position behind the tanker, than when hearing the refuelling operator confirm that your aircraft is taking on fuel."*

The author would have no argument with that. Ultimately, the tankers came into view as planned and all the aircraft took on the fuel they needed for the next leg. Another aircraft fell out when Lieutenant Dick Reese was unable to extend his probe for the second 'prod' and had to divert to Chateauroux in France. The remaining seven aircraft pressed on to Laon, where the weather demanded instrument penetrations and GCAs in pairs. Dense cloud at low level caused one wingman to lose visual contact, but he sensibly carried out 'lost leader' procedures to complete nearly nine hours of flying from Bermuda.

Reese also remembers the trip well, suffering a severe attack of vertigo on a night which he now describes in a vernacular too graphic for sensitive ears but so black that he believed either he or Bill Kirk flew most of the trip upside down! He lavished praise on his element leader, recalling that when their tanker started a 30-deg turn left, Bill enquired *"Where the hell are you going Roadie?"* to which Roadie replied *"I feel south of track"*. More words were exchanged, which resulted in Bill Kirk bringing them back on to a heading which coasted them in just where they were meant to be in Portugal. For a Voodoo leader without any navigation aids this was good airmanship - but here was a general in the making! Bill Kirk also ended up leading the three other lieutenants who made it back to Shaw together on schedule, General Ford welcoming them but wanting to know where their senior officers had got to.

CASF and AAR were now firmly on the Voodoo's agenda. In February 1960, the 20th

Return Ticket. (L to R) Lieutenants Bill Kirk, Bill Hicky, Dick Reese and Jake Sorrenson, welcomed back from Europe at Shaw by Brigadier General Ford, 363rd TRW.

Shaw AFB via Dick Reece

Now the Questions. Having congratulated the lieutenants on completing their mission to Europe, General Ford wanted to know the whereabouts of the lieutenant colonel, majors and captains who had started out on the flight. He himself then came under interrogation from Master Les Kirk, Nancy Kirk much concerned that the young Kirk had one button undone for this auspicious occasion. Bill Kirk

TRS sent six RF-101s across the Atlantic again in Operation Quick Span, starting with a non-stop flight to Spain and continuing on to Turkey, Iran and Pakistan, while two months later Shaw-based RF-101s and RB-66s, with full support units, went to the Panama Canal to participate in Exercise Banyan Tree. In May, six RF-101s flew direct from Shaw to Larson AFB, Washington, to provide support for the US Army in Operation Elk Horn and in June eight Voodoos went to SEA for Exercise Mobile Yoke. Things did not always go as planned. In February 1961, Shaw RF-101s were off again to the Far East, via George AFB, California, Hickam AB, Hawaii, Anderson AB, Guam and Clark AB in the Philippines. During this deployment several aircraft ground aborted with technical defects while others had to divert to alternates, their pilots acquainting themselves with the bases at Wake Island and Midway. However, recovery to complete the mission was part of the exercise, and complete the mission they did, flying the required recce missions out of Don Muang AB, Bangkok, and

Clark AB, while four aircraft flew to Taiwan to test operational readiness at Tao-Yuan AB. 140 missions were scheduled and 140 were flown, for a total of 474 hours.

The camera equipped Voodoos were also in great demand on the home front for tasks varying from simple public relations photography to operational support. The author, having taken over the RAF exchange post from Paddy King in September 1959, and destined to succeed him as an instructor pilot on the 4414th CCTS, underwent operational orientation on the 20th TRS in early 1960. In his own words:

'To this end I flew to Nellis AFB, Las Vegas, with my mentor Captain Al Runyan for my first 'operational' task, a mosaic of 11 lines over a weapons range in the Nevada desert. The task had been attempted several times before but had met failure for a variety of reasons and this one seemed to be heading the same way when Al was called back to Shaw, leaving a novice to attempt the mission. The 6-inch KA-2 vertical camera was used to produce the mosaic from high level, to a scale of 1:50,000, with all the photographs on 11 parallel lines given the required overlap and sidelap. This was a tall order for a hitherto low level fighter recce pilot only recently introduced to high level photography, and there were few landmarks in that part of the desert to achieve the required precision. Furthermore, clear skies below were essential and at that time of the year could only be expected in the very early mornings. Denying myself the pleasures of downtown Vegas, I rose at 0400 hours on 11 June and was over the target area by 0530 hours. Perhaps astonishingly, all went well. Later that day, hundreds of photographs littered the floor of a huge room in the operations block at Nellis, the intelligence staff eventually declaring themselves satisfied*

Speed Run. Camera magazines were off-loaded from the RF-101 without delay. Shaw AFB

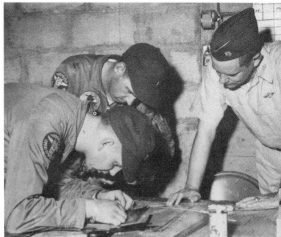

Super Vision. Lieutenant Colonel Sid Crews, Commander 20th TRS, PIs and pilots anxious to see the end product, what the camera saw. Shaw AFB

Jig-Saw. PIs piece together a mosaic from a Voodoo's vertical camera. Shaw AFB

with the result. A few beers were then in order - given that what might have been a long stay in that wonderful desert oasis seemed to be coming to an end. In fact, it ended almost immediately when a senior person from Nellis, invited to view the results of the mission, was aghast to see that it had been flown by a 'foreigner' without the necessary clearances to fly over a most secret area. This worthy officer, who probably saw stars falling before his very eyes, gained no solace from pleas that the pilot, while concentrating heavily on his flying, could have seen very little of consequence and recognised even less from such a high altitude. All this fell on deaf ears and I was ordered back to Shaw forthwith -

to be re-assigned to the 4414th CCTS as an instructor pilot'.

This training squadron was not exempt from extraneous tasks, with the author being required on one occasion to photograph the outcome of a tragic night accident when two RF-101s from one of the operational squadrons either collided after take off or flew together into the distracting lights of a chicken farm to the north of Shaw AFB.

Mobility may have been the hallmark of the Wing but routine on-base activities continued unabated with continuation training, the domestic programme and special tasks, many of which capitalised on and helped enhance the essential individuality of the recce pilot. So it was that the pilots, photographic specialists, photographic interpreters, and sometimes squadron supervisors could be found poring over film on the light tables, while men worked on their aircraft well after normal working hours. Nor were these busy men excused from such perennial activities as the annual inspections, hence a parade at Shaw of men and machines of the 363rd TRW on 6 May 1960.

Before returning to the United Kingdom the author rejoined the 20th TRS for instruction in air refuelling by day and night. The only tanker available at that time was the KB-50 Superfortress, and the only system in use then was that of probe (Voodoo) and drogue (KB-50). At heights of between 20,000 and 30,000

On Parade. The 363rd TRW on parade at Shaw AFB, with its RB-66, RF-101 aircraft and mobility equipment, for the annual inspection on 6 May 1960. Shaw AFB

101's history is littered with AAR horror stories, especially in these early days with the KB-50. The original, rigid probes on the Voodoo did not take kindly to hoses which failed to 'reel in' to the KB-50s refuelling pod when contact was made, hence their replacement with flexible probes. However, the difficulties were not all over; drogue 'baskets' continued to be damaged (or 'spoked') by the probe, there were cases of hoses becoming detached from the tanker and wrapping themselves around Voodoo fuselages and some probes broke off. Such was the case on the author's first 'prod', a self-inflicted incident when he closed too fast, hit the basket fair and square in the centre and passed the tanker still attached to the hose (to shouts of alarm from the refuelling operator in his fuselage blister. As the RF-101 drew line abreast with the tanker's wing-tip, the probe twisted in sympathy before snapping off and falling harmlessly into the Atlantic Ocean. Presumably for such a contingency, Myrtle Beach AFB was within reach with the limited (internal only) fuel remaining available, and it was to that safe haven that a much chastened pilot took his damaged Voodoo. Back at Shaw, men in the crewroom had been taking bets that their tame Limey would either hit the basket first time or break something, but since he did both all bets were off! Fortunately, some RAF pride was restored in subsequent AAR sorties when all went well, even on one dark and stormy night when it would have been better to be in the Stag Bar. In

ft, with 'four turning and two burning' the bomber turned tanker could reach a maximum indicated airspeed of only 210-215 kts (the minimum speed at which the Voodoo could prudently take on fuel), and only then in a slight dive or 'toboggan'. The RF-101 pilot would approach the tanker with flap down and speed brakes ('dive brakes' or 'air brakes') out and one engine in afterburner (trimming out the slight asymmetric affect), attempting to 'hook up' with a two to three knot overtake. He would then use one throttle up to full (military) power to stay in position, easing in the air brakes incrementally as fuel was taken on board. This was sometimes easier said than done, particularly for beginners when the weather was unfriendly or either aircraft had a technical defect, and the RF-

Bird's Eye View. What the KB-50 refuelling operator sees from his fuselage blister. Jim Ifland

Trophy Tip. Captain Chuck Lustig's refuelling probe broke off and came home lodged in the horizontal stabilizer. Chuck Lustig

recovery of a free-falling AAR probe. The fighter pilots had to be ready for anything, and there are several stories from SEA (Part Two, 'Conflict') of thirsty Voodoos being diverted unexpectedly to tankers without their pilots having had any previous instruction in AAR, or arriving at a tanker to find that it could offer only one option (boom or probe and drogue) when their only training had been on the other. There was rarely time, opportunity or inclination to query such orders and invariably the Voodoo pilots did what they were told and did it successfully. Against this background AAR was an invaluable adjunct to operational effectiveness, this amply proved in SEA, and things did become easier for the Voodoo pilots when 'boom' refuelling (the onus then falling more on the tanker's boom operator) and higher performance tankers (especially the KC-135) became available. After the KB-50, Bob Gould found the boom procedure, often carried out at the Voodoo's cruising altitude and speed, 'a piece of cake', with the later tankers often staying with them throughout a deployment, inter alia acting as their navigator.

the case of AAR at this time, it might be going too far to say that practice makes perfect; wise Voodoo pilots spoke of those who had spoked a basket and those who would; indeed that anything could happen, even to the best.

Captain Chuck Lustig was one of many experienced Voodoo pilots who knew this to be true. Despite making normal contact with the basket trailed from a KC-135, the probe of his RF-101 broke off, smashed his canopy and lodged in the horizontal stabilizer. At the routine pilots' meeting on the following Friday, Chuck was presented with the probe tip in recognition of the only known airborne

There was action of a different kind in August 1961 when Shaw AFB became involved in Exercise Swift Strike. Said to have been 'the largest peacetime manoeuvre of its kind (in the US) since 1941', the base hosted many USAF and Air National Guard tactical aircraft, including 24 C-119 Boxcar transports to deliver 789 paratroopers with full supporting equipment into huge areas of South Carolina. The author recalls that the social mix of airborne soldiers and base personnel on the ground was not always harmonious!

Life for the nomadic recce men was rarely dull or static. The Voodoos were soon off

Airborne! In August 1961, 24 C-119 Boxcars launched from Shaw AFB, to drop the 82nd & 101st Airborne Divisions into South Carolina, in "one of the biggest joint exercises since 1941".
Shaw AFB

Cold Soak. The Shaw-based Voodoos were regular visitors to Elmendorf, Alaska, in the 1960s, for Arctic exercises such as Great Bear and Polar Siege. Jim Tidwell

one of the main gear legs of his aircraft proved crucial. Of course the undercarriage failed to retract and Paul would not have continued the mission in war but, with several reputations at stake in such a prestigious competition, he kept his speed below that permitted with gear down, 250 kts, even then noticing the wing flex alarmingly, and covered all his targets. This laudable 'press-on' effort failed to impress the judges; the sortie was disqualified and the overall trophy handed to a pilot from USAFE. There but for the grace of God! This was believed to have been the only year when the tac recon force was invited to take part in what was essentially a weapons competition.

The pattern of continuous movement within the United States and world-wide remained the norm for the RF-101s and their RB-66 brothers

again, six from the 20th TRS, Lieutenant Colonel Ralph Finley in command, to reinforce NATO in Exercise Check Mate II at Incirlik AB, Turkey, followed by eight from the 29th TRS, Lieutenant Colonel Joe O'Grady now commanding, to Elmendorf AFB, Alaska, for training in arctic conditions. There was also plenty of work to be done in-country, from a major detachment of eight RF-101s to Eglin AFB, Florida, to support a firepower demonstration for President Kennedy, down to the commitment of single aircraft to demonstrations and static displays.

The competitive spirit, rampant among airmen throughout NATO in Europe, was mirrored in the US at the USAF Fighter Weapons Meet William Tell. In September 1962, participants from USAFE, PACAF and TAC participated in William Tell '62 at Nellis AFB, Nevada, with three RF-101s from the 363rd TRW representing TAC in the tactical reconnaissance phase of the exercise. Captain Paul Hodges, an instructor on the 4414th CCTS at Shaw and veteran of NATO's Royal Flush Reconnaissance Competition, was one of the chosen men from the 363rd TRW, but in this competition he was out of luck. His team was leading in this time-critical contest, until failure to remove a safety pin from

Trade Training. Under the eagle eye of TAC Commander, General Sweeney, Captain John Linihan, 363rd TRW, on Static Display at Eglin AFB, FL, explains to the Secretary of the Air Force, how to 'kill'em with fil'm'. John Linihan

in arms within the 363rd TRW, often in self-supporting, composite squadrons, improving continuously their capability to move anywhere at any time, doing all that was asked of them, and there was no better proof of this than their reaction to the crisis in Cuba.

In that autumn of 1962 events in Cuba predominated, committing the whole of the Voodoo recce force and its organic support at Shaw. This story is told in Chapter Ten; suffice it to say here that the 363rd TRW excelled in showing what the aircraft could achieve, albeit highlighting some weaknesses in the reconnaissance organisation and equipment overall. The Wing was honoured for its contribution to a successful conclusion of the crisis with an Outstanding Unit Award from President John F Kennedy, presentation of the H H Arnold Trophy, and many individual awards.

The practical problems of deploying air forces over great distances with aircraft that can never be 100% reliable, and in often unpredictable weather, were underlined again in another mission to Elmendorf AFB, Alaska, for Operation Timberline. The plan called for Lieutenant Colonel Robert O Crabtree, now commanding the 29th TRS, to lead six of his aircraft non-stop from Shaw to Elmendorf on 6 February 1963, taking fuel twice from KC-135 tankers, but it was not to be. Owing to a radio problem in one aircraft, failure to refuel in another and a hydraulic defect in a third, one pair of RF-101s diverted to Offurt AFB and a second to Richards Gebaur AFB. When the faults were rectified all these four aircraft returned to Shaw to mount a further attempt on 10 February, the new plan being to stage through Minot AFB with a single air refuelling scheduled from a KB-50. This time, three of the aircraft made it to Elmendorf, but there was further trouble ahead. On 22 February, Captain Al Brunstrom was on a test flight at Elmendorf when a major fuel leak caused the left and then right engine of his Voodoo to flame out, leaving him with no alternative but to eject. He was picked up uninjured 20 minutes later by a rescue helicopter from the same base. The accident was attributed to a technical defect and the

Exercise Bare Base. RB-66s and RF-101s of the 363rd TRW, with supporting units, demonstrate a rapid deployment to North Field Airfield, SC. John Linihan

detachment returned to Shaw on the following day. Distance was not a problem when it came to the deployment of a composite force of RF-101s and RB-66s to a nearby 'bare base' airfield at North Field, SC, in July 1963 for Exercise Swift Strike III.

It was very different for the eight RF-101s of the 20th and 29th TRS tasked to fly to Ramstein AB, Germany, in October for Exercise Big Lift. Captain Chuck Lustig remembers the outbound trip to Europe well. After staging through Dow AFB, they flew east over the Atlantic with their KC-135 tankers, to be treated to the full glory of the Northern Lights as they approached Iceland. Chuck commented later:

"It was a magnificent sight, with wave upon wave of all the colours of the rainbow; I was so mesmerised by this beautiful sight at 35,000 ft that I damn nearly ran into the tanker".

Such sights were the privilege of the few. Bob Gould was there too, fresh from his tour in Okinawa and now going in the opposite

'Big Lift'. The 20th TRS reinforced NATO in October 1963, with eight RF-101s deployed from Shaw to Dow AFB, Maine, then flown direct to Ramstein AFB, Germany. (Rear, L to R): Major 'Hoss' Linscomb, Captains Quinn Born, Henry Scherer, Warren Pierce, John Linihan, John Leaphart, Robert Gould. (Front, L to R) Lieutenant Colonel Clyde East (CO, 20th TRS), Captains Lennie Severtson, Carl Overstreet, Marvin Lindsey and Chuck Lustig. Gene Morris Collection

direction, but it was during the return to Shaw that he was particularly grateful to be accompanied by a KC-135. When his drop tanks failed to feed, he was able to jettison them over the Atlantic and take 'a tow' behind the tanker, refuelling every 20 minutes until they arrived back at Shaw.

Notwithstanding the interest and excitement (sometimes too much) of the many world-wide CASF deployments, many men looked forward to the homecoming, a few rare days of stability and a little time to socialise with friends in familiar surroundings. In the early 1960s the old, wood-built Officers Club was a cool haven for all, especially for the bachelors who lived without air conditioning in the new brick-built Bachelor Officers' Quarters (BOQ). The Stag Bar, manned by the wonderfully irreverent barman Tom, was a favourite meeting place after a hard day's work, in a Club which was thriving with diverse attractions seven days a week.

Welcome Home. Family welcome for Bob Gould - back from 'Big Lift'. Bob Gould

Home Stretch. A Voodoo nose camera's view of northerly runway at Shaw AFB. John Linihan

'Break a Leg!' The 363rd Flight Line Four strut their stuff in the Shaw Officers Club. (L to R) Ken Collins(manager) Larry Cooper, Jerry Rogers, Mike Tschida & Tom Curtis. Mike Tschida

Cool Haven. The Shaw AFB Officers Club 1959, sanctuary for the hot and weary. Shaw AFB

February 1963 saw more reorganisation at Shaw. The 363rd TRW remained the parent organisation at the base, responsible for all support functions, but the 837th AD was deactivated and redesignated the USAF Tactical Air Reconnaissance Center (TARC), a tenant unit at Shaw embracing the 4411th Combat Crew Training Group, with its 4414th CCTS (Voodoo), 4415th CCTS (Destroyer) and newly activated 4416th Test Squadron fielding a mix of aircraft.

Major Don Lang, who flew the Voodoo first with the 29th TRS at Shaw in 1959 before joining the 15th TRS at Kadena, returned to Shaw in 1963 to become a test pilot on the

Test Pilot. Major Don Lang, who began his Voodoo flying with the 29th TRS, returned to Shaw from the 15th TRS at Kadena in 1963, to take up test pilot duties with the newly formed 4416th Test Squadron. Don Lang

4416th Test Squadron. Don ferried one of the RF-101s assigned to the squadron from USAFE, where it had sustained damage while on TDY with the 66th TRW in North Africa. The aircraft had been patched up for its return to the United States but its drop tanks failed to feed over the Atlantic and he lost his primary flight instruments; with determination and continuous help from a KB-50 tanker he completed the journey to Shaw. Captain George Cowgill was also assigned to the TARC, from July 1963 to early 1964 carrying out the duties of flight test maintenance officer before being appointed Commander, 4411th Organisational Maintenance Squadron (OMS), with four officers and 66 aircraft, as part of the TARC. The squadron comprised 18 RF-101s of the 4414th CCTS, 18 RB-66s and 18 RF-4Cs of the 4415th CCTS, together with assorted RF-84s, B-66s, RF-101s and EC-130 aircraft of the Composite Test Squadron. This was big business. In the summer of 1965, George shipped out to the 45th TRS in Japan.

In May 1964, Bob Gould took part in Exercise Desert Strike, which involved hiding the Voodoos when on the ground from the prying eyes of airborne intruders, using every possible ruse including sheltering them among 1200 other aircraft at the Litchfield Park Naval Storage Area, under the wings of Super Constellations. They were never discovered. At the same time a trial to test camouflage schemes for the RF-101s was set up at Shaw, allegedly as a result of Lieutenant Ross Shaw berating the TAC commander for sending the Voodoos to war over Cuba in bright, silver aircraft. An all-black Voodoo had already been evaluated for use at night when Dewey Hemphill, 29th TRS, became the project officer tasked with looking at alternative colour schemes, including one in 'solid green' and another in camouflage. Dewey's group flew all over the States, being photographed against many different landscapes. The result was a colour scheme adopted for all Voodoos assigned to the war zone in SEA, the first combat aircraft in the theatre to be camouflaged. Interestingly, not all Voodoo pilots agreed with the need for,

Bright Warrior. Before warpaint, this RF-101 displays its original beauty. Jim Ifland Collection

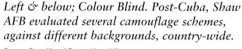

Black Beauty. This 29th TRS Voodoo painted black to evaluate a night camouflage scheme, seen at Elmendorf AFB, Alaska, in Exercise Polar Siege. Shaw AFB

or effectiveness of, the camouflage. Bob Archibald belonged to those who thought it might be of little value. He had done similar work on the F-106 in Air Defence Command (ADC) where the conclusion had been that, in terms of visual acquisition, there was little to choose between the schemes trialled.

Dewey Hemphill was also a participant in what might have been one of the greatest air refuelling disasters in the history of the RF-101. By early 1964, when Exercise Tidal

Wave/Dhanara Jata was planned and the KC-135 was well established as the tanker of choice, this deployment of four Voodoos to Thailand for a month must have seemed little more than routine for the experienced globe-trotters of TAC, but nothing was routine when it came to AAR. Dewey travelled outbound on a KC-135, acting as Tactical Air Advisor to the Mission Commander flying in the lead tanker. He joined them at Castle AFB, California, for

Left & below; Colour Blind. Post-Cuba, Shaw AFB evaluated several camouflage schemes, against different backgrounds, country-wide.
George Cowgill and Dewey Hemphill

the leg to Guam. Voodoo pilots were not accustomed to using all the runway on take-off but Dewey found that the tankers needed every yard, and began to see their pilots in a new light. It all started well, the four RF-101s flown by Tom McNierney (lead), Tom Hennigan, Fred Muesegaes and Jack Weatherby taking fuel twice before flying on to Don Muang without incident and the tankers then returning to Guam. From Guam, Dewey hitched a lift on a C-124 for Don Muang, but the aircraft went unserviceable en route at Udorn, Thailand, and he transferred to an RAF Beverley for the final leg. To his surprise, this huge transport was crewed solely by a junior pilot and a sergeant, for whom he also gained great respect when they penetrated very poor weather to land in a monsoon downpour at Don Muang with no more than an ADF to assist them. Whilst Tidal Wave was ostensibly a Thai exercise it was managed well by the US Military Advisory Group in Thailand (MAGTHAI) and the recce men completed their flying programme (mostly area covers over vast tracts of poorly mapped Thailand and into Laos) on schedule.

On the return trip Dewey flew one of the RF-101s while Jack Weatherby took over as Tactical Air Adviser in the lead tanker; no problems were envisaged. It was not until the four Voodoos were 100 miles short of their first refuelling point, 300 miles west of Clark AB, that the alarm bells started ringing. They met up with three tankers on time at 33,000 ft and the first refuelling went well, but the weather was now deteriorating fast, both at the next refuelling point and at Clark AB (their designated alternate) where the cloud base was already down to 300 ft with a visibility of one mile and a crosswind of 40 kts. The Voodoos were now flying on the wings of their tankers, so there were no rendezvous problems when it came to the next off-load, but by now they were clearly in a typhoon with dense cloud, very heavy turbulence and driving rain which severely hampered their ability to stay in contact. In Dewey's words:

"The tanker began to yaw, with the wing-tip moving fore and aft in increments which were difficult to counter with throttle movements. Finally the tanker's wing-tip light made a very rapid movement to the rear and I almost lost contact as I pulled back the throttles rapidly. The relative movement then reversed but when I *increased the throttles my engines stalled with explosive bangs, the tanker was gone and I was in a rapid descent on instruments".*

Despite cautious management of each throttle in turn the engines continue to surge, bang and stall until eventually behaving normally at 18,000 ft, when Dewey was able to begin a cautious cruise climb for maximum range. He felt sure that icing had caused his engine problems, believed that there was now little chance of successful AAR and that survival, with or without the external fuel tanks, depended on reaching Clark - or close enough to be rescued after an ejection. While he pondered the problem of climbing into a dinghy in a raging sea, he may not have considered the ramifications of ejecting in the prevailing conditions, whether his parachute would collapse in the high and erratic winds of the typhoon and at what lateral speed he might hit the water.

Meanwhile, the radio told him that all the RF-101s and KC-135s had also become separated with the four Voodoos and three tankers now milling about in the murk. The tanker crews were able to see each other on their radars but for some reason not the fighters - whose pilots had no idea where anyone was; it was a flyer's nightmare. The Voodoo pilots put off the decision to drop their external tanks and, by judicious use of their ADF, careful calculations on basic EA-6B flight calculators and good eyesight, each eventually joined up on the lead KC-135, neither of the other two being visible in the dense cirrus. With great relief they all took on enough fuel to get them to Guam, but left that tanker with barely sufficient for its own safe recovery. In fact, the tanker commander advised SAC Operations at Guam that they would be recovering with a mere 2000lb of fuel, well below permitted minimums and fuel gauge tolerances. He then compounded the problem by overshooting from a US Naval Air Station, having mistaken it for his destination at Anderson AFB, to subsequently land at Anderson as the engines of his big aircraft began to wind down through fuel starvation. It had been a close run thing, with many lessons learned and SAC relieving the KC-135 captain of his command. The remainder of the trip from Guam was relatively uneventful, with the four Voodoo pilots

Homecoming. Returning with the Voodoo detachment from Exercise Tidal Wave/Dhanara Jata in SEA, Captain Dewey Hemphill receives the traditional welcome to Hawaii from Linda Bell and back at Shaw from his wife Betty and daughter Teresa. Dewey Hemphill

welcomed in traditional manner both at Hickam AB, Hawaii, and of course by their families at Shaw.

Back in the relative peace and calm of Shaw AFB, 27 February 1964 was a special day for the 363rd TRW as it celebrated its 21st birthday, but the pace of work remained relentless. The TDYs were endless, often new and interesting with the Voodoos going to Trondheim, Norway, in June on Exercise Northern Express and finishing the year with the unusual deployment of six RF-101s of the

20th TRS to Peru for joint manoeuvres in Exercise Ayacucho, before the squadron went north again to Alaska in January still in their jungle camouflage. In Bob Gould's words: *"aircraft camouflaged for the tropics sure do show up nice in snow country"*.

At the end of 1964 Lieutenant Colonel Ray Lowery assumed command of the 29th TRS, but the arrival of the first RF-4C Phantom for the 4415th CCTS on 28 January 1965 signalled that the RF-101's operational days were now numbered. It was announced that the 16th TRS

Happy Birthday. The 363rd TRW celebrated its 21st birthday on 27 February 1964 with the USAF's Pipe Band in attendance. Shaw AFB

was to be fully equipped with the new aircraft by 30 April, but with ominous events developing fast in SEA the life of the Voodoo force was far from over. Ever more Voodoo aircraft, personnel and equipment were being drafted piecemeal from Shaw to SEA, and there were now rumours that a complete RF-101 unit would soon be committed, not only to raise the number of recce aircraft available but also because of its unique (36-inch split vertical) camera configuration. In the meantime, however, there was no let-up in the number and diversity of the mobility exercises.

Then it happened. In November 1965 a large force of RF-101s from the 20th TRS was ordered to Tan Son Nhut AB, Saigon, for combat duties. Many pilots on that squadron had already flown in SEA on TDY and completed the 100 ('countable') missions required, so the squadron would contain a large number of new men, volunteers from other RF-101 units, ex-Voodoo pilots withdrawn from staff assignments and newcomers from other roles hastily trained by the 4414 CCTS at Shaw (Chapter Three). On 1 July 1966 the 4411th CCTG was deactivated,

the Voodoos of the 4414th CCTS and RF-4Cs of the 4415th CCTS coming under the command of the 363rd TRW. The 29th TRS and 4414th CCTS were released from operational commitments from 1 August, to concentrate wholly on the training of RF-101 replacement pilots for the units serving in SEA and the 4414th CCTS then became the 31st Tactical Reconnaissance Training Squadron (TRTS).

Veteran Voodoo pilot Major 'Norm' Huggins, who had survived an ejection over the Bay of Tonkin in 1965 and a courageous brush with the North Vietnamese before being rescued at sea (Chapter Seventeen), was now back at Shaw as Flight Safety Officer on the TARC, flying RF-4s with the 4416th Test Squadron. It was in his primary role that he was recalled urgently from the local town of Sumter during an emergency landing at the airfield on 3 June 1968. There he found that the undercarriage of an RF-4C had collapsed during the landing and that the aircraft had veered off the runway on to the ramp and come to rest beneath the wing of an RB-66. The pilot and navigator had jettisoned the canopy and

Too Close for Comfort. Major Norman Huggins, Flight Safety Officer, 363rd TRW, was commended for his action in minimising the damage resulting from this wayward RF-4C. Norman Huggins

Farewell. Lieutenant Colonel John Zartman, commander of the 18th TRS, salutes the departure of his RF-101s to the Air National Guard. John Zartman

escaped from the aircraft but had left one engine in full afterburner gauging a furrow in the concrete ramp; the other engine had ingested debris and ground to a stop. Without hesitation Norm went to the burning aircraft, reached into the cockpit and stop-cocked the offending engine in time to prevent the fire chief attempting to do the same by throwing his axe into the engine intake, and before the inferno reached the fighter's fuel cells or the RB-66 loaded with JP-4 kerosene. For his quick thinking and total disregard for his own safety, Norm was awarded the Airman's Medal.

So ends this résumé of the RF-101's operational life in TAC at Shaw AFB. This spectacular, venerable aircraft had served in numbers at the titular home of tactical reconnaissance for nine years; it had broken records, roamed the world and produced many miles of photographic evidence of its worth. It would, however, remain at Shaw in the training role for several more years, this story taken up in Chapter Three. Front line RF-101s were back at Shaw briefly in December 1969, the 18th TRS returning from 10 years of equally successful service in France and Great Britain, and coming under the command of the 363rd TRW during its conversion to the RF-4C in November 1970. The honour of commanding the 'Lone Polecats' in their last days with the Voodoos went to Lieutenant Colonel John Zartman; he took the salute as the last of his aircraft departed Shaw for the 186th TRG, Air National Guard (ANG) at Fort Smith Arkansas.

CHAPTER THREE
TRAINING THE BEST

'In no other profession are the penalties for employing untrained personnel so appalling or so irrevocable as in the military'

General Douglas MacArthur 1933

There may be practitioners in other fast-jet roles from the 1950s and 1960s who argue that the successful prosecution of their particular specialisation, be it air combat, ground attack, maritime strike attack et al, was as demanding as that of single-seat tactical reconnaissance, but it would be heresy to suggest such a thing in this proud history of the Voodoo force. Certainly the 'alone, unarmed and unafraid' role called for a particular type of man, one who could think for himself, prepare assiduously for each mission but be ready to change his plan radically in mid-air, to be able to navigate well and to have a retentive memory. In addition he had to fly essentially high performance aircraft at near supersonic speeds and very low levels, often having to avoid heavy defences and in the target area hold his aircraft steady for as long as it took to take the necessary photographs. His mission would, of course, be a failure if he was then unable to get his in-flight report back and photographs home, perhaps through another gauntlet of fire from friend and foe alike and with a damaged aircraft (Vide Part Two: 'Conflict').

In ideal times, therefore, it was axiomatic in the USAF and RAF that the flying men selected for this job promised these attributes, perhaps with the added criterion that they had previous fast-jet experience on the front line. This latter prerequisite was challenged and the author was among those who believed that first tour pilots who exhibited the right attitudes and potential in advanced training could, if handled properly on their squadrons, acquit themselves well. Trials to this end proved the point in both air forces, with this and later chapters giving examples. In the dark, latter days of the conflict in SEA, as the more experienced recce pilots completed their 100 missions and had to be replaced with volunteers or pressed men, all

these truisms were well proven, but this chapter deals primarily with the basic conversion and recce training of the 'chosen men'.

With so many front line squadrons converting to the RF-101s as soon as these aircraft became available in large numbers from 1957, transition programmes were set up on the squadrons. Captain Paul Hodges, who had been serving on an RF-84F squadron at Sembach AFB, Germany, was one of many who would take this route into the Voodoo world, in 1958 converting in theatre to the aircraft. There was no such luxury as a dual aircraft or flight simulator but he and most of his peers found no problem with the transition, made easier by a detachment to the better flying weather conditions at Nouasseur AB, Morocco. They had been used to the heavy, underpowered RF-84F and to graduate to the Voodoo was, in Paul's words: *"like going from a bicycle to a Harley Davidson"*; he admits that the acceleration provided by the two big J-57s in afterburner *"required instant concentration from the start"*, he and his peers soon realising that this otherwise responsive aircraft had a very limited turning performance. 'Mixing it' with aircraft optimised for aerial combat was soon declared a 'no-go' area. Paul flew many hours in the Voodoo in peacetime and competed in the NATO reconnaissance competition Royal Flush before joining the author as an instructor on the 4414th CCTS at Shaw AFB. Later, he would apply his expertise in combat with its successor, the RF-4C Phantom.

Paul's induction is instructive; while he was undertaking advanced flying training at Luke AFB he had expressed the hope that he would be selected for air defence fighters, but this was at a time when the USAF was looking for men with the right potential to give a sensible mix of talents in the Tac Recon force, and Paul fell into that category. Subsequently, far from being

Above left to right; Veteran Commanders. Major Doug ('Grumpy') Brittian was promoted from the 4414th CCTS, here a lieutenant colonel on the 18th TRS at Laon AFB in 1963. As with one of his flight commanders on the training unit, Captain Chuck O'Connell, he was a veteran of WW2, and both had one more war to come! Doug Brittian and Shaw AFB

disappointed, Paul would revel and excel in this challenging role.

The front line RF-101 squadrons were fully formed when the 4414th CCTS was set up at the southern end of the flight line at Shaw in the spring of 1959. This squadron was tasked primarily with training pilots for the Voodoo Tac Recon force, but with a temporary commitment to provide some initial training for the F-101 fighter bomber pilots of the 81st TFW in the UK. The instructional expertise was drawn from pilots already acquainted with the role and the aircraft; Major Doug Brittian was in command, Captain Bill Lyle the Operations Officer, Captain Chuck O'Connell and Flight Lieutenant Paddy King, the latter transferred from the 17th TRS, the flight commanders. Initially, the squadron was equipped with a mix of single-seat RF-101 'A' and 'C' models, all of which had the standard operational camera fit, but in 1960 two-seat F-101Bs (without a 'stick' in the back) and F-101F dual trainers, neither of which carried cameras, were added to the inventory. Paddy had already made his

The Hard Word. Flight Lieutenant Paddy King (centre) and Captain Ken Stephens brief Lieutenants Bill Dault and Tom Malone on the 4414th CCTS.
Paddy King

Training Colours. RF-101A, 60179, on the busy 4414th CCTS flight line. Fred Muesegaes

presence known at Shaw, not only in the air but with his irrepressible spirit and Irish sense of humour at work and play on the ground; however, in common with most foreign nationals, he had the odd brush with stringent USAF security perceptions. In his case, an over-zealous unit security officer confiscated his copy of the 'Flight International', despite the magazine's unclassified, world-wide circulation, and even mooted his arrest, simply because it carried pictures of US rockets.

By the summer of 1959, the newer, heavier and faster jets then in service had been churning up paved surfaces at Shaw, and the base was

Training Ground. An RF-101C joins the traffic pattern at Shaw AFB from the south, abeam the 4414th CCTS home at that end of the airfield. George Cowgill Collection

closed to all jet flying while the necessary repairs were undertaken, the RF-101s deploying to nearby Myrtle Beach AFB. Paddy King went too, his social attributes rewarded in a symbolic gesture in which local worthies made him an honorary Mayor of Myrtle Beach; he would not enjoy this prestigious appointment long, returning with the 4414th CCTS to Shaw and handing over the post of RAF exchange officer to the author in September 1959.

The new incumbent got off to an interesting start. It all began when this obviously very English person, clad most unsuitably in a natty gents suit straight from London, arrived at Sumter railway station on a hot and humid South Carolina evening to be met by a very un-English looking officer attired quite differently and far more appropriately. The two went directly to a very kind welcoming party which had clearly been in full swing for some time and where the new boy was treated to innumerable shots of a drink hitherto unknown to him, called a 'tini' (Martini). Some time later, the two 'Brits' made their unsteady way to the bachelor quarter allocated to the new arrival, where they found the door to essential facilities firmly and unwisely locked. Gentle pressure to secure access revealed an inherent fault in construction when the complete doorway and framework gave way, leading to the first of several discussions with the USAF officers in charge of housing and the Officers Open Mess. The author takes up the story:

"I continued my introduction to the base institutions by day and my social programme by night in a borrowed car while my identification papers were being processed, and was caught short when

Speed Bird. A 'clean'(no external tanks) RF-101 was a joy to fly. Norman Huggins.

stopped by the air police who found me driving somewhat aimlessly around the married quarters late one evening. The problem was that I had forgotten the name of my host or where he lived, and who had lent me the car; I had no means of identification and tended to speak with anything but a southern accent. It would be generous to say that the rather bemused police understood my plight and I became a marked man from then on! There is no truth in the story that I left the borrowed car in the Wing Commander's parking slot at the Club, in the certain knowledge that it would soon find its owner".

Perhaps fortuitously, the very short handover briefing between the two exchange officers, much of which seemed to be carried out in the bar of the base golf course, soon came to an end but, from all that was said and several tearful farewell parties, it was clear that Paddy the professional and social ambassador was going to be a very hard act to follow - and so it turned out to be.

The Air Force Manual (AFM) 51-101 called for five, two-hour instructional sessions in the static flight simulator followed by 11 transition flights, each sortie requiring proficiency in specific areas of flight, with the final two consisting of an evaluation check and night familiarisation. Before the two-seat Voodoos became available, an instructor pilot flew 'chase' in a second RF-101 on selected sorties and for check rides, in what the author found to be a well balanced and supervised programme:

"The unsophisticated, first generation simulator served its purpose well, enabling me to feel at home on my first flight in the aircraft, and the measured pace of the subsequent transition engendered the right level of confidence. The single seat RF-101 was a joy to fly - particularly without its external tanks".

Little power was needed to get the Voodoo moving, and only idle thrust to taxi at normal speeds. The nose gear steering was very effective as were the differential toe brakes, but the Dash-1 included a dire warning that the main gear might collapse in any sharp turns at

Trainer. Until the F-101B and dual control F-101F (60247 was one of the first) arrived on the 4414th CCTS in 1960, all the units at Shaw were equipped solely with the single-seat aircraft RF-101. John Turner

speeds of 15mph or above. Take-off in afterburner was indeed impressive, each engine producing a plume of air with temperatures of 200 deg F and speeds of 55 mph out to 230 ft behind the aircraft. The rudder became effective at about 70 kts, the nose wheel normally raised at 150 kts and the aircraft lifted off at 175 kts. Without external tanks and in cold weather take-off runs of less than 700 yds were not unusual, but there could be problems. Pooled water ingested into the engines from the nose-wheel wake might cause compressor stalls and afterburner blow-outs, while the afterburners were known to ignite excess fuel vented behind the aircraft, but in both cases this was often more disconcerting than dangerous. Also, those with little experience in 'fast jets' could be caught short by the awesome acceleration and short take-off runs in afterburner, perhaps failing to raise the undercarriage before the 250kts limit on the nose-wheel, but they suffered no more than the delighted taunts from expectant onlookers.

Typical climbing speeds in afterburner could be achieved within a minute of brake release, requiring excitingly steep climb angles. The zero delay lanyard which, when attached, opened the parachute immediately after ejection, had to be detached at a safe height above the ground to avoid the possibility of serious injury in an instant deployment at high level. Pilots were also warned to ensure they engaged the 'stick pusher' on the climb (off during take-off), as an added precaution against pitch-up.

Pitch-up could occur at any stage of the flight so during the transition phase and on the squadrons much attention was paid to its characteristics, warning signs and the remedial actions. Adjuncts to avoidance and recovery included a warning horn and stick pusher, but some Voodoo pilots claimed to be able to recognise its onset and in certain flight conditions flew with the pusher 'off'. The Dash-1 for the RF-101, as amended in 1965, prescribed the following pitch/spin recovery (abbreviated and simplified here). Warnings from horn or pusher required an immediate reduction in aft control stick force and/or angle of attack. If a pitch developed, full nose-down stabilizer should be applied, with rudder and ailerons neutral and the brake parachute deployed at the peak of the pitch (when the speed should be less than 150 kts - well below

the maximum brake 'chute speed of 210 kts. If engaged, afterburners should be deselected to avoid blow-out and subsequent fuel torching which might destroy the brake 'chute. At the first sign of negative 'G' resulting from these actions, the stick should be returned to neutral. Uninitiated manoeuvres might continue during the recovery, the aircraft being virtually out of control for up to 8 seconds, after which all initial control movements should be gentle and no attempt made to pull out of the dive (during which the brake 'chute might be allowed to detach automatically) until reaching 350 kts. Should a full pitch-up occur below, or control of the aircraft not be achieved by 15,000 ft, the pilot should eject.

The manual stated that a spin was 'virtually impossible without first entering pitch-up'; it followed that a spin (a prohibited manoeuvre) was only likely to result from the failure to recover from a pitch-up. Should this be the case, an incipient spin was likely to be 'highly oscillatory in pitch, roll and yaw - probably with repeated reversals in direction'. No attempt should be made to control the aircraft, the stick merely held forward, rudder and stabilizer neutral, until the first signs of negative 'G' when pitch-up recovery procedures could begin. In the event of a flat, steady state and rapidly rotating spin, recovery was most unlikely and ejection should be 'accomplished with at least 15,000 ft terrain clearance'.

This résumé of the notorious pitch-up and its consequences should not have caused undue alarm. True, pitch-up led to the loss of some aircraft and lives, but there was a general acceptance that if the flight regimes conducive to the phenomenon were avoided and clear rules observed, the risks were much reduced. Of course there were situations, especially in combat but also in peacetime (such as in taking vital avoiding action), in which this was easier said than done but in all normal conditions, published flying techniques allowed sufficient margins for safe operations. Greater restrictions applied when the pitch-up warning system was inoperative.

In flight, the single piece, controllable horizontal stabilizer provided highly responsive and effective control at subsonic and supersonic speeds. This was particularly so at low altitude and high indicated airspeeds when over-control and excessive 'G' loading could result. The ailerons also provided excellent control, but again caution had to be exercised at high speeds when extreme or rapid aileron movement could impose twisting loads on the wing. Power operated rudder control became available from 70 kts, with assistance from a yaw damper in flight throughout the speed range Two-position flaps (fully down or retracted) added stability in certain flight conditions (flight refuelling), also considerably reducing landing speeds and distance, while infinitely variable, forward-hinged panel speed brakes on the rear fuselage were similarly effective in reducing speed.

Other than at the low speeds and high angles of attack associated with possible pitch-up, control within the recommended speed ranges was responsive and positive; the aircraft was stable at the very high speeds of which it was capable, an invaluable asset at low level in hostile environments, and the transonic zone at height was almost unnoticeable. Guidance on manoeuvring loads, inertia coupling, recovery from dives and avoidance of excessive 'G' was standard for aircraft of its type and again gave no cause for alarm. Using the prescribed techniques, the aircraft handled well on instruments and in formation.

In addition to Ultra High Frequency (UHF) AN/AIC-10 communications, ancillary navigation equipment could include a UHF homer, VOR or TACAN, ILS, radio compass, IFF/SIF, a Ground Position Indicator (GPI) and radar altimeter. An autopilot eased the pilot's workload but the author found, at least in the early days, that it should be monitored continuously. The AN/APS-54 radar warning system, which provided visual and audio warning of pulsed radio signals, generated little interest in those early, peaceful days in South Carolina, but its time would come.

Restrictions on RF-101 operations included maximum speeds of 700 kts and Mach 1.57 above 25,000 ft and 600 kts below that height (clean); 500 kts and Mach 1.3 with external tanks fitted. As for 'G' limits, 'A' models were limited to +6.33/-3, 'C' models to +7.33/-3 and both types to + 4/-2 when carrying external tanks; these were typical figures for the type at the time. 'No-go' areas included snap manoeuvres, rolls beyond 360 deg, intentional pitch-ups/spins and negative 'G' conditions in excess of 15 seconds, while many dramatic incidents throughout its life underlined the need to avoid thunderstorms

As with any jet aircraft, rapid reaction to emergencies in the Voodoo was all-important. Many procedures were largely common practice, clearly documented and readily available in check lists, but afterburner malfunctions were new to some. Up to 35% of full (dry) power could be lost if an afterburner failed and its exhaust nozzles remained open; so deselection in that event was essential to close the nozzle and stop the fuel flow to that system. Again, actions in the event of an engine fire or overheat indications were generally standard, always to be treated seriously even though there were many spurious warnings in the Voodoo; afterburner blow-out and simple failures of nozzles to open or close were relatively rare. Double engine failures were similarly unlikely and the author is not aware of any successful double flame-out landings from height, although the Dash-1 claims that the aircraft would glide successfully at 250 kts (which could maintain sufficient hydraulic pressure for essential services) and cover some 30 miles from 20,000 ft.

The Voodoos flown by the 4414th CCTS were tested rigorously by carefully selected pilots of proven ability such as Major Jack Coghlan, a 4411th CCTG test pilot, who was also accomplished in the recce role on the RF-80, RF-84F and RF-101. He was sorely tested himself when, in June 1960, at 800 ft after take-off on a test flight, his aircraft 'suddenly yawed and snapped to the left, followed by an equally abrupt snap to the right'. Somehow Jack managed to regain control and climb to 6000 ft clear of populated areas as he prepared to eject if the same happened again - but when it did it was with such violence that he could not reach the ejection seat handles. He then

Test Pilot. Major Jack Coghlan, test pilot on the 4411th, was commended for recovering an RF-101 with severe control problems.
Mary Coghlan

attempted to induce a stall and pitch-up by pulling back the stick to reduce speed, only to find as he neared the vertical that control seemed to revert to normal. From this he concluded that his aircraft had a defective rudder boost lock-out system, which kicked in at 290 kts, and that if he kept the speed below that figure he might be able to recover the aircraft. Accordingly, he completed low speed checks in the landing configuration to his satisfaction, had the traffic halted on the Columbia Highway and was able to land safely. Major Coghlan's flying skills, knowledge of his aircraft, coolness and courage under stress fully justified a recommendation for the coveted 'Well Done' award in the Aerospace Safety Magazine.

Because the RF-101's on-board role

1960. One of the first courses to include students direct from advanced flying training (Lieutenants Menees, Nimmo and Linihan).

1960. Rear, left: Lieutenant Colonel 'Pete' Stuyvesant, Cdr (designate) 78th TFS, 81st TFW (Chapter Six). Rear, centre: Author

1960. Students destined for F-101s of the 81st
TFW, RAF Bentwaters/Woodbridge (Chapter
Six)

1961. Rear, right: Flight Lieutenant John
Turner RAF; front, second right: Captain
Norman Huggins and second left: Lieutenant
Burt Waltz (Chapter Seventeen)

On the Job. 4414th flight commander Captain
Bob Tarrant, shows Lieutenant Mike Nicholas the
way. Jim Tidwell

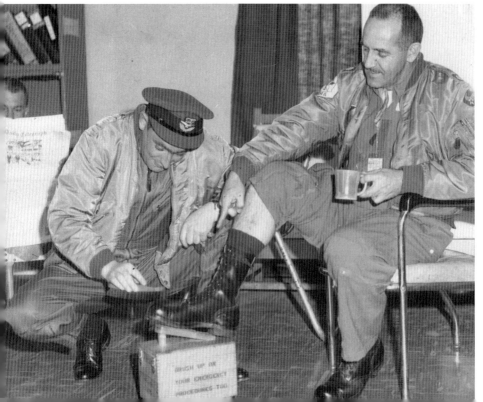

Trade Training.
The author
learning the art of
shoe cleaning, US-
style, fellow
Voodoo students
Lieutenant Colonel
Peter Stuyvesant
(destined for the
81st TFW)
supervising, while
Captain Peter
Collins (who would
become an SR-71
pilot) studies from
another British
contribution, the
Daily Telegraph.
Shaw AFB

Watching Brief. Already an experienced fast-jet pilot (F-104) Lieutenant 'Newk' Grubb needed little help from the author on the Voodoo course. Newk died in captivity in Hanoi (Chapter Nineteen). Author

equipment and operating techniques were new to most students on the 4414th CCTS, even those who already had tac recon experience, all the recce students were given the full course. Following the transition phase the second part of the course consisted of applied flying, instrument and formation training, night familiarisation and instruction in the operational role. The latter concentrated on the rudiments of aerial photography using the three camera stations, generally the KA-2 nose and side oblique cameras for low level work, the KA-2, 6-inch vertical for high level pin-points and mosaics, and the KA-1, 38-inch split-verticals for area covers. The targets for this initial orientation to tac recon were necessarily easy to find and locate in the aircraft's viewfinder; while this was a useful adjunct in training and academic photo recce competitions most Voodoo recce pilots would quickly develop a 'sixth sense' which enabled them to photograph the target automatically and adequately, without burying their head in

The Name of the Game. Operational training on the 4414th CCTS concentrated on airborne photography, seeking the ideal of centring the target and placing it a third from the bottom of the frame. The rationale of the valley crawl in the Grand Canyon is not clear. Author & John Turner

the viewfinder, a potentially dangerous practice when flying at very low level and high speed, especially in a highly hostile environment. The purpose of this course was solely to acquaint the student with the systems and their operation, together with the tactics and techniques best suited to their use. There was no low flying over South Carolina at that time below 500 ft.

For reasons which some found hard to accept at the time, the syllabus also included one sortie devoted to 'artillery adjustment' in which the RF-101, in huge and vulnerable orbits at low level ahead of field guns, attempted to adjust their fire. These sorties were considered to be great fun but of very dubious value operationally. The author cannot recall how these exercises were assessed, but fortunately they did not seem to be crucial to passing the course. Certainly, many of the students from that time will have abiding memories of those confident calls from their ever-enthusiastic army liaison officer of "on the way, wait!" Little did anyone know then that, some eight years later, the RF-101s of the 45th TRS at Tan Son Nhut, Saigon, would be flying artillery adjustment sorties in support of US Navy battleships off the coast of Vietnam.

The author took comments from a number of pilots who, contrary to an earlier dictum, were selected for the RF-101 school at Shaw without any previous experience on an operational front line fast-jet squadron, and found common consensus. Lieutenant John Linihan was one of the men chosen from volunteers who were not keen to remain on the F-86L in the homeland night/all-weather fighter force, leaving them with little immediate chance of going overseas after their training. John could have spoken for others of his kind at the time, such as Lieutenants Ken Nimmo, Stan Menees and Howard Myli, when he said that he found the aircraft imposing, compared with the T-33 and the F-86L on which they had trained, but not difficult to fly, and the volunteers may not have been disappointed in the demanding aircraft and its recce role. To be sure, they had to learn new skills, such as

those required in formation take-offs at such high acceleration rates with little power to play with in the afterburner throttle range (perhaps resorting to the unusual practice of using the speed brakes in lieu) and John remained sensibly wary of the pitch-up throughout his time on the aircraft.

Don Karges went to the Voodoo school with 1600 hours flying experience, albeit mainly in relatively low performance aircraft in Training Command. Although admitting to have been a little intimidated at first by the size of the Voodoo, he too found it easy to fly, had no significant problems and was not daunted by pitch-up. His attitude in SEA was that of many of his peers in a choice between spending the rest of the war in the Hanoi Hilton by ejecting from a pitch-up, or being shot down: "I decided not to push the bird too far but let the bad guys try to hit me". He didn't and they didn't. Don would fly many 'test hops' in the RF-101 and placed much of his confidence in the aircraft down to properly calibrated angle of attack

Newcomer. Lieutenant John Linihan, among others, proved that pilots selected in their advanced training could cope well with the RF-101 and its role. John Linihan

indicators and pitch-up warning devices. Fire warning lights led to several expeditious single engine landings, but most warnings were spurious and overall he can recall only one dramatic incident in his many years with the Voodoo force. This occurred in a rapid climb when overpressure in the cockpit of an old 'A' model shattered part of its windscreen, leaving him in a swirl of fragments and dust. In the deafening noise of the slipstream he was not aware that fragments of the canopy had entered one engine, the valiant Pratt and Whitney J-57 digesting all without complaint to allow Don a successful landing. It was all in a day's work, and perhaps in measure down to good training.

The Extended Day. The author (centre) continues debriefing Captain Robert O Case well into the evening. Author

So it was that, under the sage guidance of Major James E Tidwell, the Operations Officer of the 4414th CCTS from 1960, few of the students (the 'first tourists' included), found the course too demanding. Indeed, they all went on to become highly respected recce pilots, thus vindicating the protagonists of what to some was a trial of the inexperienced - and giving the Voodoo force a new and sometimes refreshing dynamism.

It was far from 'all work and no play' in the

Voodoo Ritual. A young lady, back from a trip in a Voodoo (for reasons unknown) flown by Captain Bill Lyle, gets the standard water treatment for all after the first flight. Jim Tidwell

Major Jim Tidwell, Operations Officer, 4414th CCTS. Shaw AFB

halcyon, pre-SEA days of peace at Shaw AFB. First sorties in the Voodoo were always celebrated with a ritual 'shower' and as a matter of routine (as was the way with the RAF in those times) officers from different units on the base mixed and relaxed over a few drinks in the Stag Bar after work, mulling over the day's work in that engaging vernacular for which fighter pilots of the day were so well known. In the Shaw bar, they had the added attraction of baiting the British exchange pilots, pointing to the history of a Revolutionary War which had raged locally in bygone days and was graphically portrayed (if with some bias) in the evening TV editions of 'Swamp Fox'. The author retaliated by re-establishing a British enclave in Camden, South Carolina and raising the Union Jack at this one time scene of several notable British victories;

> *"I shared a converted stable, purported to have once accommodated horses belonging to the British General Cornwallis, with a 'good ole boy' from North Carolina; he was born of loyalist stock in the shadow of 'Cold Mountain' and we ran an 'open house' offering traditional British ways".*

There were also, of course, the regular 'meet and greet' beer calls for the incoming students of the 4414th, who reciprocated in kind when they graduated, but in those days even the most flimsy pretext could bring the pilots and their ladies together in that old, probably original,

character-filled and much revered wood-built Officers Club which throbbed with activity on most evenings. It was on one such evening that a selection of pilots in the Stag Bar suddenly found themselves unintentionally, uninvited and certainly 'illegally', in the main body of the club. The soirées were not always sedentary, incumbents of the Stag Bar sometimes indulging in physical fitness exercises which could lead to trouble. So it was on one evening when the more energetic were learning to play the traditional RAF game of 'high cock'alorum'. With no hesitation, two teams of prime beef took up the challenge and it was 'game on' until an internal wall collapsed, spilling improperly clad officers into better dressed, more sedate, VIP company in the cocktail bar. As a result, the foreign person held responsible was invited to forego his visits to the Club for the following two weeks, previous counts of leaving his mark on the Stag Bar ceiling (again by courtesy of dubious friends) being taken into account.

In the summer of 1961 Flight Lieutenant John R Turner RAF arrived at Shaw with his family to take over the post of RAF exchange officer. Rumours had it that both air forces had agreed, for the sake of international relationships, that a 'well married' officer might be preferable to a bachelor and John was the ideal choice. He was well married, an excellent fighter reconnaissance pilot, a member of the winning team in the 1959 Royal Flush competition and experienced in high level photography from his tour on Meteor PR10s in Germany, a skill which would play well in the RF-101's role. The author remained in residence until John completed the standard course on the 4414th CCTS, very sensibly with an USAF instructor as his mentor to ensure that the two foreign nationals did not resurrect any unacceptable habits from their own air force. That said, the squadron hierarchy, surely with some apprehension, did authorise the two to fly together on a long weekend in a two-seat Voodoo to 'wherever they wished', wherever they wished turning out to be Las Vegas via San Antonio and on to Biggs AFB, conveniently on the border with Mexico. The wise psychology of those in charge proved well-founded because the trip went without a hitch, perhaps the two explorers knowing that they had a point to prove; they also learned much on many counts, but the story is best left there!

Because of the long overlap, the final change-over between the RAF officers was less intensive and eventful than had been so with Paddy King's departure and the author's introduction two years before. However, it was celebrated in the rather un-American way with a pyjama party, notable by the clear need for some of the guests to purchase pyjamas - an apparel with which some were clearly unaccustomed.

So the author left Shaw AFB after an eventful tour, reflecting later;

"I had some near misses professionally and socially, owing my survival to the kindness, guidance and consideration of my hosts, and I learned much. Among my abiding memories was the utter calm and tranquillity of misty cotton fields and swamps, Carolina's tranquil dawns and starlit dusks. Plentiful flying in the spectacular Voodoo had been a real joy - the task to be done, pace of life and company wholly agreeable. What more could a man have wanted?"

John Turner found no difficulty flying the aircraft or with its role, but admits that to become an effective instructor pilot he had to make a few changes to his very British ways. He would soon learn about the aircraft's limitations, performing a loop from a rather ambitious speed and height being one salutary lesson, but he seemed to avoid the scares which beset many in their familiarisation with air refuelling. It was while undergoing a short consolidation period on one of the operational RF-101 squadrons, following completion of the training course, that John soon had the opportunity to prove his worth professionally. He was flying as wingman to a seasoned Voodoo pilot tasked by no less a body than the

'Low Level Nevill' Flight Lieutenant John Nevill, RAF, replaced John Turner on the 4414th CCTS in 1963. Shaw AFB

White House to photograph large areas of South Texas ravaged by Hurricane 'Carla', when his leader's aircraft became unserviceable at a refuelling stop. John offered up his aircraft but the leader insisted that he attempt the task himself, and this he did with great success, the prints gaining much praise at the White House. Another credit followed, John coming to the rescue when a large buzzard shattered a forward panel and rear of a student's cockpit canopy at low level. The unhappy student, uninjured but deprived of oxygen and communications and subject to a debilitating air blast, pulled up and indicated by hand signals that he needed serious help to return to base. Under John's precise leadership a potentially serious incident was averted and the sortie terminated in a copybook emergency recovery and landing. John Turner handed over to Flight Lieutenant John Nevill, RAF, in the autumn of 1963; John, known to his hosts as

Rest and Recuperation. Officers and ladies of the 4414th CCTS bid farewell to the author (centre) on his return to the UK. John Turner

The Last Song. The author (left) and successor John Turner render an old RAF song in a final duet. John Turner

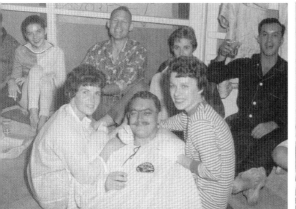

VOODOO WARRIORS

'Low Level Nevill', was the last RAF officer to fly the Voodoo, converting to the RF-4C Phantom midway through his tour.

The pattern of training on the 4414th CCTS would continue into the mid-1960s, but with pressure to replace the experienced RF-101 pilots who had completed their 100 countable missions in SEA, the selection criteria for the incoming students had to be progressively relaxed. Of necessity, more were having to be drawn from roles which were less than ideal for the demanding tasks ahead (the heavy bomber force, basic flying instructors et al), with their training taken at a measured pace and supervision at a premium. Towards the end of the decade the 29th TRS took on some of this training while the 4414th CCTS was deactivated and the 31st Tactical Reconnaissance Training Squadron (TRTS) formed in its place, staffed by highly experienced RF-101 pilots best able to look after the diversity of students. Major Rich Richardson was one; he had rejoined the 4414th in 1968 and transferred to the 31st

Instructor Pilot. Every expertise was needed to train the last pilots entering the 4414th CCTS - Rich Richardson up to the job. Shaw AFB

TRTS, serving initially as operations officer under Lieutenant Colonel Doyle Williams, then as a lieutenant colonel in command of the squadron.

With a depleting Voodoo force in PACAF and USAFE now converting to the RF-4C, the

The Instructors. There was no lack of rank or experience among the instructor pilots of the 4414 CCTS in July 1966. (Back row, L to R) Captains Lou Ravetti, Anon, Bill Dault, Monte Adkins, Chris Jesson and Gordon Newman. (Front row, L to R) Major Lou Picciano, Lieutenant Colonel Don Lang (Commander), Major Chuck O'Connell (Operations Officer), Major Cal Russell. Shaw AFB

FLIGHT ORDER

(If more space is required, continue on reverse, identifying items by number)

1. CREW MEMBERS LISTED BELOW WILL PROCEED IN AIRCRAFT INDICATED AND UPON COMPLETION OF FLIGHT WILL RETURN TO PROPER STATIONS.	2. EFFECTIVE ON OR ABOUT 16 February 1971	3. RETURN ON OR ABOUT 20 February 1971

4. FROM: (Place flight will originate)

SHAW AFB, SC

5. TO: (Itinerary, list complete address, variations in itinerary authorized)

SELFRIDGE AFB, MICH
SHAW AFB, SC

6. MISSION

FERRY AIRCRAFT

7. CREW NO.	8. TAKE-OFF TIME	9. DURATION OF FLIGHT	10. SECURITY CLEARANCE FOR PERIOD OF FLIGHT DUTY	11. SPECIAL INSTRUCTIONS
	N/A	N/A	TOP SECRET	None

12. CREW (See AFTO 00-20-5 for position codes) NO. A	13. POSITION B	NAME (Last, first, middle initial, AFSN; indicate commander of aircraft by placing asterisk next to his name.)	14. ORGANIZATION AND MAJOR COMMAND (If not issuing agency)	15. AIRCRAFT TYPE A	SERIAL NO. OR TACTICAL CALL SIGN B	FUEL LOADS (Lbs/Gals) C
1	Pilot	*HARBIN, KENNETH E. LT COL 307-32-3980	THIS HQ	RF-101	158	N/A
2	Pilot	*CROWDER, D.W. CAPT 370-26-8779		RF-101	160	
3	Pilot	*LENTS, JERRY D. MAJOR 405-36-6198		RF-101	511	
4	Pilot	*MOORE, KENDALL B. LT COL 426-14-2548		RF-101	512	
5	Pilot	*VAN DINE, WILLIAM A. MAJOR 049-24-7866		RF-101	521	
6	Pilot	*VENUS, JOHN D. MAJOR 379-30-0827		RF-101	497	
7	Pilot	*WHITFIELD, EDWIN P. CAPT 227-42-1463		RF-101	508	
8	Pilot	*KIMMERLY, john w. MAJOR 382-34-2673		RF-101	507	
9	Pilot	*JESSEN, CHRIS MAJOR 557-42-0392		RF-101	161	
10	Pilot	*WOLFE, C.W. LT COL 191-12-9180		RF-101	510	
11	Pilot	*LAWRENCE, WENDEL B. LT COL 270-20-5544		RF-101	155	
12	Pilot	*MERCER, ROGER N COL 348-18-3818		RFG101	156	
13	Pilot	*RICHARDSON, ROLAND L. LT COL 521-42-0312		RF-101	516	

16. RESERVE PERSONNEL NOT ON EXTENDED ACTIVE DUTY, ARE SUBJECT TO THE PROVISIONS OF THE UNIFORM CODE OF MILITARY JUSTICE WHILE PERFORMING THIS DUTY.

17. DATE OF ORDER 12 February 1971	18. ORDER NUMBER 035

19. DESIGNATION AND LOCATION OF HEADQUARTERS
DEPARTMENT OF THE AIR FORCE
31 TRTSq
Shaw AFB, SC

20. FOR THE   Commander

21. SIGNATURE ELEMENT OF ORDERS AUTHENTICATING OFFICIAL

KENNETH R. HARBIN, Lt Col, USAF
Operations Officer

Last Orders. This rank heavy 13 took the last RF-101s from Shaw to the Michigan ANG at Selfridge AFB. Shaw AFB

Last Out. Lieutenant Colonel 'Rich' Richardson, commander 31st Tactical Reconnaissance Training Squadron (TRTS), flew the last of his unit's RF-101s out of Shaw on 17 February 1971. Shaw AFB

requirement for RF-101 training petered out in 1970 and Rich led the last 13 aircraft in a rank-heavy formation from Shaw to the new owners, the Michigan ANG at Selfridge AFB, on 17 February 1971. They arrived at Selfridge in light snow and landed on patchy ice to a reception committee of one major on an otherwise empty ramp, the civilian orientated groundcrew having completed their statutory daily schedule and gone home. This did not impress the Voodoo men from Shaw, especially the full colonel Wing Director of Maintenance,

who announced to the major that he had 30 minutes to re-muster his troops or the pilots would refuel their own aircraft and return with them to Shaw. This had the desired effect; as ever the men of Shaw had completed their mission, with the trainers of the 4414th CCTS, the 29th TRS and 31st TRTS having fulfilled their purpose; the Voodoos would no longer grace the skies over central South Carolina.

CHAPTER FOUR
EYES OF NATO

'From Stettin in the Baltic to Trieste in the Adriatic, an iron curtain has descended across the continent'

Sir Winston Churchill, March 1946

By the mid-1950s, the Republic RF-84F Thunderflash had taken over from the RF-80, to become the mainstay of NATO's fast-jet tac recon force in Europe. Where the United States Air Force Europe (USAFE) led, the Dutch, German, Italian, Norwegian, Danish (at this stage the French) and other air forces followed suit with the aircraft; only the RAF, with its Meteor and Swift armed reconnaissance fighters, was different.

The RF-84F, with its strength, comprehensive array of cameras, fair turn of speed and very long range with external tanks, seemed a good vehicle for the job; it had a roomy cockpit and was not difficult to fly. However, it was too heavy, underpowered and lacked sufficient manoeuvrability to make it ideal, and it would have been particularly vulnerable in combat against the fast-developing family of MiG fighters. Early teething troubles included a tendency for the shroud ring around the engine compressor to shrink in the moist air of Europe, and while this could be cured by shaving the tips of the compressor blades, an associated reduction in the thrust available

further increased the already too long take-off runs. Flight Lieutenant John West, the RAF exchange officer at Shaw before Paddy King, enjoyed flying the aircraft on the 18th TRS but remembered that the external tanks rendered the aircraft a little unwieldy and that it could give an uncomfortable ride above 450 kts.

Lieutenant Paul Hodges, who flew the Thunderflash on his first operational tour with the 303rd TRS at Sembach AFB, Germany, part of the 66th TRW, on his first operational tour, remembers that in some conditions, coupled with a notorious 'hump' in the middle of Sembach's runway, the aircraft was very reluctant to get airborne without Jet Assisted Take Off (JATO) rocket pods. JATO was a mixed blessing; if the rockets failed (and they did) their added weight and drag exacerbated the take-off problem. When Paul's mentor and friend, Captain Jack Bowland, had this happen to him he only just managed to stagger over the trees at the end of the runway and bring his heavy aircraft round to jettison the recalcitrant pods over the prescribed area on the airfield, sadly killing two sheep going about their duty

Line of Succession. In the mid-1950s, USAFE RF-80s (left) were replaced by RF-84Fs, the 303rd TRS shown here on parade at Sembach AB, Germany, in 1958. Mary Coghlan/Paul Hodges

keeping the grass down but fortunately missing their shepherd. This was a rare case of Cold War 'fracticide' or 'friendly fire'.

The RF-84F had two .5-inch machine guns built into its engine air intakes and a relatively basic gunsight, but the guns would not have been very effective against either air or ground targets. Perhaps their primary purpose was to mark targets and some gunnery training was carried out in USAFE and other NATO air forces, inter alia allowing the recce pilots to retain some proficiency in the skill. USAF policy differed from that in the RAF. Guns were never intended for Voodoos built for recce from the start, while the gun-armed F-101 fighters converted later to the recce role had their guns removed to make room for the new nose and its cameras, with a commensurate weight saving. Likewise, the RF-101's successor in NATO, the RF-4C, would be unarmed, although some RF-4s were later equipped with guns and Sidewinder missiles. RF-101 pilots at Shaw told the author (perhaps with tongue-in-cheek) that getting rid of the guns had a more sinister reason, that of removing any temptation among the more aggressive recce pilots to engage in combat at the expense of their all-important primary role. RAF recce pilots readily accepted that their first duty was to return their intelligence reports to friendly hands but welcomed the chance to defend themselves with guns if needs be to keep enemy heads down en route to and in the target areas, or for air combat they could not otherwise avoid. Also, in clearly defined circumstances they might be ordered or permitted to attack specific 'targets of opportunity' encountered unexpectedly (say a nuclear missile convoy), when high explosive or armour-piercing ammunition from the 30-mm cannon carried by their Swifts and Hunters, (the Voodoo contemporaries) could have been decisive. The debate continues.

It was all change in 1958; the 66th TRW Headquarters moved to Laon AB, France, in September, with the RF-84s of the 302nd and 303rd TRS, while the runways and overruns there were still being made ready for the Voodoos. Captain Keith Kuester, a graduate of the first class at the newly established Air Force Academy, also arrived at Laon in 1958; he had been posted in to fly the RB-57 but with this aircraft being phased out he contrived a re-assignment to the RF-84F and then to the RF-101, as the Wing Flight Safety Officer. It was primarily in this capacity that he would continue to fly the Voodoo in succeeding years at Shaw, back in France and later in SEA, inevitably becoming involved in the flight safety aspects of many sad incidents.

Meanwhile, the 32nd and 38th TRS of the 66th TRW continued to fly RF-84s at Phalsbourg AB, an airfield in the foothills of the Vosges Mountains of north east France, while an RF-101C Mobile Training Unit was set up there in March 1958 to begin the transition of all four squadrons to the Voodoo. Captain 'Scotty' Schoolfield, already a fully qualified RF-101 recce pilot with 100 hours on the aircraft from his time on the 17th TRS at Shaw, arrived on the 32nd TRS before the Voodoo and had to revert to flying the RF-84F for some months, before becoming a great asset to the squadron when the new aircraft arrived.

Before their new aircraft arrived, Scotty and another established RF-101 pilot from Shaw, Captain John Leaphart, and seemingly the

'The Phalsbourg Aircraft Carrier'. Phalsbourg AB, so named because of its relatively short runway and steep drops off at both ends. Scotty Schoolfield

60099

U.S. AIR FORCE

Early Arrivals. Before the end of the decade, the RF-84Fs gave way to RF-101s. 'Balls 99'(60099) became the personal mount of the commander of the 38th TRS, Major Jack Nelson. Lieutenant Dick Reece (left) and (below left) Captain 'Scotty' Schoolfield were among the first to fly the RF-101 at Phalsbourg. Scotty Schoolfield & Dick Reece

whole of Phalsbourg witnessed the arrival of a 'goodwill mission' by four RF-101s from Shaw led by Colonel John Foster. With a cloud base of 2,500 ft and visibility of 10-15 miles, the multitude spotted the smoke trails well before the aircraft, to be suitably impressed by the unprecedented speeds and especially by what followed. When overhead the airfield, the leader pulled up abruptly into cloud and the two wingmen pealed off to their respective sides, to cries of *"What sort of manoeuvre was that?"* Before Scotty and John, the only Voodoo 'experts' around, could think of an answer, the leader and his aircraft re-emerged separately from the cloud, he beneath a parachute canopy, the Voodoo in a flat spin. So ended a very dramatic arrival; the effects of this 'goodwill' visit by the aircraft which would make a home at Phalsbourg was anyone's guess. It was said that Colonel Foster had lost the bellows in his control system en route across the Atlantic, and this led to the loss of all effective control of the aircraft during this impressive arrival.

Given the perennial poor weather throughout northern France, much of the conversion programme and subsequent Voodoo training was carried out in North Africa where there were few impediments of any sort. Lieutenant Dick Reese was serving on the 32nd TRS, the first of the 66th TRW squadrons to get the RF-101 in the fall of 1958, their aircraft arriving via Nouasseur AB, North Africa, where the

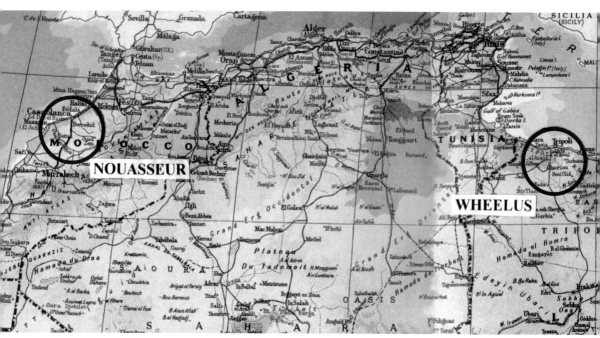

Wings Over Africa. Much of the 66th TRW transition to the RF-101 was carried out at Nouasseur AB, Morocco, the map above also showing the weapons range and air base at Wheelus in Libya. The four RF-101s in transit to North Africa carry pre-1962 tail markings while the single aircraft passing Gibraltar has the later signature.

George Cowgill Collection

Mobile Duty. Captain Scotty Schoolfield on watch at the runway threshold in Mobile Control at Nouasseur. Scotty Schoolfield

Playtime. Captains Dick Reece, Mike Tschida and Keith Keuster on the beach in Morocco. Mike Tschida

pilots carried out their conversion. Dick recalls that they smelled 'like a new car', except for one in which the ferry pilots had a small accident en route! Many pilots from the 66th TRW remember with great fondness regular detachments to their 'Sun Base' at Nouasseur, near Casablanca in Morocco, a huge SAC Reflex forward operating base; it had near perfect weather and very few flying restrictions. Moreover, when the day's work was done, there were the extraneous attractions of the warm Mediterranean, plenty of cold beer and the mysteries of Casablanca and Marrakech to explore. Life was not at all bad.

Paul Hodges was one of the many who carried out his initial conversion from the Thunderflash to the Voodoo at Nouasseur, and it was there that he got to feel the onset of pitch-up. His aircraft showed all the symptoms on landing when he raised the nose, perhaps a little too high and too quickly, to maximise aerodynamic braking. It did not happen to him again. Also at Nouasseur, Captain Bob Case remembers overflying a club just north of Casablanca at Fadala, known as 'The Sphinx', very visible from the air and with the roof sometimes adorned by ladies sun-bathing 'au naturel'. This was grist to the mill for the recce pilots, always anxious to improve their visual acuity and get as much information as possible from their targets, visually and on camera, and in this case doing both before having to 'plug in the burners' and go hard port to avoid a restricted area; it was all good training. No doubt he was not the only one to follow up his

noisy calling card with the photos he had taken, hand-carried to the Sphinx to an enthusiastic reception.

The Phalsbourg Wing would be blessed with good commanders. Major Jack Nelson, a West Point graduate, arrived to take over the 38th TRS ahead of the Voodoos, but kept his hand in on the new aircraft with the 32nd TRS. Jack had been destined for a desk job in Europe but was reassigned when the commander of the 38th TRS was killed landing short of the infamous Phalsbourg runway during a night transition sortie. As the senior squadron commander there he chose RF-101 60099, called affectionally 'Balls 99', as his personal aircraft. In those early days of autonomous squadrons, the fin of his aircraft would have carried white stars against a green background, identifying the 38th TRS from the yellow background of the 32nd. In 1969, Balls 99 went to the Air National Guard, where it remained until April 1976 before taking its place as gate guard at the Shaw AFB.

Looking back, Captain George Cowgill considers Jack to have been the 'best commander' he had in his long career, a very good but uncompromising 'boss' who did what he thought right rather than toe the party line. He was known to believe that the aircraft could be handled rather more aggressively than was originally thought, and by example proved his point. Scotty Schoolfield agreed, meeting Jack at work and play many times then and thereafter at Shaw when Jack commanded the 4414th CCTS and later when he was in charge of the 45th TRS in SEA, but Scotty thought similarly of his boss on the 32nd at Phalsbourg, Major Ralph Findlay. Ralph was able to engender loyalty and trust in all with whom he served, and was known to be an able and fearless pilot. The 32nd and 38th were indeed well served.

Scotty Schoolfield was one of many Voodoo pilots who became very grateful for the aircraft's strength in adversity. It happened at Phalsbourg on 22 January 1959, on a cold, dark and very wet night, with low cloud and a strong, gusting wind crossing the none too long runway (its steep drop-offs at both ends giving the airfield its name the 'Phalsbourg Aircraft Carrier'). These conditions were hardly ideal for instrument approaches at the speeds required of the heavy aircraft in a tight GCA pattern, but the rule was that a pilot who had not flown at night for 45 days must remain in the GCA pattern for the whole flight and Scotty, despite his previous experience on the aircraft, was no exception. With the weather just above published minimums in an era when

a squadron was judged, among other criteria, on its achievement of monthly flying hours and training requirements, night flying and instrument procedures among them, Scotty prepared to launch.

RF-101 60209 had been on the alert pad for a couple of weeks, a job which some pilots believed was often given to the more troublesome aircraft, but it's tyres had been changed before this trip and that boded well. Start up was normal, except that Scotty had to erect the artificial horizon manually; he thought no more about this until he turned downwind on his first GCA and was alerted to the now clearly malfunctioning instrument when he spotted guiding lights below him through a gap in the clouds. By his own admission he had failed to cross-check with his turn and slip indicator, on which he would now have to depend, itself now behaving erratically in the severe turbulence. To be on the safe side he left the GCA pattern to burn off fuel in a clear area nearby, but now the weather was deteriorating rapidly and Captain Mike Tschida in Mobile

Accidents Will Happen. Phalsbourg suffered a spate of accidents in the first months of 1959; Scotty Schoolfield lost a wheel in a night landing (above) and Scotty Wetzel 'pitched up' during an overshoot from short finals. Both had carried out GCAs at night and both escaped without injury. Scotty Schoolfield

Control recalled all Phalsbourg's aircraft. There was no cause for alarm at this point but who was to know what was going to happen next?

Scotty's GCA went well, albeit flown at a higher than normal speed because of the turbulence, and he was able to touch down normally at the runway threshold. As soon as he deployed the drag 'chute, the aircraft pulled violently to the left forcing him to jettison the chute and depend on nose high aerodynamic braking. Unbeknown to him, however, the left wheel had spun off its hub and now caused the nose to slam down on to the ground, the wheel strut shearing as the big Voodoo careered off the runway, the left wing then striking an electric junction box and partly detaching. Fortunately, Scotty climbed out uninjured, but the whole event and its immediate aftermath was not how he and his wife had intended to celebrate her birthday.

The subsequent enquiry revealed that an essential ring had not locked the single centreline nut holding the wheel in place, thus allowing it to unscrew and bounce, with the tyre still fully inflated, some 5000 ft across the airfield. Scotty was exonerated from all blame and later would be greeted in the Officers' Club with a variation of the popular song, '*You picked a fine time to leave me Loose Wheel* (Lucille)'.

Scotty Wetzel was another to have a lucky escape landing one night at Phalsbourg, again from a GCA. It is believed that he pitched up on an overshoot from short finals and literally backed into the ground, his aircraft momentarily 'silhouetted against the ramp lights in a near vertical position'. Fortunately, the Voodoo then flopped back into an upright position and he too walked away unscathed.

Despite the frequent poor weather and accident rate, life at Phalsbourg was not all bad and, as with military aviators everywhere, they made their own fun when work was done. Typically, the pilots let off steam go-carting with highly competitive spirit around ready-made race tracks on the airfield, but there was a far more demanding professional competition to come.

It was to the great credit of the 66th TRW Voodoo men that, in August 1958, only a few months after receiving their new aircraft, they took part in NATO's annual and very prestigious tac recon competition Royal Flush, an exercise which demanded the best of recce

All Work and No Play. Pilots from the 32nd TRS and 38th TRS took to four wheels and a somewhat slower speed for their relaxation at Phalsbourg. Scotty Schoolfield

expertise and resources in the air and on the ground. It said a lot, therefore, of those who flew the new Voodoos, in the weather which prevailed, and those who provided that essential support on the ground, that they acquitted themselves so well. The author, flying as part of the RAF's Swift team, recalls that neither the RF-101s nor RF-84Fs were able to penetrate a cloud covered valley in the Sauerland to search a winding route, and their limited turning performance would always put the Voodoos of the 66th TRW at some disadvantage. No-one expected the Voodoos to carry the day, the honours being shared between the RAF and the FAF, but they showed themselves to be a force for the future.

In fact, the 302nd and 303rd TRS, now firmly established at Laon, did not convert to the RF-101; these squadrons were deactivated in June 1959 with the 17th TRS and 18th TRS having arrived from Shaw AFB in May to take their place (their red and blue tails respectively soon taking to the very different skies of Europe). Neither squadron had an easy passage across the Atlantic, planned to be non-stop with AAR. With their commander, Lieutenant Colonel William H Laseter leading, eight aircraft of the 17th TRS were prevented from 'tanking' by a thunderstorm at their rendezvous and had to divert to Bermuda. A few days later, to the rallying cry 'Head 'em up and move 'em out', Lieutenant Colonel Clyde East, CO of the 18th TRS, led the first section of his squadron's aircraft to Laon, Captain Ernest E Holland following with the second and Captain John Stavast bringing up the rear with the third. It was from this last section that two pilots had to be plucked from the sea after their aircraft collided. Their story is instructive:

A pair of Voodoos, led by Lieutenant Lee Skinner, launched from Shaw AFB and joined up successfully with Stavast's flight before 'topping up' with fuel from a tanker and climbing to 35,000 ft, where they relaxed in a well spread formation and began taking refreshment. The wingman in that pair, Paul Carrodus, recalls taking off his oxygen mask, opening his lunch box and then looking up to see Lee's jet pipes fill his windscreen, a collision unavoidable (perhaps as a result of him losing consciousness momentarily when he removed his mask?). On impact, the nose of his aircraft 'folded back to my canopy' and he had no choice but to eject at 35,000ft. In the haste of their departure from Shaw to join up, Paul had omitted to disconnect his D-ring lanyard and his parachute opened immediately, causing him to lose consciousness again. He came to in the lower airspace *"in a cold white mist and with a loud ringing in my ears"*, all manner of survival tips coming to mind as he approached the cold Atlantic Ocean. He then needed all his wits about him after losing his survival kit in the descent and being enveloped by his parachute canopy when he hit the water with only half of his life jacket inflated. However with many salutary lessons learned, he lived to tell the tale.

Meanwhile, Lee Skinner's aircraft had also been fatally damaged in the collision, and he too had problems after his ejection. Although his parachute opened at 14,000 ft as expected his ejection seat became entangled in its shrouds and kept hitting him on the head until it parted company with him on entering the water. Fortuitously, a WB-50 weather guard

was in the immediate area and found both pilots when smoke from Lee's flares drifted over Paul; the US Coast Guard cutter 'Mendota' was then vectored on to the downed pilots and both were recovered without serious injury. The Shaw AFB newspaper 'Recon Record' carried an account of this double deployment to Laon (but not of that accident) underlining the rivalry between the two squadrons. It seems that when the 17th TRS commander 'popped' his drag 'chute at the fuel stop in Bermuda, a banner emerged proclaiming '18th TRS Leads the Pack'. Incidentally, de rigueur for the 18th TRS pilots on this trip were blue and white chequered neck scarves and bow ties. The rivalry would continue to be manifested in many ways at Laon.

The double loss during the Atlantic crossing could not be attributed to aircraft maintenance problems or technical defect, but others in the first half of 1959 could. Following Scotty Schoolfield's accident on 22 January, Tex Thompson ejected successfully in North Africa on 23 February when the undercarriage of his Voodoo failed to come down, and on 13 April, Bob High was killed when his Voodoo dived into the ground shortly after take-off. In the latter case a nut securing the actuator to the stabilator was subsequently found to have been missing. Then, because of continuing problems with the hydraulic systems, all RF-101s in the 66th TRW were grounded for two weeks in August.

These accidents were not thought to have been responsible for the amalgamation of all maintenance functions at Phalsbourg in July 1959; this having been already ordained as a general policy throughout the USAF in AFM 66-1, a result of the prevailing SAC influence. There were many who argued that these SAC ways, pursued in the name of efficiency and economy, were inappropriate in the tactical fighter force, but reason fell on deaf ears. Likewise, the intelligence and photographic facilities of the 32nd and 38th TRS were centralised. Whatever the benefits on paper, the aircrew and many of the maintenance men deplored the loss of direct allegiance to the flying squadrons, with the associated benefits of camaraderie, morale and will to work.

Along with the 'pooling'of all base aircraft in consolidated maintenance came a succession of new colour schemes for the RF-101s starting in

1960 with a black and white 'skunk stripe' on the fin. This was followed by a star inside a circle in front of a 'sunburst' depicting the colours of the four squadrons, with the star giving way later to the 66th TRW emblem. It was not until the mid-1960s that all RF-101s were given the SEA camouflage scheme.

Another very spectacular accident occurred when Captain Walt Ray led the second pair of four RF-101s on departure from Torrejon AB, Spain. Rolling at the standard 10 second interval after the first pair, the nose of Walt's aircraft rose uncontrollably to take the aircraft some 50 ft into the air before it crashed back on to the runway. Miraculously, Walt became yet another Voodoo pilot to walk away from his stricken aircraft and was able to contribute materially to the subsequent inquiry by Captain Paul Routhier, one of the 66th TRW accident investigation officers.

In his most laudable efforts to get at the truth, Paul examined in great depth all the evidence available on the effects of wing-tip vortices and reasoned that, in certain circumstances such as those which prevailed at Torrejon, they could so disrupt the airflow over an aircraft following close behind that all effective elevator control could be lost. His argument convinced the hierarchy; wing-tip vortices were found to be the cause of this accident and the interval between pairs of Voodoos in stream take-offs was increased from 10 to 30 seconds.

Sensibly, a core of 66th TRW RF-84F pilots had been retained to serve on the Voodoo squadrons, thus preserving all-important theatre and role expertise, and with those in maintenance support also learning fast, the RF-101 squadrons were now making a name for themselves with good aircraft serviceability, high sortie rates and increasing success in their missions. By the time Royal Flush came around again in June 1959 at Eindhoven, Holland, the 66th TRW was raring to go, and while it did not win in its class improvements were made on the promising start of a year before, with some unprecedented route times. The author, in attendance to manage the RAF's low level team and little knowing that he would soon be flying the aircraft himself, watched the Voodoos streak away to cross the North Sea to England at supersonic speeds, speeds which no other competitor could match. Captain Dick Vaughters, a much respected tac recon pilot who had participated in Royal Flush III at Spangdahlem was at Eindhoven again representing the 66th TRW with the RF-101. He claimed that the Voodoo's two J-57 engines had been 'souped up' by raising the maximum RPM and Jet Pipe Temperatures for the event, thus drawing on power available (but regulated for peacetime training) to enable a speed of some 645 kts 'on the deck'. It is said that there were many reports of mysterious 'booms' at about this time from the good people of western Holland and East Anglia in the UK, but no explanation was volunteered.

The 32nd and 38th TRS were now at Toul AB, France, fortunately not far from Phalsbourg because, although much work had been done on their new home, the facilities were far from adequate and many personnel

Royal Flush IV. Captain John Vaughters, representing the 66th TRW, prepares to taxi out at Eindhoven AB, Holland, on a Royal Flush mission. George Cowgill Collection

had to make use of Phalsbourg's domestic accommodation. The amalgamation of support facilities having been deemed a success, the system was retained after the move, albeit stretched with ever-increasing demands on the squadrons. For some of these difficult early months, the 32nd and 38th were joined at Toul by the 17th and 18th TRS while the runway at Laon was being resurfaced. Here the 18th TRS lost both pilots on 23 May 1960 when two RF-101s collided during a formation take-off at night, the aircraft burning in full view of ten other pilots waiting to take off to simulate a mass raid on the UK. The raid was cancelled. In a bizarre story which beggars belief, another RF-101 was lost when confusion between two aircraft under radar control at night led to one 'bouncing off the top' of a mountain in the French Alps the pilot, Captain Hank Scherer, ejecting successfully.

Royal Flush V in 1960 was hosted by Bremgarten AB, a French base in southern Germany. The exercise was now becoming notorious for malpractice, a competition of will to win at any price as much as it was of skill. Captain Paul Hodges, a member of the composite 66th TRW Voodoo team, believes that a near perfect mission flown by the host nation's team in the venerable RF-84F led the judges to examine the details and discover that,

while all the targets had been photographed and reported on without fault, the pilot would have had to fly the route at Mach 1.2. Knowing the aircraft himself, Paul commented:

> *"This could not easily be done in an aircraft which was supersonic only when going straight down at high altitude!"*

The French won in that class.

The author, despite he himself having benefited much from earlier Royal Flush exercises at Spangdahlem and Eindhoven, believed then (and still does now) that these largely academic peacetime exercises, in which the rules were adjusted continually by the well-meaning organisers to placate the loudest voices, were a very mixed blessing. To be sure, Royal Flush brought together several contributors to the final product and offered the opportunity to increase the overall efficiency in each component part and the collective team effort, but it could be highly detrimental to realistic training for war, objective assessments of operational effectiveness and the very ethics on which intelligence staffs depended. Contrasting views polarised the tac recon community and led, at least among the trophy hunters, to an excessive diversion from operational to very different competition-style training. It would also be naïve to claim that these meetings led to true

Chosen Men. Captain Paul Hodges, Lieutenants John Wood and B J Williams were chosen to fly for the 66th TRW in Royal Flush V. Paul Hodges

Target Study. Lieutenant Larry Church, 66th TRW Intelligence Officer, prepares a Royal Flush mission. Paul Hodges

Team Effort. With Major Ernie Holland as Team Manager (top left), every man in the team representing the 66th TRW at Royal Flush V, FAF Bremgarten, was a crucial player. Paul Hodges

Proud Possession. A momento for all RF-101 team members. Paul Hodges

Target Cover. This photograph had a Royal Flush V target well positioned and fully covered in the frame. Paul Hodges

and honest cross-fertilisation of ideas which would help others to succeed in war, most competitors kept their good ideas to themselves in what became increasingly a game of 'dog-eat-dog'. All this should not deny great credit to the 66th TRW team, however, with Royal Flush V showing clearly another marked improvement in its overall performance.

Not every activity of the flexible Voodoos was necessarily directly connected with competition or fully operational training; this ubiquitous force was also able to serve humanity, community and public relations, earning respect and credit from the uninitiated, nationally and internationally. Such was the case in 1960 when RF-101s of the 18th TRS in Morocco photographed the devastation caused by the earthquake around Agadir, their widely publicised photographs contributing significantly to rescue co-ordination and the raising of relief funds. In very different but equally successful tasks, the squadron photographed 8000 square miles of desert in North Africa to assist in the discovery of a WW2 B-24 Liberator while HQ USAFE, ever conscious that their presence in France was viewed with concern by some, put much into public relations activities such as 'Open Days', flypasts and the like. This was all good training for the RF-101 pilots with their presence as part of the Cold War deterrence in very visible peacetime contributions.

Captain George Cowgill had a desk job in the Command Post at Laon, but completed all the RF-101 pre-check out requirements in his spare time and persuaded General Kyle Riddle to let

Lonesome Polecats. 'Rich' Richardson, 18th TRS, 66th TRW and a squadron aircraft at Toul AB in 1960. Rich Richardson & George Cowgill

Flying The Flag. With public relations always high on the agenda, the 66th TRW RF-101s from Laon were always ready to put on a show. Paul Hodges, Scotty Schoolfield & John Linihan

him take that final step and fly the aeroplane. He then contrived a posting to the 66th Field Maintenance Squadron at Laon, followed by an assignment as the Flight Line Maintenance Officer for the 32nd and 38th TRS at Toul, which gave him plenty of Voodoo flying. As a result of such determination George would serve for many years on the RF-101 with great credit, but not without incident. It was on a ferry flight from Laon to Toul on 1 July 1961 that George had the first of many emergencies in the aircraft, the left engine of his aircraft catching fire when a fuel manifold split, burning a 12-inch hole in the outer casing. George carried out all the requisite drills and completed an uneventful single-engine landing. That one had been easy but others would not be. When tension over Berlin increased in 1961, eight RF-101s of the 66th TRW were deployed to Spangdahlem AFB, giving their pilots the unique opportunity to fly a rotation of 'single-ship' missions to and from Berlin, up one corridor and down another. It is not known whether they were authorised to take photographs, even whether their cameras were loaded, but it is hard to believe that the hierarchy could forego this valuable opportunity to update intelligence on Warsaw Pact activities either side of the corridors. This operation drew plenty of attention from the local MiG fighters, which failed in their many attempts to ease the Voodoo pilots out of the authorised airspace.

Toul AB closed in February 1962, with the 38th TRS going to Ramstein AB in Germany and the 32nd TRS, commanded now by Lieutenant Colonel John Bull Stirling, deploying to Laon, George Cowgill accompanying the latter as Scheduled Maintenance Officer. It was at Laon that George, on 20 February 1963, had another serious emergency. Whilst on a GCA to land below a 200 ft cloud base and in half a mile visibility, with 'everything hanging' (gear, flaps, speed brakes), he experienced an engine failure with the loss of all his ancillaries (fuel and oil pumps, fuel control, generator etc). Afterburner on the good engine saved the day, allowing him to 'clean up' and manoeuvre for a successful single-engine landing. There were lighter times for George at Toul. While on a 'test hop' he found a formation of 16 French Air Force Voutour aircraft and tagged on to the end, adding a new dimension to a clearly well-planned VIP flypast over a French base and giving the large audience there 17 for the price of 16. Interestingly, this unauthorised initiative drew no comment or reaction from the French.

The decision to move the 38th TRS to Ramstein and arm its aircraft with nuclear weapons was almost certainly precipitated by tensions in Berlin and Warsaw Pact harassment of NATO aircraft transiting the corridors. The F-100s of the 417th TFS resident at Ramstein had a nuclear role, but it was now thought that they might be required for escort duties with their gun armament, so the 38th TRS was to take over the special weapons commitment, with every operational pilot allocated at least one (fully memorised) war mission. This squadron would be required to retain two aircraft on 15 minutes standby at all times with the pilots' alert quarters some 100 yards from the aircraft. The other RF-101 squadrons in USAFE were also given the capability and pilots were trained in the role but, based as they were in France, loading of nuclear weapons in peacetime was not permitted and they could not, therefore, hold a similar alert posture.

This role did, of course, have a precedent in the Voodoo force with the 81st TFW F-101s which were equipped with a radar optimised for low level mapping and the Low Altitude Bombing System (LABS) for nuclear deliveries. From these developed two automatic, computerised nuclear delivery techniques for use by the RF-101s, they too being practised assiduously by the 66th TRW at El Outia Range, close to Wheelus AB in Libya, and Suippes Range in northern France.

RF-101s of the 38th TRW on the flight lines at Ramstein AB, Germany.
Fred Muesegaes & Don Karges

Happy Landings. Captain George Cowgill, on a ground assignment with the 66th TRW, soon contrived to get back to the flight line - seen here landing an RF-101 at Toul AB in 1961.
George Cowgill

Farewell Fred. Captain Fred Muesegaes presented with his score in flying hours on the Voodoo, by Lieutenant Colonel Hurlburt, commander 38 TRS. Fred Muesegaes

Bull Stirling was detachment commander at Wheelus when George Cowgill was charged with maintaining eight RF-101s allocated to the initial nuclear qualification programme. All the pilots involved, plus George, achieved what was wanted of them with two weeks to spare and George was awarded the Air Force Commendation Medal for his contribution and the efficiency of his unit back at Laon. In time the recce pilots would achieve very creditable results in both delivery modes and seriously challenge the scores posted by the dedicated fighter bombers. Captain Don Karges, 38th TRS, remembers Wheelus well, not only for their successes on the range and in navigating across vast tracts of desert without reliable maps, but generally for 'those carefree days, with virtually no local restrictions to low and fast flying', but he had a serious job to do as a squadron nuclear weapons training officer. On the 38th TRS he taught the Laydown and Low Altitude Drogue Delivery (LADD) delivery modes. The Mk 43 bomb was used exclusively for Laydown, with a drogue 'chute to retard weapon and a spike in its nose to trigger the warhead after a predetermined penetration of the target. Running in for Laydown at 100 ft and 400 kts (or higher) rendered the RF-101's Viewfinder redundant, because the target would not enter the field of view during that approach, so the 'pickle button' was depressed when the target passed through an imaginary point at the top of the pilot's rudder pedals. This was the more accurate of the two options. LADD was designed for an airburst, using a

similar run-in to a pre-planned timing point, at which the pilot pressed the release button and held it down while continuing towards the target until the computer called for a pull up at 4 'G'. The bomb then released automatically, after which the pilot executed an immediate escape manoeuvre and departed the area with all speed.

The nuclear targets for the 38th TRS, selected both for their tactical importance and to minimise civilian casualties, were mostly within an hour's tactical flying time of Ramstein. With their RF-101s able to carry the nuclear weapon on the centreline pylon between their two 450 gall external tanks, this meant that their missions could be flown operationally at low level throughout, or at worst with only the last leg in friendly airspace at height. However, this was small comfort to pilots who knew the effects of the nuclear blasts which would surround them en route. They were also aware that, even with the sophisticated recovery procedures introduced later (which many considered of very dubious value), friend and foe alike would inevitably be very trigger-happy, and that their home base might not be usable if they did manage to return. It is also believed that some of the strike targets assigned later to the RF-101 squadrons at Laon lay outside their optimum range profiles. Deterrence was, therefore, the name of the game - and who can say now that it did not succeed?

In the autumn of 1962 came the Cuban Crisis, with 'brinkmanship' between the USA

Recce Bombers line up in Libya. Fred Muesegaes & Don Karges

Competition Time Again. Captain Luster 'Vic' Vickrey and the 66th TRW team practiced hard for Royal Flush VIII in 1963. Vic Vickrey

A rare photograph (below) of an RF-101 at the USAF museum carrying a 'special' (nuclear) weapon on the aircraft's centreline station. Fred Muesegaes & Don Karges

Tanks Gone! Reacting promptly to a fire warning light, Vic Vickrey jettisoned his tanks on the designated area at Laon and landed safely. The warning was spurious. Vic Vickrey

and the Soviet Union having global implications. Every tactical unit in USAFE was brought to a high state of readiness in an overwhelming show of resolve to use all means necessary to bring the crisis to a sensible conclusion. The 66th TRW was tasked to retain half its RF-101 force at cockpit readiness from dawn to dusk, the pilots studying their well-prepared war mission folders for what might be one final sortie, while perhaps reflecting on the meaning of life!

With competition due again in 1963, Captain Wes Brooks, who had done well on the 4414th CCTS during the author's time there, was practising hard, sadly too hard. Attempting to stay below cloud in his determination to reach

the next target, Wes suddenly found himself in a blind canyon and, despite an emergency climb in afterburner, he failed to clear the mountain ahead. The aircraft hit a vertical cliff some 60 ft from the crest, scattering wreckage over the top and below into the valley. It was another salutary lesson for the many who, with such laudable intent, did their best for all to win those prestigious accolades. Captain Luster 'Vic' Vickrey, who had arrived on 32nd TRS during 1962, also took the competition seriously and had his share of incidents in the aircraft. During one take-off from Laon he reacted correctly to a fire warning light which would not go out when he throttled back, by jettisoning his tanks over the designated area on the airfield and carrying out an uneventful single engine landing. The warning turned out to be spurious, but he was not to know that.

RF-101 pilot Captain Kay Berry was posted to the 32nd TRS at Laon after Voodoo training on the 4414th CCTS in 1963; he found that most of his fellow pilots were captains, thereby underlining the policy at the time of bringing in to the RF-101 force only those with previous fast-jet experience. Kay believes that only one of the 66th TRW squadrons at Laon was required at this time to maintain currency in AAR, sharing the KB-50 resources with the F-101s of the 81st TFW from the UK. He was on hand to take a photograph of two RF-101s and two F-101s

Captains All. Conrad Binyon (right), and the pilots of B Flight, 32nd TRS at Laon AB circa 1963; (L to R) Conrad Binyon, Ed Lucas, Harry Dewitt, Kay Berry, Paul Nelson (flight commander) and Vic Vickrey were all captains, underlining the original policy of having only those with a minimum of 500 hours fast-jet experience in the RF-101 force. This would change. Kay Berry

Taking Turns. Refuelling from this RAF Sculthorpe KB-50 tanker, two F-101 pilots from the 81st TFW stand off while two RF-101s of the 66th TRW 'plug in'. Captain Ray Scott is in the basket, while Captain Kay Berry waits and Major Paul Nelson takes the photo. Kay Berry

Boom Time. The KC-135 added a new dimension to AAR for the 66th TRW. Fred Muesegaes

refuelling from the KB-50 before this obsolescent tanker was replaced by the KC-135, thereby allowing future refuelling at greater speeds and heights, and with the additional 'boom' facility.

Western Europe provided a feast of targets for recce aircraft in their operational and competition training, and the RF-101s made full use of them with their very long range capability. The abundance of static targets (bridges, airfields, missile sites, dams, barracks, electronic sites et al) were usually easy to acquire and photograph, while mobile and camouflaged military targets in the field were often very challenging. At that time all the NATO ground troops looked to air recce as

their primary means of beyond visual range intelligence gathering and there were many official and unofficial exercises to mutual benefit. Deployment of ground forces could also give the recce men invaluable training in route reconnaissance, a primary role in war, and undefined 'opportunity' targets were welcomed to test a pilot's reaction.

The 32nd TRS had a good flight safety record during Bull Stirling's tenure, but one accident could have changed the statistics had it not been handled sensibly. One of Bull's flight commanders, Major Paul Nelson, felt a jolt while flying on a routine mission over France at 500 ft and turned to see a Jodel light aircraft spinning into a field; on landing the leading edge of one wing of his Voodoo was found to be slightly damaged. Bull was dispatched at once to the local flying club involved to find

Route Recce. A likely task in war, route recces could be simple or difficult. Vic Vickrey

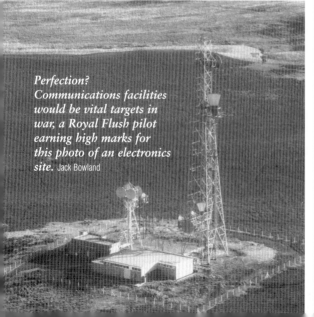

Perfection? Communications facilities would be vital targets in war, a Royal Flush pilot earning high marks for this photo of an electronics site. Jack Bowland

Urban Jungle. At the speeds and height flown, pin-point targets in towns could be hard to find. George Cowgill

Chance Find. Unexpected, opportunity targets could provide valuable information. Vic Vickrey

Field Exercise. These three battalions of the French Army were easy to find, less easy to report visually in detail in a single pass at 480 knots. Vic Vickrey

Inset & below; Honest John. Military units learned about the spy from the sky from recce photos - and the need to conceal themselves, not draw attention with smoke! Jack Bowland

that the teenage French pilot of the Jodel was shaken but not hurt, and was being treated as a hero. Funds were found to pay for the club's aircraft, the Voodoo was repaired on the unit and the accident did not appear in the statistics. Both parties were happy and parted good friends, in a victory for common sense.

It was a different story on 3 May 1963 when Captain Tom Saunders of the 18th TRS, treated his hierarchy and others at Laon to a spectacular new Voodoo dance. It was perhaps fortuitous that his RF-101 was 'clean' (no external tanks) for his take-off in afterburner, with the left main wheel going off on its own just as he raised the nosewheel at 150 kts. At first, Tom was able to retain some directional control as he aborted the take-off, but then the aircraft took over, shedding bits when the wheel stub hit an arrester wire, swinging the Voodoo through 140 deg to continue its waltz tail first down the runway and then on to the grass. The Wing Commander's call to the control tower, for all to hear: *"Get Crash out, he's on fire"* did nothing to steady Tom's nerves as the leg bearing the remaining main wheel folded, the nosewheel sheared off as it hit a runway light and the right wing tried hard, but fortunately failed, to dig in and turn the aircraft over. The noise of screaming metal then came to an abrupt end, leaving only the sirens of the emergency vehicles to signal that it was not yet all over. In fact, it was the maintenance van from 18th TRS Operations which reached the spot first, its roof providing an escape route for

a grateful and uninjured Tom; the great strength of the Voodoo had prevailed again that day. When the regular crash crew and flight surgeon arrived they were unable to find the pilot who was already back at his squadron, but in the end he could not escape that ritual medical inspection at the base hospital. Despite its ordeal the aircraft was repaired at its birthplace in St Louis, only to be lost in combat over North Vietnam.

Misfortunes were shared around. A year later Captain Nick, 'Pish' Pishvanov, 18th TRS, had his own dramatic problem on 8 June 1964, when his cockpit and eyes filled with smoke following a fire caused by a hydraulic leak during a practice nuclear laydown delivery at Suippes Range. He jettisoned the canopy (an exciting experience in itself at such high speed!), but was still unable to determine whether he was 'right-side up, climbing or what-have-you', so he ejected. Despite being at 500 ft and 480 kts plus, the ejection was successful, although Nick wrenched his knee on landing and was grounded for a month until he recovered. It was a well supervised accident, Nick being accompanied on the flight by his Director of Operations, a squadron commander and the head of the Command Post, he was of course exonerated from any blame.

On his first flight back in business on 8 July, Nick flew as wingman to Major Howard Austin who, unbeknown to him, had swapped the two assigned aircraft 'for luck'. Lucky it

Strong Survivor. Captain Tom Saunders had a wheel come off this RF-101 on take-off.
Tom Saunders

Lucky Escape. Captain Nick Pishvanov, his aircraft catching fire during practice nuclear deliveries on Suippes Range, ejects successfully (Note the second Voodoo top left).
Nick Pishvanov

Lucky Escape. Howard Austin regretted swapping aircraft with Nick Pishvanov, when a fire in the air caused him to eject. Nick Pishvanov

was for Nick because during take-off a fractured fuel line in Howard's left engine caused a massive fireball and left a 30 ft streamer behind the aircraft - both engines still in afterburner. Nick opined that the controller in the tower may have been having 'a neurocirculatory collapse as he yelled unintelligible things at the pilot on the radio, something about ejecting'. Despite being close to pitch-up when he ejected and his parachute becoming entangled with his seat when he landed in a tree, Howard was largely unscathed. Perhaps the 18th TRS was having more than its share of bad luck, another aircraft being lost shortly thereafter when one of its younger pilots, on pulling up from low level into cloud over the North Sea in afterburner, lost control and had to eject. Fortunately, particularly since he had lost his survival pack, he was spotted in the descent by the pirate radio ship 'Radio Caroline', and rescued quickly from the very cold sea, while the whole epic story was transmitted for all to hear as it happened.

Was it fate, intention or simply an accident that kept bringing Lieutenant Colonel Doug ('Grumpy') Brittian into contact with 'The Brits'? He first got to know them in Italy when Limey medics took care of him after he crash-landed a P-47 on their lines in Italy during WW2. He was fulsome in his praise for them

then but perhaps a little less enamoured with the antics of the RAF exchange pilots thrust upon him on the 4414th CCTS at Shaw AFB, first Paddy King and then the author. In his next command, the 18th TRS at Laon AB, the two-way NATO exchange programme then brought him into annual contact with RAF squadrons. The first of these squadrons he would get to know (some say too well) was No II (AC) Squadron ('AC' for Army Co-Operation) which was then serving at RAF Gutersloh in Germany.

The countryside around Laon, other than that of the nearby Champagne district, was of no particular interest to these guests of 18th TRS, but here was a chance for them to fly legitimately over otherwise almost prohibited territory (the French rules were a deterrent to the RAF's operational flying training) and they knew that there was plenty of cold beer to be had with their kindred spirits, so all seemed set fair for a professionally profitable and socially agreeable experience. So it was that Squadron Leader David Thornton took four Hunter FR 10s and his most resilient officers to Laon in the spring of 1963, the visit getting off to a good start when they were welcomed at the aircraft by Doug Brittian himself and his project officer Captain John Reeder, with of course cold beers all round. In the fall 2004 edition of the 'Recce Reader', Johnnie Reader provided a reminder of this two-way NATO 'jointery' and the excellent flying and socialising it afforded,

Above & below; Welcome to Laon. In 1963, Lieutenant Colonel Doug Brittian and the pilots of 18th TRS greeted Squadron Leader David Thornton and their opposite numbers from No II (AC) Squadron, RAF, for a NATO exchange visit at Laon. II Squadron

albeit with some memory loss due to the nocturnal activities which completed each day.

Memories of the return match at Gutersloh seem clearer, perhaps because a USAF flight surgeon was included in the party to administer liberal quantities of 'milky stuff that coated the linings of our innards'. Johnnie reports that even their flying, judged on a vaguely competitive basis, was more impressive at the RAF base, with each visitor flying in the two-seat Hunter, an infinitely more agile, if slower aircraft than their Voodoo. Despite fundamental commonality between the two services in most things, the more perceptive could detect small, cultural differences. It was Johnnie who noticed that while the USAF did their social duty on the dance floor with the RAF officers' wives, the Brits continued the serious stuff at the bar. That suited everyone, especially the wives who were not used to such attention! Perhaps the Brits also took their golf a little less seriously when, in the final act of the exchange, hosts and guests did battle on the airfield's rudimentary six-hole course. Good shots or bad were, by consensus, rewarded instantly by a generous 'slug' of a sinister brew transported in a custom-built container strapped to a golf cart, the recipe known only to II Squadron. It is said that after dealing gallantly with one such reward, veteran aviator Doug Brittian (growing visibly older and 'grumpier' as the hours ticked by), walked seemingly unconcerned into a nearby lake, presumably to prove that he could walk on water. He couldn't - and had to be rescued by his loyal pilots.

In 1964, there was more mischief when the

Welcome Back. Flight Lieutenant Ken Tatem, II (AC) Squadron, hands a beer to Doug Brittian on his arrival with 18 TRS Voodoos at RAF Gutersloh, North Germany. II Squadron

Collectors Pieces. Somehow, this picture of 'Jeannie' au naturel, treasured by 17th TRS, found itself on a Canberra of 17 Squadron, RAF, after an exchange visit to Laon and, somehow, a 17 Squadron WW2 souvenir gun found its way into Tish Lynn's Voodoo, but both were restored later to their respective owners. Doug Brittian

18th TRS and No 17 (Canberra recce) Squadron hosted each other at Laon AB and RAF Wildenrath respectively. It was more of the same at work and play, but things could have got out of hand when cherished squadron momentos changed hands. It was the RAF visitors at Loan who were said to have precipitated the near crisis, when a much loved picture of a naked Jeannie, which had adorned the wall of the 18th TRS crewroom, somehow found its way into a Canberra and thence back to Wildenrath. Incensed (since he was known to be inspired by Jeanie), Doug dispatched Captain 'Tish' Lynn to Wildenrath in an RF-101 to retrieve their loved one. There could have been no better man for the job, but by then the Brits had placed Jeannie in safe keeping and even Tish failed in this mission as briefed but he was not a man to return empty-handed. Somehow, he became the proud possessor of machine gun extracted from a German JU 88 downed by a 17 Squadron Spitfire in WW2. The gun then found its way on to his Voodoo and back to Laon making the score one-all. International negotiations followed, involving the RAF Air Attaché in Paris, and the two 'prizes' were soon restored to their rightful owners. Perhaps Doug Brittian had had enough by this time and left the 66th TRW in 1964, his squadron revealing then how they saw him in an appropriate but affectionate memory.

However, the Voodoo men of Laon then agreed to host No II Squadron again in 1965, this time in a one way 'exchange' to the 32nd TRS. The author had hoped to lead the squadron to France but it was not to be, he having to stay behind at their temporary base at RAF Laarbruch to answer an allegation of low level aerobatics over the airfield during the

Mixed Message? The other face of Lieutenant Colonel 'Grumpy' Brittian, commander 18th TRS at Laon AB, as his squadron saw him on leaving his command in 1964. Doug Brittian

"GRUMPY"

Back Again. Flight Lieutenant Bob Hillman, who led the Hunter FR10s of No II (AC) Squadron RAF back to Laon in 1965, greeted by Major Tom Temple. II Squadron

previous night's night flying (Laarbruch was a Canberra bomber base and its hierarchy did not take kindly to the ways of the fighter pilot). It fell to the senior flight commander, Flight Lieutenant Bob Hillman, who had been on the previous visit to Laon in 1963, to lead four Hunters back there on 22 July 1965; the 'boss' following later.

'I See it This Way...'. Bob Hillman briefs Major Lawrence, 32nd TRS, how he intends to fly a training sortie in France. II Squadron

Captain Rich' Richardson', who had been on the initial deployment of the 18th TRS to France in 1959, had gone back to Shaw in 1962 to be an instructor pilot and returned to his old squadron at Laon in late 1964. He found that the standard of recce training had progressed very little since his first tour there, attributing this to the amount of time the squadron had devoted to the secondary role of nuclear delivery, and he had no difficulty achieving operational status again, thereafter working his way up to become a flight commander.

Lieutenant Colonel Al Simmons was now commanding the 18th TRS and Rich paid tribute to his leadership qualities. He remembers that when a recalcitrant SNCO, a man of many qualities but subject too often to some misdemeanour, was brought before him

Above & below; Flying Visit. The author joins his squadron at Laon, one of the Hunters photographed over the sad landmark at Verdun. II Squadron

Friends Old ..... Major 'Rich' Richardson visiting a German Air Force RF-104 squadron at Leck AB, Schleswig Holstein. Nick Pishvanov

once again, Al tore up his charge sheet and offered the man a final chance to start again with a clean sheet, no doubt a few more words of 'encouragement' followed! The gamble worked, the SNCO becoming, all round, one of the best in the business. Morale on the 18th TRS was good.

Rich also remembers that their heavy programme at Laon included many VIP, liaison and exchange visits with other NATO air forces, typically his squadron enjoying a close relationship with a German Air Force 'sister' recce squadron flying RF-104s at Leck AB, Schleswig Holstein. Germans and others sometimes made the mistake of thinking that their British and American colleagues would not understand what they said in their native tongues, and so it was when German pilots branded the Pishvanov's dog 'Ein Kuchenhund', a 'kitchen hound'. In fluent German, an indignant Mrs Pishvanov was quick to point out their error; their pet was a prize Weimaraner from their German Province of Weimar. Every effort was made by all to maintain good relations with host nations, with frequent visits to and from units of the German and French Air Forces.

....And New.   RF-101s of the 66th TRW escorted over Spain en route to Nouasseur by friendly Spanish F-86 Sabres. Nick Pishvanov

Teach-Ins. Captains Mike Tschida explains the Voodoo's nose camera to NATO officers and Don Karges the oblique cameras to French officers. Mike Tschida and Don Karges

Professional and social opportunities and temptations during these visits were sometimes too good to miss, but there could be a price to pay. Such was the case when unnamed officers of the 17th TRS found themselves in a spot of bother while they and a French Mirage squadron were on an exchange visit to the German Air Force at Ingolstadt AB in Bavaria; here was an ideal chance for a unique illustration of NATO togetherness. After a full briefing on all safety aspects, a German F-104 led a formation of two Voodoos and two Mirages in good flying weather over the Bavarian countryside for all to see, the resulting photographs finding their way into the public domain and entering into the archives of the three air forces. Inevitably, this memorable event came to the attention of the hierarchy at Laon and USAFE who had not given the requisite permission for such a non-routine task. The author was not made unaware of the outcome of this heinous crime.

Fly-In. This unauthorised photo of a German Air Force F-104, French Air Force Mirages and RF-101s of the 66th TRW, earned undue interest from the latter's hierarchy. Recce Reader

Jack Bowland returned to Europe as a major in 1964, initially as operations officer on the 32nd TRS at Laon before being transferred a year later to the same post with the collocated 18th TRS. When it came time to hang up his flying boots Jack would have served in three wars and on six tac recon squadrons in 13 years, becoming one of the most respected practitioners and leaders in the business. On the down side, and for no reason or fault of his own, Jack often seemed to be around when (in his own words): *two aircraft would try to occupy the same piece of sky at the same time, and when pilots tried to land their aircraft without wheels;* he also noted that, more often than not, the aircraft involved had blue tail markings. This had been so when he was with the 303rd TRS in the mid-1950s, six RF-84Fs having three mid-air collisions in 45 days, and three more landing with their wheels up, one pilot blaming Jack at the inquiry for not telling him that he should put his wheels down for landing! However, Jack was not involved when a 66th TRW RF-101 collided with a T-33 of the Royal Canadian Air Force, neither pilot seeing the other aircraft and neither having been warned by the French radar agency controlling them. The pilot of the robust Voodoo felt a jolt at the time but did not notice that his left elevator was missing until he glanced at his rear view mirror during the recovery to land, uneventfully to incur no more than a 'non-reportable' incident. The 'T-bird' lost a wing, but both of its pilots ejected successfully. There would be another mid-air collision story to tell when Jack Bowland commanded the 45th TRS in SEA, but again the RF-101s and their pilots would survive.

Others confidently predicted, albeit perhaps in jest, they would come to grief in the Voodoo. One of the more colourful characters, who added spice to the lives of his peers and perhaps grey hairs to his supervisors, was heard to say: *"Every time I go out to that big son-of-a-bitch I'm just an accident waiting to happen".* In fact, he was deceiving them all, never having a serious accident in the aircraft; perhaps his words warded off the evil spirits.

Political unease over the presence of USAF warplanes on French soil had now been on the increase for some time and came to a head in April 1965 when an RF-101 pilot from the 38th TRS at Ramstein overflew the nuclear facility at Pierrelatte, to the French a highly sensitive area but not one which had been included as such on the USAF's flying maps in use. Be that as it may, the Voodoo was intercepted by French Mirage fighters and the 'violation' reported at the highest levels. The very surprised pilot was met back at Ramstein by the base hierarchy and some very excited French officers who predicted dire consequences. So it was that plans were put in hand to move the Laon Voodoos to RAF Upper Heyford in England.

The 26th TRW took command of the 32nd and 38th TRS in July 1965, both squadrons now beginning their conversion to the RF-4C; they would not have a nuclear role. Lieutenant Joe Whitt carried the 32nd TRS flag to RAF Alconbury in October 1966 and the men returned to the US to settle their families 'where they wished' before mustering again at Mountain Home AB ten days later. There they were reunited with their aircraft, ferried there by other crews, and left shortly thereafter to SEA as the 12th TRS.

The 17th and 18th TRS would leave France on a high note, Captains Nick Pishvanov (the 'Mad Russian') and 'Doc' Cramer, 18th TRS, representing the 66th TRW in the 1966 Royal Flush XI, having been awarded the highest ever marks for USAFE Voodoo pilots in any Royal Flush competition, with Nick placed first in his class. In his verbal commendation, Al Simmons, the 18th TRS commander, said:

"Everybody pulled together, the pilots and the groundcrew, on any job you could think of. It was maximum effort all the way and we're proud of the results".

The men of the residual 66th TRW left Laon with their 36 Voodoos for Upper Heyford on 11 September 1966 after a job well done. The spring 2002 edition of the 'Recce Reader' carried accounts of the move by John Lashuay and Carlos Higgins. John remembers that he took over the command of the 18th from Al Simmons on 1 September 1966 and was able to lead the squadron over, having purloined locally all the parts available and necessary to remedy a gear problem, whereas the 17th had to fly their aircraft back with the gear down and locked. All the 18th TRS pilots flew productive training missions en route and co-ordinated their arrival to taxi in together. Carlos confirmed that the 17th flew to the UK with the gear down, Jim Waugh leading a tight

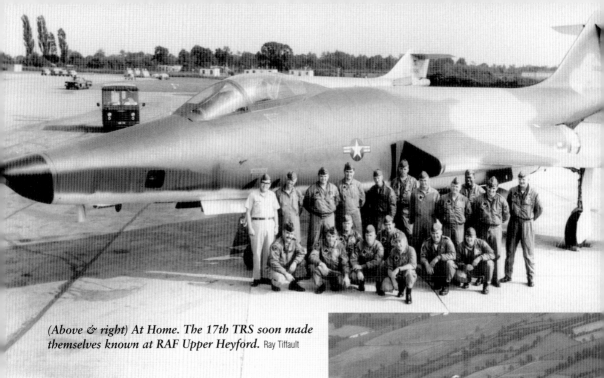

(Above & right) At Home. The 17th TRS soon made themselves known at RAF Upper Heyford. Ray Tiffault

18-ship formation down into the English murk (carefully avoiding the WW2 barrage balloons moored for RAF parachute training at Watchfield) for a grand arrival at Heyford, 'exhibiting their usual higher level of spirit, morale, flying skills and derring-do...'. Inter-squadron rivalry lived on.

The 17th TRS took up residence on the south side of Upper Heyford close to all the operational, support and domestic accommodation, with the 18th TRS occupying the more remote north side. All 36 aircraft arrived resplendent in their natural metal finish but soon they would be camouflaged, some of their pilots still wearing their orange flying suits, but the news from SEA was grim and the squadron would soon be dressed in more warlike garb. The 66th TRW now came under the operational control of 3rd Air Force at South Ruislip, within the 4th Allied Tactical Air Force, but the roles remained the same.

Public relations (PR) remained high on the agenda at Heyford, not least to help ameliorate many complaints about the noisy Voodoos. Heading the attractions were the Open Days in May 1967 and 1968, which also helped to demonstrate the station's contribution to the Cold War. Of course, the resident Voodoos topped the bill but the base's HH-43B Huskie crash rescue and fire suppression helicopters added exciting demonstrations, while visiting

RB-47s, KC-135Rs, RC-135s, the C-97 'Miss Oklahoma City'('Talking Bird') and the RAF's Vulcan bomber generated great interest.

The 18th TRS achievement in Royal Flush XII, held in May 1967, also enhanced Heyford's reputation. Lieutenant Colonel Thomas H Temple now commanded the squadron but Jack Bowland had free rein in the preparation for and running of this competition; he was given all the pilots and aeroplanes he wanted and every priority in their work-up. This was important, but perhaps

Cold War Dress. Pre-1966, the 66th TRW Voodoos retained their natural metal finish, and their pilots could be found training in standard orange flying suits - but this would now change. Nick Pishvanov

Royal Flush Supremo. Jack Bowland, spare camera at the ready, who took the 18th TRS to victory in Royal Flush XII, makes a point to a rather sleepy looking RAF umpire. Jack Bowland

crucial was Jack's influence on the training itself, his meticulous attention to detail and a rather liberal interpretation of the usually inviolate rules, standard procedures and non-essential air traffic regulations. Came the day, 12 of the squadron's pilots each flew two missions comprising three targets on three successive days, no sortie or target being missed throughout the competition. As a result, the 18th TRS won the competition in their class, this time Majors Ed Satterfield and Nick Pishvanov taking first and second places respectively. Of course all the pilots came in for high praise, but the 'back-room boys' were not forgotten, with much credit also heaped on Captains Henry Scherer and George Howard for their work on target allocation, and John Lashuay, who ran the in-flight reporting cell. The Field Maintenance Squadron played its part, changing a Voodoo's engine in two-and-a-half hours, two hours less than usual, and the resident McDonnell engineer, Bob Zaeny, got a special mention for his tireless efforts throughout the rehearsals and the competition

Pride of Place. Major Ed Slatterfield was named best low level day pilot in Royal Flush XII, Lieutenant Colonel Tom Temple seen here pinning on his well-earned patch.
Ed Satterfield

Even in the sometimes tense drama of the competition, the Voodoo men found time to play games. It may have been the 1967 ace, Ed Slatterfield, who bore the brunt of a cruel joke played by the camera men on the line. These men too excelled themselves in Royal Flush XII, off-loading and rushing the camera magazines to the photo labs without mishap. It might not have been so if the curses and screams of anguish which emerged from below the aircraft when a canister of film spilled 200 ft of film on the ramp had been real - but of course it was not.

Victorious airmen do not allow their achievements to go unnoticed, and the 18th TRS were especially keen that their close rivals on the 10th TRW at RAF Alconbury, now flying the much vaunted two-seat RF-4C Phantoms, were fully aware of their successes in Royal Flush XII. To this end the men from Upper Heyford treated Alconbury to a 'Victory Flypast', their refuelling probes raised in irreverent 'horse dong' salute. Usually, airmen do not permit such pride to be enjoyed for long, particularly accompanied by such gestures, but no

itself. On reflection, Jack Bowland believes that this achievement was the high point in his peacetime service with the Voodoo force, not least for the satisfaction of beating the French and (as he likes to remind the author) the British. Jack was promoted to Lieutenant Colonel soon after Royal Flush XII, and would soon be given a squadron of his own.

Below left & right; Winners All. Lieutenant Colonel Tom Temple with members of the victorious 18th TRS Royal Flush XII team. Ed Satterfield

Rubbing It In. RF-101s of the 18th TRS, winners of Royal Flush XII, overfly their close rivals at RAF Alconbury with their 'Horse Dong' probes raised in obscene salute.
Nick Pishvanov

retribution was forthcoming from the Phantom warriors on this occasion, giving the One-O-Wonders an even greater sense of superiority.

Likewise, it has always been axiomatic that individuals be brought down to earth after a brief parade of self-congratulation, the squadron executives being considered particularly fair game. Only too aware of this, and that he must continually 'check six', Nick Pishvanov, now a major and flight commander on 18th TRS, still got caught and photographed in the air, he thinks by one of his own, Tish Lynn, while he was head down in the cockpit changing his IFF settings (not that this would ever be an acceptable excuse!) Then, on his last trip in a Voodoo at Upper Heyford before going to war in SEA, Nick was caught by another of his flight, possibly John Boyer, who was waiting for him at 5000 ft in the English gloom when he took off, capturing him on his nose-facing camera as he turned out of the traffic pattern. Again, Nick knew what every fighter pilot knows, that man must be on the look out for adversaries as soon as he and his aircraft moved on the ramp, but this was

England in the halcyon days of peace and even the marauding Brits would surely not hit him as soon as he was outside the protection of air traffic control, it would just not be cricket. He had not bargained for his own, and on landing was welcomed to the light table in the photo lab to see himself, tail on, surrounded by a realistic facsimile of a gun sight reticule, a salutary warning of the real world and what he might face in less peaceful climes to come. The 17th TRS did not take part in the 1967 Royal Flush; with Lieutenant Colonel Paul Nelson now in command the squadron continued with the Wing's normal Cold War business, with the ever-vigilant Jack Bowland not averse to lending them a hand. On a USAFE exercise alert, Jack noticed that the sister squadron had misinterpreted a crucial signal and acted at once to prevent its aircraft from taking off when the order was to taxi to the runway threshold only. Such an error would have caused more than grave embarrassment. Friendly rivalry was one thing, serious business was quite another.

Nick Pishvanov was not the only one to be reminded, however unkindly and unjustly, that pride comes before a fall. Early in 1969, when the weather was bad at both their bases, the 17th TRS Voodoos from Upper Heyford and the 38th TRS Phantoms from Ramstein went

Underhand Tactics. One of his flight had laid in wait to get this 'nose-facer' of Major Nick Pishvanov after he took off from Upper Heyford, the negative then circumscribed with a gun sight reticule by the Photo Shop to remind Nick what he was soon to face in SEA. Nick Pishvanov

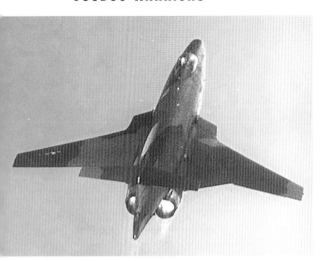

Play Time. In true fighter pilot spirit, Captain Bob Gould chanced his luck against an RF-4C over Sarragossa, Spain - and lost - as the Phantom's nose-facer shows. Bob Gould

together to continue their separate training at Moron AB, Spain. While they were there Captain Bob Gould crept up behind a 38th TRS RF-4 in his 17th TRS RF-101 and took a picture with an accompanying "Gotcha!" on the radio. Red rag to a bull, the RF-4 pilot was soon on his tail taking pictures as Bob tried hard but with no success to shake him off; although a very experienced RF-101 pilot, his machine was no match for the Phantom when it came to this sort of play.

PR initiatives were not limited to the area around Upper Heyford. Low flying over the UK generally was causing increasing concern and the ultimate solution, that of giving up all low flying over land, was of course unacceptable if NATO was to keep up its guard while the Cold War raged. Accordingly, the RAF and USAF continued to do all that was reasonable to enhance safety, avoid disrupting community activities and minimise noise nuisance. Showing off the impressive Voodoo in the air and on the ground was part of this joint PR campaign and the One-O-Wonders were only too happy to oblige at other Open Days, Battle of Britain celebrations, the Farnborough International Air Display et al.

In the final analysis, would the Voodoo recce pilots have been able to achieve their missions at low level in the NATO area of responsibility, survival being implicit in this effectiveness? Based on his own experiences in Germany, in trials against Allied state of the art defences and

from discussions with ex-Soviet and East German air defence radar specialists, AAA gunners and MiG fighter pilots since the end of the Cold War, the author believes that they had a good chance of doing so, given certain prerequisites and the right circumstances. Oberst Alfred Lehmann, who manned East German early warning and aircraft control radars in the late 1950s and early 1960s and went on to command a comprehensive network of sites, was confident in their ability to detect intruders, either single aircraft or mass raids, and to provide some form of fighter control, provided they were not at very low level. He admitted, however, that these early systems would not have been able to detect or trace aircraft flying at the heights and speeds of which the Voodoos were capable. It is believed that the Warsaw Pact did have visual observers

RAF Benefit. During their time in Europe the RF-101s of the 66th TRW were regular visitors to RAF stations and participants in UK air displays, one seen here at RAF Leuchars and, with its camouflage standing out among its USAF and USN contemporaries, another at the Farnborough Airshow. George Cowgill & Mike Stroud

at strategic points and in depth along the Inner German Border (IGB), equipped with radios to report the headings and estimated airspeeds of Allied aircraft entering their airspace, but it seems unlikely that, at the outset of general war at that time, this system would have been sufficiently well rehearsed or the defences responsive enough to make best use of such warnings. Later, an enhanced network was made to work to good effect in SEA but the circumstances were very different to those at this stage in Europe. It is not known how effective their Electronic Counter Counter Measures (ECCM) would have been against the limited ECM available to NATO at that time. Likewise, ex-MiG pilots Klaus Baarz, who became Deputy Commander of the Luftstreitkrafte/Luftverteidigung, the East German Air Force/Air Defence, and Klaus Heinig, while again proud of their capabilities, agreed that they would have been very lucky to catch Voodoos flying 'in the weeds' at the very high speeds, especially without early warning.

Similar opinions came from Dr Dusan Schneider, who served in the Czech Air Force from 1952 to 1969 flying the MiG-15bis, MiG-17PF and MiG-21. He recalls that on the day before Stalin's death in 1953, Czech MiG-15bis from Pilsen shot down a USAF F-84 from Bitburg AB in Germany, one of two which had strayed into their airspace, and that in 1959 Czech MiG-19s forced an Italian Air Force F-84 to land at Hradec Kralov AB. The embarrassed pilot left his cockpit muttering: *"Mamma mia, Mamma Mia, Madonna mia, Madonna mia"*; he was returned later to Italy by train. Dusan Schneider had no such stories of meetings between the earlier MiGs and Voodoos, or indeed about MiG-21s that were better able to take on the new recce aircraft.

Finally, the author obtained a highly reliable account of MiG-15 capabilities and limitations from an exceptionally able ex-RAF fighter pilot, Mark Hanna who, when chief pilot of the 'Old Flying Machine Company', flew the aircraft in mock combat against F-86 and Hunter fighters. Mark found the Russian aircraft to be directionally unstable, the light but rather ineffective ailerons giving a poor rate of roll, and to have a tendency to 'dutch roll' and 'pitch-up' well within the permitted speed range. He was not comfortable in the MiG at the high speeds required to attempt to intercept the mighty Voodoo, and it seems unlikely that

the MiG-17 would have been much better. However, given sufficient warning and effective intercept control, the MiG-21 could have posed a much greater threat, especially in the event of the Voodoo slowing down or venturing above 'the weeds' to take the photos with the KA-1 and KA-2 cameras.

Whether it was as a result of clandestine intelligence or simply from sensible, professional deduction, the author was able to confirm that MiG satellite bases had been set up close to the most likely penetration points for NATO aircraft, shortening response times and perhaps making the maintenance of Combat Air Patrols (CAPs), with the vast numbers of fighters available, operationally viable. A 'Diensthabendes', equivalent to the NATO Quick Reaction Alert (QRA) force had to be airborne in eight minutes by day and ten minutes by night. Even in the 'quiet' years of the Cold War, the East German Air Force, heavily biased to air defence, had to meet a 'Koeffizient Technische Einsatzbereitschaft' of 0.9, or maintain 90% of its fighters combat ready at all times, every 12-aircraft squadron holding four aircraft at 30 minutes readiness. The numbers of aircraft training and rehearsing war procedures in the airspace close to the IGB were so high that half the force would fly training sorties on alternative days only. Although the actual proficiency of the pilots in the air cannot be judged, it is known that they flew approximately half the number of training hours allocated to NATO pilots, but of course much depended on the content of each flying hour. In any event, these accounts favouring the Voodoos became less persuasive with time and the development of new technologies.

The Warsaw Pact SAM threat to jets flying in Europe at very low level did not become significant until well into the 1960s, even with the introduction of the Soviet SA-4 'Ganef'. However, with its infra-red detection and guidance system optimised for low level defence, the portable SA-7 'Grail', introduced into Eastern Europe in very large numbers during the 1960s, would have been very hard to avoid, and this would impact on the conventional wisdom of low level operations.

In the Voodoo era AAA remained the main threat at low level, the author bowing to the hard lessons learned later by those Voodoo pilots who attempted to use NATO tactics against similar defences in SEA, which exacted a heavy toll on the USAF even before integrated defensive networks were fully established. When the RF-101s entered service in Europe in 1958, Soviet 57-mm S60 guns, with PUAZO-6-60 fire directors and SON-9 fire control radars, were already thick on the ground in East Germany, being deployed in regiments of 24 accompanied by similar numbers of 85-mm guns. These were supplemented by other regiments of 37-mm guns and, in the early 1960s, by the formidable ZSU-23/2 and 23/4 Shilka mobile, radar-laid AAA. A warm welcome awaited any NATO aircraft going east.

Unlike the scenario which the Voodoo warriors faced in SEA, NATO aircraft which survived the Warsaw Pact defences would than have to run the gauntlet of myriad NATO air defences on return to their bases. Crude plans for 'safe lanes', defined laterally and vertically, rendered complications for pilots who would have much preferred the direct route home, particularly with crippled aircraft or to detour to avoid bad weather. Also, many would have been loath to climb to prescribed heights for fear that either they or 'friendly' defences had unserviceable IFF equipments, or had the wrong code selected (it changed every 30mins), in which case they would be fired upon. Cynics believed that even if everything was in order they would have faced friendly fire. Although recovery procedures were continuously updated and improved, and were practised seriously, it is believed that many returning pilots would have taken their chances on what seemed to them to be the most sensible route for them in the circumstances, probably heading for home as low and as fast as they could fly.

What tactics would the RF-101s have employed to complete their reconnaissance and nuclear strike missions? There was no panacea solution to mission effectiveness and survival, the first counting on the second; among other factors, so much depended on the disposition of home bases, the distances to be flown and the weather at these bases, en-route and over the target area. Operating from Upper Heyford, it must have been desirable to conserve fuel by flying as far as possible over friendly territory at high level and dropping down well before detection by enemy early warning radars, but with no reliable on-board navigation equipment and Allied radar assistance unlikely to be available in war, descending through cloud to low level on the Continent when uncertain of position could be fatal. Certainly in the Voodoo era, with little or no ECM cover, low level penetration of the Eastern Bloc countries may have been the only sensible option. Survival was then dependent first on surprise, eluding enemy radar and delaying visual acquisition as long as possible, by taking the less predictable routes, using terrain masking and flying as low and as fast as possible while in hostile airspace. The theory was good but the practice more difficult; the perennially poor and unpredictable weather would often frustrate ideal, well thought-out flight plans, requiring pilots to re-route around areas of low cloud or poor visibility, thereafter having to recover to the original planned track with all the accompanying time, fuel, range and speed implications, difficult in any event but more so for the single seat pilot.

Tactics in the target area had to be determined first by intelligence requirements, with photos taken at heights and speeds compatible with the capabilities of the RF-101's cameras, the greater the cover required the greater the risk. Simple requests, down to that of a visual/in-flight report, offered the best chance of success and survival. Unlike previous wars of attrition where photography was the primary requirement in order to build up and maintain a current intelligence picture, what was likely to be needed at the outbreak of war across the IGB in the 1960s, with fast-moving events on a broad front, was the timely acquisition of intelligence and an immediate response, and in this tactical air reconnaissance would probably be invaluable. Typically, service commanders and their battle managers would need to know, there and then, whether a particular bridge over the Oder Neisse River had been destroyed, whether a satellite airfield was occupied and if so by what or a particular route was in use and if so by what. These were the sorts of answers which tac recon aircrew could provide in flight or immediately on landing without exposing themselves unnecessarily for comprehensive photo coverage, and live to fly another day. If, however, they were required to take pretty pictures, Royal Flush style, for which they had to climb and slow down for the cameras, their chances of surviving and succeeding were significantly less.

The first and crucial question for the

intelligence, targeting and tasking staffs was, therefore, whether the request itself was really necessary, whether the aircraft being considered was likely to be able to achieve the task, survive and return with the results in time for them to make a significant impact on the land/air battle? If the answer was 'yes', then what were the essential elements of intelligence required, given that the greater the detail the greater the risk? It follows that overall mission effectiveness was dependent in the first place on the experience, understanding of the role and aircraft capabilities, in short, the wisdom of the battle managers. Following this filter, supervisors and pilots on the flight line should then have the opportunity to comment on the viability of the mission from their own perspectives, and be given at least some discretion on how it should be flown. It was all about understanding needs, capabilities and limitations, what was vital and what was not, and this started at the top of the battle management tree and applied all the way to the roots.

In this context George Wehling tells an amusing story from his time as a captain on the 66th TRW at Toul AB when a visiting general asked an RF-101 pilot at random to tell him how he would execute his war mission. Having listened intently to the reply and studied the warrior's well-prepared map, the general suggested that he might be prudent to take another route, to which the war-fighter, not known for his diplomacy, replied: *"This ain't no weekend cross country General"*.

With similarly rapid and decisive reaction, the same forthright officer might have saved the day for Nick Pishvanov at Upper Heyford, had the incident in question not turned out to be a false alarm. It seems that white smoke was issuing from one of Nick's engines as he taxied out, causing a much concerned young One-O-Wonder to warn him from nearby that he was on fire and should vacate the aircraft post-haste. Nick duly stopped the aircraft and unlocked the canopy but it would not open electrically and he was forced to wait for help, as the same would-be friend called on him to: *"Blow the canopy, blow the canopy, you're on fire!"*, but groundcrew had now surrounded the cockpit and might have been injured had Nick done so. By the time a crewchief had cranked open the canopy the mysterious white smoke had disappeared, the cause unknown, and everything returned to normal in the otherwise peaceful English countryside.

Flying in peacetime from bases in the UK had its attractions, with the addition of many interesting targets for 'happy snaps', but there were also problems. Airspace congestion and many diverse restrictions frequently led the RF-101s back to the European Continent for

Sightseeing. Stonehenge and the Giant of Cerne Abbas, in Southern England, were popular attractions for the photo men of the 66th TRW at Upper Heyford. Nick Pishvanov

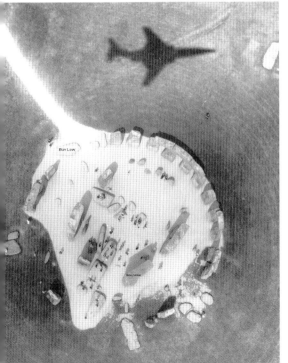
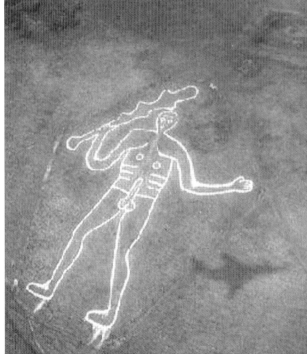

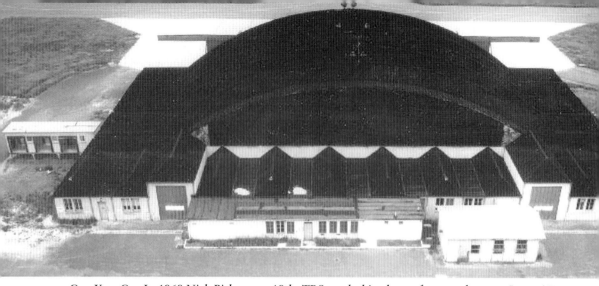

One Year On. In 1968 Nick Pishvanov, 18th TRS, took this photo of a now-dormant Laon AB.
Nick Pishvanov

realistic flying over the very ground they might have to cover in earnest if deterrence failed, perhaps nostalgia taking Nick Pishvanov to his old home at Laon to view the once very active but now dormant base with mixed feelings. Getting there was no easy matter; stringent air traffic procedures applied in transit, complicated flight plans had to be adhered to and, in practice, the French were far from co-operative.

The 17th TRS began its transition to the RF-4C at Upper Heyford in March 1969. The squadron would operate primarily in the night/all weather role, moving with its new aircraft to Zweibrucken AB, Germany, in 1970. In a daytime role the Voodoos of the 18th TRS continued to provide that unique capability with its KA-1 split vertical cameras and did very well in 1969's Royal Flush, before vacating Upper Heyford in 1970 for its titular home at Shaw AFB.

So ended the RF-101's 11 years of dedicated service in Europe; they had done their job well.

Out in Style. In their final year at Upper Heyford, the 18th TRS did well again in Royal Flush. USAF

CHAPTER FIVE:
PACIFIC VOODOOS

'The central task and the highest form of a revolution is to seize political power by armed force, to settle problems by war'

Mao Tse-tung, 1954

RF-101 Voodoos began arriving in the Pacific theatre of operations in mid-1958 to become part of the USAF's 67th TRW, PACAF. Operating remotely from their parent Wing at Yokota AB, Japan, they would replace the RF-84Fs of the 15th TRS (Cotton Pickers) at Kadena AB, Okinawa, and the 45th TRS (Polka Dots) at Misawa AB, Japan. Later, a total of eight RF-101s went to the Chinese (Nationalist) Air Force in order to maintain a force of four aircraft on the island of Taiwan (Formosa).

The story of the Cotton Pickers and Polka Dots in their early years with the RF-101s may have been overshadowed by the high profile events involving their Voodoo contemporaries elsewhere, typically the World Speed Records and Sun Run, together with events in Lebanon and Cuba, the activities of the RF-101 squadrons in TAC and the main force in Europe. In their later years, of course, the news from PACAF was all about the conflict in SEA, in which the 15th and 45th bore the brunt with regular detachments from Okinawa and Japan. This tended to place in the background those who toiled at Kadena and Misawa to provide that essential back-up and the families who, in mutual support, waited with trepidation

Badges of Pride. The badges of the 15th TRS, based at Kadena, Okinawa, and the 45th TRS at Misawa, Japan (taken from George Cowgill's flying suits), were worn with pride by the many who served there and in South East Asia.
Harry Runge & George Cowgill

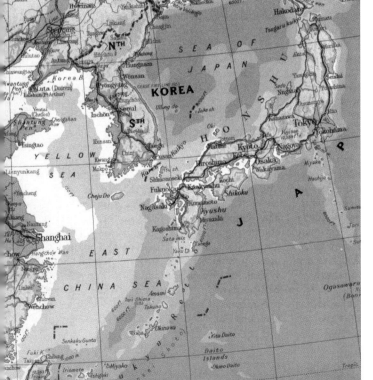

Pacific Playground. PACAF Voodoos would roam the skies from Northern Japan, over Korea, down to Okinawa and across into South East Asia. Author

for news from the front; these were the unsung heroes of Voodoo heritage. The story of the two squadrons in SEA comes later in the book with this chapter concentrating on the preceding years, their routine tasks, numerous detachments and lifestyles. It is a tribute to all those who did their duty in so many ways back at their home bases; albeit in relatively more agreeable conditions they too had their difficult times and should not be forgotten.

Misawa AFB, Japan, is situated on the north east coast of the island of Honshu, surrounded by rice paddies and small vegetable plots with a mountain range to the west parting the coastal area from the apple growing region in the main part of the Amori Prefecture. Another range of mountains to the south separates this region from the more highly populated part of the island. With the coast a few miles east of the runway and the mountain range to the west, the weather consists of abundant snow in winter and sporadic fog in the warmer months. Captain 'Burgie' Burgeson, Training Officer and latterly Assistant Operations Officer on the 45th TRS, has very fond memories of the squadron but remembers that the weather could be unpredictable, with the nearest suitable alternate at Chitose having similar problems and the other suitable diversion at Yokota AB a long way away. When returning from Yokota, Burgie was known to call his wife to get her estimates of visibility locally by reference to specific landmarks.

Tokyo is some 300 miles to the south and was accessed by a largely unpaved road more suited to the Japanese tricycle or pickup truck than big American vehicles, a difficult journey then perhaps taking more than 30 hours by car. That said, life for the families of the 45th TRS on the base was good; all the usual domestic facilities were in place with eight new accommodation blocks, each with eight apartments, built by the Japanese to their interpretation of American specifications. However, in the early years off-base quarters in 'Battery B' were described as 'pretty grim', with the houses small and difficult to heat, the roads unpaved and muddy. Initially, operational facilities for the Voodoo squadron were three miles to the north side of the base but later its operations were moved to a hangar on the main base.

Captain Gene Morris was more than happy with his life at Kadena on the island of Okinawa, 'a beautiful base with great facilities, well maintained and as close as one could get to being overseas and still have comparable facilities to an air force base in the States'. At the start of his tour he and his family lived off base in a house near the village of Awase, on a steep ridge with beautiful views over Buckner Bay and the surrounding countryside, but after two years they moved into what he called 'very nice family housing' on base, where help with the house and children was cheap and plentiful. Kadena seemed a veritable oasis to the fliers when they returned from their frequent TDYs, Gene likening it to paradise as they flew in over green and peaceful landscapes of Okinawa. He would spend the four years from 1962 to 1966 at Kadena and played a very significant part in setting up operations at Udorn AB in Thailand.

At Kadena, the 15th TRS was organised as an Air Force Controlled (AFCON) unit, assigned to the 313th AD but attached to the 18th TFW for operational control and logistical administrative support. In the early, relatively peaceful days, the Voodoo Cotton Pickers on Okinawa were commanded first by Major Russell Oaks, followed by Lieutenant Colonels Earl Butts and then Alexander Butterfield, the latter taking the squadron to war in earnest in SEA. The 15th TRS was one of four squadrons in the 18th TFW; its aircraft were assigned solely to the squadron and carried its insignias (the pooling of all RF-101s in PACAF and SEA coming later). At Misawa the 45th TRS was similarly structured.

Lieutenant Dewey Hemphill recalls that the first RF-101s arrived at Misawa for the 45th TRS in mid-1958; they were flown in by Captain Don Holman and Lieutenant Tom Davey, to be welcomed by the squadron and its commander, Major Frank O Lux. Tom, the wingman, landed first with fuel complications after which Don, at the behest of the welcoming committee and with the full authority of the hierarchy at Misawa, performed what he called 'the best low altitude show I have ever done', his vertical manoeuvres topping out in cloud. This impressed the resident F-100 pilots, countering their jibes about the Voodoo's alleged limitations. The 45th TRS pilots had already completed a ground school, with systems mock-ups as training aids at Kadena, before carrying out their own transition programme at Misawa under the guidance of Captains Elder and Johnson, who had checked

First In. Major Frank Lux, commander 45th TRS, welcomes Captain Don Holman and the first RF-101 to arrive on the squadron at Misawa in mid-1958. Dewey Hemphill

out in the aircraft at Shaw. First to be converted were the RF-84F instructor pilots, who then carried the task forward as instructor pilots on the RF-101. A contingency force of RF-84Fs remained operational until the programme was complete and the role could be taken over by the new aircraft.

The early routine at both Kadena and Misawa was much as it was elsewhere in the RF-101 squadrons, with a mixed programme to satisfy basic currency and operational training requirements, including specific photographic tasks for operational and public relations purposes. While the RF-101s in USAFE concentrated, of necessity, on low level recce, much of the work in PACAF required transit at height in order to reach their targets at great ranges and for high level photography. Despite the prevalence of jet streams, sometimes at speeds of 300 kts, and paucity of navigation equipment, the RF-101 pilots became adept at DR pilot navigation and would frequently descend through cloud to find themselves

Just Rewards. The recce men earned high rewards in some spectacular sightseeing (Captain Don O'Connell 'snaps' Frank Tiffault over Mount Fuji). Frank Tiffault

within sight of their targets, and some of the terrain over which they flew was spectacular. There were many detachments, with the 45th TRS given a considerable number of tasks operating out of Osan AB, South Korea, one of its pilots, Lieutenant John Linihan, remembering three TDYs to Osan and another to a Chinese Air Force base on Taiwan in eight months.

What made the programme a little different at Kadena was the disruption caused by typhoons. Some Voodoo pilots experienced similar evacuations from Shaw AFB in the face of hurricanes on the east coast of the USA and

there were equally rapid, often overdue, departures from Okinawa during typhoon alerts. The 15th TRS frequently sought refuge at Itazuke AB, Japan, but more than once typhoons chased them on to Yokota and then to Misawa, while it was not unknown for them to go as far as Clark AB in the Philippines. The normal plan was to launch in 'Condition Three' but Captain Don Elwood recalls that at times they were held until 'Condition Two', and once when the crosswind had reached 40 kts. On this occasion Don was sent off first: *"they figured that if I could make it anyone could"* and he did, by holding the Voodoo's nosewheel

Many Hands - Light Work? Lieutenant Bob Miranda gets help in his flight planning from (L to R) Abe Tanaka, George Bernert, Bob Miranda, 'Grand Dad' Warring & Dewey Hemphill. Ray Tiffault

Voodoo Writer. A2C Robert F Dorr, who would write well of the Voodoo in later years, with an RF-101 of the 15th TRS on detachment at Osan AB, Korea, in May 1959. Robert F Dorr

on the runway well into flying speed and then 'jerking the aircraft off the ground', at which point it immediately drifted off the runway as predicted. The rest of the squadron followed his example and all was well. Bob Gould endorsed this technique, by which they would literally 'leap into the air', he himself taking off once at the last minute in a 50 kts crosswind gusting up to 100 kts, entering a turbulent cloud almost at once and remaining in afterburner until breaking into the clear at 30,000 ft. The flight line pilots had a saying: *"Save a few bucks - lose a few planes!"*

Non-standard take-offs were not the only unorthodox practices developed by the Voodoo pilots as their confidence in the aircraft grew. Don Elwood watched with apprehension two RF-101s deploying their drag chutes in the air before a formation touch-down, and get away with very short landings.

It was during one typhoon evacuation in April 1960 that the 15th TRS lost Captain Charlie Lavender. It is believed that some catastrophe occurred while he was flying on Captain Linwood Roberts' wing in cloud as they recovered to Itazuke AB after a routine training sortie. Triggered by something in his peripheral vision, Linwood looked for his wingman but could neither see him nor raise him on the radio, only spotting Charlie again as he emerged below cloud, apparently safely on his parachute just before he hit the sea. Overflying the spot, he could see that the pilot had deployed his liferaft but was still attached to his parachute, which was dragging him, spinning, below the waves. Nearby Japanese fishermen heard an explosion, saw the burning aircraft plunge into the sea and raced to the drowning pilot, but they were unable to save him.

Bob Gould recalls 1959 and 1960 as 'reasonably routine years' for the squadron, but they were not without tragedy. Pitch-up was said to have downed several PACAF Voodoos in the early years, Captain Chuck Lustig being on the accident board involving one pilot who had a very narrow escape. It happened to an RF-101 from Misawa approaching Kadena for a single-engine landing, low oil pressure having caused the pilot to shut down that engine. On the final approach the aircraft was seen to have 'all the garbage hanging' and, although afterburner had been selected on the good engine, the speed brakes were extended and the

aircraft got 'behind the power curve', pitched up and hit the sea one wing low just as the pilot initiated the ejection sequence. An observer reported that 'the seat separated as the pilot went screaming across the water on his back like a water scooter'. It seems that the poor unfortunate was then propelled against a barely submerged coral reef which shredded his back pack parachute, ripped through his flight jacket and the shoulder of his flight suit and landed him eventually in three feet of water. An old Okinawa man, watching the whole show from the shore nearby, complied readily with the pilot's request to *"G-G-G-Gimmee a cigarette!"* As part of the accident board's deliberations, Chuck conducted tests in the same conditions and configuration, confirming that the speed brakes must be retracted or afterburner selected before reducing speed below 185 kts on a single engine approach.

Premeditated ejections were less common, but on 8 November 1959 Lieutenant Dan Waddle was persuaded to eject after his RF-101 had utility hydraulic failure and he could not get an indication that his gear was safely down and locked. He headed his aircraft out to sea and ejected, to be rescued uninjured by helicopter, but his aircraft had a mind of its own and returned to dry land, crashing in an open field. A local boy may have suffered a minor leg injury from flying debris and was taken to the base hospital at Misawa.

Just Another Day. Lieutenant Dan Waddle, 45th TRS, looks unperturbed as he walks from his rescue helicopter after ejecting into the sea off Misawa on 29 November 1959.
George Cowgill

Polka Dot Pilot. Lieutenant Frank Dunn, 45th TRS, October 1959. Frank Dunn

Voodoo Team. (L to R) Staff Sergeant Brooks (Crew chief), Lieutenant Frank Dunn (pilot) and Airman First Class Hatch, Misawa AB October 1958. Frank Dunn

Weather problems in PACAF were not confined to typhoons. Lieutenant Frank Dunn, who had joined the 45th TRS direct from primary flight training to fly the RF-84F and then transitioned to the Voodoo, remembers being talked down successfully at Misawa in 'zero-zero' conditions. This was on a day when the usual early morning fog was forecast to drift out to sea and stay there provided the wind direction did not change. Frank got airborne, completed his planned photo runs over a dam, power plant and marshalling yard as tasked and then made for a rendezvous with another Voodoo pilot for a spot of 'rat-racing' (simulated combat) over Lake Towata. They agreed to meet at 20,000 ft, but a little 'gamesmanship' could be expected from whoever got there first and Frank positioned himself accordingly, up-sun at 35,000 ft. With such an advantage he should have won the day, and he did, with a close-up photo of his adversary taken on his nose-facing KA2 to back his claim.

It was at this point that Misawa Tower recalled all its aircraft, the fog rolling in fast with IFR imposed shortly thereafter. Frank joined the queue for a GCA when the weather was given as 300 ft, visibility one mile, but worse was to come. The final controller had 'a thick Japanese accent', which suggested a trainee on the consol, but Frank followed his instructions 'to the letter' only to spot the runway well to the south when it should have

been dead ahead as he broke out of the undercast at 250 ft into very poor visibility. He had to abort this and the next two approaches with the same operator as the cloud base lowered progressively, until his fuel state was such that he declared his intention to fly out to sea and eject. Not before time, the senior controller took over, calmly announcing *"No sweat, Lieutenant, I can get you down"* and he did. This confident and highly competent sergeant gave the best GCA of his life with a sensibly long and low angle final approach, his calls on the aircraft's position proving to be accurate to a matter of feet when the Voodoo touched down where he had predicted. No-one watching with great trepidation on the ground saw the aircraft land, Frank Lux, who was close to the approach end of the runway, seeing 'only a grey blur'. While Frank Dunn waited for a 'follow me'(which promptly got lost in the fog) the engines of his Voodoo ran down; he had landed in 'zero-zero' and out of fuel, on a day to remember. Celebrations were now in order, Frank starting them off by presenting his best bottle of elusive Jack Daniels Black Label whisky to the NCO who had saved the day. By the time he handed over command of the 45th TRS to Major Cecil Bush in 1959 Frank Lux had probably had his fill of excitement.

Trail Blazers. (L to R) Captains Wayne Elder, 'Burgie' Burgeson, Lieutenants Reg Johnson, Abe Tanaka & Frank Dunn (spare), chosen to go to Australia for Exercise Hand Clasp in 1959.

In addition to the routine photographic tasks, the Voodoos of Misawa remained ready to scramble rapidly to intercept Russian 'intruders', usually Badger and Bear bombers or reconnaissance aircraft, often returning with interesting, close-up photographs. Likewise, they would provide intelligence staffs with useful information on Russian 'picket ships' monitoring allied electronics systems. Such inoffensive 'cat and mouse' games were all part of Cold War deterrence.

The PACAF Voodoo squadrons were also roving far and wide, showing the flag and spreading goodwill, and it was for that purpose that four aircraft from the 45th TRS deployed to Australia in 1959, in Exercise Hand Clasp. Captains Wayne Elder and Burgie Burgeson were accompanied by Lieutenants Abe Tanaka and Reg Johnson (Frank Dunn nominated as the spare), the successful quartet returning with Wallaby insignia adorning their aircraft.

As part of the Military Assistance

Memorabilia. Polka Dot Voodoos returned from Australia adorned with Wallaby symbols. Fred Muesegaes

First of Few. The first five Chinese pilots from Taiwan to be instructed on the RF-101 by the 15th TRS at Kadena AB (rear). Captains Bob Gould, Gayle Coffman and Bob Caudry (front). Bob Gould

USAF presence, typically with Captain John Summers posted officially from Shaw to the staff of Detachment 1, USAF 13th Air Force, Taipei (known as Taipei Air station) for two years from the spring of 1963. In effect, John was an adviser to the Chinese, flying with them in the RF-101 and T-33. He found them competent at work and very agreeable company socially, recalling that one, Captain C T Yeh, had 'the fastest reflexes I have ever seen' when it came to the game of 'drop the dollar bill' (catch the note falling to the table). Ostensibly, the Chinese nationalists had the Voodoos to watch for intruders into international waters between the mainland and Taiwan but with such a fast, long range aircraft (and with air refuelling facilities from 1965) this was clearly not the limit of their intentions and it is generally assumed that the RF-101s (among other aircraft) penetrated deep into mainland China. In fact, the communists claimed to have shot down a Voodoo and captured its pilot. The Chinese RF-101s ceased operations in 1970 but one remains on static display in Taiwan.

Programme, the USAF supported the initially clandestine Operation Boom Town from November 1959; it's purpose to keep a force of four RF-101s on the line with the 4th Composite Reconnaissance Squadron (CRS), Chinese Air Force in Taiwan. The 4th CRS contained a mix of RF-84F and RF-101 aircraft, reputedly flown by the best of the Chinese fighter pilots, who may also have had some influence in high places. The nationalists modelled these operations on the well-proven USAF pattern, and took instruction from the PACAF Voodoo pilots. Gene Morris, 15th TRS, remembers that his squadron trained some six of their pilots during 1961-1962, in what he described as a highly classified operation. In their gratitude, the Chinese invited the 15th TRS to their base at Tao Yuan on 16 April 1964; six pilots accepted the invitation, meeting two Chinese Voodoos en route for an eight-ship formation flypast at Tao Yuan. Within 15 minutes of landing all eight aircraft were sheltered out of sight below ground; this was indeed a classified operation.

The 4th CRS retained a token

Frank Dunn was well known as an enthusiastic flier, he himself claiming to have amassed some 1000 hours flying during his tour in PACAF, close to double the average for the same time period, but it so nearly ended with a tragedy, in a story he tells at length and most graphically elsewhere. This is a mere synopsis of a very dramatic accident.

Frank's last trip at Misawa was scheduled to be an interesting, classified task, involving a detachment of four RF-101s to Yokota AB, Japan, headquarters of the 67th TRW whose RB-66s could not take on this particular

Transition. USAF and Chinese Air Force RF-101s on the flight line at Taipei AB, Taiwan (Formosa). Gene Morris

Going It Alone. Four RF-101s of the Chinese Air Force over Taiwan. John Summers

Getting to Know You. Captain John Summers (second left) and Chinese Air Force RF-101 pilots socialising incognito. John Summers

assignment. When his aircraft was found to have a hydraulic leak Frank swapped it for another, starting up and taxiing out as part of a now three-ship flight to take off as a single aircraft, without afterburner, behind the lead pair. The weather was perfect and all seemed set fair on the roll until, immediately after he became airborne and as the gear was retracting, his aircraft was rocked by an explosion; the left engine fire warning light came on and the mirror showed fire torching from a gaping hole behind the cockpit. Frank stop-cocked the engine and steered away from a village below while climbing and turning towards the sea, at the same time declaring an emergency. More explosions followed with the right engine fire warning light coming on and the controls freezing as that engine too was closed down. This was clearly time to go, and Frank jettisoned the canopy to be treated to a blast of hot air as he tried in vain to eject from the now uncontrollable aircraft, his flight leader shouting due encouragement. The ejection system failed him and Frank had no option but to unstrap from his seat and climb out under

his own steam, the tail no longer in the way having split from the aircraft and fallen to earth. With a welcome 'thump' the parachute opened at no more than 100 ft and a couple of seconds later Frank dropped on to his back within yards of the fireball created by the remainder of his Voodoo.

Bits and Pieces. The tail section of Frank Dunn's RF-101C impacted in a rice paddy field - five miles from the nose section. Frank Dunn

Going Places? It is hard to believe that the Chinese Air Force Voodoos needed AAR solely to fulfil their officially published task of surveillance over coastal waters. Bill Bernert

The farmer and horse he had missed narrowly in the final throes of his descent were now plodding towards him but his problems were far from over as he was dragged across the snow-covered paddy field. Finally coming to a stop he succeeded, with the help of the farmer (albeit without a common language) and despite being in great pain with badly burned hands, in operating the so-called 'quick release' fasteners to free himself from his parachute. Together the two men spread the badly burnt, multi-coloured 'chute across the snow to attract the rescue helicopter, but failed to get the URC 4 radio working before the 'chopper' came into view and rescue seemed imminent. Unfortunately, when Frank's back was turned the friendly Japanese had packed the parachute neatly to hand to him, as a result of which the helicopter failed to spot them and continued on to land at the crash site. By now some 50 or more Japanese men, women and children had joined them and the badly injured pilot was half-carried towards the burning wreckage, finally to be noticed by the rescue crew. As Frank said, *"the look on their faces wasn't reassuring!"* Morphine and lying flat on a stretcher did little to relieve the pain on the five-mile journey back to the Misawa where an even less reassuring voice from the reception committee was heard to mutter: *"My God - he's dead!"* - but Frank soon put him right. Very soon he was on the operating table and sent into blissful oblivion.

There followed a month or so of alternating pain and darkness, in long and difficult days while the burns healed and the pain receded very gradually, ameliorated a little by continuous injections of morphine, which became painful in themselves. However, Voodoo pilots are nothing if not resilient; within a couple of months Frank's scars were minimal and, after proper recuperation in the States, he was back in the air as an instructor at Reece AFB, Texas. A Reserve Officer, Frank Dunn would complete his time in the USAF and go on to a successful career in the family furniture business. The old Japanese farmer who had come to Frank's help with the utmost calm was honoured at a ritualistic formal lunch attended by the great and good on the base, from the local headquarters and the local community, an event which clearly petrified him. As Frank said:

"Find a good Samaritan and make him as miserable as possible - that's how the system works!"

The October 1960 edition of the PACAF magazine Flyer featured the 15th TRS, now commanded by Lieutenant Colonel Earl A Butts, in glowing terms. To quote:

"If industry, perseverance and just plain hard work, blended with intelligent planning and a keen desire to excel and to be on top, are indicators of a top-notch organisation, then keep an eye on the 15th".

Under the auspices of the squadron operations officer, each of the three flights took turns to fly, run operations (the operations desk, mobile et al) or carry out ground training (including use of the flight simulator). A normal flying day would begin with a squadron briefing at 0715 hours, conducted by the operations officer and covering matters of direct operational and training interest, flight safety and training etc. Throughout the day, all information necessary for local flying operations was kept up-dated by the desk officer, who would also conduct the final briefings before the pilots walked to their aircraft. Wherever possible, and within given guidelines, minute-to-minute organisation and supervision of flying and ground training programmes was delegated to the flight commanders, who would normally lead the frequent off-base deployments as task force commanders. Central direction also prescribed crucial matters of flight safety, stressing the need to learn the lessons of the past, to adhere to published procedures and proven check lists for all operations in the air and on the ground. In the 'Flyer' article, Earl Butts believed that this system resulted in closer supervision of the pilots, more continuity in training to cover an individual's weak areas and safer flying by the judicious use of experienced pilots.

Many PACAF Voodoo pilots got to know very long transit flights to and from the USA, with Bob Gould and John Gardner being among the first to return aircraft from Okinawa to Hill AFB, Utah, for modification programmes. Their trip would involve overnight stops at Guam and then Hickam AFB after two air refuellings, before the final leg to McClellan AFB on which they would take fuel once more while airborne. This early flight was uneventful other than that the two pilots and their aircraft had to spend what Bob described as 'a rough ten days in Hawaii' waiting for an engine change, but others would not be so fortunate. As elsewhere, the only tankers available at the time were the KB-50s, flying at heights and speeds which could make refuelling with the probe and drogue very difficult in poor weather, but trips across the Pacific were made much easier with the introduction of the KC-135. Captain Chuck Lustig was another who endured a marathon trip back from Okinawa, with five refuellings being necessary on the nine

That's Progress! In the early 1960s the KB-50J tankers serving PACAF were replaced by the faster and higher flying KC-135.

Fred Muesegaes & George Cowgill

hour leg between Hickam and Richards Gebaur AFB, Missouri.

PACAF pilots could also be called on to ferry the Chinese Voodoos back across the Pacific for deep maintenance in the USA, tasks which could be difficult enough in themselves without the complications of the Chinese language which beset one such 'volunteer'. On arrival at Taipei AB to pick up the aircraft, he found that the Form 1 contained two red crosses (no fly items), with accompanying words which he could neither understand nor for which he could find an explanation so, in a measure of the confidence the pilots had in their aircraft and its redundant systems, he elected to find out what the problems were for himself. The first fault became apparent immediately after he became airborne when the undercarriage failed to retract and he had to land back at Taipei for an accompanying USAF crew chief to carry out appropriate rectification. Airborne again, he was well en route to Guam before the second defect made itself known, the fuel gauge falling to zero. By this time, our intrepid aviator was in no mood to return and so hitched a ride behind a KB-50 tanker for the rest of the trip back to the United States, taking on fuel whenever he considered it prudent.

Fred Muesegaes, one of seven bachelors in the 45th TRS at the start of the 1960s, remembers that life was good, with plenty of satisfying flying, interesting TDYs and a great sense of comradeship on the squadron. With the 45th an autonomous squadron, individual pilots and crew chiefs were authorised to name the aircraft assigned to them. Rather irreverently, given the nature of the bawdy bar song from which he took the name, Fred called his aircraft 'Mary Ann Burns'; he figured that this was most appropriate for the 'big, heavy aircraft with an infamous reputation'. Mary Ann Burns was one of the first four RF-101s to go to Don Muang AB, Thailand, on Able Mable Task Force duties. It was into this happy situation that Lieutenant John Linihan was pitched for his first operational tour, and he would acquit himself well at Misawa, on Project Field

109

Enjoy! Lieutenant Ray Tiffault, happy with his lot on the 45th TRS. Ray Tiffault

Polka Dot Men and Machines. With the 45th TRS operating autonomously at Misawa, the pilots were allowed to name their personal aircraft. Fred Muesegaes chose 'Mary Ann Burns' of stag bar ballad fame; it would be one of the first aircraft to deploy to SEA for 'Able Mable'. Fred Muesegaes

Calm Before the Storm. Crews of the 45th TRS at Misawa in the relatively peaceful days before the conflict in South East Asia.
Fred Muesegaes

Below: Loner. Captain Fletcher Cook, after hearing in October 1960 that all dependent travel to Misawa was to cease 'to stop the drain on gold' - leaving him on his own! John Linihan

Goal and Able Mable in SEA.

From the end of 1960, the bachelors of the 45th TRS were not the only ones living a single life, all dependent travel to the theatre having been suspended to 'stop the drain on gold', Captain Fletcher Cook being one of many married officers to suffer. Life went on, however, and while four of the bachelors (Lieutenants Ray Tiffault, Fred Muesegaes, Ben Welch and Joe Williams) were quenching their thirst in the VOQ they came up with the idea of designing unique blazers to distinguish

B Flight, 45th TRS. (Left photo, back row, L to R) Danny Waddle, Dewey Hemphill, Homer Lee. (Front row, L to R) John Humphrey, John Linihan, Ralph DeLucia.
John Linihan

Above & below: Polka Dot Playmates. Featuring 'Norm' and Mary June Huggins, Jack Woody, Bud McVay, Don and Nancy O'Connell, Sam Clark, Stu Matthews, Dick Campis, Joe Lyons and others, 'strutting their stuff' at Misawa, 1962-1964. Norm Huggins

Dressed to Kill. John Linihan, Ben Welch, Ray Tiffault and Fred Muesegaes ready to play. Fred Muesegaes

themselves from lesser mortals, especially those on the collocated F-100 squadrons, whose blazers they thought dowdy. The Polka Dot motif had to be central, so blue satin jackets would be spotted with white dots and, at Fred's suggestion, a Playboy Bunny badge was embroidered on the breast pocket. Then, as the beer flowed and enthusiasm grew, it was agreed that the words '45th TRS' should be added above and 'Bachelors' below the badge. Despite using local traders all this took time, but the secret was well kept until the blazers were

properly finished and the seven wearers came together for the grand launch. Proof that the impact had the desired effect came in a dictate from the squadron commander, now Lieutenant Colonel Osborne, that regardless of the bachelors' opposition, the coat would be adopted forthwith as de rigueur for all squadron officers. At this time the 45th TRS was particularly active socially and this very visible 'trademark' only increased pride in squadron membership. The blazers can be seen at reunions to this day and, at the time of writing, one belonging to the late Colonel

Anything They Can Do.......F-100s of the 18th TFW at Misawa AB. John Linihan

'Curley' Walker was being donated to the Wright-Patterson Museum, at the family's request.

The 45th TRS found other ways of making their mark; Ray Tiffault, one of the bachelors who served with the squadron from 1958 to 1962 (and again between 1964-1966), recalled that in a maximum effort the squadron generated 16 of its aircraft in May 1961 and 'wired' the airfield several times in close formation. With Major Art Osborn at the helm and the other three flights of four led by Captains Doug Kimball, Danny Waddle and Fletcher Cook, this spectacle did much for the morale of the squadron while surely incurring some envy if not admiration among the resident F-100 squadrons? However, this laudable effort

We Can Do Better..... The 45th TRS, Major Art Osborn leading Pat Murray, Pete Dekeyser, Lenny Severtson, Doug Kimball, Joe Williams, Bob Rieck, Danny Waddle, John Linihan, Dewey Hemphill, Jack Weatherby, Fletcher Cook, Ray Tiffault, Bill Whitten & Stu Matthews. John Linihan

may not have been seen by the hierarchy as the best use of operational assets and it is believed that it was not repeated.

From the beginning of the 1960s war clouds were gathering fast over SEA, with both PACAF Voodoo squadrons becoming increasingly involved in detachments to South Vietnam and Thailand. Project Field Goal, Exercise Air Bull and Exercise Pipe Stem got the ball rolling, leading to Operation Able Mable Task Force in 1961, the prelude to the full scale conflict (Part Two). All this was foreseen and sensible preparations were put in hand, exemplified by more intensive in-theatre survival training. To this end, Gene Morris attended the RAF Jungle Survival School at RAF Changi, Singapore, in 1962, in his words

The Chorus. Blanche Wallin, Marlyn Dault, Marj Gould, Jo Waltz, Betty Gibson & Pat Elwood. Bob Gould

'a gentlemanly course' from which those taking part learned a lot without being overstressed', at least until a rigorous escape and evasion exercise at the end which Gene had good cause to remember. Paired with a very tall New Zealand pilot, the two had reached what they thought was a deep canal barring their way as they fled from RAF Regiment guards intent on finding candidates on which to hone their somewhat sadistic interrogation skills. At this point the New Zealander announced that he could not swim, and there was nothing for it but for Gene to carry him over on his back, he half under water in what turned out to be a vile smelling sewer. Gene's abiding memory is of a very English voice proclaiming *"I say, Gene, did you detect a distinct odour of s*** whilst we crossed?"* Fighter pilots always find a way, and camaraderie has no limits.

On the night of 22 January 1962 the 15th TRS had an RF-101 pitch up at high level while the pilot on a proficiency check

tried to 'hang in' on the wing of his leader during some very demanding tight turns. After his aircraft had 'gone vertical and become violent - with flames coming out of the intakes', he made two attempts to recover *"mostly by rote as I had vertigo so bad that I could not read the instruments"*, before ejecting at an estimated 6000 ft, to be plucked from a cruel sea in winds gusting up to 35 kts by a valiant Marine helicopter pilot. He learned much from this terrifying experience, not solely about

Joint Play. Lieutenant Colonel Alex Butterfield and the 15th TRS welcome Canberra aircrew of No 45 Squadron RAF to Kadena, for Exercise Joss Stick.
Bob Gould

Return Match. Captain Bob Caudry, 15th TRS, welcomed at RAF Tengah, Singapore, by RAF officers, for a joint exercise with RAF Javelins and Hunters. Bob Caudry

pitch-up, and would be the better for it.

Although this chapter deals primarily with the two PACAF squadrons from their re-equipment with the RF-101 until the beginning of the major commitments in SEA in 1962, it should be remembered that Misawa and Kadena provided sanctuaries and essential support for the Voodoos throughout the conflict, while continuing to have their own domestic agendas. In 1963, for instance, Bob Caudry took part in a joint exercise at RAF Tengah, Singapore, involving USAF Voodoos and F-100s together with RAF Javelins and Hunters and, in 1964, the 15th TRS hosted RAF Canberras of No 45 Squadron on behalf of the 3rd Bombardment Wing (BW), USAF. The 3rd BW flew the USAF equivalent of the Canberra, the B-57, with the British in Exercise Joss Stick. On another occasion, two RF-101s were flown to Tengah by Major Allan L Parks and Captain Donald P Beck, supported by a PACAF Photo Processing Cell (PPC). There they completed the task of six sorties over 24 targets, impressing the British with the speed and efficiency of the operation and the quality of their photographs.

With all this going on at Misawa and Kadena while their RF-101 squadrons were being committed increasingly to the conflict in SEA, it seems right to include a glimpse of life and work back at the home bases in the later years, and the 15th TRS at Kadena has been chosen for this snapshot.

It was now rare for all the Cotton Pickers to be together at one time but when they were, photo calls were the order of the day. On 1 January 1965, the squadron had a nominal strength of 12 aircraft, 26 officers and 29 airmen, Robert O Crabtree in command with Major Richard G Thompson his operations

officer. Their aircraft were still in a natural silver finish and adorned with squadron insignia, but they were soon to be camouflaged for SEA.

In January 1965, the men and machines of the 15th TRS excelled in a stringent Operational Readiness Inspection (ORI), leaving the squadron in good shape for the return of their warriors from SEA on 31 January 1965 when the 45th TRS took over the Able Mable operation at Tan Son Nhut. The Cotton Pickers were now together on Okinawa with their families but they were given only a brief respite. In addition to the comprehensive war role training required for SEA, the squadrons had to keep all their pilots in current flying practice with check-outs, theatre

All Together Now. For the first time in four years of continuous TDY, the officers and men of the 15th TRS we all together at Kadena in 1964. Gene Morris

U.S. AIR FORCE
RESCUE

Colour Sense. After flying their Voodoos for seven years in their natural finish all the PACAF Voodoos would be camouflaged, Captain Howard Davis, 15th TRS, seen here getting airborne from Kadena in 1965. Harry Runge

orientation and follow-on role training for pilots arriving from Shaw to make them combat ready in minimum time. In addition, they ran a transition programme in accordance with AFM 51-101 for other pilots posted in direct from local staff appointments. Great ingenuity went into deriving as much training as possible from every flying sortie while maintaining a comprehensive ground training programme incorporating briefings on new equipment, tactics et al. Tired aircraft also had to be serviced, tasks set by 5th Air Force and the 18th TFW satisfied, while further detachments were planned. To everyone's credit, all the essentials were achieved rapidly and in good order.

A month earlier, in December 1964, the unit had been warned that it would be required to set up and pioneer operations at the old Japanese air base of Udorn in Northern Thailand. Gene Morris, the squadron's operational pilot-cum-administrative officer, had been earmarked to head an advance recce party and this departed in January 1965 to set in motion a rapid train of events which would get operations there underway in April (the Udorn activation story is told in Chapter Eleven). The already busy life on Okinawa became busier with the detachment of six aircraft moving to Udorn in March, to become the 'Green Pythons'.

Even with their commitments in SEA, the Voodoo pilots could not escape the myriad ground duties which called for their expertise, and many of them were drawn from the flight line to this end. Although this freed up a number of aircraft for others to fly, the squadrons were often left with too few resources overall to meet all the tasks set and it was a constant struggle to make ends meet.

The maintenance men, their number already depleted by TDY in SEA, were further stretched by the 18th TFW Project Limelight which was introduced in December 1964. This training programme, spanning four months, included on-the-job training with the 15th TRS providing the mentors, to generate an additional cadre of RF-101 maintenance personnel for SEA units. Exacerbating the problem of keeping enough aircraft on the line were the Project 1181 camera modification programme, which was now in full swing, and the major servicing schedule which took squadron pilots and aircraft away for those

long flights over the Pacific to and from the depot at Olmstead AFB, Pennsylvania. Kadena was designated the Main Operating Base (MOB) for all 1181 modified aircraft and, as such, was responsible for maintaining 12 RF-101s both at Tan Son Nhut and Udorn in SEA. The camera programme was completed very much as planned, all but three aircraft returning fully modified within six months. Inevitably, it was not long before the two Voodoo squadrons lost sole ownership of their aircraft, all PACAF and assigned TAC RF-101s then being pooled for a central authority to allocate as priorities demanded.

All this was accomplished while building work was carried out to provide additional briefing facilities for the 15th TRS between the squadron's two existing buildings. The photo men were also sorely stretched. Despite having 12 of their number on TDY in SEA during the first half of 1965, they were required to process 59,000 ft of film and produce some 14,000 prints, while at the same time improving their photographic laboratory using self-help with materials begged or borrowed. Whoever and wherever they were, life for the men of the 15th TRS was busy.

Notwithstanding every pressure, an incident at Kadena on 15 April 1965 involving Captain Charlie E Shelton was in no way attributed to any deficiency in training or maintenance practice. When Charlie was unable to get the main wheels of his RF-101 down, he landed 'gently, on the aft section and nosewheel' on a foam strip, causing very little damage. For his airmanship skills, Charlie was nominated for the 'Able Aeronaut' award, in a year when the squadron earned a USAF Safety Award for completing 12,561 hours of accident-free flying.

It is timely to pay tribute to the wives who waited anxiously for that dreaded knock on the door of their quarters in Japan or Okinawa and the news that their man was injured, missing or worse in SEA, and the number of such cases was now increasing. Murph Lustig recalls the fright of being woken in the early hours of one morning at Kadena, while Chuck was at the front - merely to be told that the typhoon alert state had changed. They who waited also served.

The Voodoos of the 15th TRS returned from Udorn to Kadena in April 1966, for the squadron to begin its transition to the RF-4C,

Pythons at Home. Lieutenant Colonel Crabtree (centre) and the officers of the 15th TRS, home at Kadena after TDY at Udorn, Thailand. Harry Runge

but many of its pilots would serve again in SEA.

The author finds it interesting that those who called the tune in Japan, at Okinawa and back in the United States, continued to maintain such heavy pressure on the weary pilots and their aircraft when they returned from the war in SEA to their home bases. Chuck Lustig put it another way:

"With the turmoil the 15th and 45th TRS were going through trying to support both Udorn and Tan Son Nhut detachments while continuing with the SIOP commitments at Kadena and Misawa, plus all the c*** such as ORIs, firepower demos, happy snaps around the Western Pacific for whoever wanted them, typhoon evacuations, caring for the wives of lost or missing pilots and training new guys from Shaw, it was almost a relief to head back to Udorn to fly combat".

Relief or not, from 1961 onwards the men of the PACAF Voodoo squadrons would all have more than their fill of combat in South East Asia.

CHAPTER SIX
VOODOO BOMBERS

'By carrying destructiveness to a suicidal extreme, atomic power is stimulating and accelerating a reversion to the indirect methods that are the essence of strategy - since they endow war with intelligent properties that raise it above the brute application of force'.

B H Liddell Hart, 1954

Earlier chapters tell of the controversy over the future of the early Voodoos which culminated in 1957 after the first F-101As were accepted by the 27th SFW at Bergstrom AFB that summer and were then rejected by the bomber barons of SAC who lost all interest in the aircraft, both as a bomber escort and a reconnaissance platform. This was fortuitous for TAC which saw the potential in this very fast, long legged jet in the tactical nuclear bomber and reconnaissance roles, while ADC foresaw its use as an all-weather fighter. Accordingly, the 77 F-101A and 47 F-101C fighters were reassigned to TAC's 27th FBW/TFW in the fighter bomber role at Bergstrom in July 1957, after which McDonnell switched all Voodoo production to the reconnaissance, all-weather fighter and trainer variants.

Lieutenant Colonel John Bull Stirling had been a strong believer in the Voodoo since he first flew the aircraft at Edwards AFB (the 50th pilot to do so) and inherited the operational test project for the aircraft in 1955; he would come to play a significant part in its life. An articulate staff officer, Stirling was the 'front man' in the Pentagon's efforts to persuade the Commander of USAFE, General Frank F Everest, and the

USAF Vice-Chief of Staff, General Curt E LeMay, that the Voodoo fighter bomber had a place in Europe. More specifically, he argued that it should replace the ageing and far less capable F-84Fs of the 81st TFW at the twin bases of Bentwaters and Woodbridge in East Anglia, to be employed primarily in the tactical nuclear bomber role over the relatively short distances to primary targets in East Germany, Poland and the Soviet Union. The case was made and General LeMay ordered the F-101s to the United Kingdom.

The unusual complex of two huge airfields at Bentwaters and Woodbridge, on the Suffolk coast only 3 miles apart and each providing long, wide runways, had been a very welcome landfall for many WW2 aircraft in emergency situations, some 4,000 said to have found safe haven there in times of great need. This seemed to be an ideal home for the noisy Voodoo, being a flat area beside the sea, just clear of major cities and controlled airspace and in a relatively sparsely populated area of forest and reed beds. Those who did live locally, especially music lovers at Aldeburgh some 10 miles away, were understandably less happy with the idea, but the Americans were very aware of this and would take many community relations

81st Tactical Fighter Wing: 'Le Nom Les Armes Le Loyaute'

91st Tactical Fighter Squadron: The Blue Streaks

92nd Tactical Fighter Squadron: The Avengers

78th Tactical Fighter Squadron: The Bushmasters

initiatives to placate their hosts. Unfortunately, there was only so much that could be done about the huge bird population which inhabited these otherwise perfect surroundings for them, they themselves always a threat to the low flying jets. However, in keeping with measures adopted throughout the country, flying was limited over specific areas during known migratory periods and 'bird scarers' were employed to reduce their activities over the airfields. There was also enough space for the large American communities (some 8000 service personnel and dependents) implicit in this 'occupation', many of the incumbents melding into local communities and coming to appreciate the surrounding environment, its kindly people and the proximity of London. The scene was set for another 'One-O-Wonderland'.

The mission for the Voodoos of the 81st TFW, 3rd Air Force, was 'to conduct special operations against any aggressor forces in Europe, in support of NATO as directed by higher headquarters'. They would take over the Operation Blast Off from the F-84Fs (renamed 'Victor Alert' in December 1958) to hold a number of aircraft armed with atomic weapons at high states of readiness. There were those who claimed that it would not be cost-effective to operate one wing of this relatively sophisticated aircraft for such a purpose in the theatre, but others counselled that it added to all-important deterrence in the Cold War. Robert F Dorr, in his excellent résumé of the situation in 'McDonnell F-101 Voodoo' suggests that the deployment of such a high performance nuclear bomber rang alarm bells in the Warsaw Pact. He quotes an article in the Soviet Air Force's journal 'Herald of the Red Air Fleet' which harangued the Americans for 'bringing a new type of atomic bomber to England'. There had to be the possibility that this would lead to counter moves in the East with strengthened air defences demanding a re-appraisal of NATO tactics.

The 81st TFW had as its emblem 'a dragon in azure holding in its dexter claw a stylized boll weevil and proclaiming a French motto 'Le Nom Les Armes Le Loyaute' ('The Name The Arms The Loyalty'), displayed against a yellow background. Heraldry spells out the significance of this intimidating creature breathing fire to subdue all enemies, depicted by the boll weevil, the blue alluding to the sky,

the primary Air Force environment, and the yellow the sun and excellence required of Air Force personnel. The Wing, which had been in residence at the twin bases since 1951, had its headquarters at Bentwaters together with the Voodoos of the 91st TFS (the 'Blue Streaks') and 92nd TFS (the 'Avengers'); the 78th TFS (the 'Bushmasters') flew from Woodbridge. These were big squadrons, each comprising some 26 aircraft in an amalgam of F-101As and F-101Cs. The two versions of the aircraft were indistinguishable externally or in their basic handling characteristics, but structural modifications had raised the clearance of the former from 6.33 'G' to 7.33 'G' with the latter for a small increase only in the aircraft's overall weight. Each squadron would be manned by four flights of seven pilots.

In December 1958, the Voodoos of Bergstrom moved to England, Major Eichelberger leading seven F-101A/Cs non-stop to Bentwaters with AAR in 11 hours; 70 more officers and 600 other ranks were airlifted from the 27th TFW to the UK before the end of 1958. The majority of the RF-84F pilots from the 81st TFW who were to convert to the Voodoo had their basic orientation to the aircraft at George AFB, California, before returning to the UK with their F-101s; there they were joined by the men from Bergstrom who were already well acquainted with the aircraft. Meanwhile the F-84s, which had been brought to a high state of alert during the Lebanon Crisis of August 1958, maintained a full operational posture for the remainder of the year before being transferred progressively to Lemweder airfield, on the River Weser in Germany, destined for the new German Air Force. By the end of 1958, the 81st TFW had 48 Voodoos on strength and 90% of its pilots achieved combat ready status in the first six months of 1959.

The basic colouring and insignia of the 81st TFW Voodoos changed three times in their eight years at Bentwaters/Woodbridge. Initially, each squadron could be identified by two coloured stripes on their fins: blue for the 91st TFS, yellow for the 92nd TFS and red for the 78th TFS. In 1961 the stripes gave way to fins painted overall in these squadron colours, emblazoned with 13 stars. Finally, when all the Wing's aircraft were pooled a year later, the fins carried three star-studded segments, each in one of the squadron colours. Major exceptions

Bushmasters Airborne.
Four F-101s of the 78th
TFS, airborne from RAF
Woodbridge. Wynette Wolf

were 56-0036 and 54-1457, all in light grey, perhaps for a trial. There were additional means of identification on wingtips, stabilizers and undercarriage doors. The fin of the Wing Commander's Voodoo sported three sets of two stripes in each of the squadron colours, while those aircraft belonging to the three squadron commanders each tended to have additional distinguishing features. For instance, Lieutenant Colonel 'Pete' Stuyvesant, commander of the 78th TFS, had four white stars painted on the main undercarriage doors of his personal aircraft (perhaps with a touch of optimism?). Pete was one of the Wing characters, actually christened Ernest DeVerd Stuyvesant but as a direct descendant of Peter Stuyvesant the famous governor of New Amsterdam (now New York) it was inevitable that he should be called 'Pete', or 'Colonel Pete' to his squadron.

Bushmaster. 'Pete' Stuyvesant, commander
78th TFS, RAF Woodbridge in 1961. Wynette Wolf

Early Bird. F-101C, 91st TFS at Bentwaters in 1959 - with blue sunray stripes. Mike Sudds via Doug Gordon

Powerful Visitor. Unidentified F-101 at RAF Whethersfield in 1960 - with sunray strips.
Alan Johnson via Doug Gordon

All Change. Yellow fin F-101C of the 92nd TFS at Bentwaters in 1961. Mike Sudds via Doug Gordon

In addition to the few conversion courses carried out at Shaw in 1960, for pilots with experience on other century series fighters (Chapter Two), a similar F-101 transition programme had been developed on the 81st TFW making use of a Mobile Training Detachment and flight simulator positioned there in July 1958. Ten hours training 'in the box' was followed by a 10 sortie transition phase, with all check rides monitored by chase pilots in single seat F-101s (there were no two-seat F-101Bs or dual control F-101Fs at Bentwaters/Woodbridge). Regardless of where this initial training took place it was followed in the UK by an extensive programme of theatre orientation and role training, on satisfactory completion of which a pilot was awarded combat ready status and was ready to go to war. He then took his turn as a qualified 'bomb commander' on Victor Alert, initially for the delivery of weapons in visual conditions only, with nuclear-armed aircraft ready to launch at a moment's notice during daylight hours only.

All this went very smoothly with the Wing Commander, Colonel Henry L Crouch, quite rightly demanding a high degree of standardisation across the Wing but leaving reasonable discretion with the individual

Blue Fin Voodoo. F-101C of the 91st TFS at Bentwaters Open Day in 1961. George Cowgill Collection

On Display. Post-1962 F-101 taxies out at an RAF Open Day. Alan Johnson via Doug Gordon

Wing Voodoo. Post 1962, fins of most 81st TFW F-101s carried three colour segments. George Cowgill Collection.

squadron commanders. This worked well, the 81st TFW showing its mettle as early as March 1959 with an impressive show for the US Ambassador to the Court of St James, the Right Honorable John Hay Whitney, senior USAF and RAF officers.

Well aware that the noise generated by the afterburning Voodoos was generally unwelcome in the local area, the Wing placed community relations high on the agenda from the start, and it remained there. On 12 September 1959 the bravery of a local farm worker, Mr Richard Mael, in helping to rescue a 91st TFS pilot who had ejected into the River Alde, was recognised with a full ceremonial presentation to him of the USAF Exceptional Service Award. USAF servicemen and their wives, at all levels, became heavily involved in local activities and charitable projects and these collective efforts did not go unnoticed at a US Ambassador's Reception in London on 19 November when the Wing was commended for having the best USAF community relations programme in the UK. It cut both ways; in recognition of the 81st's contribution to local charities, the East Suffolk County Council held an unprecedented reception for the Wing's officers in its Chambers. Responding with many individual and collective invitations to the base the Wing then held an Open Day at Bentwaters in June 1961, to celebrate a decade of tenure at the twin bases; that day they treated some 30,000 people to a convincing demonstration of their Cold War commitment, the Voodoos thundering overhead to the sound of freedom.

With the nature of the job and continuing teething troubles with the aircraft, accidents had to be expected. In August 1959 hydraulic failure caused Lieutenant Stirling H Lee to lose control of his aircraft on the final approach to Woodbridge and he failed to survive a very low level ejection. This and other hydraulic defects

led to the grounding of all F-101s between 25 August and 19 September for a Technical Order Compliance. No sooner were they back in the air when Lieutenant Colonel Charles Simpson, commander of the 78th TFS, made a miraculous recovery from a pitch-up when he was forced to break away hard from his leader, who had himself taken similarly violent action to avoid an unwarned C-124 transport approaching head-on at 2,500 ft. The Voodoos were recovering to Wheelus AB, Libya, from a weapons training sortie at 300 kts, a speed at which the Voodoo was severely limited in its manoeuvrability. Probably with little hope or expectation of recovery Simpson coolly deployed the drag 'chute, arresting the pitch-up and bringing the nose back through the horizon; he then jettisoned the 'chute and applied full military power, managing to bring the aircraft back to stable flight very gently some 200 ft above the desert. On inspection, the airframe was found to have sustained a loading of 5.9 'G', but suffered no structural damage. The colonel deserved much praise for achieving this unlikely pitch-up recovery and he was strongly recommended for an award.

In an equally remarkable feat of determination and flying skills, which could have otherwise ended in disaster, Captain Jack E Shephard brought another F-101 back to Bentwaters unscathed to enable a rapid diagnosis of the causal defect. In October 1960 he was unable to maintain height on a GCA to Bentwaters in instrument flying conditions, his throttles locked solid. He reported that, having unstrapped himself from his seat, he used all the strength in his legs to manipulate the throttles sufficiently to make a safe if unsteady landing. Captain Bye, 78th TRS, was less fortunate; he had no alternative but to eject when his Voodoo developed a massive fuel leak and fuel starvation while on a bombing sortie off the Isle of Man, but he did survive. Given the circumstances overall, the Wing deserved the Commendation it would receive for its flight safety record in 1960.

Work continued to improve domestic support in the Victor Alert facilities as the nuclear delivery systems, equipments and techniques were perfected and more Mk 7, Mark 28 and Mark 43 bombs became available. In earnest, the F-101 would carry a single nuclear store on the centre pylon between the two external tanks, simulated by a 'shape' in training. The four M-39, 20-mm cannon were considered very much a secondary option, perhaps of some use in keeping heads down as the Voodoos sped to and from their targets or against highly lucrative opportunity targets; they had little application in the air-to-air mode. Weapons training was a perennial problem from the start. The F-101 could dispense six 25 lb practice bombs from a container on its centreline pylon, on the local range at Holbeach in East Anglia, Jurby off the Isle of Man or even further away at Suippes Range in France. However, with the possibility of inadvertent releases over that part of Lincolnshire which lay below the range pattern, Holbeach was not a popular option; bomb scoring at Jurby in any rough seas was difficult if not impossible while frequent violations of the Suippes range by French and other NATO aircraft also rendered this choice less than ideal. Operation Camel Saddle provided the solution, taking the Voodoos on regular detachments to Wheelus AB, Libya, 75 miles from Tripoli in North Africa. From there they used the nearby El Outia range in the sparsely populated desert where there were very few restrictions and the range programmes were rarely affected adversely by the frequent poor weather in Europe. These deployments entailed a 1500 mile trip which, with a fair wind, could be covered in little more than two hours and was thus easily achieved in 'one hop' at high level with the two full 450 gall external tanks. Transit across France, denied on the slightest pretext, was invariably frustrated by the French air traffic authorities who often refused to authorise the heights requested en route needed for range considerations or to avoid bad weather. When the transients could not, for flight safety reasons, comply with the alternative heights they merely carried on, thereby attracting the immediate attention of French Mystere or Mirage fighters scrambled to

interrogate the miscreants. Perhaps no words would be exchanged, but the Voodoo pilots were able to make their feelings known by raising their refuelling probes in an unmistakable gesture.

Despite hydraulic problems and temporary groundings, Foreign Object Damage (FOD) which required 13 engine changes in December 1959 alone and difficulty in securing sufficient time on the weapons ranges, the Wing met all its operational commitments and training requirements in the second half of its first full year with the Voodoo. All requisite weapons qualifications were satisfied and 95% of the pilots achieved combat ready status. The Wing then went from strength to strength in the first half of 1960, flying 13,000 hours and progressing from an unsatisfactory to a satisfactory performance rating, passing a USAF ORI and doing well in a NATO taceval.

In practical terms execution of the Wing's war mission was clear and simple, if unenviable in concept for those in the cockpit. The F-101s were required to penetrate deeply into hostile territory at very high speeds (c.600 kts) and ultra low level (c.50 ft), each with a single atomic bomb. In constantly changing and ever-increasing commitments at greater distances from their bases, many targets were soon beyond the safe range for the fuel they carried on board and, while the pilots were now undergoing AAR training using the KB-50 tankers stationed nearby at RAF Sculthorpe, some thought it unlikely that they could depend on this facility in war. Their targets were predominantly in the 'offensive counter-air' category (airfields, command, control and communications centres (C3) and SAM sites), to 'soften up' enemy air defences for any offensive to follow. The Wing was provided with a comprehensive dossier of information on their targets and the defences they might face in their operating area in an 'Annotated List of Airfield Radar and Missiles'. With continuous up-dating this document was invaluable in mission planning, but it did involve a much increased work load on the ground for the already hard-pressed pilots and support staff.

1960 had been a busy year of mixed fortunes for the Wing; it started slowly, with poor weather over the East Coast of the UK curtailing flying, the records showing that the 91st TFS, for instance, flew 564 hours in January and 469 in February, but then averaged

600 hours in the following three months. This was a laudable achievement when in March airframe corrosion was discovered, leading to increased 'G' constraints on those aircraft which had flown more than 600 hours, and a one way ticket to the depot at Chateaureaux, France, for all those above 700 hours, where modifications were carried out to the main spar carry-through strut.

Colonel Eugene Strickland took command of the Wing in July 1960, with a headquarters staff consisting of 32 officers, 19 airmen and no civilians (due to a need for the highest security on the base). The squadrons were now operating an approximately equal mix of F-101As and F-101Cs; each squadron had some 37 officers and 80 airmen assigned but shortages in qualified manpower, both on the squadrons and in other sectors of the Wing, were now severe. Crucially, there were insufficient bomb commanders to fulfil all requirements, and this would remain so for much of 1960, exacerbated by the rapid turnover of pilots, inadequate range time and the fact that it took a minimum of 112 working days to train replacements. This came at a critical time for the Wing as it developed its expertise in all-weather radar navigation and bomb deliveries for round-the-clock operations. The aircraft themselves were modified for the role under Project Lampshade, its progress impeded by lack of qualified technicians. When the necessary equipment became available 'daylight only' bomb commanders underwent further intensive training before graduating to 'radar qualified bomb commander', committing him to all-weather Victor alert duty. For this he would be incarcerated with his aircraft in the Victor Alert site protective shelters for 24 hour periods, perhaps five or six times a month and more in times of tension. He also had to be ready for a surprise examination at any time on his assigned war missions. Gradually the manpower deficiencies were resolved, 10 bomb commanders qualifying fully in September 1960 and more thereafter to bring the total to 41 by the end of the year. The 81st TFW then became the first single-seat, all-weather tactical nuclear strike wing in NATO.

The original MA-7 fire control system (its nose radar originally optimised for air-to-air gunnery) had been adapted to give the fighter bombers a ground mapping capability and the M-1 high altitude dive/toss manoeuvre was abandoned in favour of an MA-2 Low Altitude Bombing System (LABS). This 'over the shoulder' delivery option allowed the aircraft to approach at 100 ft and 540 kts for a 3 1/2 'G' pull up at the target, the LABS gyros then releasing a free-fall weapon at a pitch angle of about 117 deg from the level, at about 15,000 ft. The bomb would then continue upwards to top out above 20,000 ft before descending to its target while the Voodoo executed an 'Immelman' manoeuvre to escape, rolling over and diving towards the ground in an attempt to get ahead of the effects of the atomic explosion. This procedure was practised endlessly by day and night in all weathers, continuously improving pilot skills and equipment accuracy. The more accurate LADD system, with the ground-mapping radar enabling the aircraft to approach the target at various heights and in all weather conditions at very high speeds, was introduced later. The timer released a parachute-retarded bomb automatically, enabling the aircraft to clear the area at ultra low level before the bomb detonated. In all, the 81st TFW pilots would have to become proficient in five visual and blind delivery modes. The ground mapping radar allowed the Wing to double its Victor Alert commitment with enhanced automatic deliveries, using the LADD manoeuvre against an increasing number of targets which hitherto could be tackled only in visual conditions. 'Defence of the UK' was also added as a secondary role, an interesting, perhaps notional concept for this mark of Voodoo? So, to the credit of all, the Wing again did all that was required of it, and more, attributing much of its success to 'the improved quality of Wing training.'

Because of the nature of the job the 81st TFW pilots tended generally to be older than those on other tactical fighter squadrons and some were already familiar with the area, which could be embarrassing. In 1961 Don Wolf, 92nd TFS, was showing Vern Covault, a 'new boy', the local tidal flats and how land and water in that area contrasted on the Voodoo's ground mapping radar, to discover after they landed that Vern had 'bellied in' a P-51 on those very flats in WW2, and Don decided that he needed no more local orientation.

The twin bases had also become 'home' to some big names in the fighter world, and it

Wing Commander. Robin Olds aboard his personal Voodoo 'Balls One'. Robin Olds

92nd TRS. Command of the Wing passed from Colonel Strickland to Colonel William C Clark in July 1962 and in August 1963 to that legendary fighter pilot Colonel Robin Olds. By this time Chappie James had been given the prestigious post of Director of Operations (DO), to begin the happy saga of 'Blackman and Robin'.

Robin Olds had fought with distinction in WW2 and he, as an 'ace' fighter pilot who excelled in the cut and thrust of air-to-air combat, may not have seemed to be the best choice to command a nuclear bomber wing. However, with his well-known enthusiasm and skill he soon proved his adaptability, continuing to mould the 81st TFW into a highly credible deterrent force with a convincing war fighting capability.

Captain Bill Kirk, already an accomplished Voodoo pilot from the 29th TRS at Shaw, was assigned to the 92nd TFS at Bentwaters in July 1961. Later, he would forge a mutually happy relationship with Robin Olds and Chappie James, despite Colonel Olds commandeering his previously assigned F-101 with the serial ending '001' - on the grounds that the 'boss' should have 'Balls 001' as his personal mount.

Of course Bill took part in the regular weapons training at Wheelus, remembering a social incident which gave the Voodoo men much pleasure at a time when racial issues were making headlines in the USA. The story goes that the Bentwaters pilots were relaxing outside their billets on a Sunday afternoon, when an F-100 squadron arrived to join them at Wheelus.

would continue to be so. Lieutenant Colonel 'JJ' Burns, who helped pioneer the LABS technique for the Voodoo, and Major Adrian Drew, the one-time world airspeed record holder, were joined by Majors Harry K Barco, Brian 'Cadillac' Lincoln and Charles Cleveland. Cleveland was a Korean War 'ace' with four MiG kills to his credit; he had worked with the Voodoo since the beginning, the 56th pilot to fly the aircraft, and was now the first to achieve 1000 hours in it. Then came the redoubtable Lieutenant Colonel Daniel 'Chappie' James, a coloured officer who had flown P-51s in WW2; he would demand much as commander of the

Practice Makes Perfect. Training weapons ready to be loaded on to 81st TFW F-101s. Gordon Macadie

Wheelus Warriors. This multi-rank group from the 81st TFW went to Wheelus for weapons training in 1962. (L to R) Captain Bill Kirk, Lieutenant Colonel Kolas (CO, 92nd TFS), Colonel Clark (81st TFW Wing Commander), Captains Don Wolf and Danny Sharron. Bill Kirk

One of the newcomers spotted a coloured man outside the VOQ office and ordered him, in the way of the day, to take his luggage to his room and begin unpacking. The man did as he was told, to be found minutes later hurling the 'Hun' driver's belongings around the room with gay abandon. He then introduced himself as Major Clark Price, 81st TFW. Time spent in identification is always worthwhile.

The pilots enjoyed uninhibited flying on El Outia Range, with its two long tracts of graded sand which led to the strike targets, favourite tracks also for the local Arabs and their camels plying to and from their oasis water holes. To the flyers surprise, these itinerants took no notice of the fighter bombers overflying them as low as they were able and at speeds well above 500 kts. Even more surprising was their habit of collecting the brass cartridges dispensed by the Voodoo's 20-mm cannon when the range was in use and climbing up the target supports, knife between teeth, to cut free the canvas gunnery panels.

The author was not privy to all the precise tactics adopted by the 81st TFW F-101s, and of course these depended on the range of the targets, weather, defences and availability of AAR etc. Suffice it to say that the 81st TFW pilots gave a great deal of thought to planning their initial war missions (which might have been their last) and were wholly realistic as to their survival chances. They might fly a first leg with pre-strike AAR at high level in friendly airspace to conserve fuel before descending

below enemy radar cover or be able to transit throughout at low level, fly direct to their targets for maximum range or have to skirt heavy defences, use terrain masking or avoid bad weather. In the various scenarios they faced there was no simple solution to survival and mission success. Enemy defences continued to develop and proliferate, typically with the introduction of the 'Barlock' early warning radar, new MiG fighters and increasingly effective SAMs. They could not expect any effective protection from on-board or external ECM, to obscure them at high level from enemy radars or air defences, depend on having fully serviceable IFF equipment or guarantee to change the codes precisely at the required intervals, to survive what would surely be trigger-happy defences in war. Friendly radar was unlikely to have been available to assist with their navigation; this invaluable peacetime facility and its vital communications almost certainly jammed out or used for other priorities. If a high-low-high option had to be used, perennial cloud cover and poor visibilities throughout Northern Europe could obscure navigation features and exacerbate the hazards of descending to low level (perhaps into the mountainous terrain of the Sauerland of Germany?) before detection by enemy radars. The low-low-low alternative would often have been preferred but this too could have its problems. Comfortable low level heights would have been flown over friendly territory but the Voodoos would have had to descend into 'the weeds' and increase speeds (to c. 600 kts) as they entered a hostile airspace thick with MiG fighters and a carpet of AAA of all calibres, much of it radar laid, all brought together with a crude but perhaps effective network of early warning communications. Flying the single-seat aircraft at these extreme speeds and heights, in the notoriously poor low level conditions of Central Europe, trying to avoid predictable and unpredictable defences while maintaining track for long periods of time, would have imposed great demands on the pilots. Pilot navigation, specifically map-reading, would have been the name of the game then, the efficacy of the MA-

7 radar in the ground mapping mode dependent on how discrete the landmarks were to the radar en route. Likewise, the TACAN installed in place of one of the four 20-mm guns would have been of no help in hostile airspace. The aircraft did carry a APS-54 radar warning system, able to distinguish between defensive radars, but its value would have been severely degraded in the cacophony of sound and signals likely to have been emitted from Eastern bloc defences.

That said, these F-101 pilots had much going for them. They had an aircraft endowed with great acceleration, speed and range, which rode comfortably at low level. After the Cold War the author was able to confirm, albeit anecdotally in conversation with ex-Russian and East German fighter pilots, radar and AAA men, that they did consider the Voodoo bombers a real threat. Although these one-time Warsaw Pact warriors were intensely proud of their abilities, they conceded that at the heights and speeds the Voodoos intended to fly, their warning system and early MiGs would have been hard pressed to find, let alone track, catch and destroy them. With little likelihood of classic aerial combat in this role the poor turning performance of the F-101 might have seemed of lesser importance, but it did limit the aircraft's ability to evade, take avoiding action or use mountainous terrain to best advantage.

Although never put to the test against the Warsaw Pact the Voodoo would show later in SEA that it could absorb a great deal of battle damage, return to base and fly again. The author's view, therefore, is that the F-101 was a significant asset in NATO's armoury. This, however, would only have been so if the pilots had been carefully selected and well trained - and they were. Initially, role expertise had been assured by the retention of seasoned F-84F strike/attack pilots on the Wing, while guidance on the aircraft was on offer from the men who had joined them from Bergstrom with their F-101s. The author underwent his initial training on the Voodoo with some of those destined for the 81st TFW, notably Pete Stuyvesant, and can vouch for the fact that they were 'chosen men'. This careful selection was borne out by the fact that, between 1960 and 1963, the 92nd TFS had on its books many high flyers of the future, to wit: two four-star generals, two 'three stars' and two 'two stars'.

At times everyone on Victor Alert must have thought the unthinkable, that provocation or miscalculation would lead to all-out nuclear war, a conflict in which the Voodoos of the 81st TFW would have been in the forefront. What the target planners knew, and surely the pilots too, was that if all political and military means failed, triggering a mass launch of nuclear weapons at what would have been Armageddon, the air through which they would have to fly to do their duty would be full of blinding, polluting multi-nuclear explosions. In these circumstances their chances of survival let alone success were very slim, certainly with the nuclear, bacteriological and chemical (NBC) protection given them at that time. This consisted solely of a single black eye patch, which USAF and RAF pilots would wear over one eye in the forlorn hope that this would enable them to continue on their mission when they were blinded in the other. Of course in that scenario there would have been many more than one explosion ahead of them. The widespread deployment of an increasing number of the Soviet SA-2 Guideline, an effective SAM at medium and high levels now added weight to the argument in favour of the low level penetration and egress but with the ever-increasing range of new targets this would necessitate AAR on the return and the pilots earmarked for these missions knew that this could not be depended on, concluding realistically that they would indeed be on one way tickets. They also knew that it would be nigh impossible to hide away and survive in possible 'safe areas' or walk back undetected through the nuclear fallout.

The Wing had to be ready for any contingency and the Cuban Crisis of October 1962 put this to the test, additional aircraft and pilots being brought immediately to higher states of readiness. Pete Stuyvesant was commanding the detachment at Wheelus when the word went out for them all to get home as soon as possible, and this they did. With Pete leading, the Voodoos climbed up and dropped their empty external tanks to give them the flexibility to cope with French air traffic and unpredictable weather in England. Bill Kirk was on a barge off the coast of East Anglia (UK) at the time, taking part in the recovery of a Bentwaters F-101 from which the pilot had ejected safely, and witnessed the Wing's aircraft 'hot piping' back to their base. Needless to say, he demanded to be returned to his squadron to

Looking Good. The 92nd TFS in late 1962. Don Wolf

play his part, and was soon on alert himself. It is difficult to imagine the emotions of the 81st TFW pilots on cockpit alert during this game of 'brinkmanship' which might have led to WW3, but it must have set many hearts and minds racing. In the event the Wing performed with flying colours; the aircraft did not launch and everything returned to normal, a normal state of continued tension.

On all counts demands on the Voodoo pilots of Bentwaters and Woodbridge in war would have been very high. To summarise, many would have had to fly excessive ranges, perhaps far into the Eastern Baltic, with the obvious uncertainties as to whether they could recover safely to a friendly base through a gauntlet of heavy defences both sides of the front line. Throughout the flight, with very limited help from their on-board navigation fit, they would have to depend on their pilot navigation skills, at extremely low level and probably in very marginal weather, in the target area relying on the LABS and LADD systems to deliver their weapons as required. All being well, they would then face similar difficulties on the return journey, with the added risk of fracticide as they entered an inherent friendly airspace greatly confused by the fog of war. Their's was not a happy lot but none of this seemed to affect the Wing's morale, so evidently high when the author visited his old friends at Woodbridge in 1963.

High spirits on the twin bases can be attributed in no small part to Robin Olds' leadership, being quick to recognise the realities of the task but also the potential of the aircraft. He had been introduced to the Voodoo on the F-101B at Tyndall AFB and would observe later that this was a lesser aircraft than the F-101

Celebrating Silver. Pete Stuyvesant (left) and his wife Elma (third from left) at RAF Bawdsey, helping to celebrate the station's 25 years of service in 1961. Wynette Wolf

which, with its rock-like stability, he found a true pleasure to fly at low level. He was soon at home in the single-seat aircraft, and fully aware of what was required of its pilots, commenting later "*and a damned fine challenge it was!*" The Wing was now working hard, playing hard and making its presence felt throughout the United Kingdom at every opportunity.

The F-101, with its very large turning radius and potential for pitch-up, together with the limited effectiveness of its four 20-mm cannon (three when TACAN was fitted) seemed a poor

Silence for the President! Against a Voodoo background, Pete Stuyvesant, President of the Mess at RAF Woodbridge, with Colonel Robin Olds to his right, in formal mood at a Dining-In Night. Wynette Wolf

Memorial Cup. On behalf of the 78th TFS, Pete Stuyvesant receives the McCarter Weapons Cup, named after the late CO of the 92nd TFS, from Colonel Robin Olds. Robin Olds

choice for Close Air Support (CAS) of troops in the front line, but it was to this role that it was committed in its dying days. In fact, this interesting and demanding experience for the nuclear bomber pilots was to prepare them for the role in F-4Cs which, it was announced late in 1964, would begin replacing the F-101s of the 81st TFW in 1965. So it was that the 91st TFS Voodoos joined Royal Danish Air Force F-100D Super Sabres on their base at Karup in the spring of 1965, for a CAS exercise over the Jutland Peninsular; it was, in effect, the beginning of the end for the Voodoo bombers.

Perhaps it came as no surprise when, in the spring of 1965, Olds raised and led a Voodoo aerobatic demonstration team, a natural initiative for a dyed-in-the-wool fighter pilot who had flown in the first ever USAF jet aerobatic team in early 1946. He chose his team carefully, selecting Captains 'Ski' Fantaski, Tom Hirsh and 'CR' Morgan, with Bill Baugh co-ordinating with the team as a solo aircraft. This dynamic initiative provided a little relief from the very serious work in hand, trumpeted the attributes of the aircraft, showed that it was more manoeuvrable than many believed if handled sensibly, and contributed to the morale of an already spirited Wing. However, Robin knew that without authority and with long, standing, often exaggerated horror stories of pitch-up, it would incur the wrath of those above him at a time when he had been notified of promotion to General, and so it did. The promotion was stopped and a well-earned citation was said to have been torn up before his eyes. Initially he was reassigned to a staff appointment but in nine months he was back flying on a 15-day conversion to the F-4 at Tuscon, Arizona, overseen by a formidable team comprising the Wing Commander, Colonel 'Speedy' Pete Everett, the Director of Operations, Colonel Chappie James and the Chief of Staneval Bill Kirk. Bill flew with Robin three times a day for the 15 days, in his own words: *"taking the aircraft as far as it would go"* and finishing with a live missile firing. Robin Olds rewarded him with the farewell words *"We'll meet again soon"*, as he departed for SEA to command the elite 8th TFW, the F-4 'Wolf Pack' at Ubon AB, Thailand. He was right; Chappie James and Bill Kirk joined him there shortly thereafter, the old firm soon excelling in the serious business of war fighting. Perhaps it was at Ubon that

Togetherness. Four F-101s from Bentwaters meet two USAFE F-100s over the patchwork countryside of Suffolk, England. Robin Olds

Goodwill. Bentwaters F-101C visits the KB-50 tanker base at RAF Sculthorpe in 1962. Gordon Macadie

Colonel Olds decreed that no recce pilot should ever buy a drink in his bar, mutual respect being the name of the game in SEA.

The change-over from the F-101s to F-4C Phantoms at the twin bases coincided with Colonel Old's departure, he leading one of the aircraft to its new owners, the ANG at Little Rock, Arkansas, as part of Project All Ashore in June 1965. The conversion to F-4s was led by the 78th TFS in 1965, under the auspices of a Mission Coordinating Board at Bentwaters, while the residual F-101 force maintained the required operational readiness states until the Phantoms were ready to take over a year later. In the meantime the Voodoos continued as they had started, showing themselves and demonstrating their prowess with every opportunity.

After their withdrawal from active service with the USAF those F-101As and F-101Cs which still had life left in them were converted

Grey Lady. Wearing nothing but the 81st Wing badge, 56-0036 has yet to receive its colours. Doug Gordon Collection

Good Company. F-101A at RAF Bentwaters in May 1963. Gordon Macadie.

Career Move. This F-101C, its duty done with the 81st TFW, arrives back in the USA for conversion to an ANG RF-101H. Courtesy ANG

Winner Turned Warrior. Fire Wall winner F-101C, 56-0014, turned bomber on the 81st TFW. George Cowgill

Party Piece. F-101s fly by with refuelling probes raised in irreverent greeting. Doug Gordon Collection

to RF-101Gs and RF-101Hs respectively, destined for the ANG. Each was modified with a different nose to carry reconnaissance cameras, and these aircraft would soldier on until the end of the 1970s. Some would then find their final resting place in the massive open storage area at Davis-Monthan AB, Arizona, ultimately going for salvage, the more fortunate to air parks and museums.

It is not possible to quantify the impact the 81st TFW Voodoos had at critical stages during the Cold War, but it would be reasonable to claim that they were an integral and important part of the all-important deterrence. The sleepy county of Suffolk may not have appreciated the roar of the Voodoo engines but they came to care for the good people of the twin bases who worked so hard to integrate into and contribute to their community. At the time of writing, a local initiative is underway to convert the old, hardened and filtered operations block at the now defunct base at Bentwaters into a museum, a tribute to the 81st TFW. Of course there were good memories and bad, inevitably the Wing losing F-101s and pilots during its tenure. However, at a time when attrition within the USAF's century series fighter force was causing much concern the F-101 loss rate, over its eight years of very demanding service, was not excessive. The Voodoo men of the 81st TFW left with their heads held high - they had been well chosen and they had done well.

Friends Farewell. Robin Olds says farewell to 'Balls One' after its trans-Atlantic flight from Bentwaters to its new home with the Arkansas ANG in 1965. Robin Olds

CHAPTER SEVEN
HOMELAND DEFENCE

'To be prepared for war is one of the most effectual means of preserving peace.'

George Washington, 1790

Following a period of indecision, during which McDonnell started work on a prototype, the firm was awarded a contract in 1955 to develop the F-101B two-seat bomber interceptor. Designated NF-101 and given the number 56-0232, the prototype had its first flight on 27 March 1957, to presage this latest variant of the Voodoo family. The fighter would serve well with the USAF Air Defense Command (ADC) and in the same role within the Royal Canadian Air Force (RCAF)/Canadian Armed Forces (CAF).

One and Only. During a period of procrastination McDonnell produced the NF-101B, 56-0232. The aircraft first flew on 27 March 1957. Robert F Dorr Collection

While the basic configuration of this Voodoo aircraft remained the same, the F-101B could be distinguished from other models by its conical black radome with a long pitot tube at its tip, coupled with a single clamshell canopy enclosing two crew members. The pilot's instrument display was of pleasing simplicity. Significantly heavier than previous variants, the F-101B was fitted with the more powerful Pratt and Whitney J57-P-53 engines, while the undercarriage was strengthened and given larger tyres. Other visible changes included the extended jet pipes and the slight bulge in the undercarriage doors.

The aircraft was equipped with a Hughes MG-13 fire-control system, the armament consisting of two MB-1 (AIR-2A) Genie air-to-air rockets and two GAR-8 (AIM-4) Falcon air-to-air-missiles (AAM). The Genie, which was housed in a weapons bay, was unguided

Ergonomics. This insight into the CF-101's front cockpit suggests an admirable simplicity in instrument display.
Gordon Macadie

Maximum Firepower. F-101B, 56-0236 armed with two Genies rockets (the two Falcon AAMs are not shown). USAF

and contained a 1.5 kiloton atomic head; it was designed to explode when in close proximity to a target, had a maximum speed of Mach 3 and a range of some six miles. The Falcon had the same range in both the infra-red heat seeking and semi-active radar homing mode; partially recessed in a rotary door beneath the rear cockpit, it was optimised to destroy Soviet bombers.

Exhaustive tests on the aircraft and weapons system were carried by McDonnell and the Air Force Flight Test Centre (AFFTC) at Edwards AFB, California, Eglin and Tyndall AFB, Florida; initial problems with engine surges were largely overcome and much time was spent on seeking solutions to uncommanded pitch-ups. ADC and the RCAF had high hopes

Testing Times. F-101Bs 56-0244 & 56-0247 both took part in trials at Edwards AFB, and would be used later by the 4414 CCTS at Shaw AFB, while MDC and the USAF carried out tests with 56-0236 at Eglin AFB. USAF & George Cowgill Collection

for this aircraft with its great speed, long range, missile combination and compatibility with the North American Air Defense (NORAD) Semi-Automatic Ground Environment (SAGE) system, and they would not be disappointed.

The weapons system operator (Whizzo) was of crucial importance in exploiting the capability of the aircraft to the full; in the USAF he was also known as the 'Guy-In-The-Back'(GIB), Radar Operator (RO) or Radar Intercept Officer (RIO). In the RCAF the term 'Navigator' was still in use but was replaced eventually by the designation Air Observer Intercept (Obs AI) - all distinguishable by their flying brevets. Spare a thought for the GIB; while he was head-down in the cockpit gazing into his radar scope trying to find the target and work out the geometry of an attack, his pilot might be doing strange, unsettling things up front. Teamwork of the highest order was the name of the game, the key to success and indeed in some cases to survival, as some of what follows indicates.

Daily Routine. A pair of F-101Bs takes off from Niagara Falls AFB and a 29th FIS F-101B recovers to Malstrom AFB. Gordon Macadie and George Cowgill Collections

The first F-101Bs entered service in January 1959 with the 60th Fighter Interceptor Squadron (FIS), Otis AFB, Massachusetts, for evaluation in the role and crew training. Thereafter, some crews were trained on the squadrons to which they were assigned or attached for flying, but the majority benefited from the 4756 CCTS and 2nd Fighter Interceptor Training Squadron (FITS) at Tyndall AFB, Florida.

The performance of the aircraft and its role also imposed new and heavy demands on the crews, Major Richard Holm, Wing Safety Officer at Hamilton, one of the first to face one of many interesting challenges during a check ride at Tyndall. A supersonic snap-up attack seemed to be going well as the auto pilot centred the dot and rotated the aircraft correctly into the snap manoeuvre, but then continued to take the Voodoo skywards until it was going straight up and running rapidly out of airspeed. Dick 'buried the stick in the instrument panel until the aircraft floated over the top and headed back downhill', losing the chase plane during this unorthodox manoeuvre, and incidentally the radio at the same time, presumably leaving the check pilot somewhat bemused. Perhaps it was Dick's immediate and successful recovery action which earned him a 'pass' on that ride. The Voodoo in auto pilot was wont to do the unexpected, especially on dark and moonless nights.

In both manual interception and SAGE modes, the F-101B crews were pitted from the start against targets ranging from the relatively low performance T-33 to a B-58 Hustler flying at supersonic speeds and approaching head-on. They passed the test, with training and re-equipment of some 20 front line USAF ADC

squadrons and subsidiary units beginning in earnest in June 1959 with the 84th FIS at Hamilton AFB, California, also home to the 83rd FIS. It says much for ADC and the aircraft that the squadrons were soon into an operational routine.

Of course there were difficulties and incidents with the new aircraft, some due to operator error and others to technical malfunction such as that responsible for the total collapse of the landing gear of one aircraft towards the end of its landing roll at Hamilton AFB, one of many strange occurrences involving the undercarriage during the history of the Voodoo. What made this different, however, was that it happened during the Cuban crisis of 1962, with both Falcon missiles recessed below the weapons door ground to half their size without explosion or fire as the aircraft slid to a halt on its belly.

The author visited the 60th FIS at Otis in 1961 in an F-101F from Shaw and learned something of its main operational role in peacetime, that of visual identification (visident) of unidentified aircraft 'bogeys' showing up on the ground radar network. For this purpose the squadron retained two aircraft at readiness in the alert hangar close to the end of the runway, each armed with two Falcon missiles and their crews fully dressed in immersion ('poopy') suits ready to launch within the allotted five minutes when the scramble horn sounded. Initial instructions, including vectors and heights to fly, were passed verbally until the interception controller ordered: *"Follow dolly"*. SAGE then took over, data-linking flight directions to front and rear cockpit displays until the RO located the target on his radar, typically at a range of some 20 miles and called his pilot to: *"Disregard dolly"*. By this stage the two fighters would have separated, the leader preparing to carry out the identification alongside the target and the wingman to take up a missile firing position. The lead RO would first endeavour to position his aircraft some five miles astern of the target, aware that rolling out too close or too fast could be dangerous, while doing so too far out or at too slow a speed could lead to a long tail chase. Assuming he satisfied the required parameters and locked the target to his radar the RO would then hand over final control to the pilot with the command *"Fly the dot"*; he would continue to advise on their relative position and overtake speed. A computer-generated 'pull-out' signal was incorporated to help avoid a collision. When in visual contact, the pilot could use the aircraft's high intensity spotlight to identify the target, relaying the information required to ground control. Following a successful visident, SAGE would take over again to bring the two fighters together and guide them back to their base.

A snapshot from the official 60th FIS records shows that in 1962 the squadron was committed to an increased alert posture, with a recurring schedule of a day's flying followed by one holding alert and then a free day. To meet the new requirements a revised flying programme, based on planning aircraft and pilots well ahead, is said to have increased aircraft utilisation. In addition, meals were now prepared on the flight line, with more transport and new alert facilities provided, but a consolidated maintenance programme embracing collocated units was rejected. At this stage a squadron could comprise 19 F-101Bs, 4 T-33A instrument trainers, 65 officers and 376 men.

In response to Russian provocation in Cuba, and in keeping with other Voodoo squadrons throughout NATO, the 60th TFS was placed on alert status DEFCON 3 on 22 October 1962,

with all TDY and leave cancelled. By the end of November the normal routine resumed and in December the squadron achieved an unprecedented 60 sorties in one day.

Despite very cold and windy weather at the start of 1963 the 60th FIS began averaging some 450-500 flying hours/month; it now boasted the 'best (flight line) messing facility in ADC, providing two hot meals a day for its officers', and much enhanced alert facilities. In these surroundings it achieved very high marks in January's Taceval, passed all phases of March's ORI in March and became the first fighter squadron to achieve the 'Outstanding Missile Safety Achievement Award'. Individual achievements included an ADC 'Point With Pride' award for Captains Martin McNulty and Donald Evans, for bringing their Voodoo back safely after an engine had blown up on take-off, an Air Force Commendation Medal for Captain Eugene Sirotnak for his earlier work with the 84th FIS, Hamilton AFB, and an Airman's Medal for Captain James Morris after he rescued a drowning girl. The 60th FIS would continue to be one of the outstanding squadrons in ADC, but manpower shortages arising from the ever-increasing demands for 'the best of the Air Force' to serve in South East Asia would soon bite.

Joe Whitt cut his teeth on the Voodoo in front line RF-101s before serving on RF-4Cs in Vietnam and then transferring to the F-101B on the 98th FIS at Suffolk County AFB, New York in October 1967 in the rank of major. He was far from enamoured with the alert states of five minutes, fifteen minutes or one hour, but revelled in the annual live weapons training at Tyndall AFB. There, for ten consecutive days, the crews would launch their Falcon missiles at towed targets, the best scores rewarded with the chance to fire live warheads at Bomarc SAM targets flying at 50,000 ft, Joe and his RO, Captain Vern Christi earning that privilege. The crews of two F-106s and two F-4E Phantoms, similarly armed, had also qualified and the five aircraft were dispatched to meet the threat, an F-102 going along with them to administer the 'coup de grace' if the chosen men failed. Make no mistake, this was a competition between men who knew their business, with Joe and his GIB bent on winning.

Of the several options open to them the F-101B crew decided on a head-on, level attack, well aware of the extremely high closing speed between target and fighter. They spotted the Bomarc climbing towards them very rapidly soon after launch from the neighbouring Eglin AFB and accelerated in both afterburners to meet it as it levelled at 54,000 ft. Vern picked up the target on his scope well out, locked it to the Voodoo's radar and handed over control to Joe saying:

"The closing speed is three thousand (kts) and the steering dot is yours - look at that thing come!"

Almost at once Joe got the firing signal and pulled the trigger to launch the Falcon at eight miles range and 52,000 ft, scoring a direct hit. The One-O-Wonders had relegated their playmates to the role of spectators only. Joe still remembers the stark contrast between this thrilling experience and training with the Genie in a synthetic environment, simply flying with a

dummy rocket to get the feel of its asymmetric effect when the weapons door rotated.

Another F-101B crew, Captain Steve Bangs and his RO, also had their share of interesting experiences while serving on the 445th FIS at Wurtsmith, Missouri. One night they locked on to a B-58 at 40,000 ft with a 200 kts overtake and all seemed set fair for a simulated 'kill'. Their Voodoo had a hydraulically tuned magnetron in its radar to render conventional jamming ineffective, but the Hustler could take the radar signal and move it off the target, leaving the Voodoo crew with a mere couple of seconds to simulate a missile firing. There would be no kill for the Voodoo crew that night as they were left gazing at the Hustler's four, fast retreating afterburners. In the vernacular of the time Steve commented: *"The gate-stealer stole my RO's launch"*.

The success of the F-101B on the regular,

On Guard. ANG squadrons supported the front line with F-101Bs from 1969, typically the New York ANG; Maine ANG; North Dakota ANG and Texas ANG. The Arkansas ANG unit changed its role from RF-101s to F-100Fs in June 1972. Courtesy ANG, Gordon Macadie & George Cowgill.

front line squadrons of ADC ensured the aircraft a new lease of life with the USAF's ANG. It is believed that, from 1969, the Guard took over the training of their own F-101B crews at Ellington AFB, Texas.

When the much vaunted Avro (Canada) CF-105 Arrow was cancelled in 1959, it did not take the RCAF long to press the point that the once rejected F-101B could meet Canada's air defence needs which their Ministry of Defence's favoured CF-100/ Bomarc SAM combination could not. What was clearly needed now was a high speed, long range interceptor compatible with NORAD's SAGE system, and this led the way to an order for 56 F-101Bs and 10 dual F-101Fs (designated CF-101B and CF-101F respectively) being placed in June 1961.

Delivery to the RCAF of what became known as the 'first batch', of 'nearly new' aircraft, began in Operation Queen's Row, with two aircraft arriving at RCAF Station Uplands, Ottawa, Ontario, on 24 July 1961. They were flown in by Flight Lieutenants Wilf Dobbin (pilot) and Michael Cromie (navigator), both of whom were well acquainted with the aircraft from their exchange tour with the USAF's 60th FIS, and a USAF crew from the 49th FIS, Griffith AFB. Other than by their external markings, the RCAF aircraft could not be identified from their counterparts in the USAF and their internal equipment remained essentially the same. In this first batch, the air refuelling probe remained fitted but it would not be used operationally in the RCAF, while the Webber ejection seat, without a zero-zero capability to enable low level ejections, remained an unpopular legacy from the USAF.

The armament and fire control system was also the same (albeit with the acquisition of

First In. Flight Lieutenants Wilf Dobbin (pilot) and Michael Cromie RCAF (Nav/RO), who had served on exchange with the USAF's 60th FIS at Otis AFB since 1960, led the first pair of CF-101Bs for the RCAF to Uplands, Ottawa, in July 1961. The second aircraft was flown by a USAF crew from the 49th FIS, Griffiths AFB (left of group). Mike Cromie

425 Squadron.

410 Squadron.

414 Squadron.

416 Squadron.

409 Squadron.

Frontier Force. The first line of air defence in North America was provided by the Canadian CF-101Bs of 425 Squadron, 410 Squadron, 409 Squadron, 416 Squadron and 414 Squadron.

some different marks of infra-red missiles) as was the all-important high powered spotlight for visident at night. In these early days the government to government agreement on the provision, storage and use of the Genie nuclear rocket on the CF-101s remained classified.

Crew training began immediately, eventually to equip five RCAF Voodoo squadrons and an Operational Training Unit (OTU) to replace the five remaining CF-100 squadrons. As a starter, 425 (Alouette) Squadron sent nine crews to Otis AFB for basic training on the aircraft and then to Hamilton AFB for operational orientation under the auspices of the USAF. From October 1961, this squadron then acted as a training unit for Nos 410 (Cougar), 409 (Nighthawk), 416 (Lynx) and 414 (Black Knight) Squadrons. The initial intake to the CF-101B force was drawn predominantly from ex-CF-100 crews, conversion to the new aircraft beginning with simulator training at RCAF Station Uplands, followed by flying at RCAF Station Namao, Edmonton, Alberta. Namao was primarily an air transport station but its

principal attraction was a 14,000 ft runway.

First to go through an RCAF Voodoo instructor cadre programme at Hamilton AFB was Flight Lieutenant Tom Murray and his navigator Flight Lieutenant Dave Mitton of 409 Squadron. Tom began his flying in the RAF and had flown Meteors and Hunters on No 43 Squadron (The Fighting Cocks) before transferring to the RCAF; he marvelled that the RCAF could have the high performance Voodoo operational in a mere six months and continue to fly it for many more without a fatal accident. He and Dave Mitton had the dual role of supervising a short Initiation Course, using the simulator at Uplands, and carrying out the RCAF acceptance test flights on aircraft delivered to Uplands for the operational squadrons. Tom's Log Book records his initial flight at Hamilton on 27 July 1961, the first test flight at Uplands on 14 December and 18 test flights in the following three weeks over Christmas - an impressive achievement.

The last conversion course at Namao was completed in June 1962, the normal six weeks

VOODOO WARRIORS

compressed into three with an intensive period of training, after which most of the crews, Flight Lieutenant 'Turbo' Tarling among them, were posted to 425 Squadron. Turbo, with 27 hours on the aircraft, and Flying Officer Bob Burnie his navigator, ferried one of 425 Squadron's new CF-101Bs from Namao, via the USA, to RCAF Station Bagotville, Quebec, the Alouettes' new home. Voodoo training was then carried out at Bagotville by No 3 All-Weather Fighter Operational Training Unit. Although this training went very well generally it was not without its dramas, there being some close shaves in the air and incidents on the ground (one wheels-up landing was narrowly averted by an alert runway controller). The

Training Traumas. The RCAF's Voodoo Operational Training Unit at Bagotfield had relatively few major incidents, considering the quantum jump in aircraft performance and employment. George Malton Collection

Canadians also had some very disturbing instrument, flying control and auto pilot failures but, to the credit of all, not one aircraft was lost during this period.

425 Squadron soon became 'combat ready' and was placed on Quick Reaction Alert (QRA), expected to be airborne within specific times determined by the alert state (DEFCON) in force. This was put to the test first on the night of 10 December 1962, when Turbo and his navigator, Flying Officer Pat Clancy, although airborne, had insufficient fuel to intercept an 'unknown'. Well within the allotted time, the No 1 QRA crew, Flight Lieutenant Ron Jensen and Flying Officer

414 Squadron Vanguard. Undergoing training at RCAF Station Namao: (Above, L to R) Flight Lieutenant Phil Harris, Flight Lieutenant 'Swede' Larsen, Squadron Leader Ken Lowe & Flying Officer Stu Whalley. (Below, L to R) Flying Officers Jerry Knight, Jim Leeson & Norm Regimbal. George Malton

First on Line. In 1962, 425 (Alouette) Squadron was the first unit to become fully operational with the CF-101B. Turbo Tarling

HOMELAND DEFENCE

Alouettes. Flight Lieutenant 'Turbo' Tarling (pilot) and Flying Officer Pat Clancy (Observer), No 425 (Alouette) Squadron, with a CF-101F dual trainer at RCAF Bagotville in February 1963. Turbo Tarling

Gerry Walker, were airborne under the direction of GCI, callsign 'Scabbard', with orders to identify the 'bogey'. With Scabbard's initial direction they soon made AI radar contact and, amidst heavy snow flurries, acquired the target visually at half a mile; it was a KC-97 tanker flying at 7,000 ft 'lit up like a Christmas tree', but this was not the end of the story. Drawing alongside the big aircraft, the Voodoo crew found all the interior lights on but no sign of anyone on board, and Ron Jenson reported as much to Scabbard. This unlikely story was relayed to Bagotville, where on

landing the Voodoo men were pledged to secrecy, but it was too late; when Turbo arrived home a mere thirty minutes later, his wife, Clare, asked immediately, *"What's the word on this KC-97?"* In fact, the crew of the tanker had been faced with an electrical fire which they judged to be out of control and as a result baled out, leaving the aircraft to wend its way north on autopilot - to where, nobody knew. For their skill and perseverance it was congratulations all round for the 425 Squadron crew, with commendations from their Deputy Air Officer Commanding and NORAD Headquarters and an interview with NBC to follow.

With the runways at airfields earmarked for Voodoo operations extended to 10,000 ft by the end of 1962, the squadrons, each initially comprising 12 aircraft, took up residence at Comox (409 Squadron), North Bay (414 Squadron), Uplands (410 Squadron), Bagotville (425 Squadron and 3AW OTU) and Chatham (416 Squadron). The QRA hangars ('alert shacks') there each accommodated two aircraft, typically holding five minutes readiness on Alert State 'DEFCON 5', upgraded to 'DEFCON 3' during the Cuban Missile Crisis of 1962 (when crews were required to be in their cockpits). If the political or military alert state required, additional aircraft would be brought to these or other levels of readiness. Colours differentiated the squadrons and by the end of 1962 the RCAS had five CF-101 squadrons and 66 aircraft on strength.

Flight Lieutenant Mike Hobbs, an RAF exchange pilot with experience in the UK's Javelin all-weather force, arrived in Canada to fly the Voodoo in October 1962, going first to RCAF Station Bagotville for instrument training on the T-33 (an aircraft on which he had trained initially at RCAF Gimili, Manitoba, in 1953). This was followed by weapons training on the CF-100 (an aircraft similar in performance to the Meteor with which he was also familiar) before converting to the CF-101B. With his past experience Mike

Colour Code. Early CF-101B PR photographs, of 410 'Cougar' Squadron (404 with red and white fin) and 416 'Lynx' Squadron (395 with yellow and black fin). Jim Gregory

was quickly into his stride, finding the Voodoo less formidable than he had been led to expect, and a lot more reliable than the Javelin. The Canadians did not share the apprehension of some RAF authorities when it came to operating from icy or snow-covered runways; Mike found that the Voodoo coped quite well in these conditions during take-offs, landings and taxiing on its wire-bonded tires, although aircraft sometimes had to be led to or from the runway by snow ploughs. From the start he flew the CF-101B with RCAF navigators, as did RAF exchange navigators with Canadian pilots, but this would not always be the case at other times or on other squadrons where the RAF crews were known to pair up together. Canada's first truly supersonic operational fighter soon became a firm favourite with its crews and, with its immense power and noise, a great crowd-pleaser wherever it appeared.

Mike joined 410 Squadron at the joint civil and military airfield at Uplands in March 1963, when CF-101 operations were being hampered by the preferential treatment given to scheduled civilian traffic. In the hope of alleviating this problem 410 Squadron gave the Senior (civilian) Air Traffic Controller an 'exciting' ride in a Voodoo to demonstrate the aircraft's strengths and limitations. This did the trick;

thereafter the Voodoo men were given greater consideration. When Mike joined 410 Squadron it was fully formed and, on rotation with other squadrons, taking its turn on QRA both at Uplands and at RCAF Station Val d'Or, a forward base on the 69th Parallel. Val d'Or was close to the 'Pinetree Line', part of the early warning system against Russian intruders, manned by RCAF personnel as part of the Voodoo acquisition agreement and responsible for monitoring the Canadian Air Defence Identification Zone (ADIZ). This was able to detect any friend or foe flying at speeds of 175 kts or more, and would trigger many QRA scrambles for the Voodoos from Val d'Or and elsewhere, with the crews never knowing when the 'hooter' sounded whether it was a practice or for real. In the main, the targets were civilian aircraft which had strayed off course or could not be identified, but some were Soviet aircraft, perhaps testing NORAD's reaction; none, in this game of 'cat and mouse' which continued throughout the Cold War, offered a direct threat.

After one such scramble at Val d'Or, a laudable initiative saved the day when the station's main power failed and the auxiliary back-up refused to 'kick-in' as expected. A CF-101B was immediately positioned at the

Safety in Numbers. By the end of 1962, the RCAF had five squadrons of CF-101 on strength, from a force of 66 aircraft.
Jim Gregory & Gordon Macadie

Listen Up! Aircrew briefing on 410 Squadron, RCAF Station Uplands. Mike Hobbs

Cougar taxiing. George Cowgill

threshold of the runway in use, its navigator pointing his radar antenna up the approach path to give recovering aircraft an improvised form of final surveillance and talk-down. This expedient had a precedent; a CF-100 navigator had previously talked down a Viscount at Val d'Or in appalling weather, the airliner's crew unaware that they had not benefited from a 'proper' GCA until they were told so in the Officers Mess; RCAF navigators were professionals. The squadrons spent a week or more at this forward base, with sufficient aircraft to man QRA and provide some flying for those on the detachment. When they returned home, the men of 410 Squadron always tried to improve their time from 'wheels rolling' to 'chocks' at Uplands. Using afterburner all the way, the record for the 300 plus miles from Val d'Or to Uplands was said to be 17 minutes.

With no provision made at the outset for inevitable attrition within the CF-101B force, and rejection of a suggestion in 1962 that another 17 aircraft should be acquired to that end, 410 Squadron was disbanded as a front line fighter squadron in March 1964, as was 414 Squadron at North Bay shortly thereafter, to make good losses across the force. Mike

Farewell Flypast. Mike Hobbs (RAF) leads a section of 410 Squadron. Mike Hobbs

Final Landing. 410 Squadron disbanded in July 1964. Mike Hobbs

Sunset Alert. 410 Squadron at readiness in the winter of 1963/64. Mike Hobbs

VOODOO WARRIORS

Signing In. (Left to Right) 'Dunc' Duncan, Mike Hobbs, Barry Done. Mike Hobbs

Voodoo Warriors. Aircrew of 425 (Alouette) Squadron, c. 1965, RAF exchange officers Mike Hobbs (pilot) third from the left and Stan Parry (navigator) on the right. Mike Hobbs

Black Knight. This 414 Squadron Knight's black armour would become more appropriate when the squadron's role changed to that of ECM. George Malton

Knight's Work. H B 'Swede' Larsen and Pete 'Lump' Levedag. George Malton

Warriors Tribute. 425 Squadron salutes the Governor of Quebec Province. Mike Hobbs

Just Reward. Mike Hobbs was promoted to squadron leader when he returned from Canada to the RAF. Mike Hobbs

Hobbs was then re-assigned to 425 Squadron at Bagotville as a flight commander and would earn promotion to squadron leader on his return to the RAF. The RAF exchange crew on 414, Squadron Leader David Blucke (pilot) and Flight Lieutenant John Wheeler, went to 416 Squadron at Chatham. Later, 410 Squadron was reactivated as the CF-101B OTU at Bagotville, and 414 Squadron became the CAF's Electronic Countermeasures (ECM) Squadron, based ultimately at CBF North Bay. This squadron would be equipped with a single EF-101B (CAF 101067), distinctive in its black finish, as an ECM trainer.

416 (Lynx) Squadron was typical of the CF-101B squadrons in the 1960s and 1970s. Formed at Peterhead on the eastern coast of Scotland in November 1941 with Spitfire Mk IIAs, this was one of the 18 Canadian squadrons created in Europe during that year to join the three squadrons deployed from Canada in 1940. The squadron served with distinction throughout WW2 with 79 'kills' and many 'probables' to its credit. It ended its post-D-Day tour of Europe with Spitfire XIVs at Utersen in Germany, where it disbanded in March 1946. The squadron was reformed with the piston-engine Mustang at Uplands in January 1951 and converted to the jet-powered F-86 Sabre fighter before deploying to Grostenquin, France, in 1952. Disbanded again in December 1956, 416 Squadron reformed at St Hubert, Quebec, in 1957 with the CF-100 Mk5 Canuck ('The Clunk') all-weather fighter, which was replaced by the CF-101B Voodoo in 1962.

Now based at RCAF Station Chatham, New Brunswick, 416 Squadron was well placed in NORAD's 22nd Region to help guard against any manned bomber threat in that area, using

Above & below: Squadron Leader David Blucke and Flight Lieutenant John Wheeler, RAF exchange crew, flew together at 3 AWF OTU, 414 and 416 Squadrons, August 1963 - December 1965. Dave Blucke was rarely if ever guilty of 'hanging' his nosewheel after take-off, certainly not on this night take-off with 414 Squadron in early 1964. John Wheeler

Black Deceiver. This single EF-101B, leased from the USAF as CAF 101067 for use by 414 Squadron in ECM training, would serve on into the 1980s, well beyond the demise of the main Voodoo force. Mike Hobbs Collection

Flight Line Chatham. 416 Squadron at RCAF Station Chatham c.1965. John Wheeler

tactics which were essentially the same as those used by the USAF's F-101Bs. Relatively simple head-on subsonic and supersonic interceptions were carried out at 35,000 ft, with the option of snap-up to engage targets at 60,000 ft or more while training heights depended on the performance of the targets available. Low level interceptions were usually carried out from a beam position or astern, with accurate instrument flying essential to success, particularly at night and in bad weather.

The far more complicated 'Home-on-Jam' (HOJ) procedure could be used in ECM conditions. Cockpit instruments would provide an azimuth bearing on the jammer, its elevation achieved with greater difficulty by banking the aircraft through 90 deg and holding it there with rudder for sufficient time to obtain a higher or lower indication, then repeating this procedure until the needle showed the target and interceptor to be level. Proficient navigators could judge relative target speed in relation to their own and the rate of change of bearings. This whole procedure was, however, very time consuming.

The CF-101B force had a number of spectacular accidents, with one to hit the headlines occurring at Bagotville on a rainy night in October 1962. Flying Officer Stuart Whalley had lined up on the runway after an Air Canada (formally TCA) Viscount had landed and been cleared to exit via a high-speed cut-off. The Voodoo pilot was then permitted to take off but, as he rotated his aircraft's nose, the Viscount hove into view beyond a hump in the runway and dead ahead. Stu recalls 'pulling back on the stick with both hands' but a collision was unavoidable. His aircraft tore off the airliner's fin and split open its fuselage, before staggering into the air. The Voodoo, on fire and badly damaged, was 'not flying at all well' but with afterburners and 'lots of rudder' Stu managed to climb to 700 ft for his navigator, Ray Jefferies, to eject safely. The Voodoo's port engine had ingested pieces of the Viscount and was now emitting huge plumes of flame 'three or four times the length of the aircraft, from both intake and jet pipe'. It now entered an uncontrollable roll and Stu himself ejected sideways, his 'chute perhaps opening only partially. He survived with scratches and bruises while Ray suffered a broken ankle landing on the stony ground. Two died in the Viscount, a passenger who had got up to get his

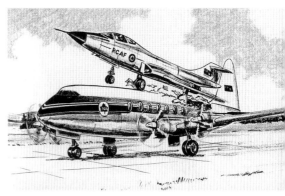

Brief Encounter. There were two fatalities on the Viscount, but the Voodoo crew ejected safely. Mike Hobbs Collection

coat and a stewardess who went to ask him to sit down; eight passengers were injured. Later, Stu went on to complete a successful career as a pilot with Air Canada and the Viscount with which he had had this brief encounter was repaired to fly again out of Montreal as an executive aircraft. Needless to say, radio frequency management and air traffic procedures at Bagotville were changed as a result of this tragedy.

Often it was the unpredictable and severe weather in Canada which at least contributed to some dramatic accidents. So it was at Chatham in March 1963 when ice, snow and wind combined to cause a Voodoo to veer from the cleared side of the runway on to a ridge of snow eight feet wide in the centre. The nose gear and one main undercarriage leg sheared off as one wing dug into the snow and the aircraft flipped on to its back, but thanks again to the strength of the aircraft the crew were uninjured when dug out from below. Again at

Drama at Chatham. Crosswind, ice and snow caused this CF-101B to slide off the icy runway in a crosswind - but the crew walked away. Mike Hobbs Collection

Chatham, a CF-101B of 416 Squadron crashed on landing in February 1966, bursting into flames, but miraculously the crew again escaped injury.

Sadly, Voodoo men did not always survive. On 28 March 1967, one pilot lost control during the break to land after a four-aircraft flypast to celebrate the wedding of a fellow officer, the two crewmen being killed when they ejected. Then in 1970, RAF exchange officer Flight Lieutenant Bill Gambold and his navigator, Nick Lundhild, survived a mid-air collision with a USAF ANG B-57; the American bomber came off worst but both aircraft managed to make a safe landing. Also in 1970 a Voodoo of 410 Squadron, the same aircraft in which 416 Squadron had given Prime Minister Pierre Trudeau a familiarisation sortie in 1968, was lost and its crew killed during a low level ejection, again begging the question whether they would have survived given a state-of-the-art ejection seat.

The dreaded pitch-up struck again in 1971, with Captain Andy Martel losing all control at 40,000 ft and not recovering until 2,000 ft. During this terrifying descent, one drop tank tore off and punctured a flap, but again the aircraft was landed safely. Inspecting the damage to his aircraft on the ground, Andy is reputed to have observed: *"the flak was hell over Bathurst"* and an inevitable cartoon was entitled: *"pitch-up recovery can be fun"*.

Air tests could also be interesting. RCAF navigator George Malton remembers volunteering to ride in the back seat of a CF-101B on a full air test conducted by the Wing Maintenance Test Pilot, Roger Shortill. This included a high 'G' recovery from a steep dive, followed by a 'bunt' to ensure that the constant

Flight Lieutenant George Malton, 414 Squadron: back seat driver. George Malton

speed drives remained on line to serve the ancillary equipment. The undercarriage was certainly not expected to come down during this exciting manoeuvre but on this occasion it did, with a resounding crash. Roger throttled back immediately and selected airbrakes 'out' but by this time the all-important utility hydraulic system had failed, leaving the undercarriage down but one leg indicating unsafe and the airbrakes fully extended. With this unsafe indication the crew had the option of ejecting but, after activating the emergency air bottles an inspection by the pilot of a passing T-33 suggested that all legs were down and locked, the pilot made a cautious but safe landing. The moral of this story: *'Never volunteer.....'*. Even with the correct and immediate actions taken following a warning horn sounding or the stick-pusher engaging, recovery from the pitch-up was never guaranteed, George Malton recalls that one

Fire Escape. This CF-101B of 416 Squadron flew no more, but the crew crawled clear. Mike Hobbs Collection

aircraft at North Bay would 'nibble' at the pusher without apparent cause and that it eventually pitched up when serving at Bagotville, again the crew having to eject. Likewise, another crew failed to recover in 1973 and had to eject, fortunately to be plucked from a cold sea by helicopter.

On his penultimate trip in a Voodoo George allowed his pilot to tempt providence in an ambitious loop when:

"it all went very quiet, save for some heavy breathing as the airspeed indicator registered 110 kts and the aircraft fell out at the top".

To give him credit the pilot admitted publicly that he had not stuck to the rules and suggested that *"we should learn from the mistakes of others"*. How true. At the start of the CF-101s life, such aerobatics and the more aggressive combat tactics were prohibited but as experience and confidence grew many Voodoo pilots succumbed to temptation, making good use of the aircraft's great reserve of power. As the Voodoo neared its end on the front line, formal training in fighter combat tactics was introduced at the OTU in preparation for the introduction of the CF-18.

Accidents on the ramp ranged across the full gamut from decapitation by propellers, being sucked into jet intakes or blown over by jet blast, all of course avoidable. The Voodoo era spawned another, John Wheeler telling of a luckless instructor navigator who, crossing the apron wearing his 'bone dome' to protect him from icy blasts of minus 20 deg, was blissfully ignorant of the approaching snow blower which all but swallowed him whole. Fortunately he survived, albeit without one ear, but wearing bone domes on the line was definitely off from that moment.

416 Squadron's first real test in a simulated war scenario came with a taceval which started at 0400 hours on 10 April 1963. The results are not known but the squadron flew a very creditable 58 sorties before termination at 1600 hours and one navigator, Flying Officer Don Parker, was subsequently awarded an AFC for 'talking down' safely his severely debilitated pilot who had been taken ill in the air. In August 1964, 416 Squadron won the Steinhardt Trophy for the best all-weather squadron in the RCAF and followed this in 1966 and 1967 by winning the MacBrien

Trophy for air-to-air weapons firings. No 416 Squadron was now hosting the RAF crews on exchange postings and in 1967 RAF Flight Lieutenants Tim Elworthy and 'Duggie' Douglas-Boyd were on the winning MacBrien team. Then there were the Call-Shot competitions, held to select the best RCAF/CAF air defence squadron for the USAF annual William Tell Air Weapons Meet at Tyndall AFB - 416 always doing well but too often pipped to the post by minor misfortunes.

'Scramble' stories abound in the CF-101B fraternity. Efforts to achieve and improve on the time taken to get airborne, or at least to the runway threshold in practices, were always impressive, Messrs Whalley and Pallen of 416 Squadron being credited with moving so fast that the controller was 'still reaching for his mike' when the 101 went screaming past the tower. Indeed, in August 1963, 416 Squadron claimed a new record of 57 seconds from 'horn to airborne'. The competitive spirit was alive and well.

Then came the epic story of David Blucke and John Wheeler, the combat-ready crew transferred from 414 Squadron when it disbanded but soon 'on state' at their new home with 416 Squadron. From being sound asleep in the QRA compound when the alarm sounded at 0646 hours on 29 November 1964, they were sprinting to their conventionally armed Voodoo within seconds. Dave hit the aircraft's two starter buttons as John called *"Chatham 01 Scrambling"*, vaguely aware that their No 2 was not with them as they emerged into the outside gloom with the security lights picking out only blinding snow. Chatham Tower replied with;

"Chatham 01 we have nothing for you, the active runway is straight ahead; we have zero cloud base in snow".

As they made their way to the runway a fire truck skidded past them in the opposite direction, to where they knew not. Cleared for take-off, the burners kicked in and they were airborne in four minutes. John now takes up the story:

"Taking off to the east, Dave pulled 5 'G' as we rotated and back-climbed to the west to meet the 'threat', going through the vertical at 5000 ft as we became supersonic. Switching to 'Guard' frequency, I called: 'Stargazer, Stargazer, Chatham 01 on Guard,

scrambled out of Chatham, passing FL200, Mach 1.1, data link unlocked demanding maximum altitude and speed". Stargazer replied, 'Roger 01, Moncton Centre - Standby'. We were in bed asleep six minutes ago and were now passing 36,000 ft doing Mach 1.3, still only 10 miles from base - with a phenomenal fuel flow. I asked Dave whether he saw the fire truck passing rather close as we were taxiing to take off, but he replied 'no' as he unplugged the burners and we levelled at 40,000 ft. Then, for all to hear [including the Russian Picket ship off the coast], Moncton came back with: 'We now have the story; you scrambled on the Fire Bells, Chatham is reporting half a mile visibility in snow with GCA on 30 minutes standby and there are no diversions, what are your intentions?"

This was a nightmare scenario for any fighter crew, but Dave Blucke announced calmly (if a little to John's consternation since it would be mainly down to him now) that they would do an 'internal aids' letdown. In fact, the GCA woke up when the errant Voodoo was on five miles final approach and it all ended well, but it might have been very different. No-one had told this new crew that Chatham QRA launched on a 'Scramble Horn' - which sounded nothing like the Fire Bells.

In their anxiety to get airborne, whether from QRA or during an exercise, even the most professional aircrew could miss something, but to taxi out without a navigator was, to say the least, unusual. That, however, is what Flight Lieutenant John 'Dutch' Stants, a highly respected pilot on 410 Squadron, did when scrambled from crewroom alert. The missing man was Brian Cluer, he had not heard the initial scramble order but when he was told of it he took a short route through a plate glass window and cut his arm too badly to fly. This event illustrates the problem a writer has in separating fact from fiction. The truth of the story, from Brian Cluer direct, is that John Stants merely taxied without him, but the preferred version, no doubt embellished with the telling in many a bar over the years, has it incorrectly that he actually got airborne on his own!

Not long after, perhaps having reflected that his services in the back seat were not properly appreciated, or that it would be preferable to

have better control over his destiny, Brian Cluer transferred to the RAF and pilot training. Having flown with him later, when he was instructing on Lightning fighters at RAF Coltishall, the author can confirm that he was entirely suited to his later role, having become a most competent and highly regarded pilot.

Another favourite bar story, which may or may not be wholly true, has it that a CF-101B navigator left his pilot in mid-air, for the Voodoo to land at the USAF base of Loring without him. There, incredulous airmen on the flight line were quick to note the ejection seat rail sticking skywards where the canopy, rear seat and navigator should have been. The navigator in question later claimed to have 'caught his watch strap in the ejection seat trigger' but other versions of the story have it that the 'back-seater' didn't like what his pilot was doing up front. In any event, the two landed independently, the pilot commenting nonchalantly to his inquisitive audience: *"never mind, could I have a new seat and some tyres please?"*

There are those airmen who allege that the 1960s saw the beginning of the demise of the real 'characters', at least in the British, Canadian and American air forces, a decade when the fun began to seep out of service flying. Others might argue that this was overdue, that the geopolitical and military circumstances demanded a more serious, professional approach to an increasingly expensive defensive shield. Having taken full advantage of the relatively relaxed atmosphere of the 1950s and 1960s, with great excitement in the air as ever-more demanding aircraft came into play in the massed aerial free-for-alls which featured regularly in the day's work, the author understood both views. However, he would claim that all three air forces would have been effective in the 1950s, with their modus operandi and way of life then against the threats of the day, and that there was still fun and satisfaction to be had in the years that followed, albeit perhaps in a necessarily more circumspect manner.

Few who served in these earlier years would deny that the Canadians were then in the front ranks of dynamic airmen, in the air and on the ground. The author, serving with a fighter squadron in Germany in the mid-1950s, can vouch for this; he flew against the RCAF's formidable Sabre 6s and drank with the pilots of 416 Squadron at Grostenquen in France; he should have known better! Similar stories came from RAF exchange crews who served on the Voodoo squadrons in Canada, with little sign in the mid-'60s of any impending 'change of life'.

One of the legendary characters of the time in the RCAF was the commander of 416 Squadron, Wing Commander Dean Kelly who, to Flight Lieutenant Doug Munro, was 'the most revered and respected squadron commander of the eleven I served in my 27 years in the air force'. Doug enthused over Dean's highly successful if rather unconventional style of leadership on the ground and his great talent in the air. His boss never carried out an external check of his aircraft before flight, arguing that the groundcrew knew this and would never let him down - and they didn't. Then there was his flying.

In August 1964, Doug accompanied Dean Kelly in a CF-101B to the 25th NORAD Region Centre, to which the wing commander was due to be posted, and it turned out to be an instructive trip. Dean strolled out to their aircraft with the customary few minutes to spare before take-off, of course omitting the external check but also having failed to get permission for the visit from the USAF or to check the NOTAMS (Notices to Airmen), the wing commander explaining that 'there was no point in giving them a chance to refuse'. When the two found out as they approached their first refuelling stop that the base in question had been closed for six months they merely diverted to Malstrom AFB for fuel before carrying on to their destination at McChord AFB.

The 'official' visit went well, but at 35,000 ft on their departure from McChord the One-O-Wonders were invited to return to pick up their luggage, which had spilled on to the runway when the weapons bay rotated mysteriously on take-off. In Doug's words: *"Dean never dropped a stitch"* replying calmly *"Roger Centre, cancelling IFR, going Tower"* and, in what the pure and pedantic would call a most unorthodox recovery, soon had the Voodoo back on the ground.

Having been offered a choice, Doug had chosen the cultural route home via Las Vegas, nursing the tattered remains of their luggage piled high on his lap; fortunately he had selected all the necessary switches correctly to keep the aircraft flying before becoming so

encumbered and they did not have to eject. Little is known of their activities on the Las Vegas 'Strip', other than that Dean managed somehow to get the Stardust management to give them the best seats at their Lido show.

Getting away on the following day was not easy, there being no high pressure air available to start their two J-57 engines (had they checked?). No problem, they would use the aircraft's internal bottles of emergency air, but (not surprisingly) the engines refused to burst into life simultaneously by this means, and the bottles were then empty. Laboriously, the two bottles were refilled from low pressure air which was on hand, and they were then used to start each engine separately. By that time the Voodoo's bottles were empty again, leaving them with nothing to blow the undercarriage down if they had an emergency, but they were off.

Landing was denied as they approached their next port-of-call, Richards-Gebaur AFB, the crew having neglected to obtain 'prior permission'. So with another nonchalant, *"Roger Centre, going Tower"*, Dean changed heading and descended, telling his navigator that they would go to McConnell AFB instead. McConnell was a SAC base, with all that implied, and this unexpected arrival was greeted by a veritable army of 'remarkably mean looking air policemen' training .50 calibre machine guns on them as they beat a hasty retreat to the TAC side of the airfield. Doug reports that the remaining legs of this eventful trip *"were conducted with their usual consummate skill"*, marred only by Dean's forty-ounce vat of 'snake killer' succumbing to gravity on their arrival at Chatham. Perhaps the moral of this whole story should be 'never assume, check,' but as is so often the case fortune favours the brave - and Dean Kelly was one of the brave.

Exchange officers David Blucke and John Wheeler had a similar tale to tell when they flew to the SAC tanker base at Ernest Harmon, Newfoundland, to buy golf clubs at the BX (Base Exchange). Once there, the two RAF men, who didn't seem to know where they were going next, were treated with much interest and generosity at the evening's beer-call. This interest persisted the following morning as the somewhat hung-over Limeys, having finally decided to go to Summerside, waded through their flight clearance, John measuring flight time with his flying boot against a map on the floor (one boot = 1 hour 30 minutes). At first, their clearance was refused, with the clerk pointing out that their endurance was the same as the route time, but they quickly remedied this by saying for all to hear that they would simply fly faster. A now incredulous crowd watched them saunter out to their aircraft and get airborne (without requesting 'engine start') in an impressively short time. The departure controller had no luck getting them to comply with his elaborate instructions and eventually approved 'a burner take-off through the vertical for a back climb'. The spectators were now treated to the spectacular, as Dave Blucke held the Voodoo down until the end of the runway and then pulled up at 5 'G', going supersonic and rolling out within view on to a reciprocal heading. That would have been a fitting climax had they not failed to check the NOTAMS and were advised on Guard (for all to hear) that their destination was closed. At this point, they decided to go home to Chatham. Never assume, check!

The Canadians were frequent visitors to Dow AFB, Bangor, Maine, if only to pick up spares for their CF-101s, for which John Wheeler believed the RCAF had not made sufficient provision. John also commented on an apparent habit within the USAF F-101B force to take off in 'dry' power (without afterburner). This encouraged the Canadians to demonstrate how they did it with afterburners, 'standing on their cans' and climbing away almost vertically. John also remembers flying with one wingman who seemed bent on being even more impressive by selecting his undercarriage 'up' on the take-off roll so that it began to cycle as soon as the weight came off the wheels. This was indeed tempting providence, as the flight leader on this occasion (the offender's flight commander, David Blucke) pointed out in a one-way interview after landing.

Official records now reveal that, in the early 1960s, Prime Minister Pearson and the Canadian Cabinet had decreed that Special Armament Storage units should be prepared at specified RCAF stations for the possible acquisition of nuclear weapons; they were to be built close to QRA hangars. Subsequent agreement with the US to move W25 nuclear warheads for the Genie rockets to Canada involved collocated detachments of the USAF's 425th Munitions Maintenance Squadron, as custodians at Chatham and Bagotville for the Voodoos in the east, and Comox for those based in the west. Later, full nuclear operations were authorised, provided weapons break-out and loading procedures had been practised assiduously and tested satisfactorily under the strictest security. All this put the RAF exchange officers in an awkward position. Initially, they were asked only to leave the room when a briefing touched on material for 'US and Canadian eyes only' but, when it was mooted that the British might be relieved from their posts, it was explained with typical political dexterity that they already had access to all the necessary top secret material from UK trials with the Genie at Farnborough - and all was deemed to be well. It is believed that no CF-101 ever flew with a live Genie aboard, airborne exercises being carried out with inert training rockets only. The Canadian government remained coy about the existence of these nuclear weapons on its soil; officially they were the property of the US and would be released to Canada only by mutual agreement under the auspices of NORAD.

Genie warheads began arriving in Canada in 1963 but Chatham, although first to be certified to load the missiles on to the Voodoos of 416 Squadron in 1964, did not receive the necessary authority for full nuclear support until July 1965. The storage bunkers were completed at Bagotville in 1964, with the station becoming responsible for nuclear support of 425 Squadron and the QRA detachments at Val d'Or during 1965. The Comox facility and 409 Squadron also passed inspection and became operational in 1965, the squadron then going on to excel in the Call-Shot and William Tell weapons competitions.

Notwithstanding the busy work schedule, there was plenty of time for socialising in the best Canadian Air Force traditions. Exchange officer John Wheeler tells of an elaborate beach party on an uninhabited island in the middle of the Miramachi River, organised by Mike Colbert during the hot July of 1965. John was charged with providing some of the liquid refreshment from his duty-free allocation, but was not prepared for the extra duties he would be called on to perform. All seemed ready for an elegant feast with all the trimmings on a well-set table when a Voodoo, reputed to have been flown by John Rose, skimmed in over the water towards them 'at horrendous speed' and pulled up in afterburner to scatter far and wide all that had been prepared so well. With little worth recovering, it was time for 'Plan B', in which the RAF exchange officer was 'invited' to swim out to some lobster pots and exchange their contents for a bottle of (his) Seagram's best; of course he passed the test to enable a party of a different kind to proceed. There are no details on the fate of John Rose, but perhaps it was agreed that in future it would be best to invite him to the party.

On 1 February 1968, the RCAF became the Canadian Armed Forces (CAF), and later simply the Canadian Forces (CF) with all the 'redecoration' of its aircraft this involved. The Red Ensign with the Union Jack on the tails of the first batch of Voodoos was replaced by the relatively new Canadian Flag depicting a Maple Leaf and, with the bilingual nature of the 'new' Canada demanding that the aircraft carry this nomenclature in both languages, 'CANADIAN ARMED FORCES' was inscribed on one side of the fuselage, 'FORCES ARMEE CANADIENNES' on the other. Later, these were both replaced simply by 'CANADA' on both sides. The size of the roundel enclosing the Maple Leaf was also much reduced on the second batch of aircraft, and this was not all. An RCAF Station became a Canadian Forces Base (CFB) and the airmen were ordered to exchange their cherished blue uniforms for the CAF common green, and later to change their proud RCAF Wings for the even more despised 'Kellogg's Cornflakes' replacements. Turbo Tarling recalls that, among other notables, the then commander of the operational wing at Baden-Soellingen in Germany, Colonel 'A J' (Arnie) Bauer, was slow to concede, and perhaps suffered accordingly. Many RCAF airmen were far from happy with these new manifestations of 'togetherness'.

Between June 1970 and January 1972, 56 of the first batch of CF-101Bs were returned to the USAF under Operation Peace Wings, 22 to be converted to two-seat recce aircraft, the RF-101B (which would serve with the Nevada ANG until 1975), with most of the remainder scrapped or committed to gate guardians. In return, the CAF received 66 replacements including 10 CF-101Fs, older than those they replaced but with fewer flying hours, and extensively modified within an Interceptor Improvement Programme. The retractable re-fuelling probe was removed to make way for

infrared (IR) sensor equipment (visible by the nose-mounted sensor ball forward of the cockpit) and an IR tracking system integrated with the MG-13 radar. This greatly improved target detection, giving target direction and tracking data but not distance; distance had to be estimated with the help of a heat-intensity indicator slaved to the IR sensor. Little, however, could arrest the general ageing process and serviceability deteriorated in the 1970s, with periodic groundings of the whole fleet; there was also a marginal increase in the accident rate.

416 Squadron took its turn in mounting detachments to Goose Bay, Labrador, and Gander, Newfoundland, to keep a watchful eye on Russian Bear bombers which were coming a little too close to the east coast of Canada. They were often rewarded with close up sightings of the bombers and in 1970 with a Distinguished Unit Citation for their efficient 'seek and find' operations. In later years the Russians grew bolder, training their guns on the Voodoos (hopefully in mock hostility) and

Lynx Pilot. Captain Turbo Tarling, 416 (Lynx) Squadron, with CF-101B 051 at CFB Chatham in 1975. Jules Plamondon

Flight Lieutenant Euan Black RAF and Captain Harry Redden CAF 416 (Lynx) Squadron airborne in CF-101 101014 at Chatham on 21 November 1975. Turbo Tarling

Mixed Crew. Squadron Leader Gwyn Williams RAF (left) & Captain Al Ruttan CAF. Gwyn Williams

using high-powered strobe lights to destroy the crew's night vision - but the 416 pilots were not put off.

Cross-fertilisation of ideas may have been the official reason for an annual 'Open House' hosted by air defence units within the 22nd NORAD Region. What better environment and timing for the purpose than a squadron's favourite social venue at a weekend? Guests would arrive, by air of course, on the Friday, and plan to depart on Sunday. As so often seemed to be the case, the task of 'catering' fell to the resident RAF exchange officer and Squadron Leader Gwyn Williams of 416 Squadron remembers driving to a local fishing port to pick up 1000 lb of fresh lobster (at $1/lb!) to ensure that their guests did not go hungry. This particular event at CFB Chatham hosted USAF F-106s from ADC and F-101Bs from the ANG, CF-100s used for ECM training from North Bay, CF-5s and CF-101Bs from 425 Squadron at Bagotville. No agenda, minutes or reports of this 'teach-in' can be found.

Undercarriage failures of one sort or another continued to plague the Voodoo men, who were within their rights to abandon an aircraft when the prescribed emergency procedures failed to get a fully safe indication. However,

when in 1983 a crew from 409 Squadron had tried all they knew but failed to get one main wheel to lock down, they decided to 'ride it in'. They did so successfully, without injury to themselves as the aircraft inevitably left the side of the runway. The last Voodoo to be lost, after an engine failure had led to an explosion and fire, was a CF-101F of 409 Squadron at CFB Comox, a week before that squadron disbanded on 1 July 1984. The aircraft entered a flat spin, losing all forward airspeed, and the crew ejected seconds before it exploded.

As with all histories of this type, it is the spectacular and dramatic which catches the eye and makes the headlines, but many

Open House. USAF F-101B and F-106 squadrons join CAF CF-5, CF-100 and CF-101B squadrons for an annual weekend 'exchange of views', the 1973 event hosted by 416 Squadron at Chatham. Gwyn Williams Collection

contributors to this book reported long careers flying the Voodoo without any major incident. Gwyn Williams was one; he recalls that he found the aircraft relatively easy and comfortable to fly and had a largely uneventful tour. By then aircraft emergency procedures had been refined and well rehearsed, with Gwyn and his navigator, Captain Bob Mitchell, benefiting accordingly. During one of their conversion sorties smoke filled the latter's cockpit following an electrical fire after take-off, the unfortunate incumbent calling for an immediate return to earth. Having no fuel jettison facility, they prepared to land with a full load by carrying out a wide circuit and, on advice from the duty pilot, keeping their approach and threshold speeds at 240 kts and 210 kts respectively. Gwyn deployed the drag 'chute below the statutory 210 kts, used maximum aerodynamic braking and released the arrester hook (which fell under gravity) to engage the wire at the far end of the runway. In fact, he had already done enough and the hook was not needed. It was easy when you knew how.

CFB Chatham was the first of the Voodoo's three nuclear support centres to close, as the USAF and CAF Genie inventories were scaled back in the mid-1970s, with all the weapons and their custodians leaving by June 1975. While 416 Squadron retained its nuclear commitment, it would now be supported in the role from Bagotville. As the only remaining centre on the East Coast, there was no fundamental change in Genie support at Bagotville, but 425 Squadron went to half strength in 1982 and its on-base alert requirement was reduced to two aircraft at 60 minutes. The station also retained contingency

Ten-Ship. Gwyn Williams RAF (pilot) & Brian Smallman-Tew (navigator) lead the formation during an air display at Chatham, 14 May 1973. Gwyn Williams

plans for the warheads in case of other commitments until June 1984. 409 Squadron (Nighthawks) on the West Coast at Comox were among the last to fire Genie rockets as the Voodoo force ran down and, when this squadron lost its aircraft, the W25 warheads were withdrawn and the last USAF custodial detachment closed in June 1984.

The Canadian Voodoo force would not go out with a whimper; as a firm and long-term spectator favourite at air shows, diverse celebrations, PR and morale-raising exercises since 1961, it would continue to perform impressively until 1984. Highlights had included participation in Canada's 1967 Centennial celebrations, a close formation of eighteen Voodoos from Bagotville which opened the Chicoutimi Winter Carnival and a spectacular duo with a CF-104, and there were none better in the business than the 416 Squadron and 425 Squadron four-ship display teams. The Voodoo would never be an ideal formation aerobatic aircraft, bearing in mind its turning performance and limitations in vertical manoeuvres, but with judicious use of

Captain Ray Dube leading Squadron Leader Gwyn Williams, at Chatham 1973. Gwyn Williams.

afterburners its size, speed and noise made it a great attraction. What follows is a snap-shot of 425 Squadron's 'Warlocks' during the 1981 and 1982 display seasons.

Major Jim Gregory took over the lead of the Warlocks from Major Keith Coulter in August 1981; he had served on 416 Squadron from 1966 to 1970 and had 1100 hours experience on the aircraft. Jim continued to follow the well tried display sequence which started with the four making two passes in 'box' formation, turning over centre stage to show first their top and then the lower sides, before the Nos 2 and 3 broke off for their individual routines. These included a level, high speed 360 deg/6 'G' turn over the airfield by No 3 in afterburner with the gear and flaps up, while No 2 completed a max rate turn in afterburner with gear and flaps down, to compare turning radii. Meanwhile, Nos 1 and 4 positioned for a flat turn pass in close line astern, separated by a mere three feet. The three units continued their separate programmes varying their speeds, heights and turns in various configurations, before coming together again for a high speed (close to supersonic) run along the crowd line and into a vertical climb finale.

Jim Gregory admitted that his first practice with the team did not go as well as he would have wished when a momentary loss of 'situation awareness' led him very sensibly to call it off prematurely. However, practice makes perfect and the team was ready for its first public show under the new leadership at the all-important Toronto Canadian National Exhibition (CNE) in September. With the display to take place over Lake Ontario, where visibility could be poor, Jim briefed the team not to depend on visual horizons and stressed the imperative of monitoring their cockpit instruments continuously, as they practiced over the local waters of Lac St. Jean.

In addition to a 24-hour delay in deploying the Voodoos to Toronto because of poor weather and a number of unreportable social 'incidents', the supporting groundcrew had their work cut out when, on arrival, an engine in one of the four display aircraft was found to have sustained Foreign Object Damage (FOD) and had to be replaced. Frantic calls to Bagotville got the new engine on its way, while the crew removed the defective unit with great ingenuity and industry (but very little sleep); as a result the replacement engine was ground run

and the aircraft ready to fly by 0900 hours on the following day. Sadly, these most laudable efforts were to no immediate avail because flying was cancelled on the first two days of the CNE owing to the weather, and the Warlock aircrew had to wait until the final two days to show what they were made of.

On Day 3, the weather was still very marginal and Jim had to amend his plan on the ground and again in the air. They were forced to enter cloud after take-off and, with a paucity of radar assistance, to descend to low level again at their own discretion as their show time approached, breaking cloud at 1000 ft above the water in haze. Their practices in such conditions now paid off and the show went well, as it did on the final day, in perfect weather.

In the following month the Warlocks were scheduled to pay their respects to the retiring CF-100 force during its 'Defunct Clunk Club' celebrations at CFB North Bay and agreed, subject to certain assurances from their hosts, to perform in a similar timeframe at the Quinte Airshow, Trenton, on the same day. The shows went well, after the leader's aircraft was grounded with a damaged speed brake and replaced by another 425 Squadron aircraft which just 'happened' to be around. However, Trenton did not honour its pledges to attend to the Voodoos' needs when the Warlocks landed there for a rapid refuel before returning to North Bay; none of the promised groundcrew, ladders, fuel bowsers or starter units being in place. Ingenuity and industry prevailed again, the visitors taking on the servicing themselves and starting the engines of two of the Voodoos from the aircrafts' emergency air bottles, for two crews to party that night at North Bay. That was not the end of the saga. The two crews who had remained at Trenton as planned were not given proper hospitality there and returned to the flight line to refuel their own aircraft in order to fly back to the party at North Bay. It is unlikely that 425 Squadron bent over backwards to help Trenton again.

In these first years of the 1980s major changes took place in the Canadian air force. By 1982, 416 Squadron had run down to half its number of aircraft and could only field a two aircraft demonstration team but the Warlocks were able to meet all their operational commitments and maintain a four-ship display team. Again led by Jim Gregory,

All Day - All Night. No. 425 Squadron continued to guard Canadian skies until 1984. Jim Gregory

the routine remained largely the same but, as with the previous year, bad weather frequently intruded on the planned programme and flexibility continued to be the name of the game. The Warlocks flew their last display at Bagotville on 27 June 1982 and, on the same day, Jim Gregory climbed out the Voodoo for the last time.

There was still serious work to be done. Operation Cold Shaft, beginning in July 1982, entailed detachments to forward bases in areas where interceptions were foreseen to be required. Accordingly, 425 Squadron moved CF-101Bs to the USAF base at Loring, Maine, to be held at one hour's readiness to fly to Gander, Newfoundland, where they would refuel before mounting standing patrols in wait for the expected Russians. At Chatham, 416 Squadron was already well acquainted with the Russians in its area of responsibility and continued to provide escorts for the Tupolev TU95 'Bears' while training hard to meet new Russian threats from supersonic bombers and stand-off missiles.

By now, however, the CF-101B force was in its death throes, and an increasing number of Voodoo men (with others from the CF-5 and CF-104 units) were transitioning to the very

different single-seat CF-18 Hornet. In June 1982, the last CF-101B went into Depot Level Inspection and Repair and 410 OTU began training CF-18 pilots; 425 and 409 Squadrons went to half strength pending re-equipment with CF-18s and ceased Voodoo operations in June 1984. The last operational Voodoo unit, 416 Squadron, continued to mount QRA with conventional AAMs until it disbanded at the end of 1984.

As with other aircraft at a time when so many new technologies were emerging and aerodynamic envelopes explored, with their pilots having to get used to much higher performance, the F-101B all-weather air defence fighter had had its problems. The aircraft had not been designed for this specific purpose but the Voodoo men made it work for more years than had been intended. With its spectacular performance, great structural strength and redundancy in engines and ancillaries, most pilots grew to love this variant of the Voodoo, handle it with sensible care and get the best out of its great potential, while maintenance men soon found ways of keeping it in the air. The author would claim that, from his own experience over 38 years of fast-jet evolution, the facts and anecdotes, the F-101B

Above & below: Warlocks - Men and Machines. Major Jim Gregory (lead pilot) and Captain Denis Guerin (navigator) led the 425 Squadron 'Warlocks' display team in their final 1981 and 1982 seasons. Jim Gregory

Swan Song. In colourful dress uniform for their final display together, Hawk One (409 Sqn) led Lynx One (416 Sqn), Alouette Un (425 Sqn) and the EF-101B(414 Sqn) in a 1984 'swan song'. CAF

performed very favourably when compared with many of its contemporaries, and that the loss of 28 Voodoos within the RCAF/CAF in its lifespan of 22 years was not excessive.

To mark the demise of the venerable Voodoo in 1984, each of four remaining CF-101 squadrons displayed one of their aircraft in appropriate colours. 409 Squadron repeated its 1977 'Hawk One Canada' scheme, a screaming black hawk behind a pale blue/grey nose, and 416 Squadron its 60th anniversary 'Lynx Squadron Canada' motif on a white background. No. 425 Squadron painted its display aircraft with a red and white Alouette stretching back from cockpit to tail, with 'Alouette Un Canada' emblazoned along the fuselage and 414 Squadron's ECM aircraft was

dressed in black - as if in mourning. Needless to say, these aircraft were much in demand at their final displays across the country. In April 1987, the ECM Voodoo of 414 Squadron flew to its final resting place in the US at the Minnesota ANG museum and the trainer went to CFB Chatham to go on display at CFB Cornwallis. Twenty four other CF-101Bs found homes elsewhere in Canada but the Voodoo would fly no more.

The men of the USAF and RCAF/CAF who produced, flew and supported the air defence Voodoo in so many ways could claim that they had done so with distinction as an integral part of the deterrence which was at the core of the Cold War. They too could look back with pride.

PART TWO: CONFLICT

CHAPTER EIGHT
OVERTURE TO WAR

'Indochina is devoid of decisive military objectives and the allocation of more than token US armed forces there would be a serious diversion of limited US capabilities.'

Joint Chiefs of Staff Study 1954

The calm and tranquillity of that beautiful, starlit South Carolina evening, on the last day of 1960, was suddenly shattered by the thunder of Pratt and Witney J-57 engines. Shaw AFB Voodoo pilots and groundcrews were preparing for deployment to SEA. With no forewarning all this came as a surprise during the seasonal stand-down but there was little need for a general call-out; most off-base personnel would be passing through the gates en route to celebrate the New Year in their respective messes and they were simply redirected to their place of work, with wives and girlfriends left to fend for themselves.

Fearing any suggestion of British involvement, an all-too alert British Embassy in Washington ordered the RAF exchange pilot to stand down and the author was banished to the Officers Club to help a handful of other officers look after hundreds of unescorted ladies. Meanwhile, flight surgeons prepared their pilots for the long flight ahead until, in the early hours of New Year's Day, the deployment was put on hold. Whether for political or practical reasons, it was to be no more than a reprieve for Shaw's One-O-Wonders, many of whom would spend much of the next decade in SEA.

South East Asia. Voodoos flew long distances to SEA from Japan and Okinawa.

The International Control Commission (ICC), established to oversee the stability in SEA following the partition of Vietnam agreed in Geneva in 1954, seemed unable to arrest the growth of nationalist and communist aggression in the area. Increasingly during the 1950s the Viet Cong interfered overtly with the independence of South Vietnam while Pathet Lao insurgents, with support from North Vietnam, became very active in northern parts

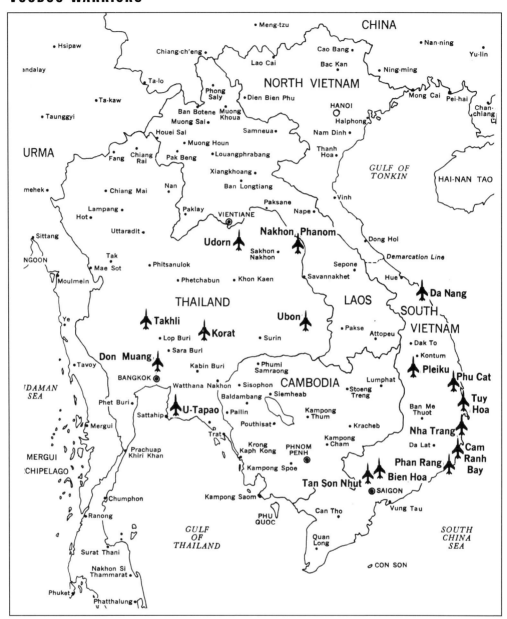

The War Zone. RF-101s operated throughout South Vietnam, North Vietnam, Thailand and Cambodia, primarily from bases at Udorn, Don Muang & Tan Son Nhut. USAF & Author

of Laos and the Plain des Jars (PDJ). Desperate for intelligence on these moves but having no effective air reconnaissance capability, the Laotian Government asked the United States for help. Initially, this was provided covertly by means of a camera-equipped C-47 Dakota used by the US air attaché in Saigon, South Vietnam, who was also accredited to Vientiane, the capital of Laos, as he plied routinely between the two cities. When the Dakota was shot down over the Tran Ninh Highlands on 11 February 1961, President Kennedy called for alternative measures to be put in place to keep an eye on the deteriorating situation in the area.

So it was that in April 1961 recce pilots who also had recent experience on the standard USAF training aircraft, the T-33, were called for from the Pacific Air Force (PACAF) RF-101

Field Goal Pioneers. Field Goal pilots Captain Bob Caudry (above) and Lieutenant Fred Muesegaes were qualified on both the RF-101 and RT-33. Bob Caudry and Fred Muesegaes

briefings on the purpose of the mission (in short, to provide President Kennedy with 'eyes' over Laos), the political situation and military intelligence. A missionary, recently returned from the country, added advice on how to approach the local people and they were shown pictures of a typical village in the expected operating area, with a Coca-Cola sign nailed incongruously to a tree. When it was put to them both Bob and Fred steadfastly resisted a plan to 'sanitize' themselves and their aircraft, thereby removing all traces of their association with the USAF to perhaps become part of Air America (the CIA-funded 'airline' flying transport aircraft and helicopters on covert operations). There was no mention at this stage of high monetary rewards for this political expedient.

The two pilots were joined at Clark AFB by Major Vermillion, who had been sent down from Korea to command the detachment but was not qualified to fly the aircraft, and by five enlisted men. Headed by a crew chief, this support team included appropriate specialists in aircraft engines, communications, cameras and structures; they were provided with equipment to support limited operations with a single RT-33 aircraft. This variant of the well-proven jet trainer was thought to be one of five built for foreign sales at Lockheed's 'Skunk Works'; it had been supplied to the Philippine Air Force under the Military Aid Programme but was now exchanged for a standard T-33. The RT-33 was a 'souped-up' version of the trainer, fitted with an RF-80 nose carrying the reconnaissance cameras (a 12-inch focal length nose oblique with 6-inch cameras in the left, right and vertical 'tri-met' stations). An additional fuel tank replaced the rear seat. Project Field Goal was up and running.

Bob Caudry found the RT-33 'a nice flying bird', heavy on take-off with the additional fuel but lighter to handle in the latter stages of flight and, after a 'test hop' on 14 April, he flew this aircraft non-stop from Clark to the Royal Thai Air Force Base (RTAFB) at Udorn, in a flight of three hours ten minutes. At Udorn he had to 'make a low pass down the runway to chase off the water buffalo and the civilians who used it as a level walkway'.

At this stage the air base at Udorn, built originally by the Japanese in WW2, was barely acceptable for jet operations. The US Navy's Bureau of Yards and Docks had built a 7,500 ft

squadrons to volunteer for 'special duties'. Captain Bob Caudry of the 15th TRS at Kadena and Lieutenant Fred Muesegaes of the 45th TRS at Misawa (the only bachelor on that squadron with the necessary qualifications) were the first to answer the call. On Easter Sunday, 2 April 1961, Bob was told to pack his bags and he departed Kadena for 13th Air Force HQ at Clark AFB in the Philippines on 7 April. There he met Fred for three days of

Making Do. Udorn airfield, rudimentary home for the Field Goal RT-33 in 1961, undergoing reconstruction. Bob Caudry

concrete runway but there were 3-5 ft drop-offs either side, no 'distance to go' marker boards, no overruns and no jet barrier either end. There were trees and a road on the approach to one runway while a 10 ft deep ditch crossed just before the threshold of the other. Although there was a low powered radio beacon (with a range of perhaps 25 miles) on the eastern side of the airfield, there were no published instrument approach procedures. With these conditions some normal peacetime regulations would have to be waved, the pilots having to improvise and exercise all their airmanship skills to operate the RT-33 safely.

When the remainder of the detachment and equipment arrived by transport aircraft on 20 April, the maintenance men went to work immediately to service the RT-33 and its cameras, a contingency force of US Marines making aircraft fuel available from mobile fuel bladders. Basic domestic facilities were provided in the Marines' 'tent city', with the officers billeted in a VOQ tent, everyone having access to the naturally heated showers (although water was severely rationed) and the slit trenches which served as latrines. The staple diet consisted of 'C' and later 'K' rations. An abiding memory for all was of the ever-present snakes, most of which were poisonous; they were particularly prevalent after frequent spells of rain, during which they found many a worrying hiding place. One man discovered that a small pit viper had spent the night in one of his boots, after which great care was taken by all when dressing in the morning. Only the

bare essentials of life were there at the start but gradually domestic conditions at Udorn would improve, the Marines building platforms to keep the tents clear of floods and the USAF reacting speedily to requests for support facilities. The expansion at RTAFB Udorn was underway.

The two pilots devised their own operating procedures, typically with the RT-33 towed to and from the runway thresholds where the engine was started and shut down to minimise the risk of FOD. Lacking some of the necessary inputs, they computed take-off runs as best they could and Fred was the first to put their calculations to the test. He admits to some trepidation as he took off in a temperature of 100 degrees, Major Vermillion and the rest of the detachment sharing his concern as they watched the RT-33 vanish off the end of the runway in a cloud of dust, but all was well. Before beginning their recce operations Bob and Fred each flew a local orientation sortie to check their unofficial procedures, which included a 'teardrop' approach making use of the low-powered beacon on the airfield. They knew of course, that when they needed the radio beacon most, thunderstorms could cause the ADF needle in the cockpit to oscillate wildly.

Although the operational missions were flown out of Thailand the pilots were tasked and briefed by the US Military Advisory Group (MAG) in Vientiane, and it was there that their film was processed and analysed. For these purposes they travelled to and fro by Air America H-34 helicopter or by any other means they could arrange. The presence of Air America, with its operations centre at Vientiane and base at Udorn, proved a godsend and the two recce pilots made good use of its rudimentary operations facilities at Udorn, especially their intelligence updates. They were soon in no doubt as to the risks they would take, particularly in such 'hot' areas as the PDJ, into which even the Air America pilots feared to go after one of their number had been shot down there in his H-34. The RT-33 pilots realised that if they ejected over Laos they were likely to be on their own.

Bob Caudry flew the first Field Goal sortie on 24 April 1961, using the vertical camera over the PDJ at 20,000 ft before descending to 200ft in Laos to take oblique photography along Route 13. It was there, at Vang Vieng airstrip,

Baptism of Fire. Captain Bob Caudry, in the RT-33, was greeted by a fusillade of small arms fire (see smoke) from this rudimentary airfield at Vang Vieng in Laos. Bob Caudry

that he came under AAA fire for the first time, ineffectively from quad 50-mm guns mounted on Dodge trucks. However, the fundamental problem for the pilots was that of flying in the very unpredictable weather without navigation aids or accurate maps. The greatest care had to be taken when letting down through cloud to obtain the photography required and when recovering to base. Fred Muesegaes recalls that his missions: *"Consisted primarily of pin point targets and vertical strips; the targets were (dirt) airfields, roads, AAA sites, suspected troop and supply concentrations and villages. We would fly at all heights, from 'the deck' to 20,000 feet, depending on the tasks and AAA expected".*

Bob Caudry recalls many pin-point targets but also the route searches, one of which gave rise to a new concern. Some five minutes after the RT-33 had made a run down Highway 7 friendly ground forces operating nearby reported that a 'swept wing' aircraft, believed

to be a MiG, had appeared and circled the area. This led to a temporary suspension of Field Goal sorties over Laos.

After flying a mission the pilot would carry his film to Vientiane and help with the photo interpretation before 'hitch-hiking' again back to Udorn. On one such occasion Bob Caudry's return to Udorn had to be postponed while his Air America pilot, who had hobbled from his H-34, had a badly bleeding leg treated; he had been hit by small arms fire on the way to Vientiane. Later Bob met another Air America pilot who seemed to be surprised to see him alive, having witnessed the RT-33 running the gauntlet of very heavy AAA fire during his target run several weeks earlier.

Despite the many difficulties, the single RT-33 had flown 16 very profitable recce missions out of Udorn before the ICC demanded a halt on 10 May 1961. With growing political sensitivities and the need for routine maintenance on the aircraft, the Field Gaol Task Force moved to Don Muang Airport, Bangkok, from where the recce missions would resume when the pause was lifted. The 15th TRS replaced Bob Caudry with Captain Don

Friendly Meeting. The Field Goal RT-33 taxies past RAF Hunters staging at Don Muang. John Linihan

Duty Carried Out. The Field Goal RT-33, its pilot having completed his task in Laos. John Linihan

Elwood and, after a four week overlap, the 45th TRS sent Lieutenant Jack Weatherby to take over from Fred Muesegaes.

The Field Goal missions were not the first sorties to be flown by USAF recce aircraft from Don Muang. In June 1960, after exercising in the Philippines and at the behest of the Royal Thai Government, four TAC RF-101s were deployed there to photograph ten targets in Thailand. Captain Bob Gould also records that 'sometime in late 1960 or early 1961', two Voodoos had been sent to reassess the turn-round and support facilities at Don Muang and Tan Son Nhut Airport, Saigon. This proved a prudent exercise when the compressed air starters provided by Pan American Airways at Tan Son Nhut were found to be wholly inadequate. Then, in March 1961, three PACAF RF-101s from the 15th TRS at Kadena went to RTAFB Takhli for the South East Asia Treaty Organisation (SEATO) Exercise Air Bull.

They were followed in September 1961 by RF-101s of the 15th TRS which provided navigational assistance to F-102s flying from their base at Naha, Okinawa, to Bangkok, there being no TACAN facilities available for them and no low frequency navigational radio receivers aboard the fighters. On the face of it this should have been a relatively simple escort role terminating in a formation descent with two 'Deuces' on the wings of a Voodoo, but it could have turned out to be rather less straightforward. Fortunately, Bob Gould had put the formation to the test at Clark AFB in good weather, and found that when he selected full flap in the Voodoo the two fighters immediately took the lead; they had no flaps. From then on the F-102s used their speed brakes. Practice makes perfect.

John Linihan, 45th TRS, may have been the first Field Goal replacement pilot who was not a current instructor pilot on the T-33. He carried out a refresher on the aircraft at Misawa and then retrieved the RT-33 from its scheduled maintenance at Clark to take it to Don Muang on 1 October 1961, where he joined Captain Grayson ('Skinny') Powell of the 15th TRS. He flew his first Field Goal missions over Thailand until overflights of Laos resumed on 9 October, after which he and Captain Horace ('Hoss') Linscombe, who replaced Powell, each flew 15 long range missions over Laos, with the only restriction

being the Royal Capital Louang Phabang. John flew his last RT-33 trip on 5 November, his replacement Captain Bill Whitten and Hoss Linscombe completing the Field Goal operation shortly thereafter. The RT-33 was handed over to non-recce T-33 pilots who would then fly the aircraft solely to ferry film and recce reports in support of the Able Mable Task Force (Chapter Nine).

The Voodoo presence in SEA began in earnest in October 1961, with four RF-101s from the 15th TRS deployed from Kadena to Tan Son Nhut with recce support facilities, for Exercise Pipe Stem. Originally, they were scheduled to take part with other aircraft in an Armed Forces Air Display in Saigon, but when the show was cancelled they stayed on, at their host's request, to photograph flooded areas around the Mekong River, perhaps surreptitiously including areas of political and military interest in the PDJ and on the borders of South Vietnam. They also sought evidence that North Vietnamese transport aircraft were parachuting supplies to their troops or the Pathet Lao in Laos, which had been cunningly avoiding those times the Voodoos were regularly programmed into the same area. When the tasking agencies refused to vary the established schedules the recce pilots came up with their own cunning plan. They launched the first pair of four RF-101s at the time ordered, then used the 'maintenance hour' allowed before launching the second pair (its aircraft having miraculously recovered from an 'oil leak'). It was while flying in the second pair as wingman to his operations officer, Major Russ Crutchlow, that Lieutenant Howard Myli of the 15th TRS, struck lucky. Their Pipe Stem task took them to the small airfield at Tchepone, just below the 17th parallel, and it was as they approached the area above broken cloud at 10,000 ft that Howard thought he spotted an aircraft below. On impulse and without breaking radio silence, he pulled away from his leader briefly to take a picture of the area with his 36-inch split vertical cameras. Little did he know then what this initiative had achieved; the photographs revealed very clearly an IL-14 transport, the Russian-built version of the C-47 with North Vietnamese markings, dropping supplies by parachute on to the airfield. The prints caused great excitement in Saigon, where General Maxwell Taylor, a former head of the Joint Chiefs of Staff of the

Needs Must. When JP-4 fuel for the Voodoos ran out at Tan Son Nhut, KB-50J tankers were flown in to transfer fuel via the AAR basket and probe. RF-101 pilot Lieutenant Stan Menees supervising this operation. Bob Gould

Armed Forces, was on a fact finding visit on behalf of President Kennedy. On the following day the evidence was hand carried to the Pentagon in Washington, en route to the United Nations as further proof of North Vietnamese aggression in the South. The Voodoos were paying their way.

The men of the Voodoo force were now learning much about operating in SEA. Bob Gould remembers one lesson which could just as well be included in Chapter Sixteen, 'Innovation, Industry and Determination'. The RF-101s were to be provided with JP-4 fuel at Tan Son Nhut by the Esso Patroleum Company, based there primarily to refuel Air France and PanAm airliners, but with JP-1 (a fuel unacceptable for J-57 engines). Too late the Pipe Stem team was advised that JP-4 was running out, which could have left the Voodoos stranded. HQ 13th Air Force came to the rescue with the practical solution of flying KB-50 tankers into Tan Son Nhut and transferring their fuel to the Voodoos on the ground - an

Team Effort. The Pipe Stem team at Don Muang in November 1961, among them Lieutenant Colonel Earl Butts, Captains Miller, Brown, Strout, Guillotte, Stevens and Lieutenant Menees, together with support personnel from the 18th TFW. Bob Gould

Recce in Earnest. Captain Jerry Miller back safely at Tan Son Nhut from another Pipe Stem mission over Laos in November 1961.
Jerry Miller

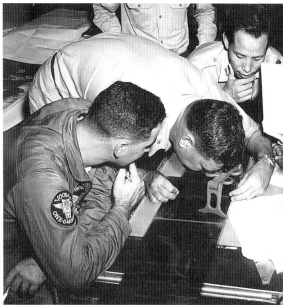

The End Result. Earl Butts, commander 15th TRS (centre) views a Voodoo pilot's film after a Pipe Stem sortie in late 1961, as Vietnamese photo interpreters (PIs) look on.
Bob Gould

expedient little known and probably never before practised. The first problem was to land and take off the tankers on Tan Son Nhut's 7,500ft runway safely, but this was accomplished with very little to spare. Next came the difficulty of getting a good connection between probe and basket on the ground, but again this was achieved with no little skill and the fuel flowed. Such team effort and ingenuity as this would overcome myriad problems in the new and unfamiliar environment.

In 31 days, 67 Pipe Stem sorties were flown successfully without loss despite cases of 'fairly accurate' AAA, before the ICC intervened again and the RF-101s were ordered back to Kadena. Fortuitously, they left some support equipment, including a Photo Processing Centre (PPC) at Tan Son Nhut, because the Voodoos would be back.

Looking back on their time in Saigon some 40 years later, Howard Myli and Bob Gould remember a 'gentleman's war', with pilots leaving the comfortable Caravelle Hotel for a leisurely first take-off at 0800 hours - returning at 1500 hours to sip beer on the veranda and watch the pretty Vietnamese girls go by 'in a little bit of Paris in the Orient'. Sadly, it would all change.

CHAPTER NINE
TASK FORCE ABLE MABLE

'Time spent in reconnaissance is seldom wasted.'

Military Doctrine.

The value of air reconnaissance in SEA having been very evident from Project Field Goal and Exercise Pipe Stem, and with the full approval of the Royal Thai government, the 45thTRS was ordered to deploy four x RF-101s with appropriate back-up to Don Muang AB 'on or about 1 November 1961'. To that end Major Herbst and three other pilots from the 45th TRS: Captain Ralph Delucia, Lieutenants Jack Weatherby and Fred Muesegaes, flew from Misawa to Clark AFB for a briefing by 13th Air Force and then on to Don Muang, initially for 30 days, as Task Force Able Mable.

They were supported by 13th Air Force through Detachment 10 of an Advanced Echelon (ADVON) at Tan Son Nhut. The senior Able Mable pilot acted as recce staff officer and operations officer responsible for all Task Force missions and the detachment was expected to generate three sorties/day beginning on 8 November 1961. Also, one RF-101 was to be held on strip alert to react to any urgent requirements from December onwards. Don Muang may have been the only base in Thailand at that time fully capable of supporting RF-101 operations relatively safely; however, as Bangkok's International Airport and with Royal Thai Air Force F-86s based there, air traffic congestion would sometimes pose problems.

'Polka Dots' Lead the Way. The 45th TRS arrives at Don Muang, Bangkok, the vanguard of Task Force Able Mable, in November 1961. Doug Gordon Collection

The Voodoo detachment was met by John Linihan and Captain Bill Whitten from the Field Goal team, both of whom would later be grafted on to the Able Mable Task Force. There was 'war in the air' and whereas the pilots had hitherto carried neither side arms nor escape and evasion equipment they would now be equipped with both. Indeed, as the conflict escalated each pilot armed himself unofficially with his choice of weapons, Captain George Cowgill admitting later that he carried a .22 calibre pistol 'doctored to stop a man', in addition to his official '38'. Rescue arrangements at this stage were confined largely to the use of any Air America aircraft which might be available when needed, giving rise to some concern over reaction times. Basic escape and evasion kits were now available, again often enhanced to personal choice, and most of the pilots had undergone survival training at Stead AFB in the United States, supplemented in some cases by specialist jungle training at the British Survival School in Singapore.

Frequent poor weather, inadequate on-board navigation equipment and external aids, inaccurate flying maps and ever-changing height restrictions continued to call for

Learning to Survive. Gene Morris shows RAF and RTAF officers how to sharpen a knife at the RAF Jungle Survival School in Singapore.
Gene Morris

Familiar Territory. Lieutenant John Linihan over Udorn AB; he had been this way before in the RT-33 on Project Field Goal. John Linihan

considerable ingenuity in mission planning, flying and the use of cameras - basic skills being the order of the day. There were other problems; overflight of Cambodia, North Vietnam, China and Burma was prohibited, with violations subject to court martial, and this made vertical strip photography in these border areas particularly difficult.

With Field Goal over, John Linihan flew a check ride with Jack Weatherby in the chase aircraft before his first Able Mable mission over Laos on 8 November 1961. He would fly 28 operational missions, mainly over Laos with the remainder over South Vietnam, before completing his first commitment in SEA on 6 January 1962, and by the end of 1961 the detachment had flown more than 130 sorties, exposing 53,000 feet of film. Rising tension and a commensurate increase in demand for air intelligence led to an extension of Able Mable indefinitely with the 45th TRS rotating its pilots every six weeks, during which time each pilot could expect to complete 15-20 missions.

Some sorties, the results from which were required urgently, were diverted to Tan Son Nhut for immediate film processing at the facilities left there after Exercise Pipe Stem. These could be very long missions and with no airborne refuelling available during these early days there was often some concern back at Don Muang when an aircraft seemed overdue, but they all returned safely. Early in 1962, to the great relief of the pilots, standard departure times and entry points into Laos (which had allowed the Pathet Lao to concentrate their guns when and where they would be most effective) gave way to more flexible planning. The need for flexibility was also recognised in

the removal of a minimum height restriction of 5,000 ft, imposed earlier in an attempt to minimise the threat from small arms fire. Later, flights of two aircraft would also replace single aircraft missions, foregoing economy of effort for redundancy, the greater security of cross-cover and, if necessary, to simplify rescue co-ordination. Lessons were being learned.

The Voodoos did take some hits. The intake and first stages of the compressor in one of Ralph DeLucia's J-57 engines were damaged by 50-calibre rounds but it kept running satisfactorily and, with basic repairs carried out after landing, continued in use until it was replaced at Misawa. Fred Muesegaes' aircraft was also hit as he approached Tchepone airfield in Laos on 9 January 1962. He was flying at 500 ft and 500 kts when a 23-mm armour piercing round whistled passed his cockpit, entered the No 2 fuel (feed) tank via the splitter vane and fuselage and severely damaged the electrics, leaving him without the right generator or fuel transfer pumps. However, with judicious management of the systems, Fred was able to complete his assigned mission and return with his film to Don Muang. As a further illustration of the determination within the Task Force to get the job done, on the ground as well as in the air, the maintenance men at Don Muang improvised a metal patch from a beer can to cover the hole through which the round had penetrated; they also found a way of repairing the electrical wiring temporarily for the flight back to Misawa where a permanent remedy kept the aircraft on the ground for six weeks. The pilots had every confidence in their maintenance support.

Not only did the Voodoo pilots have to contend now with hostile action, they were never immune from the risks inherent in their profession, flying itself, as Bob Gould was reminded while on TDY with the Able Mable force. It began during a turn-round at Tan Son Nhut, where he had landed to off-load his film. As with all Voodoo pilots he was well aware of the points system which governed tyre changes and now noted that one tyre would marginally exceed the limit during his return to Don Muang. A closer inspection suggested that it should survive one more landing and he duly departed for Bangkok. However, the tyre 'blew' during the landing run at Don Muang and Bob felt that the gear was going to collapse; that it

The 'Cotton Pickers' Arrive. RF-101 No 60051 arrives at Don Muang as the 15th TRS takes over Able Mable duties from the 45th TRS. Burt Waltz

did not was testimony to its strength. He managed to stop the aircraft in time and clear the runway, after another lesson for all to heed.

It was now clear that Able Mable was going to continue for the foreseeable future and it was decided that the two PACAF Voodoo squadrons should share the commitment on a six month rotation. Repeated requests for additional aircraft fell on deaf ears, and on 23 May 1962 the 15th TRS sent only four Voodoos to replace the 45th TRS detachment at Don Muang.

This was a very different operating environment from that with which most of the Voodoo pilots were accustomed. Heavy forestation and dense foliage concealed illusive targets and the results of air strikes in Bomb Damage Assessment (BDA) sorties, while area covers revealed little. Again, however, the main problem operating from Don Muang was the unpredictable weather, particularly during the monsoon season. Captain Burt Waltz of the 15thTRS recalled one 2 hour 15 minute trip to Northern Laos on which he logged 2 hours weather time. He had climbed to 30,000 ft, let down in cloud on time towards the first target, climbed back from safety height and done the same for the second and third targets, always failing to find clear air. When he did break out of cloud back at Bangkok he was only eight miles off track. Most of Burt's missions from there entailed single-ship, high-low-high profiles with no navigation aids available other than ADF, some limited radar control within 150 miles from base and (sometimes) a GCA back at Don Muang: *"It was all dead-reckoning and time/distance navigation and I usually cruise climbed on the way home (often from 400 miles), ending up at 43,000 ft"*. The Voodoos provided 'trade' for the Australian fighter pilots in their Mk 6 F-86s stationed at

RTAFB Ubon, who often intercepted them: *"barrel-rolling round us we tried to stay off the burble"*. Fuel conservation was imperative and often the returning pilots had to hope that they would not be 'sent around' in busy traffic.

Numerous camera permutations were evaluated during the conflict, in attempts to find the optimum configurations for SEA. There were calls for the installation of a T-11 mapping camera in the centre station, in order to up-date maps and charts, but demands for this service became excessive and the RF-101 proved to be too unstable a platform for the purpose. There were also trials with a 24-inch camera, alternative 36-inch systems, 3-inch and 6-inch KA-45s for vertical and oblique work, 6-inch Hycon KS-92 day/night framing cameras, a 3-inch KA-56 panoramic system and KA-18 high-speed strip cameras (the latter proving entirely unsuitable for SEA priorities). Each option had its supporters and opponents, according to specific, often conflicting interests. The small negatives produced by some cameras were very unpopular with army and air force customers and with the PIs, who were used to deriving their information from the larger formats produced by the KA-1s and KA-2s (9-inch x 18-inch and 9-inch square respectively). Harry Runge recalls that the KA-56 was 'particularly reviled to the point of uselessness' because of the size of its product, Very understandably, the pilots favoured those systems which offered the greatest flexibility in their tactics and best chance of survival.

The insurgent forces quickly realised that the USAF was very short of night recce assets and that they could move under cover of darkness almost with impunity; and this they did. However, the Voodoo did have a limited potential for night photography and in early 1962 an initiative had been taken in Project

169

'Toy Tiger' to make use of this. Two RF-101s were returned to the US for extensive modifications; a 6-inch forward oblique KA-45 went into the nose, a 3-inch KA-45 vertical camera and two 6-inch KA-45 oblique cameras replaced the KA-2s in the centre stations, while two 12-inch KA-45s, with special high speed bodies, took the place of the KA-1s in the aft compartment. A C-1 photoelectric flash detector replaced the B-2 terrain light detector, thereby denying automatic light settings. Eighty M-123 photoflash cartridges contained in an MB-7 pod (developed for the RF-84F) hung from a fuselage pylon between the 2 x 250 gallon external tanks to provide the necessary illumination. An APN-102/ASN-7 doppler navigation computer was also added which marginally improved navigation performance.

After delays in finding suitable film and cartridges the two Voodoos began night trials in-theatre with the new camera fit in the fall of 1962. Everything worked well mechanically but when the system was evaluated over the Mekong Delta the jungle was found to absorb too much light from the flash cartridges while paddy fields reflected too much; the PIs remained unhappy with the small negatives from the KA-45s and demands on the pilots were very high during the actual photo runs. Moreover, the cartridges provided insufficient light and the built-in two second delay illuminated an area behind the aircraft. Invariably, this type of photography required the RF-101 to fly at between 1,500 and 2,000 ft and at non-operational speeds, a very unattractive proposition in any defended areas. Before any decision could be reached on the use of Voodoos at night in SEA, events in Cuba forced the redeployment of Toy Tiger aircraft back to the United States.

Following successful offensives by the Pathet Lao in the Northern Laos, C-in-C Pacific Air Command (CINCPAC) activated Joint Task Force 116 (JTF-116) in May 1962, for the defence of Laos, and gave its commanding general operational control over all RF-101 operations in SEA. Anticipating that overflights of Laos might soon be banned, the Able Mable Task Force was called on to increase its sortie rate; this generated useful intelligence but against increasingly effective small arms fire, many Voodoos now returning damaged. On 14 August 1962, a 37-mm or 57-mm AAA round

Lucky Strike. Captain Tom O'Meara survived this hit on an Able Mable mission, but the starboard camera access door caused embarrassment when it was found by the Pathet Lao in Laos. Tom O'Meara

scored a direct hit on Captain Tom O'Meara's RF-101, detonating below his ejection seat, severing electrical and hydraulic lines and damaging an engine. Tom was able to nurse the aircraft back to Don Muang but the nose gear of his aircraft collapsed on landing, blocking the runway for two hours. It then transpired that the starboard camera access door had been blown off over Laos and found its way into the hands of the Pathet Lao, who used it as evidence that the US was operating over the country. Perhaps it was this incident and the State Department's embarrassment over the world-wide revelation that USAF Voodoos were operating out of Bangkok that denied O'Meara the plaudits he richly deserved; indeed it is rumoured that he was treated as a 'fall-guy'.

It was about this time that Burt Waltz also had his baptism of fire over Laos (Chapter 15), the experience making him even more conscious of his own combat philosophy (which made a great deal of common sense):

"Don't screw around at low level unless you have to; keep your speed up, keep changing heading, airspeed and height (unless you're on the target run); finish the photo run as soon as possible and get out of the area. Don't 'sight-see' or take 'happy snaps' and keep your head on the swivel".

Little did he know then that this would not always keep him out of trouble (Chapter Seventeen). No such advice was needed when it came to that other major commitment in SEA, looking after the many VIPs and other visitors to the Task Force, the squadron was also well up to that.

In November 1962, just as the 15th TRS was preparing to hand over to the 45th TRS at Don Muang, all overflights of Laos were suspended and when they resumed it would be with ever-changing height, routeing and other operating constraints. These restrictions would severely curtail essential freedoms in planning, flexibility in mission execution and the overall value inherent in RF-101 operations at a time when North Vietnam was increasing its infiltration into Laos and south across the Demilitarised Zone (DMZ) into South

Vietnam. With these areas now of vital interest but overflights of Cambodia prohibited, the Voodoos continued to route south of Cambodia until, in December 1962, the Able Mable force was redeployed to Tan Son Nhut, thereby halving transit flight times to their main operating areas.

With finite resources, priority given to Able Mable and very little easing in other commitments, the PACAF RF-101 force was now sorely stretched, but a plausible plan to replace the Tan Son Nhut force with ageing RF-84Fs, eminently suitable at this time for many operations in SEA, was rejected, as were initial requests for two more Voodoos from USAFE or TAC. So the Task Force was left to soldier on with four aircraft until April 1963 when CINCPAC ordered PACAF to provide two more aircraft from its own resources. The six aircraft were now employed increasingly in low level photography of large areas in the hope of finding lucrative targets, but heavy forestation made this unlikely. At the same time, the processing facilities and PIs were overwhelmed by the number of photographs then being produced daily.

The 15th TRS, now commanded by Major Alex Butterfield, took over from the 45th on 1 May 1963, with the CO and Captain Gene

Hearts and Minds. King Adulyadeh of Thailand well covered by a Voodoo's nose camera at Don Muang in 1962, his Queen preferring the port oblique. Captain Don Elwood, at his best, explains how it all works. Don Elwood

Morris going ahead to Tan Son Nhut to set things up. As the squadron's mobility officer, Gene was responsible for moving the six aircraft, their pilots and some 200 men to what would be their home for the next six months. He admits that: *"this was a big job for a young captain but I had two great sergeants working for me and they took care of me"*. It was ever thus. They worked hard for a week, living and flying with the 45th, and were ready on schedule for the ten transport aircraft bringing the rest of the detachment.

To celebrate their arrival, the officers spent their first evening taking refreshment in the Officers Club Bar at the Brinks Hotel. The hotel was in a 'rather spooky' downtown Saigon, three miles from the quarters to which they had to return before the curfew at 2200 hours and Gene recalls a race between the six pilots then present, each supposedly on the 'cyclo' (a motorcycle-powered rickshaw) of their choice. After arriving at their apartment the winner was soon forgotten when the pilots realised that one of their number, Captain George Hall, was absent and after several worrying hours they took a taxi back to the Brinks (in an even more spooky Saigon now under curfew) to find a disconsolate George sitting on the curb outside the hotel. It transpired that this new boy in town had selected a man-powered 'samlar' with which, hard as he pressed his man, he had no chance against the motorised cyclo. The driver then became lost and exhausted, George having to take his turn between the shafts to get them back to the Brinks.

The officers of the 15th TRS soon decided to improve their lifestyle, moving into a larger and more habitable villa closer to the airfield. There they hosted regular steak nights for old and new friends, including US Army advisers and 'Green Berets', many of them 'very sharp young captains and majors', with whom the pilots were able to exchange mutually interesting experiences and perspectives on the war. There is a well-worn military adage that anyone can be uncomfortable and the men of the 15th TRS, who would spend much of their time in PACAF on TDY in SEA were determined not to be guilty of that.

Saigon was still generally peaceful at this time, with only the highly sensitive areas closely guarded and few terrorist incidents to affect the social and domestic agendas. It was less so in the air but most missions involved photography of large areas of South Vietnam from high level, largely immune from AAA, and as yet there was no SAM threat or MiG fighters to worry about. The pilots were up to it, they enjoyed flying the first USAF fast-jets to operate in SEA, were confident in their abilities and cherished the uniqueness of their job. The 15th TRS was typical; they were then a bunch of highly experienced jet pilots, content with their lot and proud to belong to an elite. All this drew them together, a bunch of good friends who, in the words of one of them were 'as close as ticks on an old hound dog'. They benefited from the secrecy cloaking their role, thereby able to avoid difficult questions and demand priority in their requirements without too much explanation.

The 15th TRS men were not the only newcomers to Tan Son Nhut; two Martin RB-57Es, a version of the British Canberra, joined the Voodoo warriors there in May 1963. They were equipped with a variety of oblique and vertical cameras, had a night/infra red capability which the RF-101s could not match, better navigational equipment and a crew of two. In these early days they could fly at a relatively safe height but were slow and would become increasingly vulnerable to hostile air defences.

Recce pilots the world over were essentially individuals who believed they knew best how to satisfy the demands made on them. Accordingly, it was generally accepted that, given broad guidelines, each flight leader should then be left to plan his own missions. RF-101 pilots in SEA did not, therefore, take kindly to being ordered in great detail how to penetrate and egress hostile territory or cover their targets, particularly when it seemed that sometimes those issuing the orders were not personally or currently qualified in the role or sufficiently cognizant with the prevailing circumstances. Major Harry Runge, 15th TRS, remembers one tasking message which required a descent through cloud into mountainous terrain in the hope of emerging into clear air at the right start point for an east to west run down an infiltration route at low level. Unhappy with this suicidal plan the pilots very sensibly elected to fly the route in the reverse direction; this achieved the results required but incredibly it was not an end to the matter, the battle managers repeatedly calling for clarification on why they had not followed

Farewell Saigon. The 15th TRS ready to go after a six month TDY in Tan Son Nhut. Gene Morris

sound of gunfire and exploding bombs when President Ngo Dinh Diem was deposed and murdered, to be replaced by a military junta at the beginning of November 1963, this impressive show also marking the return of the 45th TRS to replace the 15th TRS at Tan Son Nhut. The assassination of US President Kennedy followed on 22 November perhaps presaging changes in political if not military strategies, but with an election facing the new President Lyndon Johnson in the following year the Voodoo men at the front noticed little change. In January 1964 Major General Joseph H Moore took over the 2nd Air Division, General Westmoreland becoming the head of Military Assistance Command. Publicly, it was announced that there was now 'light at the end of the tunnel' and that the war was turning in South Vietnam's favour but the Voodoo pilots saw it differently; many thought that it was rather more a turning point in a war from which their country could not easily extricate itself.

The 15th TRS took over from the 45th TRS at Tan Son Nhut again in May 1964, four of its six aircraft going first to Don Muang to take part, very successfully, in the SEATO Exercise Air Boon Choo as Reconnaissance Task Force (RTF) Bravo. At an impressive 500 ft and 480

'Jolly Green Giant'. Captain Dick Wood of the 15th TRS earned this name after trading his orange flying suit for this green version which belonged to an Australian pilot, while on the 1964 exercise Air Boon Choo in Thailand. Dick Wood

orders. Some matters were best left to the practitioners.

During the latter half of 1963 pairs of RF-101s were sent back to Don Muang at the request of the Royal Thai Government to carry out specific photographic tasks. Initially having to rely on their own photographic support and PIs they were later able to make use of the local PPC. The need for more air reconnaissance for the defence of South Vietnam was becoming ever more urgent, but collective pleas from the front line for some relaxation of restrictions on overflights of Laos and Cambodia were rejected.

In July 1963 the Able Mable Task Force was assigned to the 33rd Tactical Group at Tan Son Nhut, which then exercised control of all assigned reconnaissance assets through Detachment 1 commanded by the 2nd Air Division Reconnaissance Staff Officer. The senior RF-101 pilot served as the operations officer and the force was required to generate five sorties a day with one aircraft remaining on strip alert for any urgent tasks. The emphasis was now on oblique photography in attempts to reveal what was happening just across the border in Cambodia, but without violating that neutral airspace. Additionally, when the Toy Tiger aircraft returned to SEA in 1963 their limited night capability was subjected to further trials and modifications which eventually resulted in what some called 'acceptable' results. Others, particularly those who had to fly these potentially hazardous and often fruitless missions, may have seen it differently, but it was a case of needs must as the enemy continued to make maximum use of darkness.

The peace of Saigon was shattered by the

kts Harry Runge led the RTF back to Saigon at the end of Air Boon Choo, Captain Dick Wood in his flight earning the nickname 'Jolly Green Giant' having traded his orange flying suit for the more suitable green version worn by an Australian pilot on the exercise with them. Many of the squadron's pilots had already served their time in PACAF and returned to the United States but Alex Butterfield and Gene Morris were again part of the mixed team of old and new squadron members at Tan Son Nhut, Gene quick to observe on the changes that had taken place. On his first refresher flight there he noticed blocked roads and blown up bridges within 30 miles of Saigon and even spotted a Viet Cong soldier 'in black pyjamas' right out in the open on a road firing at him with a sub-machine gun. Things would be different this time. Immediately resuming their very social evening steak nights, the men of the 15th TRS learned from their local guests of Viet Cong successes in the surrounding countryside, of battalion-sized North Vietnamese units operating in the north of the country and of resupply columns infiltrating into all parts of South Vietnam via the notorious Ho Chi Minh Trail.

Surveillance along the Ho Chi Minh Trail, much of which was inaccessible when overflight of North Vietnam, Laos and Cambodia was denied, was a primary role for the RF-101s. The route extended from the Mu Gia Pass in North Vietnam, 300 miles south through Laos, along the heavily forested western slopes of the Annam Range and into Cambodia to feed a number of exit points into South Vietnam. During and since WW2, this crucial artery had been, and would continue to be steadily improved and expanded, to provide many alternative options for its users and a targeting nightmare for the Allies. By mid-1971, the route would consist of a labyrinth of some 2,000 miles of tracks capable of taking motor vehicles; up to 50,000 men and women, adept at the rapid repair of road surfaces and bridges after air strikes, maintained the network for use ultimately by a fleet of some 3,000 lorries, each perhaps capable of carrying four tons of supplies. The whole complex was defended by an estimated 600-700 AAA weapons of all calibres, many on high ground above the valleys and thus able to shoot down at low flying aircraft. Other than when these largely makeshift roads were rendered partially

impassable during the monsoon season, the route was in constant use when under low cloud cover and during the hours of darkness, more so when moonlight allowed vehicles to travel without lights. Sightings of major movement during daylight hours were understandably rare, while restrictions on tactics, typically an enforced minimum height of 10,000 ft, could render photography largely unprofitable; at that height neither eye nor camera could see those vehicles and personnel sheltering under foliage and trees lining a route. Low level oblique photography (known to the USAF airmen as 'dicing') was very hazardous and often prohibited, but when pilots found

Ho Chi Minh Trail. The network of tracks from North Vietnam into the South kept the Viet Cong and later the North Vietnamese Army well supplied. USAF

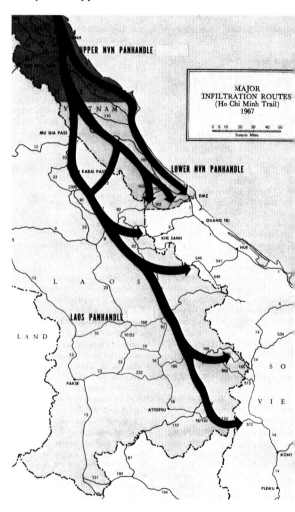

Truck Stop. This heavily camouflaged supply truck caught unawares on the Ho Chi Minh Trail. Gene Morris Collection

at Da Nang AB, where the runway was barely long enough for safety. At first, the USAF found itself unable to offer the obvious alternative of AAR but the 15th TRS came up with a solution. Gene Morris got the pilot of a visiting USN F-8 to see whether his aircraft could be refuelled through its probe and the basket used to check the AAR system of the Voodoo. The refuelling went without a hitch, proving that the Voodoo's system was compatible with that of the USN's A-3B and A-4 tankers already in daily use over the Gulf of Tonkin. Some smooth talking by Gene's flight commander, Captain George Hall (who had attended the USN Naval Academy and could speak their language), quickly secured agreement that the USN would provide tankers for the Voodoos. Such were relationships between the services at the working level. Shortly thereafter, the USAF found it possible to make their KB-50 tankers available.

Three Able Mable RF-101C aircraft were now retrofitted with KA-45 cameras in the centre camera compartment. These were more suitable for high speed, low level work but the smaller, four-and-a-half square inch negatives remained very unpopular with the PIs. With the demand for air recce continuing to rise, the number of RF-101s committed to Able Mable was increased in May.

The loss of a USN RF-8 and an F-8 to hostile

good reason to abrogate this rule, profitable targets were revealed.

In the spring of 1964 the Pathet Lao occupied the PDJ, sending the legitimate, neutralist government into crisis and persuading the Laotian Premier, Souvanna Phouma, to authorise the United States to carry out recce sorties over the besieged areas. To that end the 'Yankee Team Programme' was activated, giving the Tan Son Nhut Voodoos and US Navy (USN) RF-8s four objectives. They were to collect timely intelligence for friendly forces, substantiate North Vietnam's infiltration, provide a psychological boost to Laos and demonstrate United States determination to remain in theatre as long as North Vietnamese aggression threatened peace. Inter alia, this would provide the ICC with definitive proof of the Pathet Lao offensive against neutralist Laos in the PDJ.

The Yankee Team sorties proved very productive, with the Voodoo pilots now reporting tanks, artillery and supply trucks in strength. However, some lengthy missions required time-consuming fuel stops

Improvisation. Air-to-air refuelling for the 15th TRS, courtesy the USN and resulting from a local initiative at Tan Son Nhut, greatly improved mission flexibility. USAF

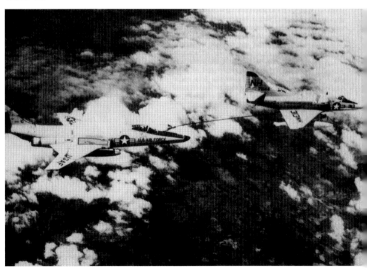

fire over the PDJ in June led to a retaliatory strike by F-100s on AAA sites at Xieng Khouang and this, together with sightings of an increasing number of 57-mm AAA with Firecan gun control radars in Laos, prompted further heated debate on whether, how many and in what manner recce sorties should continue over Laos. The result was a stop-go programme of missions, some escorted and all to be flown on strict guidelines. Now the RF-101s were also committed to daily weather recces, their pilots deemed to be best able to judge the suitability of conditions for their specialised missions. This programme consumed valuable flying hours but helped to increase the number of productive sorties. For reasons not made clear but presumably political, these single 'weather ships' were not allowed to switch on their cameras despite transiting areas of interest at high level.

Harry Runge likened the weather in which they were operating, a perpetual front moving up and down seasonally in the South China Sea, to that which he and other fellow pilots had experienced in Europe. In the summer monsoons, heavy cumulus often developed during afternoons into 'thunder bumpers' while the winter monsoons were dominated by stratus and low ceilings. As one who flew the infamous weather sorties in SEA, Harry

described breaking out under the cloud into the Laotian 'karst' (limestone hills very much like cave stalactites) as:

"really spooky, a prehistoric scene in which it would not have been surprising to see a pterodactyl on your wing. Just flying straight and level at 480 kts you could generate contrails off the wing-tips the humidity being that high. On the maps available many areas covering the all-important mountainous regions on the borders of North Vietnam with Laos and China were marked 'relief data incomplete'. Moreover, when 'slash and burn' farming took place in the dry season with negligible winds at medium and high levels, smoke and haze reduced the horizontal and oblique visibility to near zero (you could smell the smoke at 18,000ft). Vertical visibility was excellent but this provided only fleeting glimpses of landmarks and targets".

Following unprovoked attacks on two USN destroyers by North Vietnamese torpedo boats in the first week of August 1964 contingency plans were laid for retaliatory raids on the North if such aggression was repeated. The PACAF RF-101 force was also reinforced by six additional Voodoos and pilots on TDY from the 20th TRS at Shaw AFB and two replacement aircraft. Four of these aircraft and

Karst Country. The enemy could be hard to find in this prehistoric-like terrain. Nick Pishvanov

two from Misawa were then ordered to join the Able Mable force, thereby increasing its size to 18 aircraft. With thousands more US soldiers, airmen and aircraft pouring into South Vietnam and Thailand, this was now big business and things would soon escalate further. Also in August high-flying U2s revealed that MiG-15s and 17s had arrived at the main operating base of Phuc Yen in North Vietnam. This increase in the risk to unarmed Voodoos and the distance of tasks in Northern Laos renewed calls for some recce missions to be escorted by suitably armed F-100s (although the fighter's range and speed was not compatible with that of the Voodoo) and for RF-101s to be based closer to primary target areas. In October 1964 Yankee Team sorties were authorised over northern Laos in an area designated 'Barrel Roll'.

The camera configuration in all SEA RF-101s was now modified to Project 1181 standard. This replaced the KA-2 in the forward oblique station with a six-inch focal length Hycon KS-72 framing camera which could take six frames/second at focal plane shutter speeds of up to 1/4000 of a second for day photography and, for night work, a maximum between-the-lens shutter speed of one-hundredth of a second. Two more six-inch focal length KS-72s replaced the two side oblique KA-2s in the centre station. These new cameras had many teething troubles, mainly due to moisture ingress and problems with the film drive mechanisms, but by mid-1965 modifications

First Loss. On 21 November 1964, Captain Burt Waltz ejected safely and was rescued after his RF-101, 60230 was shot down by gunfire over Laos. Burt Waltz

would greatly improve their reliability. However, the smaller, 4.5 inch square negatives remained very unpopular. Essentially for low level, a panoramic KA-56A camera replaced the vertical KA-2; this used a rotating prism to take horizon-to-horizon photographs at up to six frames/second with shutter speeds of 1/5000 of a second. Both KS-72 and KA-56s had built-in image motion compensation. The KA-1, 36-inch split vertical system was retained in the rear station. The 45th TRS aircraft were modified first but this took time, causing some delay in completing the changeover from the 15th to the 45th TRS scheduled for 1 November 1964.

The 15th TRS became the first unit to lose a Voodoo to hostile action when ground fire downed the RF-101C 60230 flown by Burt Waltz in the Ban Phan Nop area of Laos on 21 November 1964. This signalled a dangerous new phase in the conflict. Burt's story is told in Chapter Seventeen.

At the beginning of 1965, for the first time in many months, most of the 15th TRS was back at Kadena AB, their aircraft now rotating through the depot in the United States for the Project 1181 modifications. Meanwhile, the 45th TRS had little time to settle at Tan Son Nhut before a significant date in the SEA conflict, 7 February 1965, the day the Viet Cong attacked a military detachment at Pleiku, killing eight Americans and wounding many more. President Johnson responded to this by removing all restrictions on air operations in South Vietnam, and went further when the communists attacked the US Army barracks at Qui Nhon, killing 23 more Americans, in authorising retaliatory raids leading to Operation Rolling Thunder. This involved selective and graduated bombing of North Vietnam (which was said by some 'didn't roll and wasn't particularly thunderous').

Bob Gould, serving on TDY with the Military Assistance Command Vietnam (MACV) but flying at Tan Son Nhut with the 45th TRS, created a little war of his own. With more than a little encouragement from his army hosts, and at some risk from friend and foe alike but under the guise of 'opportunity', he tended to add the odd unofficial request to his assigned target list. On one mission he nearly got more than he had bargained for when photographing suspicious 'graves' in several passes at low level, which sent locals 'running in all directions'. The photographs confirmed MACV suspicions that these graves were gun emplacements and that the 'streaks' clearly seen on the prints (but not noticed by Bob in the cockpit) were tracer bullets. Woe betide him had he taken a hit while covering this untasked 'target of opportunity',but he did not. Fortune favours the brave.

The single base at Tan Son Nhut for the SEA RF-101force was no longer adequate to meet the fast escalating demands on it and a decision was made to establish a second.

CHAPTER TEN
THE CUBAN ADVENTURE

'If at any time the Communist build-up in Cuba were to endanger or interfere with our security in any way......then this country will do whatever must be done to protect its own security and that of its allies.'

President John F Kennedy - 13 September 1962

On the other side of the world East and West were brought to the brink of global war in 1962 when the Russian Premier Nikita Khruschev began to send surface-to-surface, Medium-Range Ballistic Missiles (MRBMs) to Cuba. Weapons such as these, at sites less than 100 miles from the USA, were capable of delivering nuclear warheads deep into Continental USA. This was a step too far for President John F Kennedy; military alert states were raised throughout the USA and forces rushed to the Southern States.

The recce photos which first alerted the Americans to this imminent danger came from high flying U-2 aircraft. When one of these was brought down by an SA-2 SAM and the pilot Major Rudolph Anderson killed, tactical reconnaissance aircraft were deployed to monitor developments on the island, minute-to-minute. This force comprised USAF RF-101s and USN RF-8A Crusaders (originally F8U-1Ps).

The Voodoos came from the 363rd TRW, Shaw AFB, a mix of aircraft and pilots from the 20th TRS, 29th TRS and 4414th CCTS, under the command of Colonel Arthur McCartan. Sound guidance was on offer from Major Jack Nelson, the commander of the 4414th CCTS but assigned to Wing Operations, with Captain Rich Richardson, recently back from the 18th TRS at Laon, among those on hand to assist him. Rich remembers that they were left with very little authority at their level, detailed direction and target selections coming from high above. The RF-101s were deployed from Shaw with very little notice to MacDill AFB, Florida, where they were joined by six more aircraft and ten pilots of the 29th TRS which had been on TDY at Brooks AFB, Alabama. It was all hands to the pump, with Captains Fred

Muesegaes, Jim Frank and Ray Tiffault withdrawn immediately from the Squadron Officers School at Maxwell AFB, Alabama, and ordered to return to Shaw before continuing on to MacDill. Fred took his first reorientation flight in the RF-101on 29 October 1962, after six weeks on the ground, and was ready to go to war.

MacDill was crowded with some 250 jets: RF-101s, F-84s, F-100s and RB-66s (an impressive sight when they all taxied out to rehearse a mass strike) and exuded a palpable sense of excitement. Howard Myli remembered that, as he sat in the hot Florida sun for four hours one afternoon at cockpit alert, a very senior officer mounted the ladder to tell him;

"to keep in mind that the base might not be there when he returned and to think about the possibility of having to land somewhere else." As Howard said *"that kind of guy got my attention!"*

With the whole operation shrouded in secrecy, the pilots were not allowed off base for the first three weeks of the deployment, so the Officers' Club became a very busy, not to say rowdy place.

Fred Muesegaes recalls that there was some dissatisfaction at the higher command levels with the quality of photographs taken initially by the RF-101s, there being too much image motion on the Voodoo's 9-inch square prints when compared with those produced by the USN with their 4.5 inch square formats. Accordingly, some of the RF-101s were rotated through Chicago Aerial works in Illinois to have their standard fit replaced overnight with more suitable cameras for the low level, high speed work needed over Cuba.

In addition to the experience being gained in SEA, the Cuban operation provided another

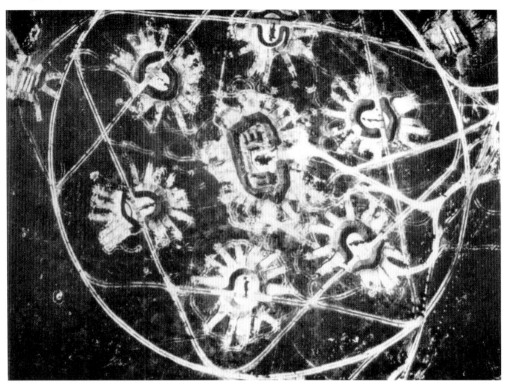

Above & below: Definitive Evidence. Photographs proved that Russia was deploying Intermediate and Medium Range Ballistic Missiles (I/MRBM), protected by SA-2 SAM Sites in Cuba. Shaw AFB

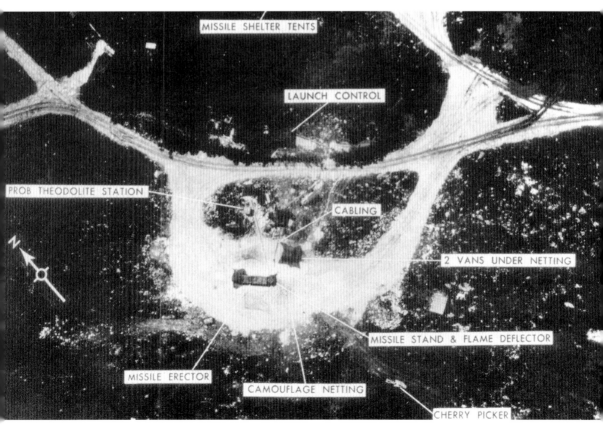

salutary test of the RF-101's effectiveness in a hostile environment, for the crews and those who had operational control, things having not always gone well at the start. Typically, one order from on high called for a Voodoo to scream overhead a missile site at supersonic speed, 'to knock down the camouflage netting with the plane's supersonic boom'. The local Voodoo chiefs argued that this was not credible and the order was rescinded.

Here was a sledgehammer waiting to crack a nut, but waiting was the watchword for the recce pilots at MacDill, there were just too many pilots chasing too few tasks, some getting the chance to fly over Cuba once or twice only. When they did, it could be exciting. Pairs of aircraft would fly at very high speeds and ultra low level, well below the minimum height for the SA-2 missiles but within the capability of the multitude of AAA units waiting to greet them. There were also MiG-17 fighters and a sprinkling of MiG-21s on the island; the former had little chance of catching the fast-flying Voodoos but the MiG-21s could have posed a threat had they been in the right place at the right time. In the event very few were seen in the air and the author can find no reports of hostile interceptions.

Fred Muesegaes flew all his combat missions over the eastern and central parts of the island, long trips which required one air refuelling (from a KC-135 tanker) on the outbound high level leg of a high-low-high profile. The Voodoos pilots would attempt to avoid detection from Cuba's early warning radar by descending to low level outside that cover, but the Voodoo's radar warning receiver picked up the tell-tale signs that they had been spotted well before they crossed the coast at low level. In an interesting role for the RF-101's wire recorder (not often used for its primary purpose of recording real time visual sightings), these hostile radar signals were recorded for later analysis of the systems being employed against them.

With dead-reckoning the only means of navigation available to the pilots, the run in to a chosen point on the coast after a long inbound leg over the featureless sea at low level and high speed could be a hit or miss affair but the Voodoo pilots were up to it. Their targets then included ships, ports, SAM sites, airfields, military facilities, communications centres, and of course the MRBM sites themselves to prove

that work was continuing apace.

The author can vouch for the fact that Howard Myli (one of that initial batch of 'first tourists' to attend the RF-101 school at Shaw AFB) confounded those critics who believed that previous operational, fast jet experience was necessary to cope with the Voodoo and its role, by achieving good results on the course and continuing this trend on his squadron assignments. One of his trips over Cuba with the 29th TRS proved the point. He had taken off as No 2 to Captain Bill Bernert for an unusually long trip, again involving air-refuelling both ways and covering 12 targets. In the event, Bill failed to take on fuel over the Bahamas and Howard took the lead, the 'spare', flown by his operations officer, slotting in as his wingman. The pair covered eight of twelve difficult targets in weather which called for many diversions from the planned route, as they braved sporadic gunfire before heading for home. It was then that Howard's heading indicator failed and he had to hand over the lead to his wingman, for a weather diversion into Tampa AFB, Florida, itself down to 'minimums'. This highly successful mission was immediately and properly recognised but, in one of those cruel ironies, the officer who wrote up the recommendations had seen the pair taxi in and assumed that the senior person in the lead had led throughout. So it was that the operations officer was awarded a Distinguished Flying Cross (DFC) and Howard an Air Medal.

Fred Muesegaes flew his last combat mission, one of the final and longest tactical recce sorties over the island, on 15 November 1962, in one of two Voodoos refuelling in the air outbound over the Bahamas before 'criss-crossing' the island for 1 hour 15 minutes (which required them to take on fuel a second time on the way back to Florida). As they approached Guantanamo Bay Fred spotted many troops running for their gun emplacements and thought; "here it comes - but then I saw them all waving so I rocked my wings in return - not all Cubans were hostile".

Good lessons, bad practices and calculated risks characterised the Cuban experience. Lieutenant Ross Shaw was credited with challenging the TAC Commander, the formidable General Sweeney, at the post-operation wash-up on the argument for camouflaging the 'shiny and easy to see' Voodoos and on the give-away 'airline time

Objective Achieved. After the momentous events of October 1962, air reconnaissance showed that the threatening missiles at San Cristobal had been removed from Cuba. USAF

scheduling of missions'. Ross achieved his aims, if the end results were slow in coming. When opposition to the recce flights was found to be surprisingly light, understandable and laudable determination to meet the demands of the hierarchy had sometimes put generally accepted good practices at risk, typically the need to confine target runs in hostile airspace to one pass and use the least vulnerable operational profiles. One pilot is said to have reported over the radio, for all to hear, that he was going to make further passes or '360s'over one target, having already alerted all the defences; he then 'went sightseeing' over Havana, thereby exceeding his predicted flight time and causing great concern right up to the lofty heights of Washington DC. Captain Dewey Hemphill also remembers that on his one and only mission over Cuba, on the wing of Captain John Leaphart, little thought was given to the air defences when completing their tasks, as they made repeated passes over some targets. At one of these, an airfield, the PIs wanted them to 'look into the hangars', which required the pair (whose aircraft were still equipped with the original KA-2 oblique cameras) to descend to below a 200 ft cloud and reduce speed to 250 kts with flaps down, a very unhealthy practice

in war. Dewey reported that the nose warning light of his radar warning receiver came on as they approached the airfield and changed to a tail warning as they departed but that 'nothing else happened beyond heavy breathing'. He opined that there was a greater danger from the powers that be in missing a target or not getting the right 'composure' than there was of being shot down taking this 'unprofessional' chance. In any event all these calculated risks, which could have had fatal consequences in an increasingly hostile SEA, paid off handsomely over Cuba and helped determine the successful outcome to this dangerous brinkmanship. A great deal of useful information had been gathered by the recce aircraft for the politicians and military men, ultimately confirming that the missiles had been removed from Cuba, the RF-101s having flown 82 combat missions over Cuba between 26 October and 15 November 1962 without loss. There were reports of flak but no evidence of damage to its aircraft and there were no exchanges with the MiGs. All this brought great credit on the Voodoo men of Shaw, recognised formally when President Kennedy presented the 363rd TRW with an Outstanding Unit Award at Holmestead AFB on 26 November 1962.

Above & below: Well Done. The 363rd TRW paraded at Holmestead AFB at the end of the Cuban crisis, for President John F Kennedy's presentation of an Outstanding Achievement Award. USAF & Shaw AFB

*Aunt Mary. The 363rd TRW remained ready
for further problems over Cuba with the
contingency exercise 'Aunt Mary', which
rehearsed the rapid collection and
dissemination of information by RF-101s.*

Shaw AFB

So ended the Cuban Crisis of 1962. The
Soviet Union bowed to the intense United States
and international pressure and withdrew the
missiles from the island, it is believed in a 'quid
pro quo' involving the removal of US missiles
from Turkey. However, there was no knowing
whether such provocation might be repeated so
a contingency plan 'Aunt Mary' was set up in
1963. This called for three pairs of Voodoos
and their pilots to stand by at Shaw for possible
commitment over Cuba again at very short
notice. An associated training programme
tested the pilots against equivalent targets in
south east USA and all aspects of the
supporting organisation in the procedures
which would be adopted should the need arise.
Both the 20th and 29th TRS took part in Aunt
Mary - but they were never used in earnest.

The operations over Cuba had exposed
shortcomings in the overall recce capability of
the RF-101 force and in so doing had helped
prepare everyone concerned for the greater
demands that would not now be long in
coming, back on the other side of the world.

CHAPTER ELEVEN
THE YEAR OF THE PYTHON AND BUSINESS AS USUAL FOR ABLE MABLE

'Home is where you make it'

With the growing need for more air reconnaissance over SEA and the prospect of offensive operations in North Vietnam, coupled with the distances the Able Mable Voodoos had to fly from Tan Son Nhut and congestion on that airfield, made the requirement for a second base closer to the main action ever more urgent, and RTAFB Udorn became the airfield of choice.

On the face of it, while just satisfactory for the RT-33 Field Goal missions (Chapter Eight), Udorn seemed quite unsuitable for the big Voodoos. Located in a huge, low-lying bowl, it was one vast watershed with several wide and shallow pools from which water never seemed to drain completely and which refilled quickly when torrential rains poured down from the towering cumulonimbus clouds in the summer monsoon season. In the hot, dry autumn weeks which followed, much of the base dried out to leave a surface layer of red dust driven by the winds to pervade all. The runway was only 7,500 ft long and 75 ft wide, with the three 25 ft centre panels often flooded and the whole surface notoriously slippery; there were no overruns or arrester gears, a deep ditch crossed one threshold while trees obstructed the other, and the parallel taxiway could not be used for RF-101 take-offs or landings. Few of the necessary support facilities existed and the buildings left by the Japanese would require much attention to render them habitable. That said, with innovation, hard work and all-important backing from on high, it was believed that the base could become adequate for its new purpose.

The plan called for the 45th TRS to maintain eight RF-101s at Tan Son Nhut (and be ready to add four more aircraft if needed), for employment primarily over South Vietnam and Southern Laos and, with a target date of 1 April 1965, the 15th TRS to begin operating six Voodoos at a refurbished RTAFB Udorn. Throughout the first year the Udorn force would be headed by the 15th TRS but include resources from the 363rd TFW Composite Reconnaissance Unit (CRU) at Shaw AFB. Also, from late 1965 some pilots from the 45th TRS would be attached on TDY to maintain the required force and experience levels as pilots from the 15th TRS ended their tours. Logistical support was to be provided by the 18th TFW and direct operational control would be exercised by the 2nd AD at Tan Son Nhut.

It was in mid-December 1964 that the 15th TRS first heard officially that it was to pioneer operations at Udorn AB and Captain Gene Morris, the squadron's mobility officer, was detailed to move there at the beginning of 1965 to assess what needed to be done and to put the necessary action in hand to make the base ready for the Voodoos 'as soon as possible'. This was another tall order for the young captain but he was up to it.

Remembering his Abel Mable experience Gene chose two senior sergeants to support him, one a specialist in civil engineering the other in Voodoo maintenance. The three of them flew to Udorn on a C-118 with $50,000 for immediate expenses and a promise that everything needed would be provided at speed. Before landing they persuaded the pilot to circle the base so that they could get a feel for its layout and immediate local area, but there was little to see other than a vast area of red soil, or laterite (an excellent sub-base for the construction to come). Most heartening, however, was sight of the Air America unit which had been so helpful to the Field Goal team and as soon as they had landed one of its

Trail Blazer. Captain Gene Morris headed the 15 TRS advanced party to Udorn. Gene Morris

Improvisation. Multipurpose elephants made Udorn AB what it was. Gene Morris

pilots told the trio what they needed to know first and then took them to the only hotel in the local town of Udorn. They found the Thais very friendly and the hotel acceptable, except for continuously excessive noise, and after a sleepless night they were up at 0600 hours to take a taxi for their initial recce of the base. Again Air America was on hand, one of its helicopter pilots, Ed Reed, telling how he had recently rescued Burt Waltz after he had ejected from his Voodoo near the Mu Gia Pass (Chapter Nine). The airline's director of operations proved invaluable, offering to provide the water essential for drinking, washing and photo processing, together with the loan of an English-speaking Thai construction expert. With his help initial building requirements were identified and planned, the work beginning at once on power plants, concrete pans, aircraft shelters, maintenance and domestic facilities. To oversee these projects Gene called for a US civil engineering section to join the advance party and true to the promises made they arrived

within two weeks. He then went back to Kadena to finalise the deployment plans and returned to Udorn on 6 March 1965 with two officers from the 363rd CRU and an NCO from the 18th Organisational Maintenance Squadron to supervise work on the base. They were soon joined by Gene's flight commander, Captain George Hall, who would help ensure that everything was ready for the Voodoos by 1 April 1965.

With some 100 Thai workers (75% of them women) five elephants and one ancient Japanese roller left over from WW2, full co-operation from the USAF and Air America, work proceeded at a remarkable pace. Operational, domestic, storage and even recreational facilities sprung up almost overnight, as did a 'tent city' for the 500 or so air force personnel who would man the new force initially. As the necessary buildings became available the service population of the

'Hands-On'. It was all hands to the pump to get Udorn AB up and running for the Voodoos, Gene Morris doing his bit on a WW2 Japanese roller. Gene Morris

base rose to 5,000 and long lines of diesel-powered electric generators thundered away, belching smoke day and night to provide lighting, air conditioning et al. All this would serve the purpose, but it would be no paradise.

A tribute to enterprise and hard work, Udorn was ready as promised on 1 April 1965; indeed the first four Voodoos from the 15th TRS, led by the squadron commander, Lieutenant Colonel Robert Crabtree, arrived on 31 March. The remaining two followed on 1 April, led by Lieutenant Commander Burton Larkins, a USN exchange pilot who had accompanied a supplementary force from the 363rd TRW. The Green Pythons, as they became known (distinguishing themselves from the Able Mable force at Tan Son Nhut) were up and running, George Hall and Gene Morris flying the first sorties from Udorn on Yankee Team missions on 1 April 1965. The Pythons would soon get to know the local area well.

The situation in SEA was deteriorating. South Vietnamese forces were unable to stem the steady advance south of the North Vietnamese and the US was now bolstering the defences with thousands more troops, deploying many aircraft of all types into the theatre and increasing its naval presence in the South China Sea. With very little flow of traffic down the Ho Chi Minh Trail during daylight hours, other than when it was concealed under low cloud, night activity, subterfuge in camouflage and deception along the route increased to unprecedented levels. Hostile troops were able to assemble in huge numbers with their equipment in the open and for all to see just over the border in North Vietnam, Gene Morris among many frustrated by such sights and the constraints which limited their operations. He firmly believed that it would be necessary to bomb the many sources of the problem in the North, and the sooner the better. However, the war was being driven by political influences and detailed management at the highest levels in the United States, determined in part by the great fear that

Cotton Pickers Arrive. One of the first RF-101s to arrive at Udorn, resplendent here in its new warpaint. Gene Morris

Communist China would be drawn into the war, while corruption in the South Vietnamese political and military hierarchies led to weaknesses in that country's contribution to its own defence.

A limited number of reconnaissance sorties over North Vietnam was authorised by the Joint Chiefs of Staff (JCS) in March 1965 but the missions would be subject to constantly changing and often inhibiting restrictions, such a minimum height of 10,000 ft in the Blue Tree programme. The nature of RF-101 reconnaissance to be provided in support of retaliatory raids in the North was outlined in HQ 2nd AD Operation Order Racing Motor, dated February 1965. This included guidance on RF-101 weather recces, escorted recce

Taxi! Captain Tom Malone, takes a slow ride from his fast-jet. Gene Morris

sorties, Voodoo pathfinder, pre-strike and BDA missions but it was quickly seen to be flawed in its detail. It was also now that the laborious, time-consuming and often hard to understand hierarchal involvement in the management of targeting and tasking became really evident. Missions over the North were very tightly controlled with many 'no-go' areas, rigid regulations and the threat of dire consequences for any transgressions or personal initiatives on the part of the crews involved, however strong the provocation or military justification. When a supply ship fired on US fighters passing harmlessly overhead and the pilots returned fire, they were dealt with very severely. Such were the rules that every target and the weapons to be used against it had to be approved by President Johnson himself in the Situation Room at the White House. The President passed his decisions to Defence Secretary McNamara who relayed them to the Pentagon, from whence they went to CINCPAC in Hawaii where they were 'fragged' (separated into fragments of an operation order) and passed to the 2nd AD in Saigon for allocation to USN, USAF or VNAF units at the front. Recommendations could be made from bottom up but with time so often the essence any approval could well come too late for it to be effective; there could be no question of reacting to fleeting targets of opportunity before they disappeared from view. The frustrations among recce and strike crews reached new heights when they sighted shiploads of Soviet guns and missiles unloading with impunity in Haiphong harbour while MiG fighters, which would be troublesome in the air later, could have been destroyed on the ground had attacks on the airfields been permitted. Likewise, allied soldiers in the land battle had to face an enemy re-equipped with the many basic necessities, supplies which could have been destroyed at source.

There were also those who came to think that BDA was as much about identifying those responsible for collateral damage caused by inaccurate bombing as assessing the damage to targets, and the frequent inquisitions did nothing for the morale of aircrew who were risking their lives to do their duty. In this context, Captain 'Norm' Huggins remembers meeting Major 'M', an F-105 pilot operating out of RTAFB Korat, telling him: *"They're accusing me of dropping my bombs in the DMZ so I'm going to quit and join the communist party"* Not a man to forsake his friends, Norm flew off at once in his Voodoo, over the DMZ and into North Vietnam at low level to take definitive photographs of the craters left by M where he had claimed, thus exonerating him from the alleged crime. Norm heard later that M had subsequently 'buzzed' the Air Force Academy in Colorado, supersonic at low level, shattering many a window therein, so perhaps he was no paragon.

Whether issued to the Green Pythons at Udorn or Able Mable at Tan Son Nhut, frags were suitably dispersed among the squadrons as required, with squadron executives then allocating missions to pilots, or pairs of pilots if that was the policy prevailing at the time, to the experienced and less experienced according to the nature of the task. However, many arrived too late in the evening for the pilots involved to carry out preparatory planning, sometimes leaving them with insufficient time the following morning to plan adequately for particularly demanding low level missions before early take-offs (two hours was normally allowed). The frag order specified the scale required, from which pilots could determine the height to fly, but this was not always adhered to if weather or hostile action rendered this impractical or imprudent. The pilots would then consider their options, seeking to remain concealed from the defences as long as possible by using low level ingress and terrain masking, taking advice from the more experienced, the weather forecasters and intelligence sources on defences, et al, before selecting their route and heights to fly. The tactics necessarily evolved as familiarity with the North Vietnamese defences increased and personal experience grew, but in mid-1965 they were seriously inhibited in their routing over North Vietnam by three prohibited areas, a 30 nm radius of the centre of Hanoi (unless specifically tasked within this zone), a 10 nm radius of Haiphong and within 30 miles of the border with China. After all this personal preparation pilots would receive a final briefing from the duty operations officer in Python Operations before walking to their aircraft. Both Python and Able Mable pilots would soon get to know their operating areas well.

If tasks were posted on the previous evening, the pilots would react in one of several ways, some concealing their emotions better than

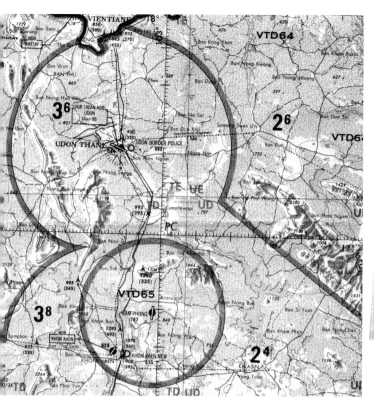

Python Country. *Most Voodoo pilots who served in SEA would have got to know this map of the area around Udorn AB well.* Harry Runge

MISSION BRIEFING

1. MISSION AND CALL SIGN
2. ACFT ASGMT - STATUS - CAMERA CONFIG
3. WEATHER (TERMINAL, ALTERNATE)
4. AIRFIELD STATUS
5. ACTIVE RUNWAY
6. TAKE-OFF ROLL
7. SPECIAL NOTICES
8. TIME HACK
9. ISSUE AUTHENTICATION
10. PERS GEAR, BLOOD CHIT, SANITIZED
11. PIF #2
12. TIME ENROUTE - RTE ON INTELL BD
13. RESTRICTED AREAS
    VIENTIANE
    LUANG PRABANG
    ARTILLERY RANGE
    SURIN (14°52'N 103°28'E) 20NM
    RADIUS - ALT RESTRICT UNLIM

Final Call. *Lengthy mission preparation ended with a final update in squadron 'Ops'.* Don Karges

Action Station. *Missions began and ended at Green Python Operations.* Norman Huggins

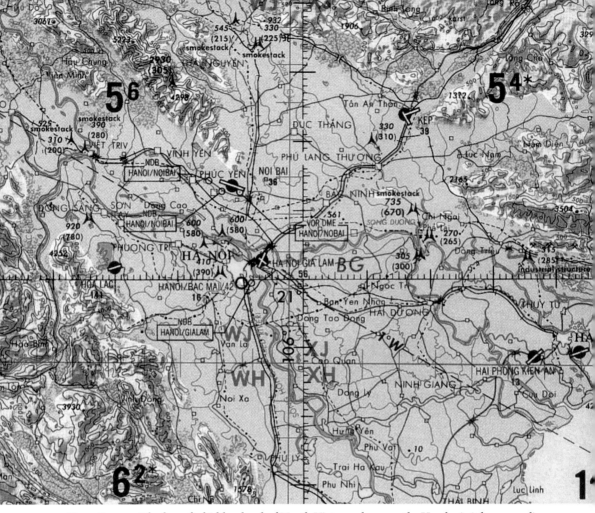

Open Season. The long forbidden land of North Vietnam became the Voodoo's 'playground' from March 1965. Harry Runge

others. One might shrug his shoulders and drift towards the bar, another go off to meditate quietly on his own. Thereafter, they would either sleep soundly, fitfully or not at all. When it came to the mission itself they would all do their duty, although some admitted that when the pressure was high they were not always at their best; this was, after all, the greatest test of the human mind that most would ever face in their lives. 'Milk runs' in South Vietnam came as a relief , but these too could be far from easy.

When strikes were authorised the Voodoos would often photograph the target on the previous day to help the bomber pilots in their planning, or they might precede the strike force to report on the weather and take pre-strike photographs. Also, with their reputation for special expertise in low level navigation, they were sometimes tasked to lead the fighter bombers to their targets, much to the chagrin of

the more experienced F-105 and F-4 pilots. One 'Thud' pilot remembers, rather reluctantly, being taken to his target by 15th TRS RF-101s but that later: *"they were allowed to stay out late, vote, carry a gun and get married without the adult supervision of the recce guys"*. Say no more. When they did accompany the bombers the Voodoo pilots might be required to seek out and pass on the exact positions of the AAA defences and, if fuel permitted, remain in the area to take the requisite BDA photographs after the dust and smoke had settled. They knew that if they failed in this other Voodoo pilots would have to be called to the area for BDA - when angry defences would be ready and waiting for them.

Many unsung heroes worked tirelessly in the background to ensure the maximum possible returns from the recce sorties and the survival of the pilots. To this end the Air Intelligence

Voodoo Pathfinders. Not all F-105 'Thud' pilots appreciated being led to their targets by RF-101s. Don Karges

Mixed Force. Was this Voodoo leading or being escorted to the target by F-4s?
USAF via Harry Runge

Section was crucial and for the Pythons at Udorn the responsibility fell to their Intelligence Officer Captain George Davenport; he had to ensure that the stringent requirements for pre-flight and post-mission debriefing were strictly adhered to. Their work on the night shift began in earnest as soon as a task was received, with the preparation of comprehensive briefing material, updates to the intelligence scenario, target material, threats likely to be encountered and reminders of current safe areas, escape and evasion facilities and procedures. Overnight, they had to compile records of all the previous day's missions within 18 hours of the last sortie landing, before briefing pilots scheduled for the early sorties and handing over to the day shift, normally at about 0730 hours. There was no let-up in pressure on the day shift, especially if 'unusual sighting' or 'incident' reports (which

could run to four pages) had to be raised. In addition to this routine intelligence staff would give periodic, collective briefings to the pilots on developments in hostile defences, updates on the capabilities of SA-2 missile systems, the SAM order of battle and all aspects of electronic warfare. Recordings of radar signals collected over hostile territory were replayed repeatedly on the ground to help pilots recognise their signatures when back in combat. So it was a busy life for the Air Intelligence Section, as it was for the essential photographic back-up described in detail in Chapter Twenty, which operated at Udorn in far from ideal conditions. They were but two elements of the total support package for the RF-101 force.

On 29 April 1965, Able Mable pilots from Tan Son Nhut used the Voodoo's active ECM for the first time in North Vietnam when three Voodoos, each equipped with four QRC-160 pods, accompanied a Rolling Thunder mission. The effectiveness of this jamming was inconclusive, but it did divert valuable recce resources from their primary role, while the increased drag seriously affected the aircraft's speed and manoeuvrability. (Chapter Sixteen)

Emerging statistics soon made it clear that if the RF-101 pilots involved continued on the current rate of TDYs to SEA, with a growing proportion of their missions flown over the North, they were unlikely to survive their statutory tours at Kadena and Misawa. It came as no surprise to the author that Captain Howard Davis, once a colleague at Shaw AFB, and Captain Tom Malone, both of whom had already flown many missions in SEA, were not slow in bringing this to the attention of a general visiting Udorn. How much they helped to initiate a dramatic change of policy cannot

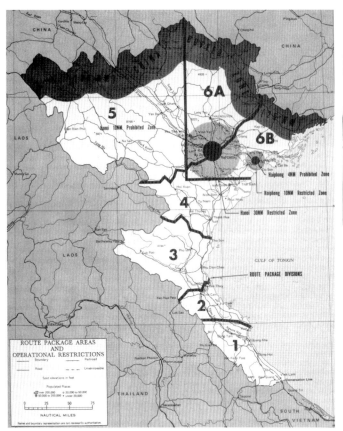

Route Packages. North Vietnam was divided into six Route Packages, RPI being the least hazardous, RPVI the most dangerous. USAF

Safely Down. The single runway at Udorn AB could be treacherous especially when wet. Norman Huggins

be confirmed; suffice it to say that shortly thereafter operational flying in the more dangerous areas of SEA for the Voodoo pilots was limited to 100 'counters'. The effect on morale was palpable.

The missions which counted towards a recce pilot's all-important score of 100, earning him a trip home on the 'freedom flight', were those flown over North Vietnam, the country being divided into six regional 'Route Packages' (RPs), each with its respective degree of risk. RPI in the south was the least hostile area while RPVI (divided into two parts) contained the most lucrative targets, the heaviest defences and the key towns of Haiphong and Hanoi, making it the most hazardous. Generally, although there was no hard or fast rule, the USN took on targets in the coastal area, the USAF those inland.

The risks faced by the Voodoo pilots did not end when they were back at bases in South Vietnam or Thailand. While the airfields were sights for sore eyes for those returning from a mission there was still the problem at Udorn of getting the big bird down safely on the potentially hazardous runway. Harry Runge remembers recovering there in the wake of a particularly heavy thunderstorm which had flooded the narrow runway, the centre section failing to drain 'worth a damn'. The standing water caused the tyre on the starboard main wheel to hydroplane with no effective braking whatsoever. Harry did not use the anti skid, believing it worthless in the circumstances, but: *"yanked the nose up to maximum angle of attack for aerodynamic braking and managed to get the beast stopped before running out of concrete"*. The story would be repeated many times on this difficult runway.

Living and working conditions at Udorn did, however, continue to improve, with the officers accommodated in single rooms equipped with cooling fans and raised off the ground in wooden 'hooches', close to toilets and washing facilities. There was now a continuous turnover of personnel, with people from all walks of life coming and going on 'courtesy' visits, fact finding forays or TDYs, but one newcomer came and stayed, 'Greenie', the real bearer of the Python name. Greenie made herself at home at once, albeit in surroundings hitherto wholly unfamiliar to her and her like, which had sprung up in their once peaceful, natural

Lifestyle Udorn. Living quarters on the left, toilets on the right; life at Udorn improved in 1965. Gene Morris

Welcome Home. Captains Tom Malone (with Greenie) and Chuck Lustig - Pythons together. George Cowgill

habitat as a veritable 'little America'. To be sure there were some 'incomers' (mainly 'townies' from the Nothern States) who found her friendship somewhat disconcerting, but the Southerners were on the same wavelength at once and Greenie sought their company with ease. Fed on liberal quantities of small chickens, her energy seemed inexhaustible as she lent a tail in squadron operations, kept maps from blowing from the plotting tables and welcomed visitors with the customary embrace (after which some seemed to find it necessary to cut short their stay at this outpost of modern day pioneers). Greenie was a true Python.

As the Voodoos penetrated further north so the risk from AAA increased. Given the

On Guard! An ever watchful 'Greenie' on patrol in Python Operations. Norman Huggins

enormous growth in number, variety and effectiveness of the guns (from 1,136 sites in January to 2,955 in July 1965), clustered as they were around high value targets in North Vietnam as well as the recognised routes to the South, the guns had become a grave concern. For what it was worth, the Voodoo men were soon able to distinguish between the types of flak aimed at them; one described the 85-mm bursts as 'little black clouds with red centres', the 57-mm as 'grey balls' and the 37-mm as 'round, orange golf ball puffs'. Altitude fused, with nearby detonations rocking the heavy Voodoos, the latter presented the greatest challenge; less worrying were the green North Vietnamese tracers, which differed from the yellow used by the allies. The dangers could be reduced by flying outside the range of the small arms and confusing the heavier weapons with constantly changing speeds, heights and headings. However, these tactics could not always be adhered to because of the weather conditions and when committed to photography.

Warm Welcome. (Above) 57-mm, 37-mm and 23-mm AAA along Route One, 30 miles south of Hanoi, and (below) machine gun fire 10 miles west of Hai Phong. Gene Morris

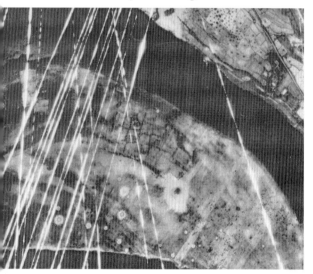

The SAM threat, first confirmed by photography from a U-2 aircraft in April 1965, now added to the problem of survival and the pilots had to learn very rapidly how to avoid these 'flying telephone poles'. An SA-2 missile site 15 miles southwest of Hanoi was the first to be completed, followed by three more in May, the first SAM victim (an F-4) being downed in July. At this stage all the sites were within exclusion zones around Haipong and PhucYen airfields - 'no go' areas for the Voodoos but whose operations just outside those areas placed them within the missile's range. Early advice was that the SA-2 became increasingly effective above 3,000 ft and a ban on flying above 1,500 ft was imposed in known SAM areas. However, this placed the Voodoos at the mercy of the guns; moreover every new missile site, be it real or decoy, active or

inactive, was ringed by strong AAA defences and 'flak traps'. Gene Morris remembers his Voodoo being *'flipped upside down by a flak burst'* and only just managing to right his aircraft at 50 ft to complete the mission; he admitted that:

"*I still get the shivers just thinking about flying over a flak trap at a missile site and it all took place 37 years ago!*"

Post-flight intelligence reports told repeatedly of 'heavy flak', 'intensive AAA' and 'excellent tracking', often with more graphic accounts. So the guns remained the main threat and it was left largely to the men at the sharp end to find out how best to brave these combined defences, and this they did (Chapter Sixteen).

The airfields on which MiG-15s and MiG-17s were being assembled, eventually to operate primarily from Phuc Yen, Kepo and Gia Lam, were now under continuous observation from USN and USAF aircraft. Then, on 4 April 1965, MiG fighters shot down two USAF F-105s, triggering an immediate response; suitably armed USN Phantom fighters began roaming the skies whenever a raid on the north was scheduled and shot down four MiGs in the following June and July. The

SAMs on Parade. An early SA-2 Site connected by bamboo road mats. Gene Morris

Cause and Effect. An SA2 (above) homes on to its target while another detonates (below) with consequences unknown. Gene Morris

Beware - Flak Trap! Multi-AAA surrounded real and decoy missile sites, this photograph believed to have been taken by Captain George Hall. Gene Morris

One Gone - One to Go. Close up photo of SA-2s, attributed to Lieutenant Colonel Crabtree. Gene Morris

Beware - Decoys! Perhaps deceiving the eye - but plain to see from photographs. Gene Morris

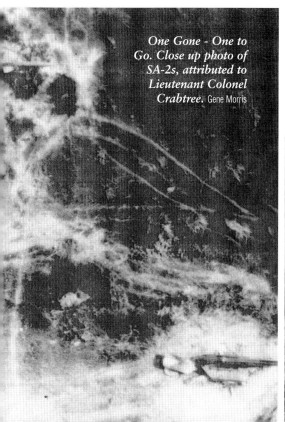

essence of survival against both SAMs and fighters was early warning for timely countermeasures and avoiding action, but the recce pilots on single aircraft missions could be heavily preoccupied with their photographic tasks just when the risk from both was at its greatest, adding weight to the argument for escorts or wingmen to provide these essential warnings. Seen in time, the ageing MiG-15 should not have been a problem, but more care had to be taken when dealing with the mainstay of the North Vietnamese fighter force, the MiG-17, an aircraft introduced in the early 1950s which would serve until the 1980s. Fitted with the Klimov VK-1 turbojet (a derivative of the British Nene engine) it had a theoretical top speed of 711 mph, was highly manoeuvrable and carried a formidable armament of one 37-mm and two 23-mm cannon. The Voodoos could out-accelerate and outrun the older MiG-15s and 17s, but what of the new MiG-21s?

With the blessing of the Thai Government the Green Python force was increased to 12 aircraft in May 1965, the six RF-101s from the 363rd TRW which were on a 'five to seven day' TDY to Udorn from Kadena being authorised to stay on 'indefinitely'. With them came Lieutenant Colonel Raymond Lowery, who became the Pythons' Operations Officer. He would be in the thick of it from the start and need all his skill on 1 July to bring back an RF-101, badly damaged by flak, to complete an emergency landing at Ubon AB. He would fly again but his aircraft would not.

On 12 May President Johnson called the first of several halts to all bombing in North Vietnam, in the hope of encouraging the North Vietnamese to negotiate. This was to be of no avail, only the enemy gaining the advantage. Reconnaissance activity increased during the ceasefire, with 184 missions flown in the three days before bombing resumed, and from this it was clear that North Vietnam and the dissident factions used every moment to strengthen their positions, repair facilities and resupply their forces at the front. Many at the 'sharp end' later surmised that their enemies were almost out of ammunition and essential supplies just when cease-fires were called. Perhaps, without these truces, the war might have taken a different course?

For the Green Pythons the priority was now North Vietnam, and to help counter the risks from the ever increasing and diversifying air defences, 2nd AD ordered that the recce missions be escorted by F-105s. However, the latter's shorter range so inhibited the RF-101s that, under pressure from the Pythons, the order was quickly rescinded in favour of the practice of flying pairs of Voodoos to provide the necessary cross-cover.

There was, however, no panacea solution to the hazards faced by the fliers. Captain Charles Shelton was the first of the Pythons to be brought down by guns over Northern Laos on 29 April 1965, followed by Captain Marv Lindsey during a mixed force raid northwest of Hanoi on 29 June and Fred Mellor, again in North Vietnam on 13 August, all of them killed. Then on 27 September 1965 Captain George Hall fell prey to the guns over the North but ejected and became a POW. Captains

MiG Threat. A MiG 17, in North Vietnamese markings, on display at the Eighth Air Force Museum, Savannah, Georgia. Author

Bob Pitt, who managed to nurse his aircraft back to Da Nang AB, and Norm Huggins who was rescued, were more fortunate. Their stories are told in Chapter Seventeen. Gene Morris and Tony Weisgarber also got away when 'bounced' by two MiGs from 6 o'clock and a height advantage, north-west of Hanoi, but the Voodoo pilots saw them coming and took the necessary evasive actions. In Gene's own words: *"There was lots of cannon fire and a missile or two but no big deal".*

Even with random scheduling and routeing the enemy seemed to have plenty of clues, hints and perhaps intelligence on where and when the Voodoos would enter their airspace, and seemed able to determine quickly where they were likely to be going and when they would get there. Captain Chuck Lustig, a 15th TRS 'Python', remembers a sortie which seemed to confirm that the communists had a comprehensive network of strategically placed reporting points to provide a crude but probably very effective early warning system, which increased the risk to the Voodoos flying at ultra-low level:

"On 2 October 1965 Captain Dick Wood led me in from the Gulf of Tonkin, towards our BDA target, an ammunition dump 30 miles north of Hanoi and close to the notorious North East Railway to China. This was a particularly nasty place to go because it was swarming with AAA, most notably 'quad 23s' (ZSU-23/4) and '37's. We coasted in north of Haiphong and ducked behind a prominent ridge about 20 miles north of Hanoi which ran approximately east to west, in the hope of masking our approach. It had always been somewhat of a mystery how the defenders always seemed to be waiting for us despite all our precautions - but we were about to find out. We were well below the top of the ridge doing 600 kts when I caught a glint coming from a bald spot on top of one of the knobs. A closer look revealed a tent, three or four men and a radio antenna. About ten miles further on, I spotted a similar position and this time one of the individuals was following us with binoculars (we were really close). We saw a couple more of these lookouts before we reached the target area and yes - they were waiting to greet us with a fine fireworks display. Apparently the North Vietnamese were copying the early warning system used by the Chinese against the Japs in 1940. It made sense; a couple of blokes with binos and radios is a lot cheaper than a radar site and a hell of a lot easier to replace in case of loss. They probably got a bonus if one of us got shot down. It was then that all hell broke loose; my aircraft taking a hit, probably from a ZSU-23 , the shell entering through the US star insignia. I felt it and smelt it as it smashed into the 16th stage air shut-off valve allowing air at some 800 deg to play on the main wire bundle with disastrous effects. All the warning lights in the cockpit seemed to come on at once, going out one by one as the circuits burned through and 'off flags' appeared on every flight instrument; a small fire also started in Bay 105, just behind the cockpit and all this below a 500 ft cloud base! I still had my hydraulics and flight controls, however, so we continued to the target and then ran out fast and low over the Red River and 'Thud Ridge' towards the relative safety of the mountains between North Vietnam and Laos. There I closed in on Dick's wing and we climbed through the overcast direct for Udorn, declaring an emergency. Having turned off the battery, I then had sufficient power to lower the undercarriage and flaps normally to carry out an emergency landing without further mishap."

All in a day's work.

Chuck's troubles were not over because he now had to face the wrath of his crewchief, who greeted him with: *"Captain Lustig, what did you do to my aeroplane?"* He had found whole areas of fuselage skin heavily blistered and on opening an access bay door 'a bunch of charred rubble hit the deck', bits that were gathered up and presented to Chuck in a peanut butter jar, a momento he has kept to this day. With typical ingenuity the technicians soon had the aircraft ready to do battle again, the sheet metal workers having filled the hole through which the shell passed with a patch shaped and coloured like a purple heart. Sadly, the aircraft which had cheated death so well on that day was shot down some months later, but for pressing on to the target and nursing his ailing steed home so competently, Chuck was awarded a DFC, presented by General Jay T Robbins, Divisional Commanding General, at Kadena AB, Okinawa.

Just Rewards. Captain Chuck Lustig, one of many who braved the hazards of SEA, receives a well-earned Distinguished Flying Cross from General Jay T Robbins. Chuck Lustig

Chuck's aircraft was only one of many which suffered severe damage, some of which was of course terminal but in other cases the extraordinary robustness of the aircraft, with its invaluable redundancy in engines and vital ancillaries, saved the day. The 15th TRS records show that, between 11 July and 8 November 1965, 20 Voodoos suffered one or other fate due to gunfire, all but two while at low level and high speed, the target areas of Viet Tri, Yen Bay and Long Met featuring repeatedly in these statistics. On 8 October, a ban on flying above 1500 ft in SAM areas was lifted, allowing the option of 'pop-up' manoeuvre and a dramatic reduction in the effects of flak (Chapter Sixteen).

By November 1965 pilots from the 45th TRS were taking over from those who had served at Udorn on TDY from the 363rd TRW and were now returning to Shaw. They were particularly welcome at a time when so many of the replacements for those also leaving the 15th TRS had no previous recce experience on the front line; one came from Training Command, one from Strategic Air Command, two were from Air Defence Command and one from the transport force. This inflow of new blood had a significant impact on the Python operations. Much would be demanded of these newcomers but also from those experienced pilots available

who had to provide essential example and supervision during what would now become an on-going and critical lead-in training period. As for the aircraft, the 12 RF-101s each at Udorn and Tan Son Nhut continued to comprise a mix from the 15th TRS and 45th TRS.

George Cowgill was on his eighth 'counter' when Captain Dick Cooper led him on Mission RTC 919, around the hot-spots in RPVI on 22 December 1965. The pair flew along the north-west railway under low cloud against the full force of 57-mm and 85-mm AAA, before the cloud broke and they were able to 'pop' to 15,000 ft just north of Hanoi to photograph Phuc Yen airfield. They then followed the north-east railway up to Kep airfield and across to the Thai Nuygen thermal power station before making for home, in a short trip lasting 1 hour 15 minutes. This had been a perilous route albeit on this occasion uneventful, but nothing in SEA was predictable and other trips over the same targets would be very different.

A policy directive attributed to the Director of Intelligence, 2nd Air Division, had decreed that, while the RF-101 pilots were to photograph their primary and secondary targets as a first priority, they were to let their cameras roll well before and after these targets while over hostile territory until their film ran out, in the hope of revealing targets of opportunity. What may have seemed like a good idea in principle to some in the hierarchy, this additional requirement placed a very heavy burden on processing and interpreting facilities. However diligent the ever larger force of photographic technicians and interpreters, the amount of film produced daily was immense and there was a danger that priority tasks might not get the proper attention. In fact, very few worthwhile 'opportunity' targets were found in this way. Equally disturbing to those at the front, reconnaissance successes now appeared to be measured in the terms of the length of film exposed rather than in the number of specific objectives satisfied.

Harry Runge had more to say on the trials and tribulations they had with the cameras available to them. Much of their work was carried out with the KA-1, 36-inch split verticals, invariably to a scale of 1:5000, either on area covers for the army in South Vietnam or for BDA photography in the North at 15,000 ft. The army was not interested in the small format cameras, these and the KA-56

January 1966. This was always a cause for celebration, but the outflow caused continuous turbulence in the pilot manning schedule to retain the necessary level of experience.

What of visual sightings of opportunity targets? In Europe, NATO recce pilots had trained hard to combine photography with the acquisition of target information visually, with some but not all nations feeding these sightings without delay into an in-flight reporting network. The author can find no evidence of any formal organisation for in-flight reporting in SEA (or use of the airborne command cell for this purpose) perhaps on the argument that with the nature of this war the enemy, the political constraints and command structure, there was no call for such a facility. However, some Voodoo pilots did quite properly draw

used primarily for 'happy snaps'. Compliance with some frags was difficult. When Harry was tasked to 'look over the border from South Vietnam as far as possible into Cambodia', he flew as close as was legal then 'rolled the bird to a 45 deg bank, applied as much top rudder as my leg would take to keep the nose level (but not for long!, and operated the split-verts'. There was also the requirement to 'look inside the caves in the Karst area of the Ho Chi Minh Trail', but the frag had taken no account of the time of day, the sun angle or weather conditions, again demanding the use of the split verts.

Gene Morris was one of the first Pythons to achieve the magic figure of 100 'countable' sorties, at the end of 1965, but others following in quick succession as 1966 unfolded, Harry Runge among them flying his 100th on 13

BDA. RF-101 confirms successful strike on bridge at My Duo, 15 miles north of DMZ.

attention to potentially lucrative, untasked targets. Chuck Lustig was one; on landing from a mission he reported a large truck park and gave a precise grid reference (his sighting was later confirmed on film). The PI passed this information up the reporting chain at once, through 7th Air Force to PACAF and apparently on to Washington DC, where a

Alternatives. Bridge down - three alternative routes available.

By-Pass. Bridge destroyed but approaches for a floating bridge (above), and pontoon bridge (below).

strike was approved. Although allegedly accorded every priority within the intelligence, targeting and tasking system which existed, 48 hours passed before the strike was mounted, by which time the trucks had been replaced at the target's location by AAA, all ready and waiting for the bombers.

1965 ended with a Christmas truce which continued throughout January, but there was no respite for the recce pilots who flew daily surveillance missions over North Vietnam with all the defensive systems ranged against them. They confirmed the inevitable, that the North Vietnamese were making the best of such pauses to repair, resupply, regroup and reinforce their forward units, again with no intention of negotiating. Everywhere, hundreds of coolies were spotted working in daylight and with impunity on the damaged infrastructure from the Red River south to the DMZ. On one mission, Major Harry Runge and Captain Jerdy Wright produced a classic photograph, which was eventually released to the public, of a hastily rebuilt bridge on Route 1 where 30 trucks were waiting to proceed south. Bridge work of all kinds was the order of the day.

1966 began with seasonally poor flying weather which seriously hampered air reconnaissance. The recce pilots logged an unprecedented amount of weather time and became adept at descending through cloud as they approached the target area, hoping that they had judged their position well enough to avoid any high ground as they sought clear weather below. To be on the safe side, many would plan to descend over the Gulf of Tonkin outside North Vietnam's radar cover, but often they could not avoid giving some warning of their coming. When they broke cloud, often as low as 200 ft, it was essential to establish their position from the map without delay and proceed en route; orbiting to find out exactly where they were could be fatal. In any event they could expect intense opposition from the moment they crossed the coast, with observers tracking them visually through to their targets.

When the bombing resumed in February a more formidable force faced the Americans on land and in the air, and the Pythons returned to pre-and post-flight photography with seasonal haze now adding to their navigation and target acquisition difficulties. Furthermore, probably as a result of the bombing moratorium, new AAA and SAM sites were now active as far south as Vinh and Dong Hoi, together with heavier concentrations of guns at choke points on the Ho Chi Minh Trail. The importance of these targets, together with those around the PDJ and Bai Thuong area, also called for some missions to be carried out with high risk at low level.

The new year brought with it a complicated rearrangement of assets, command and control. The 45th TRS had moved back to its home in Misawa when the Able Mable commitment at Tan Son Nhut was taken over by the 20th TRS from Shaw AFB in November 1965, manning 12 Voodoos provided by the 15th TRS. Many of these TAC pilots had already served in SEA on TDY but now they built on their experience during the unreal atmosphere of a bombing pause, during which there was plenty for them to do, the squadron flying 14 sorties a day and retaining one pilot at readiness throughout the daylight hours.

Back at Udorn, George Cowgill flew a mission on 14 February 1966 which was recounted first in Doug Gordon's FlyPast article 'Tactical Reconnaissance in SEA':

"The targets were all in the Thanh Hoa area, specifically a bridge we called the 'Dragon's Jaw', a nearby SAM site, an airfield under construction at Bai Thoung and a barracks in the mountains. In really bad weather we flew on dead reckoning from Udorn to Vinh, descending to 100 ft on the radar altimeter over the Gulf of Tonkin. Leaving 'roosters tails' over the paddy fields, we flew on at 50 ft, over the first three targets at anything from zero to 800 ft and 600 kts plus, while facing intense ground fire".

This combination of very low cloud, poor visibility and heavy flak made life very difficult for his wingman, Captain Jimmy Wylie, who lost contact with his leader; they got together again and pressed on to the next target, the barracks and staging area near Thiet Tra, which was surrounded by mountains up to 5000 ft. The weather then deteriorated further and they were forced to climb to high level to make their way home, but they had done well. Both George and Jimmy were recommended for Silver Stars by those at the front who understood what they had been through to accomplish so much of their mission, the leader pressing on for as long as was sensible and the wingman hanging in so well, both to produce the required photography, but the recommendations were downgraded to DFCs by higher headquarters.

During this period of intensive flying Cowgill and Wylie flew almost every day, often together switching leader and wingman positions. On the day after the Thanh Hoa mission it was Jimmy in the lead over Vinh and into the Nape Pass, George led them the next day into the Nape and Mugia Passes between North Vietnam and Laos, and Jimmy was at the helm again on the following day for an area cover of the infamous Dien Bien Phu. While they encountered light flak on all these trips they managed to complete their tasks without damage to their aircraft; the mutual confidence between wingman and leader (and vice versa) in regular partnerships was not only comforting, it paid off.

It was again with a regular partner, Captain Moe Moses, that George earned another DFC on 24 February, two weeks after the last. Moe led Mission UE605B to Vinh via a standard route and they descended to cover several bridge targets at low level on the road and rail routes northwards up the coastal strip to Thanh Hoa; it was on this leg that intense small arms fire caused a massive leak in George's aircraft. An immediate abort, cool heads and an urgent call for tanker support served them well that day, George managing to hook up with a mere three minutes of fuel remaining before flameout. Again, some targets had been covered successfully, and more importantly a valuable pilot and aircraft had been saved to fly another day. It was George's 39th 'counter'.

George Cowgill finished his TDY at Tan Son Nhut on 19th May 1966, flying back to

Misawa on the following day to complete his tour with the 45th TRS; he travelled on a C-135 with a grim reminder of the war, the bodies of 32 US soldiers, none of whom had reached their 23rd birthday. He himself would return to SEA, PCS with the 45th TRS on 30 June and go on to complete 104 'counters'.

After much debate between PACAF, 5th Air Force, 13th Air Force and 2nd Air Division the 460th TRW was activated at Tan Son Nhut in February 1966 to look after all reconnaissance assets in SEA, subordinated to the 2nd AD pending the formation of 7th Air Force on 1 April 1966. In March 1966 the 20th TRS moved with 12 aircraft to Udorn to replace the Green Pythons and the 45th TRS took over the Able Mable duties at Tan Son Nhut TDY from Misawa with 12 aircraft.

After sterling service with the RF-101 in SEA, Lieutenant Colonel Robert Crabtree led the first element of the 15th TRS back from Udorn to Kadena on 29th March 1966 where they would await conversion to the RF-4C. The squadron had not however finished with the Voodoo; with such a shortage of experienced recce pilots in SEA, some who had not completed their 100 missions would return to Udorn to supplement the 20th TRS and the 45th TRS at Tan Son Nhut. It also acted as a recce training unit for RF-101 pilots destined for SEA, provided maintenance support and replacement aircraft for the 20th and 45th TRS. In the last year, with great resourcefulness and determination the Cotton Pickers had set up a

thriving operation in far from ideal circumstances at Udorn. While in SEA their Voodoos had flown 4,349 combat sorties in 6,786 flying hours, been awarded 10 Silver Stars, 52 Distinguished Flying Crosses and 5 Purple Hearts; a very worthy tally indeed. Their conduct had been exemplary but they had lost 6 aircraft in combat or accidents, very sadly with two pilots killed, two taken prisoner and one dying in captivity. During this pivotal year in SEA the Cotton Pickers and the Polka Dots had shared the accolades heaped on the Voodoo force wherever it served in SEA.

What of Greenie? When the 15th TRS Green Pythons ceased to exist at Udorn in March 1966, some say that she was smuggled back to Kadena in a special crate in the nose compartment of an RF-101 (below oxygen height?) while others believe that she was transported back to Okinawa courtesy the US Marine Corps. In any event there is evidence that she survived the war and emigration, George Cowgill seeing her at Kadena in 1969 (some 4 ft longer than he remembered at Udorn) and Chuck Lustig spotting her again in Okinawa in 1973. Hopefully there is no truth in the rumour that she was later kidnapped by the Marines who had then enjoyed an unusual (even for them) meal! Although the trail went cold, it is generally believed that she died of natural causes. Greenie and the Green Python airmen of South East Asia had earned a major place in Voodoo heritage.

CHAPTER TWELVE
20TH TAC LEADS THE PACK

'Never trade luck for skill or fly with anyone braver than yourself'

Airmens' Creed.

Tactical Air Command's 20th TRS moved from Shaw AFB to Tan Son Nhut to replace the 45th TRS in November 1965, the twelve RF-101s they would fly there provided by the 15th TRS. These 20th TRS pilots, some of whom had already served in SEA on TDY, began their theatre orientation with sorties in the low threat areas, then graduated through the unreal atmosphere of the Christmas bombing pause to the more demanding missions up north. Whereas the communists were indulging in massive resupply and reinforcement, day and night throughout the pause without risk from the air, the recce pilots had to contend with the fast-developing air defences. This was very much a one-sided ceasefire.

Meanwhile, operations at Udorn continued apace, with the 15th TRS assisted by pilots from the 45th TRS on TDY, until the Pythons were replaced by the 20th TRS from Tan Son Nhut and the squadron returned to Kadena to

20th TRS. The 20th TRS arrived at Tan Son Nhut in SEA from Shaw AFB in November 1965. Don Karges

be re-equipped with RF-4Cs. The 45th TRS then took over the Able Mable commitment at Tan Son Nhut with a detachment of 12 x RF-101s until the full resources of the squadron were deployed there, one officer and one airman only remaining at its titular home in Misawa. During this time the PACAF aircraft were rotating back to the United States for modifications and camouflage.

At Udorn, the RF-101s of the 20th TRS and the newly arrived

Mixed Force. Captain Jim Young taxies past an RF-4C from the 11th TRS at Udorn in 1966, as the Phantom begins to replace the Voodoo. Don Karges

Going for Warpaint. George Cowgill photographs Dick Bidlack taking fuel en route from Misawa to the USA in January 1966, for modifications and warpaint. George Cowgill

RF-4C of the 11th TRS were immediately involved in an on-going recce programme against North Vietnam's energy sources, protected by very angry defences which anticipated the recce aircraft after each raid. During this campaign their photographs did more than simply confirm or otherwise that the bombers had hit their target; in the case of a major petrol, oil and lubricant (POL) site, for instance, it was possible for the specialist PIs to assess the capacity of the unit which remained following the attack. However, the numerous political and humanitarian constraints which inhibited war fighting in SEA, probably more now than at any other time or place, included a ban on those most lucrative of targets, the dykes on the Red River. Breaching these dykes was well within the capabilities of the USN and USAF and would have caused untold damage to the domestic infrastructure, industry and communications network in North Vietnam, but there was no chance of such an operation being authorised in Washington. Knowing this, the Vietnamese built POL and other facilities into or close by the dykes to ensure their immunity from attack. There were other frustrations, some of course stemming from lack of the 'big picture' at flight line level, along with suspicions that some of the hard-earned photographs were never used.

Lieutenant Colonel John 'Bull' Stirling, 46 years old and with a wealth of RF-101 experience behind him from tours at Shaw and Laon AFB, took command of the 20th TRS at Udorn in July 1966. He now faced the most daunting challenges of his long career but would apply all he had learned in the past to maximise the potential of the 20th TRS and minimise losses to his men and machines. Drawing also on the experiences of the Green Pythons, his on-going analysis of the modus operandi at Udorn and over North Vietnam soon underlined the many problems and he suggested some remedies. The 20th TRS pilots were quick to discover for themselves the hazards of operating from the narrow, slippery runway at Udorn, especially after the all too frequent torrential rain had flooded the inherently poor surface covered with oil and tyre rubber from countless landings. Stirling witnessed one of his aircraft, flown by a capable pilot (albeit with little experience on the Voodoo) skid from left to right on the waterlogged runway, the brakes and anti-skid

having very little effect, until it departed into the soft mud and slammed into a dyke, tearing off the undercarriage and snapping the fuselage in half. As was so often the case, however, the very rugged Voodoo remained sufficiently intact (if on its side) for the dejected pilot to climb unscathed from the cockpit. Practically, there was only a certain amount that could be done to improve the state of the runway but Bull Stirling pressed continuously for grooving at both ends to reduce skidding and the erection of arrester barriers, again at both ends (and it is believed one in the middle), which eventually paid off. The squadron lost another aircraft to the well-known problem of pitch-up, relatively easy to avoid in routine training but more likely to happen in the stress of an operational environment as was the case here. Some pilots managed to recover from pitch-ups, but they used a lot of sky. All that could be done here was to stress, again and again, the causal signs and recovery procedures.

Again using the lessons of the past, Bull Stirling looked to the welfare of his pilots. He knew that they had to relieve the stresses and strains built up in combat by letting off steam on the ground and:

"from a personal point of view I never regarded anything wrong with breaking up a few lousy tables and chairs in the Officers Club when we were breaking up a lot more up North; it seemed perfectly natural for a fighter pilot who had been dodging SAM missiles around Hanoi to become a bit aggressive".

However, he also knew that this could cause tensions between the pilots and those who were living and working with them in support roles on the front line but who were not subjected to the same pressures, and that this could put the careers of good men at risk. It was ever thus. He thought that the Udorn Officers Club, decked out in Las Vegas style with roof beams which invited mischief, too ornate and fancy for his men, and when it was closed for a 'cooling off period' after some grave social misdemeanour, and the 20th TRS officers went down town to find their pleasures, he decided that they should have a bar and lounge of their own. Captain Jack Langille was the man who 'eyeballed the basic structure and design, then supervised the building' of a more suitable venue for the Voodoo pilots, constructed by

Home Making. The 20th TRS pilots made themselves at home at Udorn, building a walkway between Squadron Ops and a crewroom, Captain 'Buddah' Phillips here in residence. Don Karges

self-help from materials begged and borrowed. On all counts the project was a great success, a suitable service doctor also being added to their number to help care for their bodily needs.

As the Pythons had also discovered, operating problems were exacerbated by the departure of an increasing number of experienced Voodoo pilots who had completed their tours, with many of their replacements being posted in from other roles and rushed through conversion and basic role training at Shaw. These 'new' pilots now faced the less benign operating environment in SEA and needed very careful handling if they were not to contribute unnecessarily to the attrition statistics. The majority did their best, but some were of marginal ability and the difference

between them and the battle-hardened 'old heads' who had completed their 100 missions was very noticeable. The much valued and cherished individualism for which the force was renowned now had to give way to a greater degree of standardisation in operating procedures and tactics.

There were Voodoo pilots in SEA who did not need to be there, who volunteered for or simply completed more than their fair share of the difficult and hazardous missions without complaint, who pressed on in marginal weather or damaged aircraft rather than abort and have that sortie rescheduled. Most did not seek recognition and were merely happy in themselves to have done their duty; they chose to take the ultimate risk of their chosen profession. Captain Don Karges was one: he was due to rotate back to the USA after a tour on RF-101s with the 38th TRS at Ramstein, but applied for TDY to SEA and was sent to the 20th TRS at Udorn. Captains George Cowgill and Keith Kuester, both of whom have been mentioned already, could also be counted in that number. These pilots had contrived to become qualified on the RF-101 while serving as staff officers with the 66th TRW in Europe and while George secured an assignment to the 45th TRS Keith was accepted on flying status again while continuing his duties with the flight safety staff at Tan Son Nhut. Keith would fly 87 missions in SEA at the height of the conflict, many at low level and with 14 over North Vietnam, to earn a DFC.

Then there was Captain Bob Archibald. With three weeks notice only, in April 1966, Bob was posted direct from flight test duties with an Air Defence Command F-106 unit at Loring AFB, Maine, to the recce desk in the command post of the 460th TRW at Tan Son Nhut. Unhappy with this sedentary life he requested and was granted permission to check out again in the RF-101 (which he had not flown for five years). Then short of pilots, the 45th TRS welcomed this ad hoc addition to their ranks until a glut of new pilots left little capacity for him to remain in flying practice and he was posted to 7th Air Force as the Voodoo specialist on the combat tactics team. Again Bob worked his way back to the flight line, somehow arranging

Voluntary Effort. A staff officer at Tan Son Nhut, Captain Bob Archibald flew many missions from Udorn, but had to take his turn running the operations desk. Bob Archibald

orders which allowed him to fly the RF-101 with the 20th TRS, with the full authority of no less a man than three-star General Momyer, the 7th Air Force commander. No sooner were these orders to hand than Bob was on the midnight courier (the 'Scatback') to Udorn. Initially he was treated with some caution by the 20th TRS, permitted only to 'look over the shoulders' of the resident pilots as they planned their missions. This did not last long, however, with threats of hierarchal displeasure coupled with personal persuasion and by all other means possible, including using his position as the RF-101 tactical specialist in SEA, Bob was soon back on the flying schedule. At first, he was sent on relatively low risk missions but he soon proved his worth and progressed to the more demanding tasks, flying as wingman to the best, including Lieutenant Colonels Bull Stirling and Jim Brickel. To all intents and purposes, he became a legitimate member of the 20th TRS, even 'pulling desk officer', despite the fact that all this was wholly unofficial and that he had never been sent to SEA to fly. When he rotated back to the USA, in March 1967, he had accumulated 120 operational missions with 50 over North Vietnam - not bad for a staff officer and all credit to his enterprise, determination and just a little cunning.

The 20th TRS was also quick to recognise that the key to survival was to keep a good lookout (difficult to do with the head down in the viewfinder on the camera run), and to 'jink', jink and jink again; they too accepted that when low level 'dicing' missions were necessary the Voodoos should be flown 'in the weeds' (50 ft over flat terrain), where possible avoiding roads, railways and rivers which were likely to be heavily defended. Where photography was required between 10,000 and 15,000 ft they would hope to use the 'pop-up' manoeuvre (Chapter Sixteen). They saw the wisdom of using the oblique cameras whenever possible to avoid overflying the target and that there should be no 'sightseeing'. Their tactic for escaping from the hostile fighters was simply to outrun them, knowing that the Voodoo was more stable and controllable at low level and

'In The Weeds' Advice on when, where and how to risk it at low level became very specific. This photograph was taken from another RF-101, post-1965, 'somewhere in SEA'. USAF/Don Karges

'Going Left'.   Jerry Lentz leads Ray Tiffault at low level over SEA in 1966. Ray Tiffault

outside RPVI and to abort non-vital missions if they would otherwise be forced to low level by the weather. He also challenged the policy of sending single-aircraft into SAM-infested areas and cited several advantages of operating in pairs, as a result of which many of the 20th TRS sorties now included wingmen. With lookout all-important, Bull Stirling's attitude towards the MiGs was instructive. In general he favoured a policy of dealing with them in the air rather than attempting to destroy them on the ground, especially when they were dispersed and partly concealed (leading to late acquisition), under protective cover or heavily defended by AAA, which could be very costly. He did not discourage the traditional individualism which had served the experienced recce pilots so well; he knew its value and once they had proved themselves he allowed his charges to plan their

very high speeds than the MiG fighters.

Bull Stirling also looked closely at the relevance of these tactics and techniques in relation to damage and loss rates in the different circumstances but this circumspect study was hampered by the lack of witnesses in the mainly single-aircraft operations of the time; he also understood that, under the stress of combat rather than in relatively straightforward peacetime training, basic mistakes ('pilot error') could have accounted for some unexplained losses. Of course small arms, AAA, SAM and later the MiGs took their toll, but only two of the unaccountable losses occurred in RPVI or thereabouts, when the pilots would have been expected to be very much on their toes. Bull Stirling noted that most of the unexplained losses occurred in the far less hostile areas, leading him to the reluctant conclusion that some of the 'old and bold' might have become a little complacent, perhaps a little over-confident, and he repeatedly commended to all the basic rules for flying the aircraft. He also stressed the need to keep clear of the most dangerous airspace at low level (other than when necessary to cover important targets below low cloud). Indeed, based on his own experience, he directed that his pilots should remain above 10,000 ft

own tactics according to their personal preferences and prevailing circumstances, but a mission never left the ground in his time without the squadron knowing what the pilot intended to do.

There was nothing light-hearted about the preparation for any of these recce missions. The planning room where it all started some two hours ahead of launch time did not resound to the ribaldry and banter exuded in peacetime; soft music often pervaded the scene, with the pilots and their helpers moving about their respective jobs quietly, knowing that the plan which evolved could mean success or failure, life or death. The tactics and routeing decided upon depended on the targets, photographic requirements, terrain, weather, and of course the ever-changing, colour-coded defences, inevitably most intensive in the target area. Pilot debriefing, essential to the purpose and for the collateral intelligence accrued which might help improve the effectiveness and security of those to follow, was a more relaxed affair, but the adrenalin was still flowing. Bull Stirling remembers a pilot returning from his first mission in RPVI to report, with shaking hands; *"an awful lot of welding shops downtown Hanoi"*. He would soon know better.

With the bombing of North Vietnam increasing so rapidly, even single aircraft missions could not keep pace with demands for pre-strike recce and BDA; indeed by August 1966 there was a backlog of 36 targets awaiting post-strike photographs. Also, the span of control over nine flying units was now proving too great for the 460th TRW at Tan Son Nhut, leading to the formation in September 1966 of the 432nd TRW at Udorn to control all reconnaissance units in Thailand, both Wings coming under the operational control of 7th Air Force. A further clarification of responsibilities stemmed from the realisation that the 45th TRS had flown more than half of its recce missions over North Vietnam in the first half of 1966, consuming a great deal of time and fuel in transit and often requiring AAR. Accordingly, an order went out that, as a general but not inviolate rule, their tasks were henceforth to be restricted to Laos and South Vietnam, with a consequent increase in tasks over the North for the 20th TRS.

Regardless of this guidance the pilots of the 45th TRS still went north. Captains Ralph Kral and Ray Tiffault found themselves over the notorious Than Hoa bridge again in 1966, a target which defied destruction and would cost at least five F-105s including that of the legendary Lieutenant Colonel Robbie Risner, who was to spend the rest of the war as a POW in Hanoi. That day the prospects of success for the two recce pilots also seemed bleak, with weather and the defences combining to increase the risks involved, but the mission was of the highest priority and the pair did not hesitate. They had to climb above the weather en route and descend over the Bay of Tonkin to coast in at 500 ft, before being driven down to 200 ft in a visibility of 1 nm as they approached the target and prepared to take their photographs. Then 'all hell broke loose', the North Vietnamese opening up with all they had as the Voodoos scythed their way through 'the weeds' at more than 500 kts. Miraculously they and their aircraft survived without a scratch, to take the required pictures of the bridge (as yet unbroken) with the nose oblique and pan cameras. Climbing back through the cloud, their return trip was uneventful and the back-up pair stood down thankfully. Ralph and Ray

Thanh Hoa. Photographs of this seemingly indestructible bridge at Than Hoa earned Ralph Kral and Ray Tiffault DFCs. Ray Tiffault

were subsequently awarded DFCs. In desperation, attempts were made to break the bridge by rolling a very large bomb out of the rear of a C-130 Hercules cargo plane, but to no avail. Later, a single sortie with the new laser guided bombs destroyed one span. The defenders were similarly innovative, laying decking over the remaining bridge piers, barely visible except to the PIs just below the water level, bringing the crossing back into use again.

Captain Jerry Miller, with the 20th TRS at Udorn, remembers that, pending confirmatory photographic confirmation, bombers continued to be fragged every day against high value targets despite their very persuasive visual reports that the objectives had been achieved, unnecessary losses often resulting. It was during one such series of missions that a relative newcomer to the squadron was leading a pair of RF-101s into RPVI for the first time to verify the achievements of an accompanying strike force against the heavily defended bridge at Bac Ninh on the Red River. The bombers had 'popped' to 7000 ft, 20 miles short of the target, they and the recce aircraft then coming under very heavy fire from AAA and SAM. The first of a salvo of three SA-2 missiles detonated behind Captain Vince Connolly in the number two Voodoo as he gave his leader cross-cover, but the third struck home and Connolly went down with his aircraft. The leader returned to Udorn, the unfinished business calling for a further attempt. An RF-4C Phantom from Udorn was the next to try his luck, only to suffer the same tragic fate and, pending that elusive photographic evidence another strike was scheduled. The F-105 strike leader selected for the job, who had already been to this target twice before and had visual evidence of success, argued against employing the 'Thuds' again on a further unnecessary and wasteful task, but his pleas fell on deaf ears; these missions would continue regardless of cost until photographic confirmation became available. The 'old boy net' now came to the rescue with the Thud commander having little difficulty convincing Bull Stirling of his plight. Solely on his own initiative, Bull sought volunteers to 'charge once more into the valley of death' (Tennyson) and Jerry Miller, operations officer of the day and despite being on his 'run-down' after 98 'counters', answered the call, with Captain 'Sandy' Sisco agreeing at once to fly on his wing.

Fortune favours the brave. The pair planned a 'water in-water out' approach and egress via the Gulf of Tonkin, coasting in north of Haiphong to head west among the karsts for several miles before turning south-west for the bridge. Perhaps they were not expected (there having been no preceding strike on that target) for it was only when they 'popped' to 15,000 ft that they encountered any opposition from AAA and they suffered no hits. Their task complete, the pair descended with all speed back to ultra low level and out into the Bay of Tonkin before climbing again in relative safety to report *"mission accomplished: bridge crossing confirmed destroyed"* as they started their recovery to Udorn, but it was not all over yet. They were then ordered to take on fuel in the 'Arctic Bear' tanking area and proceed with their film direct to Tan Son Nhut for the photographs to be seen without delay by the disbelievers. The photograph shown here was taken by Sandy Sisco with his pan camera as he weaved overhead giving top cover while Jerry held his aircraft straight and level to use his KA-1, 36-inch cameras. The results showed a clear break in the bridge, one third from the top, although the evidence is barely discernable in this photograph. The original print also revealed an underwater bridge in place to one side of the main route, with tracks to it on both banks; the Viet Cong thought of everything. The F-105 pilots had done their job well, their

Bridge Party. 'Sandy' Sisco flew top cover for Jerry Miller, both photographing the notorious bridge at Bac Ninh. Jerry Miller

visual reports had been vindicated, the Voodoo pilots had risen to the occasion and the hierarchy was convinced at last; the bombers would not now have to go back into that hornets' nest again, at least for some time. All this says much about the command and control system, the unoffical networking and the spirit at the 'sharp end'.

Doug Gordon, in his article 'Recce in SEA', records another typical mission in late 1966, JCS 19, which involved Don Karges and Bob Archibald. The target, a railyard north east of Hanoi in RPVI, had been struck by F-105s some ten days before and the 20th TRS had been trying since to get the photographs demanded to assess any collateral damage (and damage done to the target!) before another strike was mounted. For some reason the trip had already been cancelled that day, and when it was resurrected the original leader was not to hand and Don volunteered to take his place with Bob as his wingman. The weather forecast precluded a direct approach so the pair flew in at low level and 540 kts from the Gulf of Tonkin towards Hanoi before popping up to 15,000 ft. Despite a great deal of 'chatter' on the RHWR there was only sporadic gunfire in the area and they were able to take their photos and escape unharmed at that height directly across Hanoi towards Udorn. It was then that they heard a flight of 16 F-105s, led by the fighter-bomber ace Bobby Wayne, about to abort their mission against the same target because of the poor weather they were encountering as they approached from a different direction. Don's call that the weather over the target was clear was evidently met with mixed feelings, an anonymous voice heard to say 'Oh Shit!', but the Thuds pressed on and achieved their objective, the Voodoos following to take the BDA photographs.

After passing their *"mission accomplished"* in-flight report to the control centre 'Brigham', the recce pilots were ordered to divert to 'Red Anchor', the tanker always on station during these operations, take on fuel and proceed to direct to Tan Son Nhut, so that their photographs could be viewed by 7th Air Force as soon as possible. That the two recce pilots made no comment on this unexpected and perhaps unwelcome addition to their day is a further illustration of their positive approach. Unknown to Don, this would be Bob Archibald's first air refuelling from the boom of a KC-135 and equally unbeknown to Bob, Don had never before refuelled from an airborne tanker (a fact Don revealed to him only years later). Normally, both would have received at least the minimum if not the full requisite training in this sometimes difficult procedure, and certainly in less stressful circumstances, but these were not normal times. Without querying the order they both took fuel successfully despite heavy turbulence and the need to dodge

in and out of thunderstorms, Bob watching Don take the boom first believing he was learning from an expert. Such was the determination of the Voodoo pilots to do their duty.

The achievement of 100 'counters' was always a cause for celebration, perhaps tinged with a little envy on the part of those just starting out on this experience of a lifetime. Cooling buckets of water or cleansing foam baths were *de rigueur* and the 20th TRS at Udorn embarked on a happy spate of these sometimes riotous events as 1966 ended and 1967 began, pilots and groundcrew all joining in. Jerry Miller's '100th' on 27 November 1966 was typical. As was the usual custom, he was given a 'soft' mission to finish his tour, even bringing back his two drop tanks when frequently they had to be jettisoned to enhance survival. He recalls that after some pilots had *"buzzed the place pretty good"* the 432nd TRW wing commander had put out the word (and Bull Stirling had passed this on to him in no uncertain fashion) that *"these wild 100 mission passes must stop"*. It is not recorded what the wing commander thought as Sandy Sisco led Jerry in, now as wingman but flying inverted, for an otherwise normal break and landing, Jerry spraying the ramp with fuel (which is the Voodoo's way of objecting to flying under negative 'G'). Suffice it to say that in the spirit of the day all was overlooked and Jerry was given his well-earned send-off in style. Don Karges, the volunteer from the 38th TRS, took a little longer to reach his 'ton' in the monsoon season and because his experience on the aircraft required him to carry out many additional instructor pilot and 'test hop' duties; he reached the magic figure on 12 January 1967.

Bob Archibald would fly more of these demanding missions out of Udorn before finishing his time with the 20th TRS. In January

Red Anchor. A tanker was always scheduled to be on the Red Anchor station when operations were taking place in its area. Don Karges

Going Home! Jerry Miller gets a wash-down and congratulations from his squadron on returning from his '100th' on 14 November 1966. Don Karges

Going Home! Don Karges, completing his 100th 'counter' on 12 January 1967, was welcomed back by his crew chief and Lieutenant John 'Bull' Stirling. Don Karges

1967 he was led across the Red River and the runway at Kep Airfield from south to north, continuing up the extensive taxiway system into the hills to cover some five to ten miles of revetments (some occupied by aircraft), ammunition dumps, maintenance sheds et al, all the while running a gauntlet of heavy AAA. The North Vietnamese were making life ever more difficult.

Depending on the time available a great deal of energy could be devoted to perfecting a sortie plan to meet the task requirements, taking account of the weather and continuously changing intelligence updates, only for the mission to be cancelled (often for reasons not clear to those on the flight line). Such was the case with Bob and JPS 5110. The target was the Thai Nguyen industrial complex which Bob planned to approach in the shadow of 'Thud Ridge', hoping to achieve some surprise, before crossing over the ridge near a 4,000 ft spot height for a left hand pull up to photograph the target with the KA-1 cameras. Egress would again have been in the shadow of the ridge, descending with all speed to backtrack north-west. This would have been relatively easy for a pair of RF-101s in tactical formation, but not for larger flights of F-105 bombers, more than a few of which had been lost in that area. The profusion of weapons systems facing the mission is clearly shown in the matrix of colour-coded outlines, leaving

little room for deviation or manoeuvre. Whether this plan would have served its purpose, with the Voodoos surviving, will never be known, but it offers some indication of the forethought and care with which such missions were prepared.

Demands for more timely intelligence from air recce continued to increase with many conflicting priorities ranging from requests for

Mission Cancelled. Bob Archibald's careful planning of Mission JCS 5110, into the massed defences north of Hanoi via 'Thud Ridge', was to no avail; the mission was cancelled. Bob Archibald

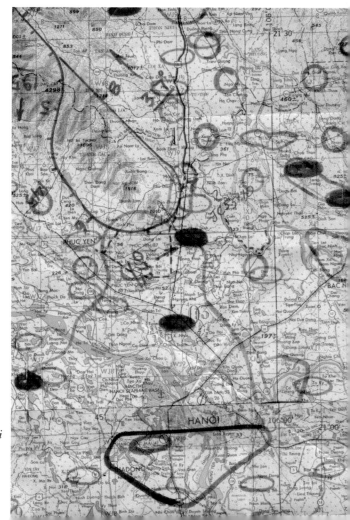

Mugia Pass. RF-101s photographed the shattering effects of this B-52 strike at the northern end of the Ho Chi Minh Trail. USAF via Doug Gordon

targeting material to BDA but continuing to concentrate on interdiction targets, especially along the Ho Chi Minh Trail. The 20th TRS was able to acquire the sort of information required quickly but getting it from Udorn to the main customers at 7th Air Force in Saigon took time. So it was that the more urgent missions flown out of Udorn were henceforth planned from the start to air refuel and proceed direct to Tan Son Nhut with the film. This satisfied the generals but the extended flights made life harder for the Voodoo pilots.

Hard Day's Night. George Cowgill, after flying three missions, feet in a 'bingo' ditch (open sewer) waits at Tan Son Nhut for a ride back to his quarters. George Cowgill

Beyond the Call. George Cowgill, who flew with the Pythons and the 45th TRS, completed 104 countable missions in May 1966.
George Cowgill

212

The war now became a cycle of intensive bombing and one-way ceasefires, from which the North was able to recover quickly and with impunity. Typically, during the first two days of the five-day Tet truce in 1967 the RF-101s from Udorn and Tan Son Nhut photographed more than 1500 trucks on the main routes leading south, with 176 vessels and 14 barges offloading cargo at the Quang Khe ferry. On the final three days they spotted 2799 trucks and 3112 boats in the south of North Vietnam, amphibious craft at Quang Khe and Hook Mi-6 helicopter activity in the area of Dien Bien Phu. In all, analysts estimated that during this ceasefire the enemy moved enough supplies to sustain all the North Vietnamese divisions then in South Vietnam for more than a year. After the truce, just when they were needed most, the Voodoos were ordered by CINCPAC not to fly below 12,000ft unless authorised specifically to do so by his headquarters, and since low cloud ceilings also contrived to help the North Vietnamese, many recce missions had to be cancelled or aborted. The order was soon rescinded.

All this was routine stuff and continuous *déjà vu*, but occasionally the recce pilots were tasked with unusual missions, some a welcome diversion. One pilot was required to fly up the beach in the panhandle of North Vietnam at tree-top height whilst operating his 24-inch focal length nose oblique to enable a detailed analysis of its coastal defences. Unable to hear the Voodoo coming, probably in afterburner at 600 kts, those on the beach must have been terrified by the huge aircraft barely above their heads and then by the crescendo of noise, the euphoric perpetrator remaining unscathed to bring back excellent photography. Another pilot, whether on an assigned task or blessed with opportunity, must have had a similar effect on a number of soldiers manhandling their guns in the open; such finds caused great delight when the resulting photographs were produced. Spectacular sorties, the inherent drama and perils of many and the routine nature of others, made a rich mixture in the flying lives of the Voodoo men of SEA, the like of which could not be easily understood by the uninitiated, while efforts were made to relieve the tensions by improving lifestyles on the bases and offering such rest and recuperation as was possible. Major Nick Pishvanov, 'the Mad Russian' who had done so well in NATO's Royal Flush in very different circumstances a year or so before, and who was now exercising his undoubted professional talents in earnest with the 20th TRS, recalls that life at Udorn overall was not wholly serious and intense. Even in sometimes dire times the Voodoo pilots retained that legendary spirit, sense of humour and banter which has always been the hallmark of a fighter pilot.

On 19 January Stirling led a pair of RF-101s,

Brief Encounter. These hostile gunners were caught in the open by an RF-101. Don Karges

escorted by four F-4s carrying podded noise jammers, against the well defended Phuc Yen airfield. This was a deceivingly uneventful mission, with light and inaccurate AAA and the one SA-2 fired against them missing by some distance, seemingly indicating the effectiveness of the jammers. The next sortie, against the equally heavily defended Kep airfield and two nearby targets north-east of Hanoi, with Stirling leading 'Savannah' Flight and covered by four podded F-4s of 'Rattler' Flight, was very different. Bull recorded that overhead Kep his Voodoo's RHWR; *"went wild with an intense array of spokes and aural warnings' followed by a missile launch light and guidance warning."* Finding this excessively confusing and distracting, Bull switched off the RHWR, allowing a cacophony of other sounds to fill the air as pilots were called to 'push it up' or otherwise evade some 20 SA-2 missiles fired against the six aircraft. Rattler Four went down as the five remaining aircraft twisted and turned to get out of the fight and return home, but the photo mission had been accomplished as required.

A third mission, led by Jim Brickel, also met stiff opposition when tasked over the Thai Nguyen steel plant. His aircraft took many hits, caught fire and lost one engine but he managed

On the Job. The two faces of Major Nick Pishvanov, ready to fly and back at his desk job. Nick Pishvanov

Target Kep. Captain Sandy Sisco photographed Bull Stirling over Kep airfield on a BDA mission escorted by four Phantoms with ECM pods, on 19 January 1967. USAF

to complete his photo run and get his aircraft back to Udorn, further evidence of the resilience of the Voodoos and their pilots. However, the value of this type of ECM cover, taking account of all the pros and cons, remained in doubt; no evidence can be found that this force mix was adopted universally but it was employed when considered desirable with a notional reduction in losses. The story of ECM initiatives, as they affected the RF-101s, is told in Chapter Sixteen.

The reconnaissance priorities for the 20th TRS continued to be centred on North Vietnam, but there remained plenty of work for the Able Mable pilots of Tan Son Nhut in South Vietnam and Laos, pre-planned and reactive, with a heavy emphasis on mosaics of large areas. To meet unpredictable tasks two RF-101s were held in readiness on the airfield throughout daylight hours, and it was they that responded to an opportunity target on 20 February 1967, to keep a convoy moving through the Mu Gia Pass into Laos under surveillance until a strike could be mounted against it. With hostilities intensifying after the Tet Truce, the ever-changing status of the rail network was also subject to the continuous reconnaissance, bombing and repair. With better weather in April and May air activity increased; on 22 May the Voodoos covered 25 primary targets and the same number of opportunity targets, one pilot successfully avoiding no fewer than 20 missiles ripple-fired

at his aircraft.

During 1967 the RF-101s became heavily involved in establishing a detection network, an 'infiltration barrier' along the Ho Chi Minh Trail. This generated signals, night and day, from seismic and acoustic sensors 'planted' along the route which were then transmitted to a cell at RTAFB Nakhon Phanom, where they were translated into specific movement. Starved of this type of detailed information from other sources, this could be invaluable to intelligence staffs and target planners. Critical to the success of this barrier was the positioning of the sensors and to this end the RF-101s, with their KA-1 cameras, were indispensable. So began an on-going task, with photographs of vast tracks of land requiring regular up-dates as more and more sensors were planted; at one time the whole Voodoo force was committed to this role with five sorties a day.

RPVI continued to be the regular venue for the 20th TRS, their RF-101s now flying these most hazardous missions invariably in pairs or with escorts, with a spare aircraft also launched when it was necessary to ensure that one did not have to 'go it alone' (Chapter Fifteen). Either option was to be welcomed but rendezvous with escorts could be difficult in poor weather, particularly in the event of late decisions to launch, while the Voodoos had to reduce their normal operating speeds when in company with the F-4 and there was always the problem of manoeuvring sections of aircraft 'in

Train Spotting. This BDA photograph, taken by the 15th TRS in August 1965, shows the damage caused by an F-105 strike on the infamous North East Railway, 95 miles from Hanoi.
Gene Morris

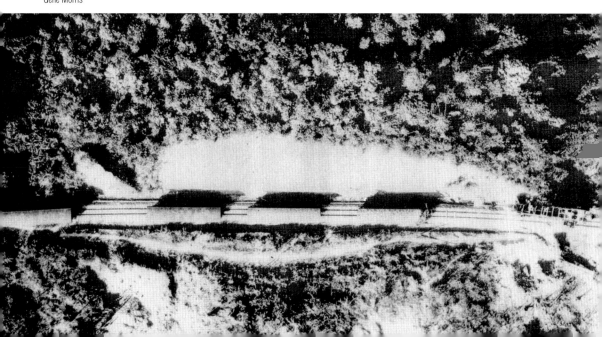

the weeds'. Multiple tasks also became the order of the day, and the acquisition of additional 'opportunity' targets was now actively encouraged. Life in the air for the Voodoo warriors in SEA had become increasingly busy.

John Bull Stirling was now nearing the end of his time in command; in the last difficult year his squadron had lost three aircraft in combat and four more to 'operational accidents', four pilots had been killed and one became a POW, but Bull never wavered in his dynamic and caring leadership, his efforts to achieve operational objectives and minimise losses. Waiting in the wings to take over was Lieutenant Colonel Jim Brickel; he had joined the 20th TRS in November 1966 with little experience on the RF-101, but had been in the thick of it from the start and very soon proved his worth in combat to earn the respect of his squadron. He had been rewarded with an AFC for his courage and tenacity during an especially difficult mission against the Thai Nguyen steel works, and this was followed by a DFC on 1 May for evading missiles and MiGs over the notoriously hostile Hoa Loc airfield in North Vietnam, again to bring back full photo cover. He took command of the 20th TRS on 2 May 1967 and, after the award of a Silver Star on 21 May for another epic trip over a target close to Hanoi, he became the most highly decorated Voodoo pilot in the SEA conflict.

Jim Brickel was of course not alone in his courageous exploits on the 20th TRS; there were too many incidents to recount here from this tumultuous period in US aviation history, with some pilots gaining well-deserved accolades while others went unobserved. Major Notley Maddox fell to the guns over North Vietnam on 20 May 1967, Captain Chuck Winston to a SAM on 1 August; Bobby Bagley and Bob Patterson were downed by MiGs on 16 and 17 September respectively, Patterson being rescued and Bagley becoming a POW.

John Summers, who had flown on the victorious 32nd TRS Royal Flush XII team at Upper Heyford in May 1967, was one of six seasoned recce pilots detached from there to Tan Son Nhut for three months TDY in August 1967. The newly arrived pilots lived in a two-story Villa in Saigon, guarded by Chinese mercenaries who, in John's words; *"made the Mafia look like a Sunday School Class"*. They were known to promise that if anyone attacked a building they guarded they would track them down and kill them, their wives, children, brothers, sisters and parents. There were no such attacks. The Heyford group spent the first month only in this comparative luxury before completing their TDY at Udorn.

In July 1967, USAF Headquarters advised PACAF that the last available RF-101 had been

Team Effort. All those involved with the 20th TRS at Udorn contributed to the achievement of 5000 sorties in March 1967. USAF

At Ease. Officers of the 20th TRS take a break in their hectic schedule at Udorn in 1967. Source Unknown

delivered to SEA, and this led to the deactivation of the 20th TRS at Udorn in the following October, most of its aircraft and personnel being transferred to the 45th TRS at Tan Son Nhut.

As with the Pythons of the 15th TRS before them, the 20th TRS had covered themselves with glory. In a team effort they had done all that had been asked of them - and more - despite the difficulties of a rapid turnover of pilots and maintenance personnel, with a commensurate reduction in pilot experience on the aircraft and in the role. Regardless of this, and some inevitable loss of the 'individuality' which had become inherent in those who had flown recce for years, the new boys had played out their role with distinction on the most dangerous stage in the SEA theatre. They had been led superbly at the front by the 'old heads' and the new executives who had to learn rapidly the stark realities of their air war.

Roll of Honour. Recorded for posterity, the names of 56 pilots of the 20th TRS who flew 100 'counters' over SEA, March 1966-October 1967. Don Karges & Harry Runge

CHAPTER THIRTEEN
THE END GAME?

'The one who does not remember history is bound to live through it again.'

George Santayana

From October 1967 all SEA Voodoos were assembled at Tan Son Nhut with the 45th TRS, under the command and control of the 460th TRW; by now they were camouflaged, carried the tail letters 'AH' and would in principle be committed mainly to southern North Vietnam, Laos and South Vietnam. With attrition continuing to deplete the force, was this the 'end game' for the Voodoos in SEA? In fact, they would soldier on until November 1970, pressured to do so because there would still be too few recce resources to meet the many demands and because of the popularity of the Voodoo's unique 36-inch split vertical cameras. So it was neither the end, nor was it a game.

Good Company. Now camouflaged, with small tail numbers and USAF insignia, RF-101C 56-096 'Iron Eyeball' with F-100 and Caribou at Tan Son Nhut in 1966. George Cowgill

All Together Now. The 45th TRS 'Polka Dots' at Tan Son Nhut. Doug Gordon Collection

Up Front. Rich Richardson making good use of the Forward Operating Location (FOL) at Phu Cat, which halved the Voodoo flight time from Tan Son Nhut to the North. Rich Richardson

It Could Happen To Anyone! This F-100 came to grief at Phu Cat AB. Nick Pishvanov

In August 1967 a Forward Operating Location (FOL) was set up at Phu Cat in central South Vietnam, closer to the forward army units and the main operating areas, thus offering improvements to response times. Already an F-100 base, Phu Cat's refuelling, aircraft maintenance and photo processing facilities were enhanced to serve the Voodoos. This proved to be a useful asset in September's Operation Neutralise, aimed at finding North Vietnamese field artillery menacing US Marine positions close to the DMZ. These gun emplacements could not be identified from the RF-4Cs cameras with the small format, but the Voodoos KA-1s revealed the positions allowing effective strikes to take place.

The recce aircraft would continue to play a full part in the intensive bombing campaign and take losses. In the true tradition of combat airmen, the fliers never seemed to lose their sense of humour, regardless of the risks and losses, and a story emerged from the first 'River Rat' Reunion dinner in 1967, hosted by 'Blackman and Robin' (fighter aces Chappie James and Robin Olds), to bear this out. A USN officer is said to have read a message, allegedly sent to Ho Chi Minh, which offered to shove a whole squadron of fighter bombers off the back of a carrier if he blew up the recalcitrant bridge at Thanh Hoa - thus saving both sides the unpleasantness of continuing as they had been. Sadly, the bridge remained intact for several more years, with USN and USAF aircraft losses mounting.

Already an experienced recce pilot, Major Luster ('Vic') Vickrey, who had learnt his trade at Shaw during the author's time there and then on the 66th TRW in Europe, got to SEA in the fall of 1967. He had been on TDY at Eglin AFB, Florida from the 363rd TRW at Shaw, helping to plan McNamara's 'electronic wall'(Chapter Twelve), when he heard on the grapevine that he and his colleagues were to move to SEA to continue this work on ground assignments, and indeed to that end each was issued with a folding chair and table. The thought of a desk job in SEA was too much for Vic, who volunteered there and then for combat duties with the Voodoo squadron and within a week he was on his way to Tan Son Nhut. With many of the 45th TRS pilots, including the supervisors, lacking his already extensive experience on the aircraft and in recce, his appointment as the Wing's all-important Stan Eval/Combat Tactics Officer would be a great asset.

Vic then made sure that this was no desk job and was soon in the air in the thick of it, flying his first mission over the DMZ on 26 September 1967. When the North Vietnamese started shelling Allied troops across the DMZ, Vic Vickrey was in his element; he defied the conventional wisdom and relative safety of the less vulnerable heights, drawing on his experience to bring back vital photography of the offending guns from low level. In his own words:

"Mid-altitude or vertical photography having proved useless, we went in at 100 ft and 550 kts, with all oblique cameras blazing, and in that way found our targets

Bombs Gone! RF-101s supported bombing sorties by F-4s, F-105s and B-52s. Gene Morris & Vic Vickrey

Chance Find. This unusual sighting of an NVA armoured fighting vehicle near Khe Sanh at the beginning of 1968 attracted much interest. Vic Vickrey

hiding under the trees and camouflage netting".

Vic led the first of these missions and flew eight in all, inter alia checking out squadron executives and others without loss. Following a particularly hazardous low level sortie on 1 October, leading a flight of RF-101s into the North, he was awarded the Silver Star. Fortune favours the brave.

As 1967 gave way to 1968 the Allies were facing major setbacks on the ground throughout the country and another truce over Christmas 1967 and the New Year did nothing but help the aggressors. It remained business as usual for the Voodoos during a further phase of

Operation Rolling Thunder, and in providing crucial support to US Marines under attack by two North Vietnamese divisions at Khe Sanh helped to bring about an end to the siege in March 1968. It was at about this time that the recce pilots' visual sightings, offering near real time information, began to make a real contribution - corroborating evidence coming from other sources confirming what they reported. For intelligence staffs who had demanded photographs this was a real breakthrough; perhaps the integration of seasoned operational strike and reconnaissance pilots into army units at all levels might have helped convince the soldiers that they could rely on this raw intelligence. Major Nick Pishvanov, who had served only recently with the 20th TRS at Udorn, was one such air adviser, he serving with the Army Corps HQ at Hue Citadel.

In the early hours of 31 January 1968, co-incidental with continuing operations at Khe Sanh, North Vietnamese troops and the Viet Cong attacked cities and military targets throughout the country. The Tet Lunar New Year Offensive had begun. Tan Son Nhut itself was the subject of an audacious raid, with mortars and rockets which damaged some RF-101s and facilities. This could have been a disaster for the defenders, had not a handful of USAF Air Police warded off the attackers when the South Vietnamese airfield guards fled, until US Army helicopter gunships and troop

Army Co-Operation. Nick Pisvanov, as Recce Support Officer with the army in SEA, desperate to get airborne again, risked flying with some 'lunatic' Army pilots in their Huey helicopters, and survived! Nick Pishvanov

Self Survival. Rich Richardson, carbine to hand, helped fight off an attack on the pilots' villa, downtown Saigon in January 1968.

Rich Richardson

reinforcements came to the rescue. Fortunately, many of the munitions fired at the airfield had failed to explode and the aircraft revetments had absorbed much of the blast from those which did. There was much excitement too downtown, some one-and-a-half miles from the airfield at the pilot's villa, where again South Vietnamese guards deserted their posts and left the pilots to defend themselves. This they did, dressed in flak jackets and armed with carbines. During a lull in the fighting the aircrew returned to the airfield to find it littered with unexploded ordnance and debris, but that their groundcrew had patched up several aircraft damaged in the raids and had all they could recover ready for flying. First, the Voodoos had a job to do very close to home, to seek out intruders in the local area and attempt to spot the hides from which the rockets had been fired at the base. To this end the pilots got airborne between fire fights, one having a brush with a bullet which beat him to his Voodoo and causing him to change direction to the spare aircraft in which he then completed his mission.

On 1 February, while the airfield was still under sporadic attack and debris littered the runway, Major Rich Richardson took off for his first sortie of the day to cover interdiction targets in the A Shau Valley, a deep cleft between high mountain ranges. He found the valley covered by cloud, but with just enough gaps for him to complete the two runs necessary to cover his first targets satisfactorily

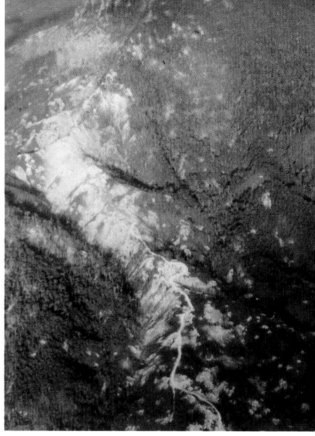

Death Valley. The A Shau Valley, a cleft between two mountain ranges in northern South Vietnam, came under constant surveillance by the 45th TRS, this devastation probably due to carpet bombing by B-52s. Nick Pishvanov

using the KA-1, forward oblique and 6-inch 'little looker' pan cameras, but he had to fight the weather and some sporadic ground fire all the way. He then climbed out to recover at Phu Cat to refuel, have his film processed and prepare for a second mission in the afternoon against three airfields in the A Shau Valley. Again dodging cloud and the high peaks ranging either side of the valley, from which came heavy flak, Rich found and photographed all three targets. He then returned to Saigon, where he completed his sortie with several photo strips of the local area, a common practice among the Voodoo pilots when fuel allowed to enable the PIs to search for the latest intruder activity. All in a day's work, but easier said than done! Rich Richardson would complete his 100 missions in 1968 and return to Shaw AFB. The recce pilots would go back to the very heavily defended A Shau Valley

All Over. Rich Richardson completes his 100th 'counter' at TSN in 1968.

Rich Richardson

repeatedly as the North Vietnamese increased construction work to improve access to the south.

The Tet Lunar New Year offensive changed everything around Saigon, including the pilots' lifestyle. There were now numerous 'no-go' areas and local movement was severely curtailed; the pilots moved on to the base into makeshift accommodation which was far from ideal, and vulnerable to well-aimed missiles. With everyone now on constant alert against attack, occasional raids on the base, less comfortable surroundings and a demanding flying schedule, sleep was hard to come by. All this led to increased stress and fatigue levels but the RF-101 pilots continued to do all that was asked of them.

The communists struck Tan Son Nhut again on 18 February 1968, with 122-mm rockets destroying one RF-101 and damaging eight others. These attacks, with crude but effective weapons fired from unprepared sites, continued sporadically for some time with little detrimental effect other than to increase tensions throughout the base and divert recce effort from much needed tasks up-country to local area defence, albeit with very little success.

The diminishing RF-101 force was now becoming progressively more limited in what it could offer. The provision of spares to replace the ever-increasing number of war-worn parts was becoming a major problem, exacerbated by a critical error in the supply chain which returned urgently required spares to the US as 'no longer needed'. It would take six months for the aircraft's spares system to recover, during which time hard-pressed maintenance crews had to resort to the time-consuming practice of 'cannibalization' to keep what they could in the air. There was more bad news in 1968, when it was discovered that the potting compound used to insulate some of the aircraft's electrical connectors when the aircraft were modified to Project 1181 was melting, leaving bare wires and every chance of an electrical fire. However, strenuous efforts by a 16-man specialist rectification team carried out the necessary remedial action for the whole RF-101 fleet at Tan Son Nhut in a month. The unsung heroes in the background had risen to the occasion again.

On 31 March 1968, President Johnson announced that, with the exception of those forces currently menacing the Allies around the DMZ, all raids into North Vietnam would cease at 0800 hours on 1 April. As usual, however, reconnaissance over the North continued; the RF-101s much in demand and very busy again between April and June taking part in Operation Turnpike, again to locate enemy movements southwards, truck parks and supply depots.

The huge losses incurred by the Viet Cong in the Tet New Year offensive did nothing to deter a repeat performance and the 'Second Offensive' was launched simultaneously against a large number of cities and military targets in South Vietnam on 5 May. Fearing for its Voodoo force on the ground, the 460th TRW had five of its RF-101s moved to Phu Cat each evening and returned to Tan Son Nhut in the mornings. With 'uncompromising' Korean regular soldiers standing guard on them at Phu Cat it was assumed that there would be little risk from ground intruders but the base was targeted on 11 May by mortars and rockets, damaging two of the Voodoos and bringing to an end the policy of nightly dispersal.

Although more attacks were expected around Saigon, keeping the Voodoos busy searching local areas and the defences in a continuous, tiring state of alert, they did in fact diminish. More sporadic raids there were, but many Voodoo sorties over the 'rocket belt' around Saigon were now returning without information on the targets and the intensity of these local operations gradually reduced. This freed up assets needed urgently for the summer interdiction programme, which began in July 1968 and became open-ended as the North Vietnamese extended the road system and poured ever more reinforcements and supplies into the south. The search for heavy field artillery pounding Allied defensive positions from across the DMZ continued, the pilots now facing new concentrations of AAA and SAMs in the area and having very limited success; natural camouflage and skilled concealment had hidden the guns well and, however hard the pilots and PIs looked they could find only a few of the many that were known to be there. Although Major Giles Harlow was brought down during these operations on 6 August 1968, Rich Richardson maintains that their losses were minimised by the pilots insisting that detailed planning of their missions be left to those who had absorbed considerable and

sometimes painful experience over many years in SEA, whereas slavish adherence to detailed orders from on high could have led to unnecessary losses. He points to one potentially very hazardous mission, for which the target planners called for a six-line area cover at a very vulnerable low level, to which the pilots applied their own tactical expertise. So it was that six pilots each planned to fly one line, in parallel and separated by one mile to ensure the right sidelap, and within the same small time window to give some element of surprise. In fact, one pilot admitted (very courageously) that, in the stress of the moment, he failed to operate his cameras on his line and, with pride prevailing over caution, had returned to his start point, against all the rules, to repeat his line. He survived and the mission was accomplished, but he was lucky.

Small arms fire remained an on-going concern, now to be expected almost anywhere in SEA. Although the pilots retained the final say, executives stressed the need for single passes only over a target, at minimum heights of 2000 ft and 3000 ft over known concentrations. Where cloud precluded important area cover photography at these heights a maximum of three lines should be flown. Paucity of assets now limited most missions to single aircraft.

Lieutenant Colonel Jack Bowland, fresh from his triumph in Royal Flush at RAF Upper Heyford, arrived to command the 45th TRS at Tan Son Nhut in 1968, to face very different challenges. By this time, most of the seasoned recce men from the Voodoo force had completed their time in SEA and, although his squadron was heavy in rank (predominantly majors and lieutenant colonels), the recce experience overall was low, so the return of John Summers to Tan Son Nhut in July was welcome.

John arrived as a captain, was promoted to major in September and remained at Tan Son Nhut for a total of nine months, adding to the three months TDY in 1967 to complete one year in theatre. There was plenty for all to do but much discussion among both veterans and 'new recruits' over who should be tasked where and with what, with particular reference to the division of allotments between North and South Vietnam. The arguments could be in logical conflict, with experience so often being a prerequisite to success and survival, but such

'At Home'. Moved on to the base when trouble flared up in Saigon, the 45th TRS pilots soon made themselves at home in their BOQ at Tan Son Nhut. John Summers

Back to the Future. John Summers returned to the 45th TRS in July 1968 as a captain; he lost no time getting airborne again, was promoted to major in September and completed his tour in SEA in April 1969.

John Summers

experience gained only with practice (and inevitably with some targets missed). This was a balance of risks. On a personal level there were also the attractions of two points earned towards an Air Medal, 'up North', compared with one point elsewhere in the war zone, with of course the desire to achieve that prestigious 100 missions, and return home.

As expected, the officers made the best of their new domestic circumstances on the base at Tan Son Nhut. How it came about is not quite clear, but the pilots assumed that concrete laid alongside their accommodation block, and the delivery of building materials were for their benefit, and they at once constructed their own recreation room and barbecue patio. This they fashioned in the style of the English pub, complete with a darts board for the sport they had grown to love at Upper Heyford, and christened it 'Ye Old Polka Dot Pub'. All was well until visiting inspectors wanted to know what had happened to the 'Training Facility' for which they had provided the wherewithal. Down came the pub notice and up went the training schedule, until the inspectors had gone.

Back at work there was an unexpected and interesting diversion from the recce routine. Up until the early 1960s many who passed through the recce school at Shaw questioned the value of including 'artillery adjustment' within the flying syllabus, albeit with only one sortie committed to it flown over a gunnery range in North Carolina. The RF-101, with its wide turning radius, would have been an unwilling 'sitting duck' within visual range of hostile fire at very vulnerable heights and speeds and could hardly have been expected to have done the job effectively in such circumstances. Little did they know then that they might apply this rudimentary knowledge in earnest in SEA to adjust naval gunfire, typically with the 16-inch guns of the WW2 battleship 'New Jersey' firing 2,000 lb shells some 25 miles from off the coast of Vietnam, and with some success.

It was during John Summers' time that the 'Paras' of the 101st Airborne Division were in town, always anxious to get on with the job. They deplored the several days it could take for an intelligence request to be fulfilled, given the speed of its collection by the Voodoos, and greatly welcomed the strictly unofficial help they got from the RF-101 pilots. It was easy; if a pilot thought he might have time and fuel to spare after a short mission or 'test hop' he could invite the soldiers to specify the photography (or a visual recce) they needed within a certain range of Tan Son Nhut. When the film arrived back (preferably all on one camera) it would be processed unofficially as a 'camera test' and the prints delivered without delay direct to the requester. John proved the value of this expedient when he brought back information by this means on a hitherto unknown enemy troop concentration which could have inflicted heavy casualties on the 101st Airborne who had planned an attack in that area. This was air recce utilisation at its best, doing much for operational effectiveness and inter-service relationships in Saigon.

Still the Voodoo pilots pursued both routine and exciting work with skill and enterprise, sometimes taking risks which might not be condoned by those pulling the strings on the ground, John Summers being typical of the breed. He had been tasked to carry out BDA after a strike but when he arrived over the target four F-100s were still hard at it and John decided to join them, to 'kill'em with fil'm'. By slotting into the attack pattern each time the number four 'Hun' pilot completed a pass he intended to get real-time strike photographs of weapons impact, but he did more. His passes attracted hostile fire which enabled the F-100 pilots to pin-point the guns and take them out on their next pass, in what indeed became a joint effort. Much impressed, someone in the F-100 force reported all this to the Vietnamese military, who awarded John their Air Operations Medal (Honor Class), an equivalent

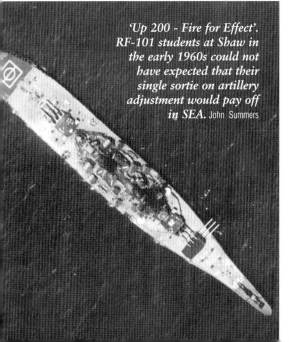

'Up 200 - Fire for Effect'. RF-101 students at Shaw in the early 1960s could not have expected that their single sortie on artillery adjustment would pay off in SEA. John Summers

Strike! While carrying out his 'instant BDA', John Summers drew gunfire for the accompanying F-100 pilots to plot and strike on their next pass. John Summers

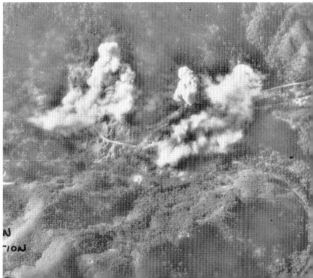

to the USAF's Silver Star. However, by the time the paperwork got back to the 'States, John was undergoing conversion to the B-58 (Hustler), at Grisson AFB, Indiana, and it was there that he should have been the star of the show at a lavish ceremony planned to celebrate the award. Sadly, when the local press advertised the forthcoming event it implied, quite incorrectly, that the medal had been won by a B-58 flyer during 'secret missions' over SEA, and this incorrect assertion so concerned the generals that the ceremony was cancelled. John had to be content with the presentation of this medal in the Wing Commander's Office to go with his Silver Star, two DFCs and 12 Air Medals, an enviable tally but perhaps not an unusual array for a long-term Voodoo man who had served in SEA. He then suffered another disappointment when the B-58 was cancelled two days before his first flight, but was consoled by a posting to the first FB-111 class.

Apart from sundry diversions, the interdiction campaign of repetitive tasks dominated operational flying for the remainder of 1968 and well into 1969. As American and South Vietnamese aircraft blocked one route, the enemy opened another and repaired the first under cover of darkness or poor flying weather, so it was incumbent on the Voodoo pilots to provide daily updates. As a matter of routine, the 45th TRS would send two aircraft north every day to cover the same infiltration routes, invariably with their KA-1 cameras. Frequently, they would land at Udorn to have the film processed and analysed without delay, while their aircraft were refuelling and reloading with film for their return sortie.

Another bombing halt at the end of October 1968 was based on the expectation of useful peace talks in Paris but as usual this proved to be too optimistic as air defences in the North Vietnamese panhandle were again strengthened and convoy activity increased. Recce flights continued, but the few RF-101s which crossed the DMZ into the North were escorted until March 1969, when they were permitted again to go alone, provided they remained below 17 degrees 15 minutes north and could keep their height above 15,000 ft. The interdiction programme concentrated again on the A Shau Valley in 'Project Mac See', but for the Voodoos it was *déjà vu*.

The 45th TRS had now standardised the

Just Rewards. Belated congratulations for Major John Summers on the award of the Republic of Vietnam Operations Medal (Honor Class). John Summers

camera fit in its aircraft, thus eliminating the delays caused by continuous changes. For forward oblique work a KS-72, 12-inch focal length camera in the nose was invaluable for the few ultra-low level 'dicing' missions. The centre station contained a 3-inch panoramic camera and pair of 6-inch KS-72A split verticals, while the much-favoured KA-1 36-inch split verticals were retained in the aft compartment. Secure 'Seek Silence' communications were also fitted on site to all RF-101s in SEA, with High Frequency (HF) communications added to some of the aircraft.

As 1969 drew to a close, economy measures brought staging operations at Phu Cat to an end, while reducing both the AAR tankers available to the recce aircraft and the pilot-to-aircraft ratio within the RF-101 force. This curtailed the number of long range missions for the 45th TRS severely and most of those flown into North Vietnam had to refuel at Da Nang, with an inevitable delay in film exploitation, but there remained plenty of work for them elsewhere. The Voodoos, with their unique camera fit, were again the aircraft of choice for a major interdiction operation Commando Hunt III in North East Laos, and again they excelled with photographs of movement along road and rail described in official papers as 'clear and sharp'. In this operation the recce pilots also developed a procedure in which they orbited close to target areas during strikes, for immediate commitment to BDA by an Airborne Battlefield Command and Control Centre

(ABC3) as soon as the smoke had cleared and before the results could be concealed (but not before the defences were ready for them). Reaction times to opportunity targets or urgent requirements were also minimised by diverting RF-101s already airborne to higher priority tasks or scrambled from an alert state. It had taken a long time for the hierarchy to recognise the value of such decentralisation and flexibility, but better late than never. However, the alert posture succumbed to further economies in April 1970, the 45th TRS then required to retain one aircraft only and a pilot 'on call'. The aircraft were now provided with overhead shelter at Tan Son Nhut.

Poor weather generally had prevailed throughout the Commando Hunt III campaign over North Vietnam but when it cleared single Voodoos continued their forays into the North, but still only as far as 17 degrees 15 minutes, sometimes escorted and predominantly at low level to minimise the risk from the new MiG-21s which were now prowling over the panhandle in an area also infested with SAMs. The North Vietnamese reacted by reinforcing low level air defence with more automatic weapons, causing 7th Air Force to raise the minimum heights for the Voodoos to 4,500 ft.

In April 1970, President Nixon ordered attacks to 'clean out enemy sanctuaries on the Cambodia-Vietnam border' and a month later, in Operation Face Value, the Voodoos were authorised to fly 60 nm into Cambodia to photograph every target which might have

Top Cover. After the intruder attacks in early 1968, the aircraft were also given added protection at TSN. USAF

military significance, but avoiding the capital Phnom Penh. These sorties revealed that the Khmer Rouge insurgents and their North Vietnamese supporters were using specific rivers extensively to transport personnel and supplies into the country. Surveillance of these routes became a primary role for the RF-101s at the expense of requirements in South Vietnam, and the Joint Services Committee eventually approved, with certain restrictions, reconnaissance over the whole of Cambodia.

The first official indication that Voodoo operations were about to come to an end came in February 1970, with a proposal to de-activate the 45th TRS later in the year, together with the 16-aircraft RF-101 training unit at Shaw AFB. 7th Air Force opposed the move on the grounds that only the venerable Voodoo could produce the much wanted, large format KA-1 photography, but to no avail. The 45th TRS ceased operations on 1 November 1970 and the last RF-101 left Tan Son Nhut on 16 November bound for the Air National Guard at

Meridian, Mississippi. The 45th TRS then re-formed with RF-4Cs within the 67th TRW at Bergstrom, commanded by Voodoo veteran Colonel George Edwards.

So ended the epic story of Voodoo commitment in SEA, a story of duty and courage among the RF-101 pilots and their groundcrew, and in which 35 of their aircraft were lost together with some 13 pilots. The information they brought back on their photographs, and visual reports, contributed markedly to the overall intelligence picture, specific operations and target analysis. The pilots had faced grave dangers from the increasing ferocity of massed air defences, unpredictable and often inhibiting weather and from natural causes, and they had done so with facilities on the ground and in the air which were far from ideal. It had been a job well done.

The chapters which follow focus on some of the aspects of RF-101 operations, in SEA and world-wide, which deserve special emphasis.

CHAPTER FOURTEEN
THE GREAT SAM HUNT
- A ROUTINE SORTIE?

'Where are we - why is he doing that......Oh S**t!'

A Recce Pilot

With the conflict in SEA in full swing by 1965 there was probably no such thing as a 'routine sortie'; although there were factors common to most, each mission had its own demands and attendant risks and was flown in very different circumstances. Those over South Vietnam and Laos were relatively simple, albeit never risk-free, but penetrating North Vietnam, particularly into well-defended areas, was quite another thing. Pilots assigned to these missions were seen to be 'taking their turn in the barrel' and they were faced with varying and very personal degrees of trepidation.

Take one trip flown by Major Marv Reed of the 45th TRS with Captain Chuck Lustig, attached from the 15th TRS, as his wingman. A pair of RF-101s was tasked on 28 July 1965 to seek out a suspected SA-2 site some 15 miles south-west of Hanoi, a similar site near the capital having been responsible for damaging four F-4s on the 25 July in one of the first major SAM actions of the war. On that day Marv had been airborne nearby with his number two, Major Ralph Kral, orbiting in cloud waiting to carry out BDA on a target nearby, so they heard the whole saga reported on the radio as it developed.

It was because the F-4s were at medium level, in a height band ideal for the SAMs, that the Voodoos were now ordered to go in low to avoid that threat and obtain close-up photos of the new missiles. However, in doing so they would be exposed to rings of AAA expected to be defending the site; the same guns which had downed three F-105s in the area on 27 July. As usual the Voodoo pilots were placed in a dilemma.

Captain Marv Reed. Marv Reed

Captain Chuck Lustig. Chuck Lustig

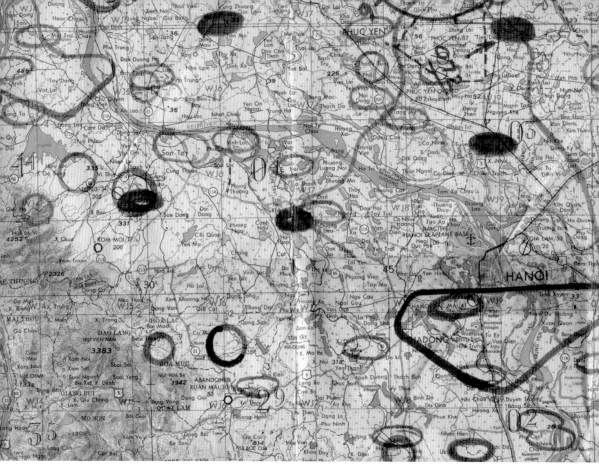

The Great SAM Hunt. The Voodoos had to run the gauntlet of heavy defences in their successful SAM hunt. Chuck Lustig

At Tan Son Nhut, the temporary home of the 45th TRS on Able Mable duty, Marv, Chuck and Ralph Kral (who would man the spare aircraft) began some rapid planning to meet a noon TOT. They would air refuel from a KC-135 on the Thailand/Laos border and proceed over the mountains of Laos, into the PDJ and up to the border with North Vietnam, then turn north-east to descend and cross the Red River near Yen Bai at low level. The pair was then to reverse south to recross the Red River and climb to 500 ft to take the photographs required in the target area of Son Tay. Egress would be south over the mountains again in the climb to refuel from the waiting tanker. The weather in the target area was forecast to be unusually good, with scattered cloud and a little haze.

The three pilots walked to their aircraft in good time but during the lengthy start-up Marv found that he could neither transmit nor receive on his ARC-34 radio, and Ralph Kral had to take the lead in the spare aircraft. Some pilots would have left it at that, happy to live to fly another day, but not Marv Reed. He demanded another aircraft and with all speed started up, secured a priority clearance through heavy traffic and took off in front of a long line of civilian and military aircraft, speeding north to catch up the pair ahead. This he did while the planned refuelling was taking place, after which he took the lead and invited Kral to return to base. As every leader knows, this is hardly the best way to start a difficult mission, and who could know what lay in store ahead?

The descent to low level also went according to plan, after which they jettisoned their external tanks and increased speed to 540 kts to cross the Red River at tree-top height with Chuck flying in tactical formation off Marv's starboard wing. That was when they were greeted by a veritable fury of flak. They could hear the booms and feel the blast from the 37-mm and 57-mm AAA, together with the infamous Russian-built ZSU-23/4, and see the gunners' faces as they fired at them from point

French Legacy. As Chuck Lustig led in the turn south from Yen Bai, Marv Reed caught these North Vietnamese gunners on his nose-facing oblique camera, firing from old French revetments. Marv Reed

Above & below: Warm Welcome. Guns of all calibres were always waiting for the Voodoos after they had crossed the Red River. Marv Reed

blank range. This was no place to hang around but high time to select afterburner to get all the speed possible from the now 'clean' Voodoos. This mission was going to be no picnic. In hindsight, Marv believes that they only survived by flying below the guns' lowest depression.

The higher than planned speed rendered the pre-planned time marks redundant and for a few moments Marv experienced every low level pilot's nightmare, he became uncertain of his position (a recce pilot is never 'lost'). They seemed to be heading directly for downtown Hanoi, where the notorious 'Hanoi Hilton' welcomed American pilots. When Marv admitted to Chuck that he was uneasy, his wingman came immediately to the rescue in an excellent example of just one of the virtues of flying pairs of aircraft; he knew where they were and took the lead.

The two Voodoos were now approaching the target with cameras operating to record the surrounding defences, Marv's nose-facing oblique camera later revealing concrete bunkers (legacies of the French occupation) and gun defences which were clearly firing at them. No doubt the gunners were also warning those ahead to be ready for them. With this early warning system in place the Voodoos might remain hidden from the radars at ultra low level, but they could not hope to achieve much needed surprise and from then on they were given a very warm welcome.

Having found their position on the map as they approached their IP on the Red River, Marv Reed resumed the lead and they climbed to the more vulnerable height of 500 ft necessary for the photo task. They were now

running a continuous gauntlet of automatic weapons which lined several kilometres of the southern bank; in Marv's own words *"all the guns were shrouded in smoke as they fired at us, a most pernicious display of xenophobia towards a couple of unarmed Yankee pilots".* How they were able to fly through this intense barrage from IP to target, unscathed, seems something of a miracle. Indeed, Marv said afterwards that: *"this was probably the most fortuitously successful event we could experience in a lifetime".*

As they approached the target, 'with bent throttles', Marv passed over a 100-mm gunsite, clearly shown in photos from his pan camera which were published in the February 1966

No Threat. This 100-mm AAA site, caught on Marv Reed's pan camera as the pair ran in to the suspect SAM site, would be no threat to the low flying RF-101s. Marv Reed

Flak Trap. Chuck Lustig, flying Marv Reed's wing, also photographed the unusual sight of 100-mm AAA in two lines, with associated radar. Chuck Lustig

Target Sighted! The suspect SAM site was sighted roughly in the position given - but the missiles were fakes; mission accomplished! Chuck Lustig

edition of 'Newsweek'. From his position, offset by a quarter of a mile in line abreast, Chuck spotted another 100-mm site, unusual in its layout, but then both pilots saw 'something white' off to the left and there, fleetingly, were the missiles they sought. As the Voodoos continued south and began their climb over the mountains to rendezvous with the KC-135, Marv remembers:

"a euphoric adrenaline rush of exhilaration, coupled with an awesome feeling of relief and accomplishment. There is no greater feeling in this world than having been unsuccessfully shot at."

They had the courage and determination to get it right, but perhaps they were also a little lucky.

Back at Tan Son Nhut, after a mission lasting 4 hours 10 minutes, the photo lab men lost no time getting the films to the light tables ready for analysis by the PIs and no lesser man than General Rockly Triantafellu, Director of Intelligence, 2nd Air Division. The results were excellent; the two pilots having covered the target area and captured the 'missiles' on their pan cameras. There were six SA-2s, set in a typical circular cluster with radar control at the centre, but they were fakes to decoy aircraft into an area bristling with guns of every description, a veritable flak trap from which Marv and Chuck had escaped.

It was an unwritten rule on the squadron that after a mission such as this had been flown up north 'in the barrel', the pilots involved would be allocated a less risky mission to follow, and Marv was not unhappy to be given an 'in country' task on 29 July, a mosaic of the Mekong Delta. This also gave him the opportunity to practise the 'pop-up' tactic

*Survivors. Chuck Lustig (left) and Marv
Reed lived to tell the tale - many times!* Don
Karges Collection

which he and Chuck had been discussing and
which was then being developed elsewhere
(Chapter Sixteen), the aim being to remain at a
highly vulnerable height only for as long as the
photographic task required. This he did to his
satisfaction, landing back at Tan Son Nhut in
mid-morning to find that his squadron had
been tasked to return 'as soon as possible' to
the same missile site at which he and Chuck

had so nearly met their maker the day before,
even though the photographs had confirmed
the decoys and a flak trap. Being the ranking
pilot available, and notwithstanding 'the rule'
about returning to the North again so soon, he
chose to take the lead again with Captain Dan
Doughty as his wingman. This time, however,
despite a great deal of scepticism and some
opposition on the part of others, they used the
pop-up manoeuvre to succeed in their mission
and found the flak significantly less menacing.

The story has a tragic and almost
unbelievable sequel. As Marv and Dan were
returning to their base they heard their mutual
friends, Captains Jack Weatherby and Jerry
Lentz, departing for the same target they had
again covered successfully only a few minutes
before. Believing that their photographs would
once more prove satisfactory for the purpose,
Marv suggested that the mission be aborted,
but the command cell ordered Weatherby and
Lentz to continue. This they did, repeating the
same low level approach which Marv and
Chuck had found so hazardous the day before.
This time the guns at Yen Bai scored direct hits
on Jack's aircraft, causing massive fuel leaks
and a subsequent fuselage fire. Undeterred,
Jack continued his photo run and turned for
home, Jerry pleading with him to abandon his
aircraft as the flames increased until the
Voodoo exploded and crashed in a ball of fire
from which there could have been no escape for
the pilot. Lentz returned to the tanker and
thence to Tan Son Nhut with his recce report.

Very few missions 'in the barrel' could be
called 'routine'.

CHAPTER FIFTEEN
GOING IT ALONE

'Alone, Unarmed and Unafraid'

Recce War-cry

Debate on the pros and cons of employing single aircraft or pairs on recce missions in SEA, whether or when they should be escorted or unescorted, within strike packages or operating independently, continued throughout the conflict and has done since. Previous chapters have touched on the revisions and reversals in policy on these matters, citing specific circumstances and the changing nature of the defences, economic imperatives, experience levels and other determinants, invariably accompanied by caveats and reservations. Inevitably, personal experiences and perceptions have added weight to one argument or another. This chapter draws some of the threads together, with particular reference to the single-seat RF-101, without attempting to suggest which option fits which occasion.

While the recce force in SEA was building up and before the risks became great, it might not have been unreasonable to fly 'single ship' recce missions. Early sorties were generally limited to the relatively less dangerous overflights of Laos and South Vietnam (with an occasional peek over the neighbouring borders); they were not devoid of risk but the gunfire came largely from low calibre AAA (compared with that which was to come) unguided by radar, and from small arms. Where flak concentrations were known to exist they might be avoided or overflown above their range, subject of course to task requirements. Before SAMs and hostile fighters threatened the Voodoos, the case for tasking a pair of aircraft was certainly arguable.

The principle of flying single seat recce aircraft in pairs in a more hostile environment would seem very sound. In the first place, the mission might call for more photo cover than could be provided by a single aircraft on what should invariably be a single pass. Also, a second pair of eyes might see assigned or opportunity targets missed by the leader, and in any event the visual report should be more accurate when covered from slightly different perspectives. Equally important, leader and wingman are able to provide mutual cross-cover, drawing each other's attention to hostile flak, missiles and fighters, thereafter assisting in any evasive action. In addition to maintaining a good look-out, a wingman should monitor closely the route being flown against an essentially joint plan (both men sharing their ideas and experience), ready and able to assist the leader in his navigation should the latter become uncertain of his position, either by helping him to recover to track or by taking the lead himself (see Chapter Fourteen 'The Great SAM Hunt'). Also, in the event of a leader having to abort the sortie on the ground with an aircraft unserviceability, or in the air with battle damage, the second man should be able to complete the mission as planned (assuming that single aircraft missions were not seen to be too hazardous in the prevailing circumstances). Finally, in the nature RF-101 operations in SEA, where communications were tenuous at low level in mountainous terrain, a second man could be invaluable should his partner have to eject, not only to report the likely cause and exact location but in helping search and rescue operations.

However, all these benefits might succumb to the need for economy of effort, and there were those who extolled the virtues of 'single ship' missions. They argued that such sorties capitalised on the individuality of an experienced recce pilot, that one aircraft presented a smaller and less attractive target, that the pilot could concentrate solely on himself and his aircraft without having to worry about a wingman and that there were no 'tell-tale' radio transmissions. A single aircraft can also be manoeuvred more aggressively and without warning, to take full advantage of terrain masking and to negotiate marginal weather at low level in difficult terrain (such as the karst country in North Vietnam), during which a second aircraft could so easily lose contact. A more balanced view is that particular circumstances should dictate when

Going It Alone. Captain Burt Waltz flew many of his Able Mable missions alone. Burt Waltz

and where pairs of aircraft are flown and when single aircraft might achieve the purpose with a reasonable chance of survival.

Burt Waltz of the 15th TRS accepted this when tasked to fly solo over Laos, but always remained weary. He recalled that (as far as he knew) he was fired on first in 1962, probably by 37-mm AAA, when he came across two Russian-built IL-14 'Crate' transports (C-47s) from North Vietnam landing at an airfield in the PDJ. Shortly thereafter he was 'chased' by what he thought was a 57-mm gun battery while using his cameras at 15,000 ft. He estimated that the first burst of 'six black puffs' was two miles back and 3,000 ft below, the second rather closer and the third too close for comfort. It was time to leave. In this case a wingman would have been able to report these shots while his leader concentrated on his photography.

As threats to recce aircraft mounted, escorts or wingmen became increasingly desirable and ultimately imperative for mission achievement and survival; so it was that in 1965 the order went out that all pairs or solo recce missions tasked above 18 deg north be escorted by F-105 fighters. These early escort missions were to be employed solely as defensive umbrellas, unless authorised specifically on an 'individual mission basis' (by no less than the JCS) to act offensively in the flak suppression role. Unfortunately, the F-105s did not have the Voodoo's 'legs' and could rarely stay with them until the latter had completed their missions, so 2nd AD withdrew the order and authorised the Voodoos to fly in pairs on the potentially more risky tasks.

Despite the advantages and Burt's story, flying in pairs or with escorts could not often help greatly in protecting the RF-101s from the guns, especially at low level; indeed 11 Voodoos were lost to AAA in the year ending 1 June 1966, throughout much of which two-ship operations in hazardous areas had been the norm. To suggest, however, that statistics such as these disproved the value of mutual support would be a calumny; these losses could be attributed variously to increasingly effective defences, the tactics necessary to get the job done in difficult weather conditions, the camera configurations and the tasks assigned, not to mention a sense of duty among the pilots. However, the doubters prevailed; flying pairs of RF-101s into the more hostile skies lasted only

Two's Company. In 1965 the proliferation of air defences in North Vietnam led to the resumption of pairs missions. Don Karges

until June 1966 when, paradoxically with the proliferation of multiple threats, the Voodoo force was ordered to revert to single aircraft operations. Thus the recce pilot's sardonic war-cry of 'alone, unarmed and unafraid' was in vogue again, even if the last condition remained very arguable.

The Voodoo books by Dorr and by Drendel and Stevens both report a mission on 28 June 1966, during which Captain Patrick Reaves might well have wished that he had been accompanied by a wingman. The target was the important and very well defended bridge over the Red River at Viet Tri, eighteen miles north-west of Hanoi, and Patrick was tasked with BDA photography in the wake of another attempt to destroy the bridge, this time by eight F-105 'Thuds' of 'Dodge' Flight, led by the well known ace Major James Kasler ('Yosemite Sam'). The bridge was notorious for its ability to survive and for the ferocity of its defensive screen of multiple 57-mm and 88-mm radar laid AAA, together with numerous SAM sites in the local area, which had already accounted for an RF-101 after a previous strike.

Patrick Reaves was up at dawn for the meticulous pre-flight preparation which might save his life. It all started well; he launched on time with a fully serviceable aircraft and checked in with Dodge leader as planned, who warned him to expect: *"all the AAA you want, all you want!"* The approach he had planned to his target was covered by cloud which had not been forecast, and he had to revert to DR navigation; this technique of holding heading and speed steady could usually be relied on over short distances and in light winds but not this time. When Patrick found a gap in the cloud cover he failed to identify any landmarks and had to return to the IP to try again. By now the North Vietnamese were watching his every move on radar but they waited until he was back on track, had found his target and begun the 'pop' before letting loose with everything they had. Reaves went on and up, the RHAW in his cockpit now bright with spokes in all quadrants until, as he was levelling at the optimum camera height, a massive explosion rocked the Voodoo, damaging the right wing and causing one engine and main flight instruments to oscillate violently. Without a wingman to assess the damage by external inspection Reaves could only assume the worst as he carried out a maximum rate

descent to low level and sped for the relative security of the hills. As he did so, he had another unpleasant surprise, an indication on the RHAW that he had been illuminated by a SAM radar. With great presence of mind, he headed for the SAM site which promptly switched off, perhaps in the belief that it was about to be attacked by a 'Wild Weasel' with anti-radar missiles, the operators still scuttling from their posts as the Voodoo passed overhead. Gingerly, Reaves nursed his stricken aircraft back to Udorn to complete a copy-book straight-in approach, bringing his aircraft, the film required and himself back home safely. He had accomplished his mission, but it might easily have been so different and a wingman could have been invaluable.

Patrick Reaves was in the air over North Vietnam again on the following day, defying the unwritten rule that after 'a turn in the barrel' he should fly a less risky sortie immediately thereafter. He went home two months later having flown his 100th counter and 168 combat missions in 286 hours. He was one of many RF-101 pilots who completed most of his missions alone, surviving at least in part because of his assiduous preparation, skill and experience, but he too might admit to a large measure of luck. Others were not so fortunate. Major Blair Wrye was on his own when he was shot down and killed on a 'counter' well into North Vietnam on 12 August 1966. It seems possible that, in the extreme heat of that day, he lost his communications when the circuit breakers popped, but there was no-one with him to confirm this or assist him in any way.

As small arms, AAA, SAM and MiG defences in the North continued to grow in number, another factor entered the equation which would challenge the wisdom of single aircraft operation in all circumstances, the influx of new pilots direct from basic orientation and recce training on the Voodoo at Shaw. However well intentioned these replacements, and however hard they tried, they were faced with a very steep learning curve in a most hostile environment, and many were ill-equipped for the demands ahead. Whether it was because they lacked the necessary basic ability or previous fast-jet experience (some were from the heavy bomber force and training roles), the concern was the same, that North Vietnam was no place for new pilots to go it alone until they had proved themselves to their mentors and

Watch Out - MiGs About. In SAM and MiG airspace, a second pair of eyes was invaluable to provide essential warnings. Luster Vickrey

experienced wingmen flying 'chase'; to do otherwise would be a false economy. So it was that, with or without dispensation from the rules at the time, local commanders nursed their newcomers into battle progressively and sensibly. However, as a result of this turbulence and additional supervisory commitment, the front line was now always short of the expertise needed to carry out the more difficult missions up north.

Fortunately, the single aircraft policy was rescinded again in September 1966 and pairs took to the sky officially once more. With MiG fighters now prowling the skies above North Vietnam, this was timely; other than when airborne, ship or ground radars were there to help, a second aircraft was crucial to provide those essential early warnings. Perhaps it is significant that no Voodoos were lost in the following two months.

Be it with single aircraft or pairs, from late 1966 the Voodoo men were now becoming more involved in strike packages designed to counter the number and diversity of the air defences ranged against them, increase mission effectiveness and reduce attrition. Accordingly,

the RF-101s were being integrated progressively into overall raid plans to carry out their pre- and post-strike recce tasks, taking full advantage of airborne command posts, tankers and early warning aircraft, F-105 Wild Weasels for flak suppression, EB-66s and other aircraft for stand-off jamming, F-4 fighters to take care of any MiGs and long range rescue assets. Unfortunately, force packages generally lacked flexibility and the airborne assembly of so many aircraft could negate any element of surprise, not only signalling the approach of a raid but often where it was most likely to take place. All that said, they could render worthwhile dividends.

In ever-changing circumstances battle staffs have always been faced with the on-going dilemma of how best to employ their recce assets and 'going it alone' was but one of many options. In SEA, the remote, time-consuming micro-management at high levels, driven by heavy political influences, complicated the decision-making of the battle staffs in theatre and those on the flight line who tried hard to optimise the use of the RF-101s.

CHAPTER SIXTEEN
INNOVATION, INDUSTRY
AND DETERMINATION

'A recce pilot is a fighter-bomber pilot with brains'

John Stavast

John Stavast may have pushed his luck with any fighter pilot friends he might have had before he claimed at the 2001 Voodoo Reunion that 'a recce pilot is a fighter-bomber pilot with brains', but Tony Weissgarber rushed to his support in the subsequent Recce Reader. He reminded everyone that in 1964-65, when fighter-bomber pilots in SEA were not getting to their targets because of poor navigation, recce pilots such as George Hall rode in the back of F-100s to guide the strike force. Moreover, General Moore, in Saigon, ordered F-105 strikes to be led to their targets by RF-101s but this unpopular expedient did not last for long. This chapter draws on and amplifies illustrations already mentioned in previous chapters, to show that the Voodoo pilots had not only special navigational skills but that they used innate enterprise and determination to increase their survival and operational effectiveness.

The enemy quickly recognised common and recurring patterns in the USAF's mission schedules and laid in wait for their visitors along routes known to be in regular use, entry 'gates' and favoured turning points, clustering their guns accordingly. They also got to know the operating parameters for the photo aircraft and could therefore site, lay and fuse their guns for best effect. The worst case scenario for the RF-101 pilot was a mission flown into the target-rich, high threat area of RPVI in North Vietnam; whether flown by single aircraft or in pairs they could be distinguished easily from the strike packages of four, eight or more bombers. Moreover, BDA sorties would normally follow as soon as the smoke from a strike had cleared, at which point the now very angry defenders would have recovered sufficiently to give these unarmed aircraft a suitably ferocious welcome, the RF-101s seen as too easy a prey to ignore.

This could of course cut both ways; the Voodoos might be seen as low value targets compared with the bombers and ground forces ignore the unarmed recce aircraft rather than draw attention to their positions by firing at them, choosing to change that location and prepare a 'flak trap' for the bombers which were likely to follow.

In any event, the North Vietnamese had learned fast and it was up to the Allies to find ways of outwitting them, with constant re-appraisals of their modus operandi, aircraft and camera configuration and defensive options. Notwithstanding recurring pressures from arm-chair warriors, that the way to go in SEA was low level 'as we did in Europe' or 'because we've always done it that way', experience at the front and sound heads on the flight line there showed that this was not necessarily so. Accordingly, there was a need to adapt to tactics and techniques, and to modify equipment to suit the different requirements and circumstances in SEA, with due regard to the inextricable and crucial matters of camera capabilities and the defensive systems the Voodoos faced. Fortunately, despite deep 'mind-sets', it was still found possible to teach old dogs new tricks.

The number of initiatives taken to enhance the effectiveness and safety of RF-101 operations, and the many who deserve credit for their promotion, are too numerous for this book, and indeed some beneficial or potentially useful ideas fell by the wayside then or have since been forgotten, as have their exponents. The best the author can do is offer a few surviving examples, some of which succeeded and others which did not, in this blanket token of praise for those who exercised such foresight, enterprise and determination.

As is so often the way, many of the initiatives came from bottom up, in this case from those who were then earning their living in hostile skies or caring for their aircraft on the ground. Equally often, some within the hierarchy were a little slow in understanding and supporting ideas which simply had to be evaluated, if not eventually adopted, to enable the RF-101s to continue to provide what was required without unacceptable attrition.

One of the earliest of these initiatives was remembered by Captain Jerry Miller. Circa 1963, Captain Bob Caudry experimented with a manoeuvre designed to allow the use of the KA-1, 36-inch split vertical cameras at higher speeds and lower levels than were prescribed in ideal conditions. This involved a steep (60 deg) climb to about 8,000 ft, acquiring the target during the climb and taking an oblique photograph while keeping the target in the viewfinder during a low 'G' push-over into a 60 deg max rate descent. Sadly, the camera's vacuum system was reluctant to accept these 'G' conditions, which caused the film to 'float' and the pictures to became unusable. Although some enterprising pilots found ways of adapting this technique and applying it with some success, this specific procedure was not thought to have been introduced into general use. However, it did open minds to the possibility of similar, alternative means of achieving the necessary photography with greater chances of survival.

Great minds think alike and, faced with a universal problem of the guns, it is not surprising that several Voodoo pilots came up with the same general idea in about the same timeframe, albeit with variations, that of a 'pop-up' manoeuvre as a means of getting the job done and living to fly another day. This being so, the author is at pains to ensure that the credit is shared between the main protagonists, rather than to single out any particular exponent. Likewise, with a paucity of official detail and differences in personal accounts, it has been very difficult to tie down precise dates in this tactic's evolution; it was certainly used as far back as 29 July 1965 (Chapter Fourteen) but the gestation period seems to have culminated in its adoption by the 15th TRS at Udorn in October.

In the beginning, conventional wisdom had it that the effects of AAA could best be avoided or minimised by flying the Voodoo as fast as possible and as low as its pilots were able, but this was not born out by experience in SEA any

more than it had been in Korea. Besides, with the aircraft's standard camera fit, optimum photography could not be achieved at these extreme speeds and heights. Of course, flak could be avoided by flying above the range of the heaviest guns, provided the weather permitted the photography required, but the aircraft would then be at the mercy of missiles and radar controlled MiG fighters which would soon enter the fray. Perhaps a mixed profile, carefully timed, could fit the bill?

Captains Gene Morris and Ernie Rutledge had been discussing the 'pop-up' idea with their peers on the 15th TRS at Udorn before they rotated back to Kadena, where they decided to put it to the test. With little guidance on how long a Voodoo could remain within a missile's effective envelope before the latter's radar achieved the necessary lock on, firing solution and the completion of an attack, they enlisted the help of a neighbouring US Army Hawk unit in Okinawa and set up a trial. There were differences between the US Hawk and Russian-built SA-2 missile but they were sufficiently alike to render some valid conclusions. So it was that Gene found himself in a Hawk control van in radio contact with Ernie in a Voodoo. Five test sorties were flown to find out what the Hawk battery could and could not achieve against the RF-101 as the pilots evaluated possible pop-up options.

They discovered that as long as the aircraft changed its heading by 30 deg and height by 5,000 ft every 30 seconds the Hawk could not reach a firing solution. This technique, while possibly keeping the Voodoos safe from SAMs might not, however, be compatible with the photography required. It followed that the second part of the trial must find how the customers' requirements for photographs could be satisfied with minimum exposure to the missile sites. In training, the recce pilots had been taught that a 60% overlap was required between successive photographs for optimum stereo viewing and mapping to a set scale with the vertical cameras. To satisfy this need, the RF-101 had to fly at a combination of higher levels and/or slower speeds than was healthy in a missile environment. However, the main demand in SEA was for area cover with the 36-inch split vertical cameras, and for this it was agreed that an overlap as low as 15% could suffice.

The tactic Gene and Ernie evolved was to

POP-UP TECHNIQUE

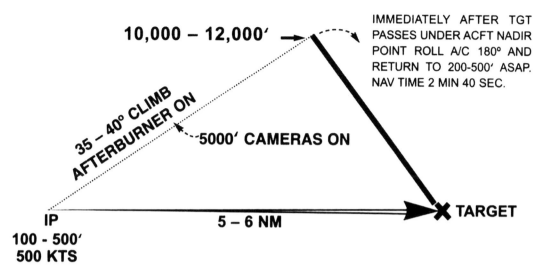

10,000 – 12,000'

IMMEDIATELY AFTER TGT PASSES UNDER ACFT NADIR POINT ROLL A/C 180° AND RETURN TO 200-500' ASAP. NAV TIME 2 MIN 40 SEC.

35 – 40° CLIMB AFTERBURNER ON

5000' CAMERAS ON

TARGET

IP
100 - 500'
500 KTS

5 – 6 NM

Pop-Up and Live. Captain Gene Morris floated this one of several options for the pop-up manoeuvre. Gene Morris

approach the target at very low level and high speed (say 540 kts), hoping to achieve some surprise, then pull up into a maximum rate afterburner climb to 20,000 ft and holding this for a maximum of 30 seconds before descending to 10,000 ft, again for 30 seconds. They would then repeat the sequence until the task was complete before descending rapidly to egress at ultra low level. In this way they avoided missile lock-on and launch in 90% of the runs made. Initially there seemed less then universal support for the idea but could refinements placate the unconvinced?

At the same time, similar trials on the pop-up were being conducted by the 15th TRS at Udorn, under operational conditions. Major Harry Runge led development of the principle in theory and practice, and was credited widely with deriving a pattern for general application. He was aware that the optimum height band for the 'split verts' cameras was 9,000-15,000 ft, where the threat from AAA was less than that from the SA-2 missiles , against which the Voodoo had no effective countermeasures. However, with area cover being the primary requirement, Harry too sought guidance from the resident PIs at Udorn on the matter of overlap and they also agreed that as little as a 15% could indeed be acceptable to them. This would clearly allow the Voodoo pilots to complete their tasks satisfactorily at speeds and

heights more compatible with survival. Harry also knew that the SA-2 could fly at Mach 3, perhaps four times faster than the Voodoo at the prescribed camera operating height, had a fused warhead and, crucially took time to acquire, launch and destroy a target. The missile also had a high wing loading which severely limited its manoeuvrability and this too could be used to advantage.

With all this in mind, Harry considered the RF-101's tactics. He knew that 'low and fast wasn't cutting it' against ground fire, while a high/medium level approach not only gave their presence away on radar but placed them at the mercy of the missiles and the MiGs. From these deliberations and careful map study, he worked his conclusions into a scenario typical of a photo mission against a target north-west of Hanoi and presented it for consideration. He suggested an approach from the south-west at the lowest possible height and highest practicable speed, with the maximum use of terrain masking before 'exploding' out of the mountains at a point close to the target in an afterburner climb to 12,000-15,000 ft. The cameras would be triggered on levelling off over the target and remain on for a minimum acceptable photo run, before a maximum rate descent in a high 'G' turn was carried out to exit back down to the relative safety of the mountains. Harry argued that, given the right weather conditions, pin-point tasks could be accomplished in this way with minimum exposure time to hostile defences, inter alia giving both SAMs and guns the problem of a target with constantly changing airspeed and altitude.

To find out what the crucial exposure time would be, Harry tasked Captains Don Bresee and Howard Davis to fly the profile outlined above at Udorn; they concluded that it could be completed before an SA-2s secured a 'kill'. Pop-up also had the appeal of simplicity, important when flying in the inevitable confusion of combat conditions against multiple threats. Over drinks on the evening following the flight trials, Harry's briefing on the general concept was greeted with enthusiasm by the pilots, who offered some possible refinements which might be appropriate in certain circumstances. This, to many, was how the 'pop-up' was born.

Gene Morris recalls that he had discussed the pop-up idea with his friend, Marv Reed of the 45th TRS, and with the F-105 force from Kadena operating out of RTAFB Khorat, which made good use of it in some of their bombing missions. Reed and his wingman, Captain Dan Doughty, were believed to have been the first to try out the pop-up manoeuvre in earnest in the latter stages of 'the great SAM hunt' on 29 July 1965, surviving with less than the usual interference from AAA (Chapter Fourteen). So it was that the pop-up was accepted in principle, perhaps unofficially at first and with subsequent variations, each with its own degree of risk depending on the situation at the time. In practice, many aircraft still sustained battle damage but losses decreased markedly. Pop-up was not the ultimate solution to survival, but it was certainly a very useful option which could enhance mission success, and it was all down to innovation and determination on the flight line. In company with Gene Morris and others, Harry had refused to be constrained by those who preached the conventional wisdom. As the pop-up evolved in sensible application he observed: *"it was a delight to me to see pilots thinking again"*, and he was able to claim that no 15th TRS aircraft was lost carrying out the manoeuvre between October and his departure from SEA in the following January.

Of course there were times when it was necessary, for operational reasons or when weather conditions precluded any other

suitable photography, for the pilots to cover their allotted targets at low level. The story of Vic Vickrey going in at ultra low level to look for enemy guns hidden under tree cover just north of the DMZ (Chapter Thirteen) exemplifies both the need on occasions for this potentially very hazardous approach and the determination of the recce pilots to succeed.

As for self-defence for the unarmed Voodoos, it was evident that the RF-101s would benefit from any warning that they were being illuminated by hostile radars, when the radar was 'locked on' and when missiles were fired. In addition, they needed active measures to confuse and disrupt, if not blind the early warning, gun-laying and SAM radars, and much effort was directed to these ends. Some stand-off jamming was provided by EB-66, EC-121 and USN aircraft but the Voodoo pilots remained uneasy over its efficacy. One recalls a sortie in which an EB-66 failed to detect the high pulse recurrence frequency of an SA-2 launched against him but that he saw the missile in time to 'dive for the deck' and escape.

The RF-101 Dash 1 of the mid-1960s tells of the AN/APS-54 Radar Warning Receiver (RWR) which provided the pilot with basic visual and audio warnings when the aircraft was illuminated by radars on certain frequencies. However, the Voodoo pilots in SEA needed more information of this type and Gene Morris recalls that their aircraft (together with the F-105 'Wild Weasels') were the first in the theatre to be modified with the APR-25/26 RHAW gear in early 1965. This equipment provided tones in the headset and lights on the tele-light panel in the cockpit, these signals determined by the frequency and pulse of the illuminating radars (SAM, AAA, EW and airborne fire control) along with 'activity' and 'launch' lights to warn of a missile lock-on and firing. The cockpit display also included a vector scope with a strobe to indicate the threat direction and signal strength. To the pilots who learned how to interpret the signals this equipment could be invaluable; Gene remembers: *"cruising around the southern part of North Vietnam at 15,000 ft, staying outside the missile rings and easily evading fire from 85-mm guns by using RHAW information on the Fire Can gun radars"*. With very careful attention to the APR-25/26, the Voodoo pilots could risk flying above 4500 ft, beyond the lethal range of small arms, steer clear of SA-2

Survival Pod? Up to four QRC-160 ECM pods could be carried on the RF-101, but with penalties in performance and no guarantees of effectiveness. George Cowgill

and GCI radars and 'head for the weeds' when warned to do so by the RHAW, procedures which were again readily adopted by the F-105s when they were equipped with the APR-25/26 in 1966.

It was still up to the pilot to remain alert and acquire missiles visually, to calculate when to break away from their flight paths; timing the break was crucial and on the assumption that the missile was limited to 3 'G' the 'break' had to be significantly greater than that. Also, the audio signals could be so numerous and distracting, perhaps masking important warning calls from leaders and wingmen, that some pilots were inclined to dispense with them. As with Patrick Reaves (Chapter Fifteen), John Summers remembers using an RHAW vector to simulate an anti-radar missile armed Wild Weasel attack by diving directly towards the emitter and thereby causing it to close down.

As for active ECM, the 15th TRS RF-101s had been modified to carry the QRC-160 pods in 1963 and the Voodoo was the first 'fast-jet' to take these jamming pods to war over North Vietnam. On 29 April 1965, three RF-101s from Tan Son Nhut, each equipped with four, wing-mounted QRC-160 pods, flew in support of a Rolling Thunder mission to jam the air defence radars. Captain Dick Wood, then

serving at Tan Son Nhut, is believed to have been among the first pilots to put these pods to the test but he was unable to judge then or comment now on whether they were a success or failure; he does recall that after one flight, when the equipment's 'tech rep' opened the pod on the flight line, some of its internal components fell to the ground in bits. To be fair, Dick had been flying very fast and very low, manoeuvring at high 'G', but that is what Voodoo pilots did and would not have wished to be constrained solely to protect these electronics. Chuck Lustig also flew with four ECM pods when TDY from the 15th TRS at Tan Son Nhut in July 1965. He reported failure lights on three of the pods halfway through the mission and felt that he was flying with half air brake extended, while having to endure a high frequency (but not uncomfortable) vibration throughout the flight. In that configuration, with such a high drag index, he doubted whether he could have achieved more than 500 kts in the aircraft, even in afterburner and, because his pods were bolted on and could not be jettisoned, he predicted that a Voodoo pilot so encumbered would be 'dead meat' in any combat. This poor start for the Voodoos in ECM was due in large measure to a dearth of understanding and expertise in the air and on the ground; the pods also suffered badly from

245

the necessarily high operating speeds and 'G' forces, while test equipment was inadequate and serviceability consequently very poor. Also, at this stage there was little if any proof of its worth, the extra commitment had to be to the detriment of the aircraft's primary recce role and there were severe penalties in combat performance. It is not surprising, therefore, that their early use petered out in a general lack of enthusiasm and confidence, but that was not the end of the story.

The protagonists of podded jammers, such as Lieutenant Colonel 'Inky' Haugen, an electronic warfare specialist at Eglin AFB, would not be put off and trials on the new QRC-160 trials at Eglin from late 1966 also benefited from the presence there of Gene Morris, who put his experience in SEA to good use. In Gene's words: *"it soon became obvious to the test team that, with the secrecy surrounding the pods, the aircrews knew too little about them to achieve best effect, while maintenance crews had no knowledge of how to set them up to jam key frequencies"*. While this was being put right the pods were strengthened and Gene was then able to observe an overall increase in effectiveness. In a van simulating an SA-2 radar, he watched four F-105s, each emitting from two QRC-160-1 pods, noise jammers which generated static on the specific frequencies used by hostile radars, leaving the SAM operators unable to achieve satisfactory missile firing solutions. It was concluded that a formation of four aircraft, each emitting from a pair of these pods, produced an optimum 'bloom' which concealed all four aircraft; Haugen described this as 'like hunting for bugs under a blanket', whereas that produced by two aircraft only could leave one of them vulnerable.

Following these trials, a further evaluation of the QRC-160A-1 pod was carried out by F-105s in SEA, with results towards the end of 1966 which helped dispel some of the grave misgivings over the earlier equipment and lead to full production of the latest variant, the AN/ALQ-72. Later pods also incorporated deception jammers, which returned incorrect positions of target aircraft. Confidence in the pods was now returning and some RF-101s would shelter in the mixed force packages which braved the ever more heavily defended North. Major Nick Pishvanov, 45th TRS opined later that: *"while they (the pods) made nasty noises, they may have kept many of us alive"*.

George Cowgill also became involved in trials of podded jammers for the Voodoo at Eglin in 1967: *"on several nights flying as many as four, very dark and boring two-hour*

Workhorse. George Cowgill deployed from Hill AFB to Eglin AFB with this RF-101C in the winter of 1967 for intensive trials on ECM and RHAW equipment. George Cowgill

sorties", but he was never privy to the results. In the same year the 20th TRS at Udorn seemed happy to give ECM pods, carried by their escorts, the benefit of the doubt, perhaps on the basis that anything should be better than nothing. In January 1967, a pair of the squadron's RF-101s flew to the well defended Phuc Yen airfield with four F-4s carrying these jammers, and met little opposition, but the next two sorties, also over the North with the same force mix, was different, again leaving the effectiveness of this ECM questionable (Chapter Twelve). Then in April 1967, the 20th TRS began carrying up to four modified pods on their RF-101s; these pods, designed for fighter aircraft, should have filled radar screens with static and clutter but John Summers, with the 45th TRS, believed they worked properly only when the carrier was flying straight and level. Again, with no proof that they were doing their job and with each 400 lb pod adding significantly to the drag and therefore severely reducing the Voodoo's speed and manoeuvrability so essential in MiG airspace, they were neither convincing nor universally popular with the pilots.

Thereafter an active ECM system was fitted to the RF-101s internally; this incurred no extra drag and continued to operate during evasive manoeuvres. John Summers commented: *"the internal jammer was supposed to capture a radar signal, spin it around for a millisecond or two then spit it back to the radar site"*, to give an erroneous position of the target aircraft, but again there was no hard evidence that it had any real impact on the air war in SEA.

Notwithstanding this progress, an SA-2 destroyed a Voodoo carrying ECM pods over North Vietnam on 1 August 1967, killing the pilot, Captain Charles Winston. 7th Air Force then accepted that current self-defence ECM technology could not be relied on and that single-aircraft RF-101 operations over North Vietnam were now imprudent. Learning from the many painful lessons of the past, and making use of all the assets available, standard patterns for RF-101 missions gave way to a more circumspect, flexible approach. Depending on the nature of the task and the risk factors, more consideration was now given to allocating certain recce tasks to other aircraft, having the Voodoos fly alone, in pairs or with escorting fighters (with or without ECM pods), or protected within force

packages. More evidence suggested that an effective protective screen could be provided by four F-4s carrying pods, spaced laterally by 1,500 ft and vertically by 500 to 1,000 ft, but this was an unwieldy formation, and it remained but one of the options.

The story of ECM in relation to the RF-101 in SEA seems inconclusive. Certainly those who worked hard to get the best out of the APR-25/26 RHAW found it very helpful if distracting in combat, but early attempts at providing self-defence with jamming pods foundered. While there were those who remained sceptical over the effectiveness of the modified pods in noise and deception jamming and regretted the drag/weight penalties, others came to believe that, with adherence to prescribed tactics, they could enhance survival. No-one questioned the continued benefits of mutual self-help and cross-cover in the air, the maintenance of a good look out and early visual acquisition of missiles, ideally prompted by warnings from escorts or other sources. All that said, it was claimed officially that with optimum use of the latest noise and deception jammers, the North Vietnamese had to fire five times the number of missiles once needed to achieve a kill against an unprotected target.

Another modification to the RF-101 which proved useful in SEA, as indeed it did elsewhere when external air starters were not available, was the cartridge starter, its only drawback being the size and weight of the cartridges. One engine could be started with a cartridge, after which a cross-feed provided the air necessary to start the other; this method was even used when a mission was fuel-critical, the pilot taxiing out on one engine and starting the other internally for take-off. It was also possible, given suitable conditions, to take off on one engine and start the second in the air by means of a normal air start, Jerry Miller having done so after a diversion to Korat while Tom O'Meara's Voodoo was cleared from the runway at Don Muang (Chapter Nine). Frustrated by an overheat warning on the right engine during start up at Korat for the return trip (and perhaps anxious to be home for 'happy hour'), Jerry did his calculations and took off safely on one engine on the long runway, without fuel in his external tanks, climbing to height before starting the second engine satisfactorily. He recalls that the take-off run was still somewhat better than that of an

RF-84F and he had avoided expensive, time-consuming maintenance at Korat to make it home for the happy hour.

The tendency has always been for the accolades to go to those who were flying or at least supporting RF-101 operations at the 'sharp end'. While high visibility developments in aircraft tactics and equipment, such as the 'pop-up'and ECM, stole the limelight, there were many lesser examples of Voodoo men enhancing mission effectiveness through personal or collective initiatives within their specialisations. Often out of sight and mind, a veritable army worked assiduously behind the lines with determination to provide the men at the front with the right tools for the job. For instance, tribute must be paid to those involved in the development of new camera systems needed to meet challenging needs and Chapter Twenty is devoted specifically to those involved in photo processing and exploitation. Above all, there were those with similarly laudable enterprise who worked long and hard on the Voodoo itself, its engines and ancillaries, on the operational flight line and in deep maintenance, to get the best out of the force and give the pilots every chance of survival. Their commitment, vital and often exercised above and beyond the call of duty is outlined in Chapter Twenty One. Even further out of sight and so often out of mind were the myriad other support functions, the weather and air traffic personnel, crash, fire and medical crews, administrators, suppliers, caterers et al. They also served and should not be forgotten, but their contributions lie beyond the remit of this book.

Some of the ideas for improvements, expedients and short-cuts in the name of efficiency, derived from experience in war and peace were quite properly rejected. Others were certainly worthy of consideration, even if frowned on initially, opposed or rejected outright by the hierarchy in the less realistic days of peace or by the more cautious in SEA. Fortunately, in times of need common sense did sometimes prevail, the conflict in SEA bringing out the best in the RF-101 force. Whatever the result, fact or opinion, nothing should detract from the laudable efforts of those who tried so hard, often with little immediate or subsequent reward or recognition, to produce initiatives which were often worth a try even if they did not ultimately succeed. This was essentially a team effort, to which enterprising individuals contributed in so many diverse ways with determination not only to do their duty but to add value; and this they did.

CHAPTER SEVENTEEN
GREAT ESCAPES

'I learned about flying from that'

RAF flight safety idiom

Most of the Voodoo pilots who braved the diverse hazards in SEA were fortunate to survive death, serious injury, capture or irrevocable damage to their aircraft to fly another day, but many had near misses, and it is to them that this chapter is devoted.

The author makes no apology for including in this chapter incidents in the air and on the ground which might seem too trivial to qualify under the heading 'Great Escapes', to make the point that (as every aviator knows) little incidents can very rapidly escalate into major emergencies, perhaps culminating in disaster. When they did not, it was often because of rapid reactions and personal skills, the strength and resilience of the aircraft, or both, and all this was true in the case of the Voodoo fliers, those who looked after them and their aircraft. Many RF-101s were brought home heavily damaged either from combat, other operational factors or from natural hazards. Then there was always the unpalatable truth of human error, be it within the command chain, in engineering or other support, or down to the men who flew the aircraft. The Voodoo warriors faced all these realities, prompting many to say: *"I learned about flying from that"*, and for completeness it seems right to mention some specific events of this nature from the life of the Voodoo.

Risks to the Voodoo men and machines began long before they encountered the dangers of combat, every pilot learns this from the moment he starts flying and the author himself being reminded the hard way on his fourth trip in an RF-101. This is his story:

"*It was an unusually cold and frosty morning in February 1960 at Shaw AFB when I calculated a very short take-off run from the desk charts and entered it on my flight clearance. On the roll, 150 kts came up after only a few yards as I raised the nose and lifted off almost immediately thereafter at 175 kts. Then it all happened at once. The*

huge nose cone reared up on its hinges, broke off and crashed through one side of the canopy, leaving a gaping hole as it spun down on to the airfield. Having ducked, most of the debris glanced off my helmet, but a blinding dust cloud rose from the cockpit floor and splinters of perspex found their way under my visor in a swirling blast of incoming air, tending to limit visibility. With all wheels in the well, flaps up and burners out, the aircraft flew well at what seemed like a safe low airspeed, and although I could hear nothing on the radio, subsequent lights and hand signals indicated that my transmissions were being received. To prepare for what might be an interesting landing, I jettisoned the two 450 gall external tanks into the swamps, narrowly missing a T-33 flown by Captain Ernie Meis who, unknown to me, had swooped up fast from below after I had cleared the area for the drop. With no forward visibility or airspeed indications, I had called for a shepherd and very shortly the unmistakable face of my squadron commander, Major 'Grumpy' Brittian was alongside to escort me down. Doug Brittian, not necessarily known for his speed on the ground, must have 'scrambled' faster than he had ever done before! Sensible leadership and more hand signals then got me back on to the runway safely. Both the crew chief and I had failed to check properly the two lugs which locked the nose cone down, an unforgivable oversight in peace which could have had dire consequences."

Of course this was inexcusable in peacetime but in the busy tensions of war it might be more understandable and this is the Harry Runge story of a similar incident. All was normal as Harry rolled down the narrow runway at Udorn to begin another operational sortie in SEA, his wingman, Captain Al Magazzine, following 10 seconds later. Then, as he lifted off

Chin-Up! Major Harry Runge waited with trepidation for the nose cone to depart but he was lucky.
USAF via Al Magazzine

at 175 kts, the nose cone also came up in its hinges, but stayed there, obscuring his forward view and denying him airspeed indications. There was nothing for it but to continue, Harry using his experience to fly blind on power settings and, as he said, 'by the seat of the pants'. The great worry was, of course, that the nose cone would break loose, hit the cockpit and injure the pilot. Fortunately, Al Magazzine was there to provide the necessary speed cues as they burned off fuel and landed with the utmost care, the nose cone flopping back into place during the deceleration. Harry taxied into the revetment to more than the usual welcome, his crew chief bearing a fifth of Crown Royal.

The author had another thrill, on 4 May 1961:

"It all began with a 'low go' from a practice approach at Naval Air Station, Beaufort, SC, when one of the oldest RF-101As on the squadron (54-1495) suffered a complete utility hydraulic pressure failure, the primary system then fluttering in sympathy. With wheels and flaps down and airbrakes out, the nearest alternates at Charleston under a rainstorm and Hunter AFB failing to return my calls, it seemed prudent to land at Beaufort. Even without a useable hook on the aircraft, the relatively short runway and a crosswind, there should not have been a problem landing safely, provided everything worked as it should. Sadly it did not; the drag 'chute fell off (defective latch?) and I had no emergency brakes (when checks were made on other Voodoos at Shaw at least one more aircraft was found to have the same problem). Consequently, I ran off the end of the runway at speed, shedding gear, wings and tailplane as the cockpit buried itself, inverted, in the swamp beyond. Resident Marines were on the spot at once but heavy lifting gear was out of the question and they went to work on a tunnel under what remained of the aircraft to pull me out. This took time, during which we exchanged views on the situation in hand and the need

to extract me in time for the party scheduled for that evening at Shaw, in two rather different languages, my hosts clearly intrigued at what they would find at the end of the tunnel. Although able to walk, with the only real injury a gash in one arm sustained when my rescuers cut me free of the cockpit harness, they insisted on stretchering me back to the runway along the trail I had blazed, between the debris and dead snakes, to the base hospital. En route, in an extraordinary coincidence, I passed the only Marine pilot I knew at that time, and we both recognised each other from a previous, very similar incident. We had met when he was an exchange pilot with the RAF, and we had both been diverted to RAF Aldergrove, Northern Ireland, because of bad weather at our respective bases. He too had experienced a hydraulic failure in an RAF Hunter fighter and had run off the end of the runway; the only difference being that his aircraft flew again and mine did not, but I had been lucky!

I did not make it to the party at Shaw that evening, but the party came to the base hospital, from which I escaped on the following day. A few days later I had another hydraulic failure in a Voodoo, this time ending in an uneventful diversion to the then Congaree AFB (Columbia). Was someone trying to tell me something?"

Mid-air collisions between aircraft were an ever present hazard, usually resulting from human error on the part of the fliers, flight controllers or others, but from which there were some remarkable escapes. Such was the case when Lieutenant Colonel Simpson, 78th TFS, narrowly averted disaster at Wheelus AB in 1959 (Chapter Six), again when two 18th TRS pilots collided over the Atlantic on the way to France later that year (Chapter Four), when one 66th TRW Voodoo hit a Jodel light aircraft and a second collided with a Canadian T-33 over France (Chapter Four). These accidents were in peacetime; in the tensions of war, often exacerbated by stress, crowded airspace and

Brief Encounter. Prompt action, good subsequent airmanship and the resilient Voodoo combined to save the day after a mid-air collision between these two RF-101s of the 45th TRS at Tan Son Nhut in 1969. Jack Bowland

less than perfect control, the chances of such incidents were greater. Two RF-101s hit each other over Vietnam on 30 April 1969, both pilots from the 45th TRS able to bring their disabled aircraft back to Tan Son Nhut (Chapter Thirteen). The nose of 56-217 was severely damaged, as was the wing tip and one tail pipe of 56-168, but in a further tribute to the Voodoo men and their machines both aircraft were repaired and returned to front line service. Other 'mid-airs' did of course have fatal consequences.

In addition to natural hazards, those attributed to bird strikes, human errors, technical and engineering problems, the Voodoo pilots in SEA (and to a limited extent in Cuba) faced the additional risks of multiple air defences. The greatest threat to mission effectiveness and survival, from the start of and

throughout the war in SEA, was from gunfire in its various incarnations. Small arms and automatic weapons dominated the airspace at very low level, fortunately with many of defenders having little understanding (at least at the start of the conflict) of the 'lead' necessary to hit a fast-moving aircraft, but there was always the risk of a chance shot finding its mark. So often there was the wall of fire through which the Voodoos had to fly when hostile soldiery merely planted their rifles vertically in the ground and fired volley after volley of unaimed fire into the air, hoping that their adversaries would simply fly into this hail of lead. In fact, all this may have been more disconcerting than lethal but many aircraft returned with varying amounts of damage, some pilots unaware that they had taken a hit until the after-flight inspection or even later, because it had failed to affect critical systems in the air. Such was the case with Captain Jerry Miller of the 15th TRS, who must have been hit while searching for a supply storage area east of Nakhon Phanom, on the border between Laos and South Vietnam, on 14 August 1962. He had no idea then, during a diversion to Korat AB or when the right engine of his aircraft overheated on start up for his short trip back to Don Muang (Chapter Sixteen), that he had sustained battle damage. It was only during a full inspection at Don Muang that, in Jerry's own words: *"we found a 50-cal hole in the bottom of the right engine intake but none on the top; the engine had swallowed the round! The last 4-5 stages of the compressor were 'corncobbed' and the turbine was a mess but she was running, maybe with not too much*

Lucky Strike. This Voodoo, its fin peppered by gunfire, survived to fly another day. USAF

power, but running."

Many Voodoo pilots had good reason to be thankful to Pratt and Whitney for the J-57 engine, and for having two of them; compared with other engines at that time they rarely failed completely due to technical defects or after suffering the perennial problem of bird strikes. When George Hall hit a very large sea bird (believed to have been an albatross) during a recovery to Kadena, Harry Runge remembers him saying: *"the engine kinda coughed once and went back to normal after it had inhaled the bird plus all the intake rivets; try that with a ** engine and good luck ole buddy!"* Harry himself had a more dramatic brush with the birds. Just as he rotated during an afterburner take-off for a dawn patrol out of Tan Son Nhut, a huge flock of the legendary doves of peace launched an attack on him from the grass beside the runway, at least 20 of them splattering themselves over the canopy and filling both engine intakes and undercarriage wells. Only by his very rapid reaction was Harry able to abort the take-off successfully. In a typically laconic manner the line chief observed: *"Hell, the birds only polished up the turbine blades!"* and left a thankful Harry to 'clean house'. He was able to think of three aircraft which had also returned safely on one engine and of course there were many more.

Captain Tom O'Meara, 15th TRS, was believed to have been the first Voodoo pilot in SEA to suffer seriously from the wrath of the guns in SEA, over Laos on 14 August 1962, but he was able to recover his badly damaged aircraft to Don Muang (Chapter Nine). It was not until 21 November 1964 that the first RF-101 fell in hostile territory, when Captain Burt Waltz of the 15th TRS was brought down as he photographed gun positions in the Ban Phan Hop region. Initially, he was fragged to reconnoitre a sector of the Ho Chi Minh Trail only, but as he climbed into his aircraft at Tan Son Nhut his flight commander, George Hall, gave him an additional target, an AAA site which had shot down an F-100 the previous day, and this would be his downfall.

Burt got airborne, refuelled from a KC-135 tanker and joined his escort of two F-105s on time. The first part of the sortie also went well; flying under the weather the three aircraft joined the Ho Chi Minh Trail at Attopeu, working their way north past Saravane, Tchepone and Mahaxay, to finish up at the Mu

Gia Pass. They then had to climb out of the bad weather towards the final target, fortuitously finding a hole through which they descended again, Burt acquiring his target at Ban Phan Hop 'on the nose' as he emerged below cloud at 800 ft, now flying at more than 500 kts. That's when it all happened. The Voodoo came under intensive gunfire, with six hits by 37-mm AAA in the wing and fuselage causing mortal damage to both engines and illuminated every warning light in the cockpit. On fire and with no control Burt ejected, Captain Chuck McClarren, in the lead F-105, telling him later that the wings of his Voodoo had fallen off just after the ejection. Burt himself takes up the story:

"I don't remember much until the 'chute opened, when I thought I was coming down faster than usual and was going to hit one of the karsts broadside, but then I was in the trees. The Voodoo hit the ground in a huge fireball close by".

Suspended from a tree high above the ground and bleeding from what he thought might be a broken nose, Burt attached himself to his 70 ft 'clothes line' and began his descent to the ground until 'something then broke' and he fell the rest of the way to sustain more serious injuries. Semi-conscious but somehow managing to get off a smoke flare: *"with one hand and my teeth"*, he helped Chuck McClarren (who, with his wingman had been pouring retaliatory fire into the offending gunsite) direct a passing Air America helicopter to his location. Burt again:

"The next thing I remember was the 'Whoop, Whoop, Whoop' of the chopper but when the first man I saw was a mean, tough-looking oriental guy I thought it was all over (and I hadn't even taken my gun out of its holster!)".

However, his rescuer was one of two Laotian Rangers, soon to be joined by a USAF major:

"They tried to pick me up until they realised that I was pretty broken up and carried me to their helicopter on a blanket. The Air America pilot, Ed Reid, then flew me to Nakhon Phanom where morphine was administered before I was taken to Korat and the 31st Field Hospital in a SA-16 Albatross".

Burt Waltz spent the next seven days in hospital, helped back to life by liberal quantities of Crown Royal whisky. He then

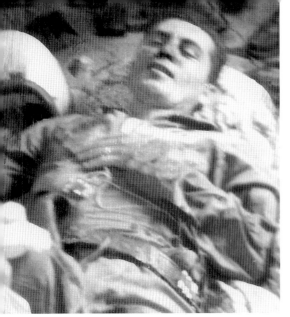

Going Home. Captain Burt Waltz had a painful ride home in a helicopter after his ejection over the Ho Chi Minh Trail but he was not complaining. Burt Waltz

spent four months undergoing traction in Okinawa, followed by five months of recuperation before returning to flying status one year and one day after nearly losing his life. It had been a very hard time but he had been lucky and as with so many of his kind he had 'bounced back' to continue doing his duty.

Again it says much for the strength of the Voodoo and its redundant systems that so many survived the increasingly effective gunfire, often able to go on to finish their mission before returning home safely. It was also an affirmation of the enterprise and industry of those on the ground, the maintenance men with their battle damage repair specialists, that so many of the damaged aircraft were recovered and returned to service so quickly. In their excellent article on the Voodoo in SEA, Drendel and Stevens suggest that in the latter half of 1965, 17 Green Python aircraft were nursed back to a friendly base after suffering gunfire damage, some very seriously, although one was destroyed on landing.

This was the aircraft flown on 5 October 1965 by Captain Robert Pitt who, with his wingman, pressed on under a 3,000 ft cloud base, within the optimum range of AAA and the MiG base of Kep, to get BDA photographs of the well defended Long Met ammunition dump, 30 nm north-east of Hanoi. With eight miles to run to their target Bob's aircraft was severely damaged by AAA, causing a massive fuel leak and fire in one engine, but he managed to extinguish the fire and turn the crippled aircraft towards the relative safety of the Bay of Tonkin before deciding to attempt a recovery to the nearest suitable base at Da Nang. Although his Voodoo was also badly damaged, his wingman completed the photo run and rejoined his leader. Unable to receive fuel from the tanker, which had hastened to his rescue, there was no time to waste, and on a straight-in approach he lowered the undercarriage and flaps on the emergency systems, before losing the rudder control which might have helped avoid a spectacular arrival on the airfield. On landing, the gear sheared off as the aircraft careered through a radio shack and came to rest, Bob climbing almost unscathed from the wreck. His wingman returned to Udorn with the film which had almost cost them their lives.

Captain Norman 'Norm' Huggins, 45th TRS also had an epic escape. On 1 November 1965, his 12th wedding anniversary, Norm and Captain Mike Thomson, of the 15th TRS, took off from Udorn to carry out BDA on three missile sites 35 nm north-east of Hanoi in RPVI; it was 'their turn in the barrel' again. With scattered cloud expected for much of the route, the plan was to fly at high level to the coast, let down over the Gulf of Tonkin, drop their tanks before turning north-west over the islands east of Haiphong until 20 nm from the border with China, then 'pop' to 10,000 ft to photograph their targets with the split-vertical cameras. At the end of their photo runs they would descend fast to make their get-away with all speed at low level, climbing when clear of the worst dangers for the recovery to Udorn. The whole trip was expected to take about 1 hour 40 minutes but it did not go according to plan.

During the descent over the sea, Norm's Voodoo took a hit in the starboard engine, he believes from 37-mm AAA, causing red lights to flash and audio alarms to sound in the cockpit as smoke billowed from the doomed aircraft. Stop-cocking the engine did not help and as the fire grew worse, accompanied by explosions, Norm told Mike he was ejecting and was soon tumbling into cloud on his parachute. He was cut and bruised from the ejection, his liferaft and survival pack were torn from him and only half of his life jacket inflated, but he landed safely in the water and

Practice Makes Perfect. Sea survival training was repeated for real in 'Norm' Huggins rescue. Norman Huggins

War Fighter. Captain Norman Huggins about to ride a Polka Dot Voodoo to war from Udorn. Norman Huggins

began striking out for a small island some 200 yds away. Sadly, the natives he had spotted there were hostile and greeted him with a fusillade of small arms fire. Returning their fire with his revolver, he reversed his direction out to the open sea and placed his faith in the air rescue service which he guessed correctly had already been summoned by Mike Thompson. Could the rescuers reach him before his enemies, now racing towards him in sampans bent on making him their guest, he ran out of ammunition or became exhausted? In the nick of time a pair of USN Douglas A-1E Skyraiders arrived to take care of the sampans with cannon fire and rockets while two USAF F-104s circled overhead to give top cover to a Grumman HU-16 Albatross landing on the water to pick him up, the furthest north any rescue had been attempted up to that time in the conflict. Norm was taken back to Da Nang to be patched up, pronounced fit for duty and allowed to return to Udorn; he was in the air again over North Vietnam a couple of days later to complete two more missions before finishing his third

tour of duty in SEA. Quite incidentally, 40 years later, the author met one of the F-104 pilots who had provided top cover during the rescue, at RAF Bentwaters, while researching the history of the 81st TFW F-101s. Bob Brown verified this story, remembering that when the flight surgeons had finished with Norm at Da Nang, he burst into the Officers Club demanding to buy any F-104 pilot a drink.

Chapter Thirteen recorded that life could also be dangerous for the Voodoo men on the ground down south in Saigon, far from the main combat zone. In July 1965, while on TDY at Tan Son Nhut, Chuck Lustig remembers suggesting (as he was wont to do) that he and a group of some 12 fellow pilots should take one more drink at the Rex Hotel, their favourite watering hole in Saigon, before departing for dinner at another of their haunts, the My Canh

Armed Escort. An A1-E 'Sandy' escorts the Albatross amphibian from the scene of Norm Huggins rescue. Norm Huggins

waterside restaurant. It was lucky that he did because a Viet Cong bomb detonated in the restaurant just as pilots approached and this was followed by a claymore mine exploding on the gangplank to catch earlier revellers there as they tried to escape. The pilots returned to the Rex, which then did a roaring trade as they celebrated one of the greatest escapes of their time, and the fact that alcohol can really be good for you!

Back at work the Voodoo pilots learned fast how to deal with new defences. On 22 May 1966 the pilot of an RF-101 homeward bound at 4,000 ft some 35 nm north-west of Hanoi, saw one of the SA-2 'flying telephone poles' bearing down on him just in time; he broke into it, sending it past him by 'little more than 100 ft'. Others who were quick to recognise each threat and react accordingly also lived to tell more tales of survival and it was the same with the MiGs. Initial assurances from above that the Voodoos would be able to out-turn these fighters must have come as a surprise to the Voodoo pilots and such claims were soon proved to be ill-founded; as with the SAMs it was vital that the MiGs be seen in time for the Voodoos to make their get-away. Without escorting fighters, self-defence weapons, fully effective electronic or infra-red countermeasures, the only sensible option was to jettison their tanks, plug in the afterburners and make best use of their very rapid acceleration and top speed. They could out-run the MiGs (except for the MiG-21s) and this was the tactic (together with seeking the relative security of cloud) that they employed.

Despite this, two RF-101 pilots given a target 30 nm north-west of Hanoi on 15 November 1965 still pushed their luck when the wingman reported two MiGs passing to the rear of them and some 6,000 ft above, in an excellent attacking position, while his leader was on his photo run at 9,000 ft, seven miles east of Yen Bai. They should have cut and run but the leader pressed on over the target while the wingman sandwiched himself between his leader and the MiGs and successfully lured them away. The two Voodoos then ran, in afterburner at around 600 kts, streaking over towns and villages at roof-top height and through heavy gunfire eventually to shed their pursuers and continue home with the precious photographs. Fortune favours the brave. On 17 March 1966 MiGs made passes on a pair of RF-101s as they left their target in the Dien Bien Phu area of north-west North Vietnam, only to lose the Voodoos in heavy haze as they too escaped at speed.

Notwithstanding the new SAMs and MiG fighters, AAA remained the main threat and the most difficult to avoid. After being shot down by gunfire over Laos on 18 October 1967, Captain Nick 'Pish' Pishvanov gave much of the credit for his survival to the woodcraft he had learned as a child, his survival training at Stead AFB and jungle training in the Philippines. The story began when he was ordered to recce a stretch of the Ho Chi Minh Trail at low level. This was consistent with the conventional wisdom for operations in Europe but not with practical experience in SEA which suggested that, whenever possible, such a task should be flown at a less vulnerable height. His aircraft was hit in the bell crank housing, causing it to pitch out of control with the horizontal stabilizer 'locked'. Pish ejected successfully at 500 ft, with little time to prepare himself before hitting the trees and ending up suspended a few feet from the ground. He had made a mental note of the direction of the hostile gun fire and saw his mount crash a couple of miles away with 'the best target photos ever' aboard! The hazardous low level ejection had the benefit of denying his would-be captors his precise location and he was able to prepare for evasion unhindered. Training and sensible forethought had rendered him well equipped in every respect for the challenge ahead, that of survival; he had the knowledge, two serviceable radios, extra water and above all no fear of the jungle. Having hidden his 'G'-suit and LPU (life preserver), he moved away from the immediate threat to a more secure location, by which time his enemies had found his parachute and fortuitously deactivated his recovery 'bleeper', which would otherwise have led any rescuers to the spot and into a trap. Then, in what turned out to be a mixed blessing, a 'big black bird' nearby began taking an active interest in proceedings, squawking loudly whenever Pish made a move, but also providing a similar alarm when anyone approached. An attempt to walk to freedom across the heavily occupied Ho Chi Minh Trail would have been sheer folly, while to look for a safer place, food or water was both unnecessary and imprudent, so Pish laid low, remained silent and resisted the temptation to smoke.

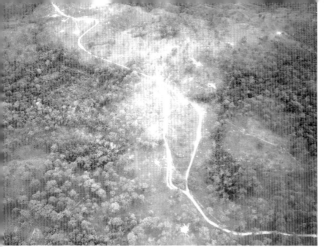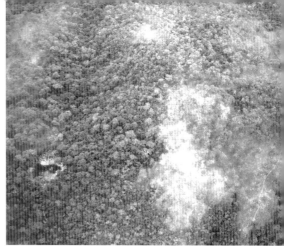

Smoke Marks The Spot. His 'perfect' photos aboard, Nick Pishvanov's Voodoo goes up in smoke but he brought back his visual report. Nick Pishvanov

Meanwhile, the rescue organisation had swung into action and an hour or so after the ejection, when all was quiet, 'Crown', the C-130 Hercules rescue co-ordinator (which had intercepted Nick's emergency signal and was orbiting at height nearby) made contact with him. After insisting on going through tortuously long authentication procedures via the Udorn and Saigon authorities, and pleading 'higher priority communications traffic', Crown set the final recovery action in motion. With judicious use of his radio, Lensatic homing device and an orange locator panel, Pish had no difficulty guiding the protective A-1Es and a rescue helicopter to the spot. Hoisted clear of the trees on a Davis Tree Sling, he was towed clear of the danger area before being taken aboard a Jolly Green Giant and ferried, via a manual refuelling stop in the jungle, to Da Nang.

Pish did not bring back the photos required but he could pin-point the hostile activity and position of the guns to which he had succumbed (and which were not supposed to be there), credible intelligence in itself. Photographs were usually demanded to confirm visual sightings but on this occasion his word and an aircraft lost were accepted as sufficient proof. Strike aircraft were ordered into the area and caused massive secondary explosions which suggested the presence of a truck park or ammunition storage and thus underlining the value of visual reporting to supplement, or provide an alternative to photographs. Pish had a copybook rescue, bringing credit to all involved; as for the man himself, perhaps he should have been rewarded for confirming his airborne sightings of valuable intelligence while on the end of a

parachute and then on foot; this was dedication indeed.

There is a sequel to this classic rescue story. Several years later, quite by chance, Major Nick Pishvanov met the co-pilot of the Jolly Green Giant involved in his rescue while on a bus which was taking them both to their offices at the Pentagon. From this nostalgic meeting he learned that the helicopter's captain had died in a subsequent rescue attempt; it was not only the combat pilots who risked their lives in the common cause.

Although such dramatic stories and losses within the Voodoo force tended to diminish in its final years of war in SEA, gunfire continued to take its toll. On 28 October 1969, an RF-101 was badly damaged in the left wing with the resulting fire destroying the utility hydraulic system and port aileron control. The pilot managed to get his crippled mount back to base and climb from it uninjured after a very fast, flapless landing, during which both tyres burst, the aircraft left the runway and the starboard gear sheared off, in yet another spectacular escape.

This chapter has offered a small sample of how some RF-101 pilots avoided death, minimised injury to themselves and damage to their aircraft, during their duels with the weather, natural hazards, technical defects and above all hostile action. Many similar incidents have gone untold in a conflict which was far from anything the recce pilots had expected or trained for in the relatively halcyon days of peace in the Cold War. That they all coped so well, in the air and on the ground, in such difficult circumstances, is a great tribute to them and to all who supported them.

CHAPTER EIGHTEEN
THE 'HANOI HILTON'

To be a prisoner of war (POW) in North Vietnam has been described as 'almost as grim as death' and too many American aircrew can confirm that the reality was indeed appalling. In the case of combat aircrew it all began with the stress of the mission itself, then the trauma of ejection and the rough handling which would almost certainly follow if captured, after which there might be the humiliation of being paraded before jeering crowds in towns and villages. Worse was to come, the infamous prisons. Here the POWs could expect solitude, starvation rations, little if any medical treatment, beatings, torture and perhaps death. Hoa Lo Prison, west of the Red River in Hanoi, earned the name 'Hanoi Hilton' which heads this chapter but in the text serves as a euphemism for the many locations to which the aircrew were taken, each with similarly sardonic nicknames.

Captain 'Scotty' Morgan was the first 'Voodooer' to be taken prisoner by the North Vietnamese after AAA had downed his RF-101 on 3 April 1965; he spent the next nine years as a POW. Many more would follow and most would not be freed until 1973. Captain Charlie Shelton would not return home. His Voodoo was mortally damaged by ground fire over Northern Laos on 29 April 1965 and he ejected. He was seen from the air to be safely on the ground and himself reported as much by radio, but the rescue helicopters could not reach him then or in the three days which followed because of bad weather, after which he was captured by the Pathet Lao and held for three-and-a-half years in the very caves he had been sent to photograph. Based on information from local villagers, informants, defecting Pathet Lao soldiers and refugees, Charlie was 'a most un-cooperative prisoner', renowned for his many escape attempts and for beating three of his interrogators to death with a chain before he was overpowered. He may then have been moved to Hanoi but all news of him ceased at that time. In 1994, 29 years after he had been shot down, the USAF finally declared Colonel Charles Shelton 'Killed in Action' (KIA); his

wife, Dorothy had taken her own life four years before.

Captain 'Newk' Grubb also paid the ultimate price while a POW after his Voodoo too was shot down by gunfire over North Vietnam on 26 January 1966, the only loss during the one-way Christmas ceasefire. From pictures made public at the time, Newk appeared in good condition after his ejection and capture but he died in captivity. Officially, he succumbed to an 'undisclosed medical condition' nine days after his imprisonment but it is generally believed that the cause was over zealous interrogation as attempts were made to find out when the bombing of North Vietnam would resume, information which he did not have. Newk had been one of the author's more promising students at the Shaw Voodoo school, a strong man of determination and tenacity, characteristics which were unlikely to have endeared him to his ultimate hosts. Major Alan Brunstrom, on Newk's wing when he was shot down and soon to be a POW himself, opined later that the 'Goon Squad' were learning the business of interrogation 'on the job', some clearly enjoying it, others perhaps finding it a little distasteful, but none knowing quite how far they could or should go.

The author wrestled long with the pros and cons of proceeding with such a sensitive subject in this record of Voodoo heritage, being loath to intrude on very personal and private memories even 30 years after the last of the prisoners was released. Attitudes among the POWs to the idea varied widely, with some understandably unable or unwilling to recall their painful experiences, but a broad consensus within the Voodoo fraternity felt that 'Voodoo Warriors' would not be complete without some special tribute to their POWs, and the author is particularly indebted to Colonel (Ret'd) Al Brunstrom, one of their number, for agreeing to share his experiences as a prisoner in and around Hanoi.

Al was flying from Udorn as Captain Bill Bradley's wingman on 22 April 1966 when he was shot down while carrying out pre-strike

Solitary. This evocative painting by Maxine McCaffery symbolizes the mood of an American POW in his Hanoi cell, the names of others etched on the wall behind him. Via Alan Brunstrom

Survivor. Alan Brunstrom. Alan Brunstrom

photography over the Cao Nung railroad bridge on the notorious North East Railway, some 60 nm from Hanoi. Two 37-mm or 57-mm rounds caused a fire in the left engine of his Voodoo which he could not extinguish and minutes later his aircraft pitched up at 1,500 ft, leaving him with no alternative but to eject. A copybook ejection and descent was followed by a 'soft' landing in the mud of a rice paddy, where North Vietnamese peasants were waiting to capture him. Curious but far from hostile, they took him to a cave, allowed him to wash, gave him food, drink and a clean set of Vietnamese clothes (which were replaced later that day by his soiled flying suit) and in the afternoon took him, sometimes blindfolded, through inquisitive crowds stimulated by blaring loudspeakers, to an army unit in the town of Lang Son. There he was questioned forcibly but refused to complete an autobiographical questionnaire and was rewarded with the first of many beatings. Heavily

bound and blindfolded he was taken by Jeep on the long, overnight journey to the Hoa Lo complex in Hanoi.

On arrival at 'Heartbreak Hotel' (HBH), the initial interrogation centre within the Hanoi Hilton, Al was ordered to sit (not lie or sleep) in what he would come to know as a typical

Hanoi Hilton. The Hoa Lo prison complex in Hanoi. Alan Brunstrom

HANOI HILTON

HOA LO PRISO

Drawn from Memory

LEGEND:

1 NEW GUY VILLAGE
2 HEART BREAK HOTEL
3 MAYO
4 CELL BLOCK
5 MAIN GATE
6 LITTLE VEGAS AREA
7 CAMP UNITY AREA
8 STARDUST
9 DESERT INN
10 RIVIERA
11 NUGGET
12 STOCK YARD
13 KITCHEN
14 MINT
15 THUNDER
16 BATH AREA
17 COAL YAR
18 MEDIC SHA
19 QUIZ ROO

one-man cell, measuring 7 ft by 7 ft, it was filthy, infested with rats and lit by one small bulb. Managing to loosen his ties brought another beating, but he was heartened by the presence in the next cell of the Korean Ace, charismatic and highly respected F-105 leader, Lieutenant Colonel Robinson (Robbie) Risner, a presence he would come to welcome. He was taken to the 'quiz room' in 'New Guy Village', where he was shown evidence from the crash site which revealed him to be a Voodoo pilot from the 20th TRS at Udorn, and subjected to persistent interrogation for the rest of the day. His captors also showed him a tape entitled 'Risner and Grubb', to suggest that they already knew much, but Al continued to give them his name, rank and number only. Later, they allowed him to talk to Risner alone, perhaps in the hope that he would be persuaded to say more, but the colonel's briefing had the opposite effect. Risner and his successor, Commander Stockdale, always exercised exemplary leadership, doing much to raise the spirits of the prisoners, as did a 'tap code' which enabled the inmates to communicate effectively between cells, albeit covertly and at great risk.

Only under extreme pressure did Al resort to the essentially simple and wholly innocuous story he had prepared; he 'played dumb', claiming erroneously that as a newly promoted major he knew nothing of value to them and

certainly not when Hanoi might be bombed. Later, he told interrogators what their predecessors had told him during previous sessions, both tactics apparently effective. Every day for a week he would be allowed a shower and given clean prison clothes on a diet of cold pumpkin soup, very stale hard bread and a few vegetables (for which he had little appetite) before being taken back to his cell late at night. There was no medical treatment. After a second week in solitary confinement at HBH, he was moved to the 'Zoo'. It was 6 May 1966.

At 12 ft by 14 ft, the cells in the 'Pool Hall' of the Zoo were almost twice the size of those in Heartbreak, accommodating two men and a host of rats, mice and snakes; they were equally filthy with one 'honey bucket', virtually no ventilation and very few concessions to personal hygiene. The complex consisted of a number of separate buildings, between which some communication could be maintained by diverse means, but with direct contact the senior officers were deprived of overall control.

With 'The Fox' as camp commandant, sadism was rampant among the guards and interrogators, Al Brunstrom coming in for special treatment from those branded 'Spots', 'J.C.', 'The Lump' and 'Elf'. 'Sewer greens', cabbage and rice were added to the inadequate and unappetizing diet and medical treatment for such prevalent problems as ringworm,

Reception. New Guy Village - but no welcome for the POWs. Alan Brunstrom

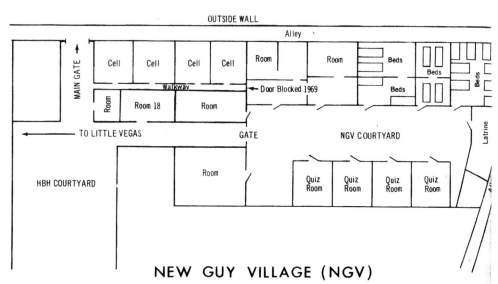

NEW GUY VILLAGE (NGV)

intestinal worms and chronic diarrhoea, was either non-existent or totally ineffective.

Failure to extract military intelligence from the POWs, despite every psychological and physical means, eventually gave way to intensive political indoctrination aimed at instilling the 'correct attitude', but this was equally unsuccessful. Al Brunstrom was accused (with good reason) of communicating with his fellow prisoners; initially he refused to sign an admission to that effect but after 12 hours of torture he finally admitted that he had attempted to do so, but failed, and that was enough to gain respite.

The US attacks against North Vietnamese fuel resources, on 29 June 1959, led to the infamous retaliatory march of POWs through the streets of Hanoi on the evening of 6 July. Again the initial reaction of the gathering crowds was that of curiosity, but they were quickly whipped into a frenzy of anger by loudspeakers and the scene turned very ugly; Al was among the many prisoners who were beaten 'black and blue, from head to toe' before their guards could get them to safety. Ten minutes after he had been returned to his cell at the Zoo Al was taken outside again, blindfolded, gagged and tied with his arms behind a tree. There he remained throughout the night, the guards returning every 10 minutes or so to kick and beat him; by thrusting the gag further into his throat with a dirty stick they broke his dentures and left him with chronic eating problems for the next six-and-a half years. At dawn, he was taken to the interrogation room where he was 'worked over' again, all for allegedly talking to the individual with whom he had been handcuffed during the march.

At about this time the POWs were told that they were to be tried under North Vietnamese law as 'war criminals' and must choose either to admit this crime and condemn US policy in SEA, in which case they would be treated humanely, or be executed. When called upon to make his statement, Al wrote that he was an officer in the military service of the United States Government, that he was proud to serve his country in any way that he could and was 100% behind the US Government policy in Vietnam. This courageous stand earned him more punishment; he was deprived of his cigarette ration (three cigarettes a day) and regular washing facilities, which seriously

affected his health. After six weeks of this intransigence The Lump had him removed to even less habitable surroundings where his arms and legs were shackled so tightly to his so called bed for three days that it restricted the blood flow, causing massive swelling and excruciating pain as the metal cut into his flesh. When he screamed in anguish the irons were loosened to give some small relief for a further day before he was taken before the The Lump once more, at which point, his pain having subsided temporarily, he again refused to admit his 'crimes'. More beatings and greater torture followed, taking him to the point of suffocation, until he finally agreed to make the required statement.

By the manner in which they were written, and in their content, it was obvious that such statements were written under severe duress and could not be believed in the world outside. On the contrary, the POWs were seen to be doing their duty courageously and no more could be asked of them. As such, this exercise should not have caused anything but contempt in the United States for the North Vietnamese captors.

Back in the Pool Hall at the Zoo Al Brunstrom was now seen to have adopted the 'right attitude' and was rewarded by a resumption of a cigarette ration and access to washing. On 22 September 1966 he was joined by a roommate who would share his cells for the next three years. Together they faced a new propaganda campaign, a futile effort to convince the world of North Vietnam's humane treatment of its POWs. When Al and his roommate refused to complete a questionnaire to that end they were punished by long periods shackled in irons in various postures of great discomfort - until it was decided to move them to 'Little Vegas'.

Looking back, Al Brunsom remembers his months at the Zoo as his worst in his captivity. He remains sure, however, that resistance to every pressure was worthwhile, in that it made interrogators work very hard in their attempts to get what they wanted, and largely denying them anything worthwhile. He emphasised again the value of the positive leadership and mutual support which existed between detainees, in helping to sustain this resistance and in maintaining morale.

When Al and his cellmate were moved to Little Vegas on 25 May 1967, allegedly because

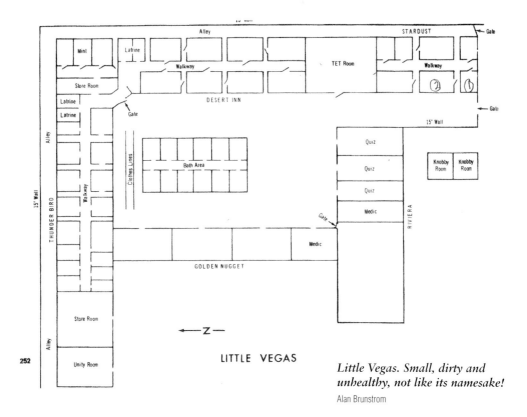

Labels in diagram: Alley, STARDUST, Gate, Mint, Latrine, TET Room, Walkway, Walkway, Store Room, DESERT INN, Latrine, Gate, Gate, Latrine, 15' Wall, Clothes Lines, Quiz, Knobby Room, Knobby Room, Bath Area, Quiz, Walkway, Quiz, Medic, THUNDER BIRD, 15' Wall, Gate, Medic, RIVIERA, GOLDEN NUGGET, Store Room, —Z—, Alley, Unity Room, 252

Little Vegas. Small, dirty and unhealthy, not like its namesake!

Alan Brunstrom

of their 'bad attitude', they expected the worst but it was not to be. True, their room in the 'Stardust' was even smaller and just as dirty, with ominous stocks at the foot of the double-decker beds, but after an uneasy night their new 'den mother', known as 'The Maggot' or 'Greasy', told them that their past had been forgotten and that they were to be given a new start, but was this a new tactic? In August they were allocated to a barely larger four-man room and then to an identical cell in the 'Desert Inn', where they were joined by two additional cellmates. This too was a great boost to morale. To further hamper contact between the prisoners the complex was built with narrow passages between each cell; no two cell doors faced each other and guards were often posted in the corridors 24 hours a day, but the POWs still found ways to keep in touch with each other. Suspecting this to be so, but lacking evidence, charges were trumped up all round and Al was ordered to write a confession revealing what had passed between them: *"I wrote that I knew I would be tortured if caught communicating with others, and since there was no information on the camp for which it was worth being tortured I had not done so and this The Maggot accepted."*

The unhealthy, dirty conditions prevailed throughout Little Vegas, with ventilation little better than that at the Zoo, but there was some relief when the inmates were allowed, if only periodically, to wash out their cells. There were also brief spells in which the food improved marginally but it soon reverted to the very bare essentials and medical assistance remained all but non-existent. The behaviour of the guards continued to be erratic and unpredictable, depending on their mood and own political indoctrination. Attempts to persuade the prisoners to make good the damage caused by US bombing failed and as time passed there was a general decrease in political education and interrogation.

Al continued to suffer the very cramped conditions of the four-man cells at Little Vegas until May 1968, when he and his original cellmate were moved to Son Tay and 'Camp Hope'. Their new home was in the 'Opium Den' of four 'suites', each with an outer door leading to a foyer and doors to one two-man cell and one one-man cell. At first Al and his cell-mate shared a two-man cell, with the inner cell doors later opened during the day to allow the three prisoners to mix (the outer suite door being locked) but in the final weeks Al was moved into the single cell to spend the nights alone. This was hardly the luxury it sounds but the three prisoners now had windows to the outside world and improved ventilation. On

10 December 1969 Al left the cell-mate he had been with for 39 months and moved into 'field grade' quarters in the 'Beer Hall' with five other prisoners. They occupied a room measuring 17 ft by 30 ft with five windows which allowed some contact with other prisoners and they had an additional room which served as a primitive latrine.

It was from here that Al drafted his first letter home on 11 December 1969.

For men who had become so used to solitary confinement, or at best the company of one or two others, the much increased communication afforded by the five-man rooms was very welcome. Their North Vietnamese warders and interrogators ('Bushy' or 'Blackie', 'Rat' 'Maggot', 'Gap', 'Mouse', 'Hog' and 'Mark') were variously intelligent, dangerous or harmless, but always unpredictable. The very poor diet continued with diarrhoea and worms rampant and medical attention wholly unsatisfactory. A new building, the 'Cat House' was opened, to which the POWs were moved in and out for no obvious reason.

Throughout the earlier days at Camp Hope punishment for poor attitudes, failure to respond to political propaganda or complete the regular personal quizzes as required, continued to range from angry verbal reaction through confinement to cruel torture. When serious threats accompanied an order that all the POWs complete another autobiography, the senior US officer advised them to repeat what they had written before, thereby avoiding unnecessary torture.

Few of the POWs attempted to escape, such moves being positively discouraged by Robbie Risner and other senior officers in the camps; they argued that it would be very difficult for the escapees to blend into the background once outside the prisons and that external help was a must. USN Lieutenant George Coker and USAF Captain George McKnight found this out for themselves on 12 October 1967, although they managed to get out of the camp and swim down the Red River for some 15 miles before being recaptured. Then, in May 1969, another of the author's recce friends from the Voodoo days, Captain Ed Atterberry, met his death in the aftermath of an abortive escape from the Zoo. Ed had been shot down on a reconnaissance mission over Ha Bac Province, 10 miles north-east of Gia Lam, and steadfastly refused to accept incarceration. After

meticulous planning, in which he used his experience as a one-time telephone linesman to deprive their captors of electric light, he and Captain John Dramesi escaped through the roof of their cell and travelled 3 miles before being recaptured. Retribution was swift and terrible, only John surviving the brutal torture to which Ed is believed to have succumbed (the Vietnamese reported that he had died of an 'unusual disease'). Not only were Atterberry and Dramesi punished severely, the whole POW community was 'systematically worked over' as a result of this short-lived freedom. Dire warnings that any further escapes would have even graver consequences reinforced the orders against such attempts unless they met stringent conditions. Within these constraints other plans were conceived but none were thought to have come to fruition.

In the spring of 1970 came the first small signs of changes in the treatment of POWs. When Al failed to agree to repeated demands that he write to President Nixon, Henry Kissinger, congressmen, his fellow pilots or US troops in South Vietnam (urging them to stop fighting) he was merely subjected to more yelling and screaming before the Rat claimed to be too busy to deal with him and that punishment would follow later. It did not and there was no more torture in the camp. In another heartening development Al received the first, very small parcel from home, heralding the start of a periodic exchange of correspondence. In all, Al received three packages and 12 letters (with photographs of home), his wife getting about the same number from him in return.

In November 1970 an attempt was made to rescue the inmates of Son Tay prison, some 24 miles west of Hanoi and as such more vulnerable than those in and around the capital. An elite raiding party of 56 soldiers, having trained exhaustively at Eglin AFB, Florida, flew from Udorn to Son Tay in six helicopters, with appropriate air support, only to find that the prisoners had been moved out four months earlier. So much for definitive intelligence!

Indeed, on 14 July 1970 all 57 POWs had been moved to 'Camp Faith', closer to Hanoi. Here, one building was divided into five cells, each with a separate, small cubicle for the honey buckets; three large windows provided light, ventilation and better contact with other prisoners, which together formed the best living conditions Al had experienced in captivity. Soon, the POWs were allowed outside on a roster to bathe and exercise, this concession extended later to full mornings or afternoons in another great improvement. The inmates now began to flex their muscles, with a 'go slow' leading to concessions in hygiene and internal organisation. Water was now adequate and washing facilities improved. Sporadically, food was supplemented by limited additions of fruit, milk and juices, candy and cookies. Interrogation and political indoctrination had all but petered out, a legitimate education programme had started and the more severe punishments were a thing of the past. Things were definitely improving.

The same applied albeit to a limited extent to the medical attention they now received, but Al's account of his own condition illustrates the magnitude of the remedial action required:

"By November 1970 my diarrhoea had slowed up somewhat, probably due to vitamins from home plus a little protein. On occasions I would get diarrhoea pills but they were totally ineffective. I had developed a pain in my left shoulder which left it almost paralysed, accompanied by a sharp pain down my left arm my left thumb and index finger losing all feeling. For a month I received no treatment and then, just as it seemed to be getting a little better, the 'medic' gave me some pain killing pills which allowed me to sleep for a few hours each night.

As I got back to normal I was given Vitamin B shots for several days before they decided to give me a penicillin shot. Although I had had penicillin many times I developed a reaction (probably from bad penicillin rather than any allergy to it) which brought about complete panic; five more medics showed up, I was given five different shots and recovered quickly. However, I then had after effects which caused my face to swell up and close my eyes for three days. Subsequent x-rays after release showed that I had had in the past a broken clavicle, the cause uncertain but probably the reason for these problems. I then lost a filling in one tooth and believe it or not a dentist came and filled it, only for it to drop out again two weeks later. My pet worms continued to cause great discomfort - especially when they crawled out to play each night"

On 24 November 1970, for reasons again unknown, all 57 inmates of Camp Faith were moved at two hours notice to Camp Unity back at the Hoa Lo complex in downtown Hanoi. At Unity all the newcomers occupied one room, each sleeping in very cramped spaces 22 inches wide along raised ridges running down the centre. There were some improvements, with primitive 'oriental-style' latrines flushed by

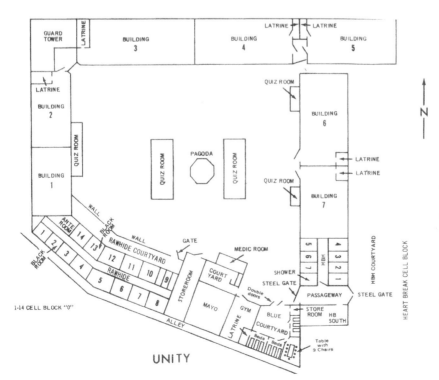

Camp Unity. In November 1970 it was all move again, this time to return to Unity in the Hanoi Hilton.
Alan Brunstrom

bathwater from a header tank, washing and bathing facilities, a small exercise courtyard and, later, a ceiling fan which provided some circulation of the putrid air. This complex would eventually host all the POWs believed to be in North Vietnam; they would live in similar rooms screened from each other but still allowing some contact between them.

'Bushy', the camp commandant and several of his minions from Camp Faith and Camp Hope, had followed their prisoners to Unity but, other than the den mother, Rat, they were now much less in evidence. Interrogation or political indoctrination may have ceased but the prisoners continued to be harassed, particularly in their educational and religious activities, with every effort to restrict personal communication; they were now treated more like criminals than POWs. Perhaps it was a degree of complacency and a tendency among the more confident to aggravate or antagonise their guards that now led to periodic, punitive crack-downs. Just before Christmas 1970, in a thorough inspection, the guards discovered a personal microfilm and an embryo, hand-made radio set. This resulted in the confiscation of US education material, together with the contents of US aid parcels which included much needed warm clothing and food items being saved for the Christmas celebrations. Thereafter, parcels from home were inspected closely and often mutilated.

The basic menu continued to be the order of the day but it was supplemented now with vegetable side dishes, more bread, milk and some candy. After 1971, the medical services improved progressively but with more attention than effect, especially with respect to the perennial worms. When 'pinkeye' hit the camp eye salve and drops were provided but the condition seemed to be beyond the capability of the medical services and eventually it ran its course. There followed what appeared to be a case of food poisoning which affected half the occupants and attracted much medical attention, including no fewer than seven doctors, but little remedial action. The POWs at Unity were now organised on a Wing basis, with a senior ranking officer at the head, an executive officer, operations officer, supply/housekeeping officer and commanders for each of four flights. Al was the supply officer and 'A' Flight Commander. There were also staff officers for communications, security,

medical, education and a chaplain. This well-proven organisational structure served its purpose but was an anathema to the Vietnamese. They created a Junior Officer Liaison programme which was intended to overrule the POW initiative and through which to communicate their orders and concessions, but when they found this to be wholly ineffective and that it was quicker to achieve their objectives through the Wing organisation their system was discarded.

With growing confidence, the Wing continued to do everything possible to enhance their life style. Perhaps controversially, a moratorium on outgoing letters was introduced in the hope of better treatment from the guards by seeking to imply to the outside world that the POW's captors were not allowing them to write home. Inevitably, some doubted whether this had the desired effect and regretted the loss of contact with their loved ones, but it was accepted generally that the internal organisation overall was of great benefit to the material and psychological welfare of the POWs.

Perhaps it was the on-going bombing of Hanoi that led to the move, again at short notice, of some 200 prisoners from Unity to Camp 'Dogpatch', via an uncomfortable 30 hour truck journey into the mountains late at night on 15 May 1972. For eight months at Dogpatch the POWs were shuffled between small, cramped and badly ventilated rooms with no electricity; such lighting as there was came from kerosene lamps and the very low temperatures were bearable only after the issue of some cold weather clothing (socks and long underwear). There were rudimentary washing facilities, crude flush toilets and a tiny exercise courtyard; the prisoners were allowed some freedom to move around the complex during the day but were locked in their cells at night. The conduct of the guards remained unpredictable. Propaganda throughout April 1972 claimed that it was the US which had sabotaged the Paris Peace Talks, but there were further improvements in the diet, with a marked increase in protein, fish, meat and soybean curd and 'goodies'. Medical attention was still far from satisfactory and one man suffering from typhoid was removed to Hanoi where it was reported later that he had died. Internal communications within Dogpatch were generally good but the internal organisation which had proved so effective in Camp Unity was now replaced by typical squadron or other structures more appropriate for the smaller, separate rooms.

The POWs were returned to Camp Unity in Hanoi in January 1973, where more changes awaited. All the screens within the courtyard, which had previously limited contact between rooms, had been taken down, as had the screens and the panels on the cell windows. There was more sleeping space for each man and much more freedom of movement overall; the end of the ordeal was clearly drawing near.

On 12 February 1973, the anniversary of Lincoln's birthday, Al Brunstrom boarded a USAF transport at North Vietnam's Gia Lam Airport for Clark AFB in the Philippines. Two days later, on Valentines Day, he was reunited with his family at Travis AFB, California, after nearly seven years in captivity. It was a day to remember.

Al's weight variations during captivity

Homecoming. This picture of Lieutenant Colonel Al Brunstrom meeting his wife at Travis AFB, California, on Valentine Day 1973, says it all. Alan Brunstrom

Back in Business. Many POWs, like Alan Brunstrom and Charles White shown here, resumed their flying careers in the USAF. Alan Brunstrom

followed the pattern of initial depravity, starvation rations and lack of medical treatment, through stages of incremental improvement: 193 lb on capture, down to 120 lb and up to 158 lb on release. He had undergone all levels of torture, resisting until the pain became too extreme and then treating his interrogators to a mixture of innocuous fact and fiction. He had endured very debilitating medical afflictions, so much due to the starvation rations and thoroughly unhygienic conditions. On the plus side, he had 'found' himself, learned a great deal about human nature, come to appreciate the value of

Above & below left: Memories. Who can guess at the emotions when Alan Brunstrom returned to the scenes of his imprisonment in 2003? Alan Brunstrom

Survival. This logo was worn with pride by those who survived every ordeal which beset the POWs in SEA. Alan Brunstrom

personal and collective discipline and learned a greater tolerance towards his fellow mankind. Again he was quick to praise the leadership of his superior officers, the comradeship engendered in such dire times and the merits of the US military ethics. As with so many of the POWs he had survived with honour and would return to active service.

Al Brunstrom's story could be that of many of his fellow captives, albeit with variations. There were those who suffered more physically, those who were less able to adapt to their wretched circumstances, those who resisted more and paid a greater price and those who were unable to find ways of ameliorating their hardships and suffered some inevitable degradation of their spirit. Who would criticise any of them?

CHAPTER NINETEEN
KILL'EM WITH FIL'M

'The camera never lies.'

So often in a story of this kind it is the heroes in the cockpits who predominate at the expense of those who provided them with vital support on the ground. In fact, there would be no story worth telling if it were not for concerted efforts at all levels, first to produce and evaluate the aircraft then maintain diverse operational, logistical and engineering support throughout the aircraft's evolution and its service life. Evolution has been dealt with briefly in Chapter One, other direct support functions such as the weapons systems for the F-101B and CF-101B, their radars and missiles, the nuclear weapons and guns for the 81st TFW, featuring where appropriate in chapters which followed. The remaining chapters concentrated on the RF-101 and its all-important cameras, dwelling on the significant part they played in the SEA conflict (Part Two). It is for the latter reason that Chapter Nineteen is devoted to photographic support as a specific illustration of the contribution made by the men behind the machines, before Chapter Twenty focuses more generally on that whole army of special men who kept the aircraft in the air - the Voodoo Medicine Men'.

Whether in NATO's prestigious Royal Flush recce competitions, disaster assessment in mainland USA, or in war, the main *raison d'etre* for the Voodoo recce force world-wide was photography. Competition and domestic photography have been touched on in earlier chapters and it is now time to say more about photographic camera support in SEA. While visual recce was practiced regularly in Europe and the requirement was written into the TAC and PACAF RF-101 mission statements, it had a low priority in SEA, where the Voodoo men's primary role was to 'kill'em with fil'm'.

What follows is an amalgam of recollections from the now retired Colonel Jimmy Ifland and his lifelong colleague and friend Chief Master Sergeant John Roddick, photographic and camera specialists respectively in the RF-101 force.

John Roddick called the Voodoo camera system 'maintenance friendly, accessible and reliable', which was just as well because in the early days spares for the operational, test and servicing equipment were in short supply and the Voodoo force might be deployed at a moment's notice over great distances to remote

Colonel Jim Ifland. Jim Ifland

Senior Master Sergeant John Roddick.

John Roddick

bases with rudimentary facilities. Somehow, as is so often the case when the need arises, the men on the line, back in the camera servicing shops and in the business of producing the ultimate product, photographs, always rose to the occasion. Again, ingenuity and industry was the name of the game and this was rarely found wanting.

Cross-training and the posting of photo men between the flight line camera system, shop test equipment and component repair specialisations enhanced their general knowledge of optics, photography, electronics and the nature of the reconnaissance mission. John Roddick remembers that the 15th TRS was one of the squadrons which proved the inherent value of having the camera men 'belong' to specific flying squadrons, with the resulting allegiance, loyalty and improved morale paying off in the workplace. However, in the early 1960s, all specialist photo resources were brought together within the 18th TFW Avionic Maintenance Squadron (AMS). While remaining on the Voodoo flight line, the photo men now became less intimately connected with the squadron while at the same time being somewhat remote in the AMS command chain. This was a less than ideal situation in the peacetime routine of a largely static flying unit but it was wholly inconsistent with the unpredictable requirements of tactical squadrons on constant alert to go anywhere in the world at any time. Despite this ill-advised centralisation of resources the dedication of the camera men to the task was utterly exceptional, as the remainder of this chapter will more than adequately demonstrate. It was not until the

late 1980s that the reintegration of these specialists into tactical flying squadrons became the norm and by far the preferred option for most of the men involved, those running the squadron and the pilots; it had taken that long for this to be accepted by the establishment.

Routinely, work on the camera systems began when the daily flying schedule was issued the previous evening, with camera and film requirements being listed against aircraft tail numbers. The night shift would then load film from air conditioned containers into magazines within a darkroom, ready for them to be fitted to aircraft for power-on checks of the complete system some two hours before take-off. The cameramen remained flexible, however, ever-ready to respond to inevitable changes in the programme with urgent but meticulous attention; even in daily training they remained conscious that in competition and war, time and perfection were of the essence.

Given the normal modus operandi within the tac recon role, that of flying single aircraft or pairs at irregular intervals, the groundcrew assigned to RF-101 squadrons rarely enjoyed the respite afforded when waves of aircraft are launched and recovered together. With a constant stream of RF-101s coming and going, the Voodoo cameramen tended to remain on the flight line throughout their shifts, pride alone demanding that film be downloaded, taken to the darkroom and processed as expeditiously as possible, without error.

Removing and replacing the cameras and magazines in the nose and side-oblique stations of the Voodoo was relatively simple but this was not so in the case of the two big 36-inch split-vertical cameras housed below and behind the cockpit, on swing mounts to facilitate image motion compensation (IMC). The combined load of 150 lb was raised and lowered mechanically by cable which had to be cut when the system jammed, an infrequent but far from unknown event. It was then that the smallest member of the team had to wriggle into the small access bay with the necessary wire cutters, while the largest of his companions would position himself below with mattress or cushions to catch this heavy weight as it fell. John Roddick recalls that however able and well practised the team, this solution did not always work perfectly, resulting in many a minor cut and bruise and a host of unwelcome questions from the maintenance office. At the end of daylight flying (few Voodoos were equipped for night photography), defective equipment was removed for attention in the camera maintenance shop, and the whole cycle began again.

The best test of collective abilities came with the frequent deployments, particularly to bases which offered only the basic facilities, but the photo men always seemed to adapt to the conditions and find the ways and means to do their job. Mobility plans took account of the specific destination, expected duration and the tasks to be carried out when detailing the photo men and equipment to support the RF-101s off base, but they could not always anticipate what was needed.

Soon after losing direct control of its photo specialists in the early 1960s, the 15th TRS began a number of detachments to Taiwan to fly reconnaissance missions in support of the government there in its territorial dispute with the Chinese communists on the mainland. With little warning, the men considered right for this purpose, many hidden away in the depths of Okinawa, had to be found and recalled while C-130 Hercules on the ramp at Kadena loaded photo equipment which would be housed in the accompanying air portable B-2 Quonset Huts. In Taiwan the host base provided all the necessary facilities for the four RF-101s in a clear and simple chain of command for this limited but intensive operation. An NCO, who reported to the Voodoo pilot acting as the detachment maintenance officer, was responsible for the work of the camera crews and for maintaining a continuous liaison between the operations centre and processing activities in support of the assigned missions. This worked well.

A similar pattern was adopted initially by the 15th TRS when it set up shop at Tan Son Nhut in 1963 (Chapter Nine). As the war gathered pace, with an increasing number of Voodoos operating from there, Udorn and forward operating bases, the manpower involved in its support rotated continuously between SEA, Japan, Okinawa and the United States. Capitalising on their experience many of these men filtered into the replacement RF-4C force and other recce units within SEA as the RF-101 force ran down at the end of the 1960s.

In the beginning, these men were well tried and proven professionals. Although many had been brought up in a peacetime environment, the unique requirement of the recce business had been drummed into them, that of getting the film to the customer with minimum delay. As time passed, however, they had to be replaced by officers and enlisted men from other, sometimes very different roles in the USAF, who took time to accept the essentials and acclimatise to the role in an operational theatre. Many of the newcomers were steeped in the conventional wisdom of USAF Manual 66-1, a doctrine which in many ways was ill-suited to an operational recce flight line. While abiding by this doctrine in principle, the 'old lags' had applied common sense to evolve the best practices for RF-101 operations, any deviation from which was initially an anathema to some of their successors. Typically, some replacements needed convincing of the need for camera men to remain on the flight line throughout flying operations, and therefore isolated from the camera maintenance shops. John Roddick remembers this time as *"an assignment from hell"*, at least until the arrival at the 460th TRW of a new, highly respected and experienced wing commander from the 363rd TRW at Shaw, where more sensible, flexible recce practices had evolved. One result of his initial visit was that the AMS acquired two new, specially-marked dispatch trucks to speed film the one mile from aircraft dispersals to the processing facilities, a simple but very profitable addition to the force. There was no substitute for experience (as the Voodoo pilots were also finding at this time).

Experience in operational conditions also paid off with expeditious improvements in mobile processing facilities, found essential when elements of the permanent Photographic Processing Cell (PPC), portable darkrooms and a variety of low capacity processing and printing equipments were rushed from Shaw to Homestead AB, Florida, for use during the Cuban Crisis of 1962. Palliatives would not satisfy the ever-increasing demands for rapid, mass production of photographs in SEA; it was now time for major surgery.

Positive reaction to this wake-up call in Cuba must have seemed painfully slow to the men on the ground in SEA, but the procurement agencies and industry back in the USA re-doubled their efforts in response to the strident and persistent cries from the front for state of the art equipment to make better use of the

VOODOO WARRIORS

wide variety of cameras which became available to the RF-101s and the RF-4Cs. Meanwhile, the Voodoo men from the 15th and 45th TRS and the 363rd TRW, who provided the photographic support for the initial operations in SEA in Project Pipe Stem and the Able Mable Task Force, had to do their best with well tried practices using tired and obsolescent equipment deployed from peacetime bases to Don Muang and Tan Son Nhut. The necessary facilities were increased in scale and enhanced progressively as the conflict grew, with relatively few problems at Tan Son Nhut, where power and water were in place, but this was not the case elsewhere.

Raison d'être. Not ideal, but the photo men made do at Udorn - and excelled. Norman Huggins

At Udorn in 1965 the photo men had to start from scratch to improvise and make do. The official history of the 15th TRS tells of the need to 'haul water to the site seven times a day', the early problems of film storage space stemming from the need to duplicate much of the material and the multiplicity of films for different camera configurations (the Project 1181 Voodoos were not equipped with plotting cameras optimised for interpretation). Also, with three different camera systems in use, there was often a shortage of trained manpower, test equipment and spare parts. Despite these difficulties the 15th TRS PI section handled an average of 14 sorties a day and the PPC produced up to 3,000 prints.

The PIs themselves were no better off. They worked primarily on the assigned targets and major tasks when these involved area covers rather than 'pin points', but they were also required to scrutinize any other film exposed en route in the hope of finding additional targets. The degree of urgency in photo interpretation would depend on that of the requirement and this would determine whether an Immediate Photo Interpretation Report (IPIR) would suffice within 12 hours, or whether it should be rendered within two hours in a Flash Report.

Wherever it was carried out, the workload for all was usually heavy and sometimes excessive, especially in the early days at Udorn with its ill-ventilated, poorly equipped facilities. After film processing, interpretation, printing, production of traces and overlays, the final products had to be packaged and dispatched to over 40 addressees daily, all to be completed for the courier aircraft by 0230 hours on the following morning. It followed that most of the photographic specialists and the PIs were working unacceptably long hours, some going for many weeks without a day's rest, but it was not until December 1965 that a better equipped, more spacious building became available and the manpower was increased.

In 1967, the Aerospace Systems Division, Air Force Systems Command, accepted from Goodyear Industries the first of the new WS-430B photo exploitation facilities for initial tests by the TARC at Shaw AFB. All eyes were now on this centre of expertise to see whether it had the flexibility of mind to keep all-important

Big Business. A full scale WS-430B comprised 22 units. Jim Ifland

mobility and bare-base potential to the forefront of their evaluation.

For a full scale, wholly bare base commitment, the complete WS-430B would comprise a complex of 22 modules for editing and inspection, processing, titling and cleaning, interpretation, printing, chemical mixing and distribution, including the provision of water and power, refrigerated storage and maintenance shelters. This was very big business; with each module measuring 8 ft by 12 ft and 8 ft high (eight of these units expandable to increase working space), and all the interconnecting hardware, the entire system would occupy a space of some 75 yds by 23 yds but for limited operations fewer units could be deployed. Designed for all likely climate conditions, key nodes were air conditioned and weather proofed; all the units were air transportable and with the increased airlift capability offered by tactical Hercules aircraft and strategic transports, the WS-430B, in part or whole, could be dispatched very rapidly world-wide. This capability was proven in trials based on the original TAC deployment criteria but fell short of the greater demands in nature and scope of SEA. Fortunately, veterans from that theatre were on hand at Shaw to identify early shortcomings and help introduce the necessary improvements, improvements which would continue to be made throughout the WS-430B's service life in SEA.

The 460th TRW, activated at Tan Son Nhut in February 1966, was firmly in charge of all recce operations in SEA (other than U-2 and SR-71) when the WS-430B (to become known as the Photo Processing Printing and Interpretation Facility (PPIF)) was deployed. The first unit went directly to the 16th TRS (RF-4C) flight line at Udorn in 1967, for use by Phantoms and Voodoos. Additional PPIFs were subsequently assigned to the Voodoo squadrons, the second for the RF-101s landing at the forward base of Phu Cat, and the third for 460th Recce Tech Squadron (RTS) at Tan Son Nhut. Problems were exposed and resolved as the whole system grew and evolved to meet ever increasing demands, magnified dramatically when the order went out to the recce pilots to expose all available film when over hostile territory, this saturating even the enlarged facilities. The knock-on effect was to slow down the processing of primary target photographs and produce bottlenecks at the

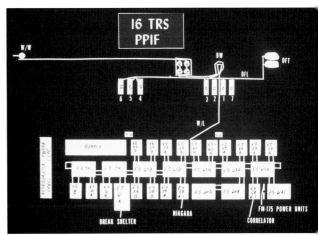

Up and Running. The first of the WS-430B was deployed to Udorn AB in 1967. Jim Ifland

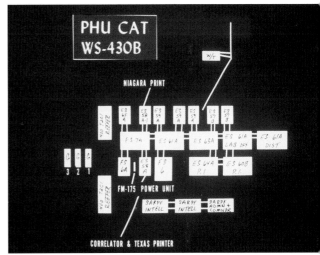

Up Front. 50% of a WS-430B unit was positioned at Phu Cat FOL. Jim Ifland

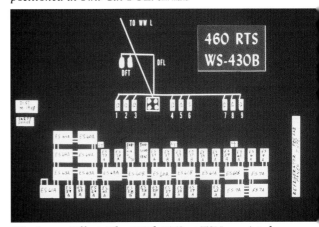

Maximum Effort. The 460th RTS at TSN consisted of 150% of a WS-430B, with two SAC vans as shown but space remained at a premium. Jim Ifland

Who Does What? Responsibilities for all SEA tac recon support defined here. Jim Ifland

Speed Run. An Eastman Kodak Niagara Printer at work in one of the 460th RTS SAC vans. Jim Ifland

later titling, cleaning and negative reproduction and printing stages. More men and equipment were moved in to lighten the load but this only added to the congestion in the finite space available and led to increased administrative problems. With typical ingenuity, the 460th RTS procured two enormous (40 ft long) SAC 'mobile' processing vans to accommodate a huge Eastman Kodak Niagara high speed continuous roll printer, a Texas printer and a Log Electronic automatic dodging printer. This solved the printing backlog and produced special prints, but at a price, yet more manpower, power resources and air conditioning. The PIs still had to work in very confined spaces until means were found to relocate them. The air conditioners also caused unacceptable vibration at the PIs' light tables when viewing targets with magnifying optics. Rapid generation of interpreted imagery from specific targets being deeply ingrained as the cardinal priority, this excessive use of film was an anathema to the recce community. The PIs would go direct to the primary targets and only

then search the remainder of the film expended with little expectation of spotting anything of value through gaps in the perennial cloud cover; they also knew that any targets found would move before any offensive action could be taken against them. The policy of continuous camera operation had serious flaws.

The 12th Reconnaissance Intelligence Technical Squadron (RITS), effectively the 7th Air Force RTS, produced in-depth analysis, briefing material and any special tasks. The overall division of responsibilities for photo processing, which had stabilised by 1967, is best summarised by the chart above. Regardless of the sensors used by whatever squadron or aircraft, in-country mission results were handled initially by the PPIF, those collected out-of-country by the 460th RTS.

Timely intelligence remained all-important. After an aircraft had landed, the clock began ticking as films were logged in and inspected for any damage which might affect processing. The film then went through the highly sophisticated Versamat processors and on to the PIs, who checked for satisfactory coverage of primary targets and any obvious targets of opportunity target for their Immediate Photo Intelligence Report (IPIR). The film was also inspected by maintenance personnel for correct operation of the aircraft camera system. If required, a Flash Report was sent at once, followed by an IPIR to the requester and interested parties; this was too detailed and usually too widely distributed to be passed by voice, but secure telephones

Everything Under Control. The PPIF Work Order Control Centre tracked every mission from receipt to final report and distribution. Jim Ifland

were used to communicate essential facts to selected customers. Later, Key Punch machines were introduced to speed up the passage of detailed information, and for security reasons, this task fell to the already overworked PIs. The PIs were also required to produce mission traces (overlays on maps to record the mission's photographic cover). Finally, the film would be titled, annotated as required and given a security grading before being cleaned and sent to the photo labs for reproduction. Duplicate negatives and duplicate positives were produced and distributed according to work order requirements, every detail of these

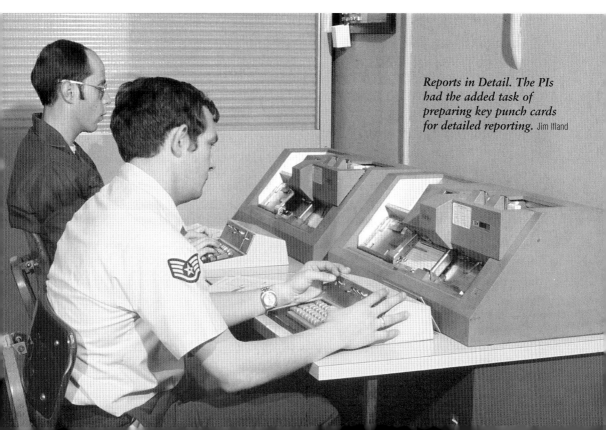

Reports in Detail. The PIs had the added task of preparing key punch cards for detailed reporting. Jim Ifland

Crime Prevention. Following the theft of a generator, security was tightened. Jim Ifland

procedures being recorded in a time log to identify any problems and areas for improvement.

The PPIFs were hard pressed, not least in the maintenance support elements, and the 16th PPIF was typical. The trials at Shaw were based on the single shift concept with optimum throughput and had not been carried out under the pressures of war; consequently, they failed to anticipate the problem areas encountered on the front line in SEA. Preventative maintenance suffered as a result of the continuous operations 24-hours a day with the availability of power and water for the expanded facilities often hovering on the marginal. Maintaining sufficient power for these comprehensive operations was a constant problem, exacerbated by the limited number of generators available and the monsoon rains. When one of the six generators vital to sustain round-the-clock operations at Tan Son Nhut was stolen, a replacement was rushed in and new security arrangements were put in place. The errant item was later recovered with a new coat of paint, fortuitously giving the 16th PPIF a much valued spare. It's an ill wind....! Then came the rains, during which the drainage system could not cope. The PPIFs were soon immersed in several inches of water, shorting out and destroying vulnerable circuits with loud explosions and inevitable power outages. Again, the lessons were soon learned and remedied by elevating the cables and connectors on perforated steel platforms.

Sufficient usable water for photo processing was always a matter of concern. With base facilities unable to guarantee a constant supply, tankers were always on stand-by and were usually required to top up the PPIF's 1,500 gallon storage tanks (elevated to provide sufficient pressure) several times a week. What went in had to come out but in war there may have been scant attention to the disposal of the chemically polluted water, adding to the drainage problem.

Keeping the PPIFs supplied with huge quantities of film, chemicals and spare parts for the equipment was another on-going challenge, with much lost, damaged or pilfered en route. Initial storage space for film and sensitized materials was soon found to be inadequate and had to be replaced by walk-in

Power Preservation. PPIF electrical cables had to be raised clear of flood levels. Jim Ifland

Cold Storage. Interconnecting, walk-in refrigerator units stretched for up to 100 ft.
Jim Ifland

refrigerated units, while 55 gall drums of chemicals, especially vulnerable in transit, were easily damaged, leakage contaminating other supplies.

Then came the Tet Offensive and the attacks which followed, with the painful realisation that the Americans could not rely on their South Vietnamese guards and had to depend, in the first instance, solely on a handful of USAF air police and their own skill at arms to defend themselves and their operational assets. What was believed to have been an 82-mm rocket destroyed a PPIF and all the equipment it contained at Tan Son Nhut, the honeycomb panelling used in the construction of the PPIFs to optimise insulation and minimise weight doing little to reduce shrapnel penetration, but fortunately this one was unoccupied at the time. As Jimmy Ifland said:

"This brought the war very close to the ground support personnel on the base and every spare moment was then devoted to protecting personnel and operational assets".

Sporadic attacks called for immediate evacuation to safer areas, often with the consequent loss of material being processed at the time.

Tet Troubles. The Tet offensive caused critical damage to a newly arrived WS-430B unit at Tan Son Nhut - but there were no casualties.
Jim Ifland

Special Protection. The PPIF's crucial electrical generators were given additional protection. Jim Ifland

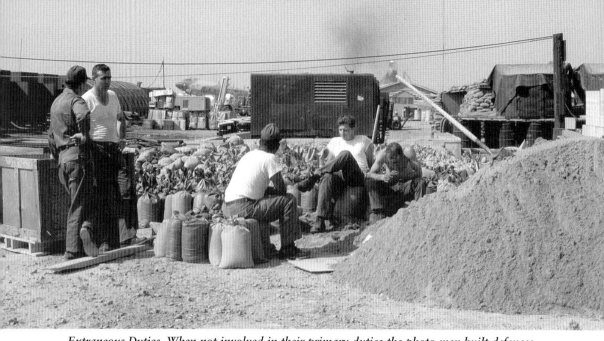

Extraneous Duties. When not involved in their primary duties the photo men built defences, with the odd coffee break. Jim Ifland

Notwithstanding all these difficulties, the whole photographic process was speeded up progressively with local innovation, experience and new technology. The introduction of the Niagara printer was very welcome but with the need for meticulous treatment to obtain precise intelligence from the imagery, together with the massive throughput and number of customers, the pressure was continuous; at peak times well over five million feet of film were being produced every month.

Fundamentally, the work of the men who in one way or another facilitated the final product of a recce pilot's mission, the photographs, was at that time similar the world over but with more than a few additional problems in SEA. In this conflict their work continued round the clock, with great demands on all involved exacerbated by the excessive film expenditure (which incidentally gave off-duty Vietnamese airmen a lucrative sideline in collecting and burning the discarded film to extract the silver therein). They were also operating in far less than ideal circumstances overall, often with rudimentary facilities in congested working space and with frequent shortages of every kind. Finally, in the latter days they had to contend with mortar attacks and Viet Cong infiltration into base areas, of necessity adding a defence role to their already heavy commitments.

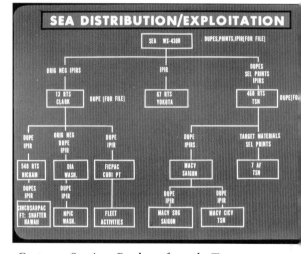

Customer Service. Products from the Tac Recce photo service were distributed widely.
Jim Ifland

It is right, therefore, to include all the camera maintenance, photographic processing teams and PIs who served in SEA in this tribute to the Voodoo warriors. Despite all the hardships they maintained the high level of support essential to effective recce operations and can be justly proud of their contribution to the war. Although so often out of sight and out of mind, they richly deserve a place of honour in Voodoo heritage.

CHAPTER TWENTY
VOODOO MEDICINE MEN

'If it ain't broke don't fix it'

Old RAF maxim

Much of what was said in the previous chapter about those involved with the RF-101's cameras, photo processing and interpretation applies to a host of other men who supported Voodoo operations in other ways in war and peace. Back-up facilities such as air traffic control, the emergency services, administration, equipment supply, catering et al, all made significant contributions and deserve a share of this tribute, but more than a brief mention of each is beyond the scope of this book on the Voodoo family. This chapter homes in on the maintenance men who were more directly responsible for keeping the aircraft flying; they were the 'Voodoo Medicine Men' and for this the author is especially indebted to one of their number, Senior Master Sergeant Edgar M Mays.

Badge Of Pride. The patch worn by Voodoo Medicine Men. Edgar Mays

Edgar came across the Voodoo first in the mid-1950s while assigned to the ARDC at Eglin AFB (Chapter One), little knowing then that he would come to work on them at Shaw AFB - and this is largely his story:

"When I reached Shaw one of the crew chiefs assured me that the Voodoo was far from difficult to maintain. Indeed, he told me that when he went on TDY with F-100 units their crew chiefs would use most of the contents of their tool boxes on their complex aircraft, whereas he would normally need only a standard six-inch screwdriver, a six-inch crescent (spanner) wrench

Medicine Man. Staff Sergeant Edgar Mays. Edgar Mays

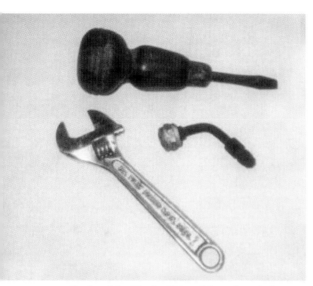

Tools of the Trade. Edgar Mays found that these personally acquired tools did most of the routine jobs he had to carry out on the Voodoo. Edgar Mays

Easy Access? Not all maintenance tasks on the Voodoo could be accessed with such ease.
Shaw AFB

and a high pressure air chuck to service the RF-101, rarely opening his toolbox."

The then Staff Sergeant Mays soon joined those whose enterprise and industry proved invaluable, working initially on the Voodoo in the Phase Inspection Dock, and in his year-and-a-half there acquired his own basic three tools (from the US Army when it left Japan). Edgar's son Terry remembers his father paying 'a whooping 10 cents' for a special wooden handled screwdriver which remained in the Mays household for years after its important contribution to Voodoo serviceability, tucked safely in Mrs Mays' hand-made holster.

When a Voodoo arrived at the Phase Dock, all the necessary access panels were removed and the fittings lubricated in strict accordance with check lists. Then came the detailed inspection using Phase Inspection Cards, followed by rectification of any defects found. Invariably the aircraft would then be raised on jacks for undercarriage retraction tests and/or brake checks. Time expired components would be replaced before the panels were refitted and the aircraft taken to Post-Dock for 'power on' systems checks; it would then be taxied to the engine trim pad for final tuning. A pre-flight inspection and functional check flight would follow to determine any remedial action to be taken, and thus how long it would be before the

Voodoo could be returned to the flight line.

However simple basic servicing of the Voodoo might have been in relative terms, access to certain components could be time-consuming, especially when there was a need to remove the massive 450 gall drop tanks in order to work on the engines and ancillaries. Removing the tanks and replacing them was simple enough, but getting hold of armourers to take out and replace the explosive cartridges (necessary for emergency jettison) and the fuel trucks to off-load fuel and refill them was another matter, and could lead to major delays.

As always there were tricks of the trade which could circumvent published procedures safely, often discovered or resorted to when prescribed support facilities were not available on TDY or during combat operations. This was the case when Edgar Mays found that a generator had failed on his aircraft during the Cuban crisis. Six hours would normally be allocated to its replacement, with an engine removed, but with time at a premium Edgar managed to squeeze one shoulder through the engine bay door, cut the safety wire, remove and replace the defective generator, all within the hour. Where there's a will there's a way.

Turning the Voodoo round between flights was also straightforward. The groundcrew would simply marshal the aircraft into the fuel pit and attach the single point refuelling hose while (perhaps against the published doctrine) a new brake parachute was installed. Then came the tyre inspection, a check on the contents of the hydraulic accumulators and a thorough look around the aircraft to see that all was as it should be. There were very few occasions when both crew chief and pilot (who had the ultimate responsibility) failed to notice a danger sign but it could happen, as in the case when both failed to notice that the RF-101's nose cone was not secure (Chapter Seventeen). With human fallibility being what it is a team effort was always essential.

The heavy tyre wear resulting from high take-off speeds, especially at maximum all-up weights, was a perennial problem. If necessary, visual assessments would override the mandatory points system used normally to determine when tyres should be replaced, take-offs with external tanks earning six points, 'clean' aircraft only four. Even if they appeared to be in good condition the tyres were required to be changed when they reached 36 points,

about a week's flying in a typical training programme at Shaw. Notwithstanding the rule, subjective judgement was sometimes exercised when this number was likely to be exceeded by a point or two, but this carried risks (see Chapter Thirteen).

The massive J-57 engines were highly reliable, but they needed to be 'trimmed' for optimum performance. This could be carried out by the crew chiefs, some of whom were also cleared to taxi the Voodoo to the engine trim pad and to the compass rose for the periodic compass swings. Edgar Mays was one who revelled in these opportunities to get his hands on the controls of the big aircraft.

As with many fast-jet aircraft at the time, the fire warning system in the Voodoo was notoriously unreliable and it was often very difficult to locate the problem. Other than as a result of combat, actual engine fires were comparatively rare, but false warnings were not, often due to some disturbance in the fire warning loop while other work was being carried out on the aircraft. Again Edgar found this out for himself while on TDY, when a persistent fault in the loop of his aircraft was resolved only after the right engine had been removed twice.

The crew chiefs were also responsible for the correct operation of the rain removal valves which blew hot air on to the windscreen, a great asset to Voodoo pilots during landing or air refuelling in rain. On deselection, these valves should return to their housings just ahead of the canopy, but if they failed to do so the continuous blast of hot air could damage the Plexiglass, and indeed this happened to one aircraft during its return from Cuba, the glass in the left side panel melting as a result. Edgar Mays knew how important it was to ensure that the valves remained clean and lubricated properly, learning the hard way.

"I was determined to ensure that my aircraft was as perfect as I could make it for a night AAR sortie and spent all afternoon checking the internal and external lights and raising the rain removal valves to clean them down to the metal using a Silicon spray recommended by a more experienced crew chief. Apparently my pilot's mission went very well but he did ask that I do something about the rain valves, which had failed to retract after he had used them, so much for the 'expert' advice I had been given!

Thereafter, I lubricated the valves with engine oil and the problem never recurred".

Another trick of the trade!

Not all rectification was straight-forward. When a recalcitrant spring in the J-57's oil pressure adjustment valve needed attention the oil had to be drained while hot and replaced with 24 quarts of synthetic oil in a laborious procedure, the engine then being run to adjust the pressure. This was one of many difficulties associated with the early century series fighters but lessons were learned and modifications eliminated the problem. There seemed no way of avoiding another lengthy procedure, that connected with the loading of nuclear bombs on to F-101s and RF-101s (in Europe only), which required high pressure air to be pumped into the upper part of the undercarriage hydraulic jack. When the rubber seals within these jacks deteriorated the aircraft had to be placed on independent jacks in the hangar for the undercarriage strut to be removed to enable replacement. Replacing a canopy seal on 'A' model Voodoos was also very tricky, given the difficulty of seating it in the grooves provided. However experienced or well versed in those little tricks (such as pre-soaking the seals in a bucket of ice-cold water for several hours in hot weather) crew chiefs were often exasperated by several spare inches of seal remaining when they reached the end to the run, by which time they were sporting red, swollen and aching thumbs for their pains. With typical inspiration they persuaded the dental clinic to part with time-expired teeth drills, which they then used to clean and re-groove the canopy seal channels and this proved the ultimate solution. Again the lesson was learned, with the 'C' models which followed having a greatly improved housing for these seals.

Lively banter between the pilots and their crew chiefs on the flight line added to the quality of life for both. Edgar Mays remembers a diminutive Voodoo pilot commenting:

"although I always stow a pack behind me, I'm shoved so far back in the seat when the burners light that I couldn't reach the throttles to abort even if I wanted to until I've pulled up into the climb!"

He is unlikely to have convinced his audience of this, or admitted the possibility to his squadron flight supervisors. This was real life on the flight line.

When it came to being allocated his aircraft Edgar Mays felt a certain foreboding when his fellow crew chiefs suggested that he was being given a 'rogue', and that he should ask for another, but was this a classic flight line 'scam'? He was told that 'his' RF-101, No. 56-60168, seemed to have developed some peculiarities since landing nose-wheel up and becoming a 'hangar queen', cannibalized to provide other aircraft with parts otherwise not immediately available. However, Edgar accepted the challenge:

"I helped put '168' together, took it to the flight line and gave it my best pre-flight check, only for the pilot to find that when the stick was displaced fully back it failed to return to the forward position, so off it went again to the hangar and the flight controls team. Concerted effort revealed that an incorrectly routed speed brake hose was restricting the stick movement and the problem was quickly resolved. This time the flight test was very satisfactory and the aircraft flew regularly for 21 sorties on the trot without a single defect, to gain an enviable reputation for its handling and reliability".

A job well done.

Edgar Mays had started as he would go on, later laying claim to two noteworthy periods of intensive flying with 168, both well beyond the two sorties on every other day which was the normal expectation at Shaw. The first trip would have started earlier in the morning had the UHF radio not been unserviceable during start-up for a test hop after an engine change, but Mays 'borrowed' a replacement set from a nearby aircraft and 168 was soon airborne. The flight test went well, followed by a rapid turn-round for the second sortie and then a third. It was during this flight that news came through that the squadron had been tasked with a special night AAR mission and that 168 was included in the programme. Then came one of those incidents which can so easily arise when signals between pilot and ground crew are incorrect or misconstrued. Suffice it to say that when Edgar was cleared by a newly arrived pilot to check that the pitot head was warming up soon after it was switched on, he found it had in fact been on for some time and burned his hand so badly that *"I couldn't open it again to straighten the fingers".*

Although he had been on duty for 13 hours, Edgar was now told to get ready to depart almost immediately, with a small party of others, on a 'Top Secret' TDY, the destination to be announced only when they were airborne in the supporting transport aircraft. Someone else would look after 168 on its return. Having hurried home to collect the bare essentials for life, with no explanation to offer his wife, he was soon airborne on a C-130 Hercules with the chosen few now told that they were bound for Myrtle Beach AFB, on the Atlantic coast some 100 miles east of Shaw. On landing, the groundcrew prepared to receive their RF-101s from Shaw, after which Edgar and several others went fast asleep in a drainage ditch close to the ramp; they were tired after 18 hours on duty. Sure enough 168 was among the Voodoos to arrive having completed its fifth trip in 24 hours. Their task at Myrtle Beach was to photograph all the fields farmed in the two Carolinas (including the watermelon patches, cornfields and vegetable gardens) pending a major exercise by the 101st and 82nd Airborne Divisions, to assist in proving or otherwise any subsequent compensation claims. An early photo revealed watermelons disappearing into an army helicopter on a pre-exercise recce.

Unlike the first, the second marathon session for 168 was pre-planned. With justifiable confidence, Edgar volunteered 168 for an infra-red (IR) camera trial which another aircraft had failed to complete. He was not to know then that this would call for five, two-hour photo sorties in one 24 hour period, beginning at 0500 hrs, but he and his Voodoo were up to it. It was still pitch black when he made his way to the flight line with his sandwiches packed for the long day ahead, to prepare 168 for a pre-dawn IR photo mission. The subsequent sorties also went ahead on schedule and by the third, when word of this maximum effort had got around, all the crew chiefs were out on the flight line to urge them on. They were not disappointed; 168 achieved all five sorties without any defects, in what was believed to

Anywhere, Any Time. Men of the 363rd TRW, Shaw AFB, ready for another deployment in 1960.
1. *Capt A F Ziemba, A2c A D McGibney, A3c L Jeffries*
2. *Capt T McNierney, T/Sgt J E Hall, A1c J W Lowery*
3. *Capt J M Pierson, A1c D E Medlen, A3c R K Harvey*
4. *Capt D L Larid, A3c C L Redditt, A3c CL Deneke.* Shaw AFB

Making Do. Airmen from Shaw purifying water in their 'bare base' exercise at North Field AB, SC. Shaw AFB

have been a record for a specific Voodoo operation at Shaw. Edgar and the young pilot who flew the latter part of the trial then took great delight in showing off 168's tyres, which were barely scuffed despite the intensity of this operation.

Crew chiefs were justifiably proud of such achievements, most probably going unobserved but some were recognized, as was the case when Edgar, who had only returned from a four month course in Denver the day before, was called on to take his beloved 168 to Langley AFB for a static display as part of a tribute to Medal of Honor winners. As an added concession, he was allowed to take his family with him to share his pride in the fruits of his labours. The men of TAC had to be ready to go anywhere, at any time and for any reason, and to 'rough it' if needs be.

Edgar Mays and 168 were soon on display again. They had been recalled to Shaw from the crew chief's fourth TDY that year, this one at James Connelly AFB where specialists from the camera firm could attend to a problem with the IR equipment. At Shaw he was ordered, with two others, to drive to McDill AFB with a load of two-way radios and other equipment, and from there to Homestead AFB to rejoin 168, where President John F Kennedy was to congratulate those involved directly in helping to bring the Cuban crisis to a successful conclusion (Chapter Ten).

At Homestead, pilots and crew chiefs were very conscious of their lack of personal preparation for this memorable event. Edgar again:

"My pilot and I were laughing about who smelled the worst as we stood sweating in the hot Florida sun, dressed in clothes which should have been changed two days before, with hair that needed cutting the previous week and wearing shoes which had not been polished for far too long".

This embarrassing situation being equally obvious to their immediate superiors, barbers and shoe-shine men were summoned to the flight line the following morning to put these matters right. Being civilians, they refused at first to turn out because it was a Sunday but, when the base commander left them in no doubt as to their future, or lack of it at Homestead, they acquiesced. Perhaps news of all this reached General Sweeney, the commander of TAC, who ordered that funds be made available to all those likely to be chosen for displays in the future, so that they might purchase new fatigues, jump boots, blue scarves and fatigue caps. This rig became known as 'Sweeney's Greenies', and was *de rigueur* at least once a month.

Many crew chiefs developed a special bond with their aircraft and often the pilots, ever-conscious of safety and with reputations hard-earned but easily lost. Edgar knew that it was an anathema to both pilots and their supervisors to conclude an investigation into a defect encountered by a pilot in the air with a 'CND' (Could Not Duplicate) in an aircraft's documents after an examination on the ground. Edgar recalls one pilot, who flew through a large flock of birds on take off, reporting *"an unusual thumping"* in his aircraft while airborne, for which no cause could be found on the ground. Not satisfied with this, Edgar went beyond the call of duty, working late into the night to bleed the hydraulics and entered 'air in the system' on the form as a believable cause of the 'thumping'. On the following morning the same pilot flew the aircraft and found it to be *"the best 101 I have ever flown"*. The pilot was happy man - and so was Edgar.

It cut both ways. Perhaps not knowing the local rules, enlisted men on TDY sometimes encountered difficulties with their host units and it was right that their officers should come

Battle Damage. With the robust Pratt and Whitney J-57, the pilot did not notice any effects from this AAA round through the Voodoo's jet pipe. George Cowgill

to the rescue. On one such base, the manager of an NCO club (the only facility open to the visitors after a movie they had attended), refused to allow the Voodoo crew chiefs to remain in the club, where they sought a simple hamburger, because they were dressed in fatigues - the only rig available to them. The local base commander failed to get the manager to relax the rule in this special case, but the NCOs would not be denied and threats by their own commanders to refer the matter to General Sweeney personally had the required effect.

After three-and-a-half years of work on the RF-101, Edgar Mays readily confirmed that the Voodoo was far from being a difficult aircraft on which to work and claimed that most crew chiefs became intensely proud of their charges:

"If you wanted a fist fight, just call their Voodoo a 'pig' or a 'hog', and you got one! Some guy put an ear of corn under the nose of one of the RF-101s and it took a long time to calm down that aircraft's crew chief".

Thereafter jokes of this nature ceased.

Looking back in retirement now, Edgar Mays believes that the Voodoo had a better serviceability record the more it flew, and that

much of this was due to its basic construction. He came to feel the same about the Voodoo's successor, the McDonnell Phantom, on which he served in the more difficult combat environment of SEA, 'his' RF-4C flying 98.5 hours in one month. He left Tan Son Nhut as a 'Crew Chief of the Month', with a Commendation Medal.

The Voodoo Medicine Men were able to show their true mettle when they went to war with the RF-101 in SEA. They deserve very great credit for keeping so many of their now obsolescent aircraft serviceable in most demanding circumstances, with very high temperatures, wind and sandstorms, rain and floods all hampering their work. In SEA they faced a new challenge, battle damage repair, which involved skills unfamiliar to many new arrivals and had to be undertaken without interruption to the daily programme. Fortunately, the Voodoo's rugged J-57 engine could sustain a great deal of punishment from bird strikes, FOD from the imperfect operating surfaces in SEA and combat. Jerry Miller had an engine 'swallow' a 50-cal round without a murmur and Harry Runge claimed that *"the second engine brought back at least three of us*

Supply and Demand. Behind the scenes, demands on equipment staff at the end of the supply chain were endless. Ray Tiffault

in my time", but engine changes were inevitable and could be very time-consuming. Over a six month period 17 Green Python aircraft of the 15th TRS required battle damage repair; 14 were dealt with at Udorn, two could be patched up sufficiently to fly them back to their home bases for deeper rectification and one was deemed to be beyond repair. This outstanding record brought great credit on the Pythons' 'medicine men'. Whatever their duties the groundcrews improvised, introduced new servicing schedules and made do, braving the midday heat which could burn their skins, and 'cannibalizing' aircraft when spares became scarce. They often worked 12-14 hours a day.

The official history of the 15th TRS, in the vanguard of Voodoo operations at Udorn in 1965 (Chapter Eleven), underlines all these problems, added to which skill levels were often low among replacement personnel in all specialisations, in a situation hardly conducive to on-the-job training. At the start there was no machine shop for heavy metal work, no maintenance shelter or de-fuelling facility, but

above all it was supply difficulties which pervaded all else, and it was the 'suppliers'(frequently undermanned) who bore the brunt of the frustrations on the flight line. It all started badly, the first pack-up from Kadena having been designed to support operations for a short period only and understandably proving inadequate for the extended commitment. There were too few serviceable ground power units, general equipment and aircraft spares were rarely adequate and delay in resupply was a continuous problem. In these early days at Udorn the maintenance men were often left waiting for replacement items due to break-downs in communication between maintenance and supply, but on the 15th TRS this local problem was largely overcome by transferring authority for supply to the unit's maintenance officer and conducting business through a joint panel of specialists from both sections. Udorn was at the end of a very long supply chain which depended on the availability of air transport which was never enough to meet all needs and was all too often purloined for

They Also Served. Sergeant Vechia, 15th TRS, Operations Clerk, Udorn.
Don Karges

perhaps taken a little for granted by the busy aircrew? His section was among those which went about its duties quietly in the background, neither seeking nor often receiving recognition.

The high morale in SEA could also be attributed in part to the integration of these men into the operational squadrons. Most of the enlisted men drafted to SEA from Shaw had been accustomed to centralized servicing, the standard practice throughout the USAF wherein technicians (other than men who worked on the flight line) were pooled at Wing level and bid for as required by the individual flying units. However efficient the system seemed to be on paper (and this in itself has always been a bone of contention), and however worthy its protagonists, the men involved at the front could not have been expected to have the same allegiance as those who belonged directly to a squadron. In SEA, everyone serving on the independent, cohesive and self-supporting operational squadrons came under the command of, and were responsible to, one master and again there was great pride in 'belonging'. The groundcrew were also dedicated to their aircraft and might get to know the men who flew them intimately, professionally, socially and domestically, sharing good and bad times alike. Typically, such a squadron would comprise 23 officers, 280 enlisted men and 12-16 aircraft, an acceptable span of control for a lieutenant colonel 'boss'. Included in this number, but again so often overlooked, were the squadron operations and administrative staff, the latter hard pressed with, among other things, all the organisation and arrangements associated with the many who were serving TDY with the squadron (60% of the officers and 20% of the enlisted men in 1966) in a constant rotation between SEA, the PACAF bases and the US. These 'back room boys' also rose to the occasion, their full integration helping to give these squadrons that inner strength necessary to withstand this turbulence and the detrimental effects of the rapid turn-over of personnel.

'higher priorities'. To make matters worse, critical items were often delivered damaged or to the wrong destination. Somehow the men at the 'sharp end' coped, but rarely could the hard-pressed suppliers expect praise for their unstinting efforts.

All the more surprising then that this history tells of the 'excellent morale' of the enlisted men, the best evidence of which was the number of voluntary requests for extensions, although living conditions were generally considered inadequate and working hours were much longer than would normally be expected. Perhaps this was because, after years of training and peacetime routine, they now had a real purpose, with personal initiatives encouraged to overcome shortages and the myriad other problems resulting in personal pride and satisfaction from achievement. As a small example of this, take Sergeant Goldworthy of the 15th TRS; he designed a replacement for the leg holster to carry a gun and additional equipment in the survival vest, appreciated but

Proud Team. The Green Pythons of the 15th TRS at RTAFB Udorn. Harry Runge

The end product of all these labours, serviceable aircraft, stood ready and waiting for their well-equipped and prepared pilots every dawn at Udorn, six pads each able to accommodate two aircraft and cared for by teams of five men supervised by a line chief and a maintenance officer. The 12 aircraft assigned (but not always available) were required to fly up to 14 sorties a day, and it was to the great credit of the men on the line that the Pythons'

records claim that only one mission was aborted 'due to maintenance difficulties'.

There is no end to the stories of energy, enterprise and determination among the men who looked after the One-O-Wonder on the ground in peace or war. This is their success story too because their efforts as team players were indispensable - and they must never be forgotten.

CHAPTER TWENTY-ONE
LOOKING BACK WITH PRIDE

'But what can you do after the warrior dead

and for the one who cradled his head?

What can you do for the long silence sighing?

What can you do for love's slow dying?'

Ernie Meis - Recce Pilot

WE WILL REMEMBER THEM

Are we not lucky, we of the Voodoo community who served in the air and on the ground, to have survived the many rigours of life to this day? Many have not, and we all know friends and colleagues who succumbed to accident, combat or natural causes, not only the men (for in the workplace most were men in those Voodoo days) but also the wives, children and girlfriends who were held dear.

One of the great strengths of our fraternity has been the enduring spirit of togetherness, shown whenever one of our number has met with tragedy or difficulty, such means as e-mail, internet, the splendid Recce Reader and annual reunions keeping us all in touch with each other. When it was once thought expedient to include the Voodoo muster within the annual Recce Reunion, stalwarts would have none of it, and since then our independent reunions seem to have gone from strength to strength. As I write, Hurricane Katrina is leaving a trail of devastation throughout the South, bringing tragedy, great hardship and expense to an unprecedented number of residents, including some of our own. The Voodoo network is swinging into action with information, sympathy and support again bringing out the best in our One-O-Wonders. This has been our strength, and long may it remain so.

All that said, it is an unpalatable fact that our numbers must now dwindle more rapidly by

the year, hence the need for this story of our times, not only to bring back memories for us but to inform our descendants so that they may look back with pride at the efforts of their forebears.

This final chapter is devoted to we who have survived and those who have not, and to what has been done, and is being done, to keep the memories of the Voodoo and its people alive. Three subjects interlink in this theme; the aircraft, the bases from which the Voodoos operated and the people, but particularly the people. It would, of course, be wholly unrealistic to try to list all those who have gone before us and those who remain, and wrong to focus on a few, but let us feature just one who may be said to have typified our type, perhaps the epitome of a recce pilot who did his duty and who, at the time of writing, has just left us, the late Colonel John Stavast.

Born in 1926, John Stavast served in three wars, in WW2, Korea and SEA. He enlisted in the Army Air Corps in 1944 to become an air gunner but was among the many rendered redundant at the end of the war and discharged in 1946. Invited back into the cadet programme in 1949, John earned his wings and became a flying instructor; he began his recce career with the 18th TRS at Shaw in 1956, and thereafter followed the familiar sequence of flying on the RF-84, RF-101 and RF-4C. He was shot down

Back in Harness. Colonel John Stavast, recce pilot, back from Hanoi, doing what he did best. Recce Reader

by a missile on his 91st combat mission in an RF-4C over North Vietnam in 1967 and spent the next six years as a POW, suffering great torture in nine prisons in and around Hanoi while acting as senior officer in five of them. After release and a slow recovery from his many ailments, he continued to serve until 1980, retiring as a colonel with 6,000 flying hours, three Silver Stars, two Legions of Merit, two Purple Hearts and three Distinguished Flying Crosses among his medals. He had done us proud, and there have been many like him.

Many of the Voodoo bases have closed but there are books and documents which tell of the fate of some of the aircraft (See Bibliography), gate guards and museum pieces providing visible evidence of our times. Again, it is neither within the compass nor the competence of this book to list the final resting place of all these venerable aircraft; the destiny of one can serve for all. RF-101C No 56-202 was delivered to the USAF on 16 August 1958, and assigned to the 363rd TRW at Shaw. Two years later it was transferred to the 66th TRW and remained there until rotating back to Shaw, thereafter to the Arkansas ANG in 1970 and then to the Mississippi ANG in 1975. At the end of its flying days, '202' was taken to the Military Aircraft Storage and Disposition Center (MASDC), Davis-Monthan AFB, Arizona. Believed to have been released from there briefly to a private owner in 1991, it was then returned to the MASDC. Bob Archibald informed the Voodoo community of its demise in the spring of 2004 after heritage enthusiasts had spotted it being prepared for final disposal, its wings and nose cut off and the carcass due to be taken to Gila Bend Range as a ground attack target. Thankfully, the authorities were persuaded to part with the nose cone, which has become part of Bob Archibald's private collection.

It is now time for the words to end and to let the pictures which follow remind us of the past and present, of those with whom we shared good and sometimes bad times, of bases now closed and our titular home which has survived, and of the aircraft which served us so well. They all played a part in the history of the 'Voodoo Warriors'.

The End of an Era. RF-101C 56-202 being cut up for scrap at the Military Aircraft Storage and Disposition Center, Davis-Monthan AFB, Arizona. Bob Archibald

Gone are the Peacemakers. Peace now reigns over this once bustling home of the 17th & 18th TRS RF-101s at RAF Upper Heyford. Author

'Balls 99'. RF-101C 56-099 in retirment at the titular home of tactical reconnaissance, Shaw AFB, SC, in 2004, the author masquerading as a local. Margreet Walpole

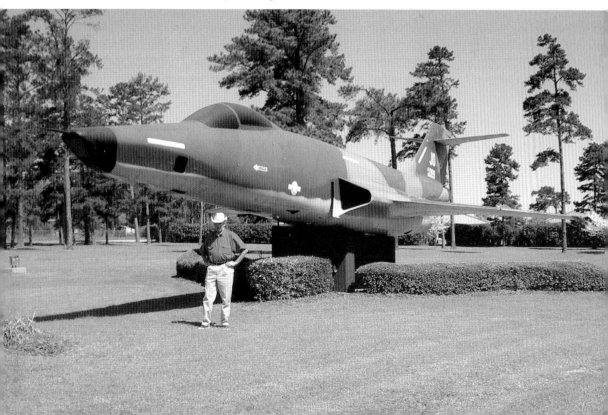

Looking Back but Still Going Strong. Chuck O'Connell (the younger), Lou Picciano (who needs aeroplanes?) and Bob Sweet with Voodoo at Pima Air Park. Chuck O'Connell, Lou Picciano & George Cowgill

Young at Heart. Carl Overstreet, looking very much as the author knew him at Shaw in 1960 but now a 'biker'! Recce Reader

Model Perfection. George Cowgill & DIY Friend. George Cowgill

Age Shall Not Weary Them. Dick Reese, Kay Berry and Conrad Binyon. Dick Reese, Kay Berry and Conrad Binyon

Back to the Roots. Veterans of the 4414th CCTS at the Sumter RF-101 Reunion, 1993. Chuck Lustig

Incognito. Believed to be Jerry and Carolyn Rogers remembering the good old days. Anon

The Heyford Mob 40 Years On. (Rear, L to R) Bob Gould, Roger Brockhoff, Carlos Higgins, Jimmy Wylie, Phil Harvell, Ray Tiffault, George Howard. (Front, L to R). Monnette Simmons, Marj Gould, Fran Brockhoff, Katherine Higgins, Mandy Wylie, Gretchen Harvell, Elios Sullivan. Bob Gould

RF-101 REUNION 2004: NASHVILLE, TENNESSEE

Photos courtesy Don Karges, Mike Tschida, Chuck Lustig, Al Magazzine & Jerry Rogers.

The Organisers   (L to R) Don & Mary Karges, Scotty Schoolfield, Cindy Thomas, Chuck &
Murph Lustig, Mike & Diane Tschida.

Won't Anyone Talk To Us? - Bob Archibald
& Marv Reed.

'Do You Remember When....?' Howard Davis,
Harry Runge & others.

I Never Could Get the Hang of It.
Nigel & Margreet Walpole.

Emergency Services Standing By. Doug Yates, Tom Saunders,
Mary & Don Karges, Mike Tschida, Chuck & Murph Lustig,
Dick Reece, Diane Tschida, Joan & Jerry Miller.

Dots on Parade. Fifty Years On.

'So I said to Him.....' Carlos Higgins & Keith Kuester.

You Really Want A Picture of Me? 'Norm' Huggins with Mary June & Carol Campis.

'It Was Like This......' Jerry Miller tells Joan how it was.

Follow Me. Doug Yates and Tay Tiffault lead the way to the General Jackson.

This Stuff Could Make You Go Blind!
Mandy Wylie gives Jimmy a helping hand.

Rest and Recuperation. One-O-Wonders rest up
after a busy visit to Jack Daniels.

They Were All Here Yesterday. Jo Kuhlmann
checks the bar stocks.

See No Evil, Hear No Evil, Speak No Evil.
Marv Reed, Chuck Lustig & Al Magazzine.

A Good Time Had By All. Joe Kuhlmann, Al Magazzine, Don Karges & Dick Reece.

CANADIAN COLLECTION

A number of CF-101Bs were retained at Canadian military establishments as gate guards or other memorials to a revered all-weather fighter.

George Cowgill Collection

414 SQUADRON - NORTH BAY

425 SQUADRON - BAGOTVILLE

409 SQUADRON - COMOX

416 SQUADRON - CHATHAM

416 SQUADRON - CALGARY

RF-101, Maxwell AFB. Author

Just Tribute. RF-101 and friends at the George Hall Air Park. George Cowgill

Record Holder. F-101A 532426 set up a world speed record of 1207.6 mph in Operation Fire Wall, 12 December 1957. George Cowgill

Chinese Voodoo? Hybrid of two RF-101Cs (56-210 & 56-229) to represent the several RF-101s flown by the Chinese Air Force at Robins AFB. George Cowgill

RF-101B at Reno AFB Nevada. George Cowgill

RF-101G No.541487. Gordon Macadie

INSIGNIA OF PROUD PILOTS

USAF Command Pilot Wings.

RCAF Pilot Wings

Chinese (Nationalist) Air Force Pilot Wings

RAF Pilot Wings

BIBLIOGRAPHY

The factual framework for this book is based largely on information from official documents made available by the USAF Historical Research Agency at Maxwell AFB, Alabama, USAF and RCAF/CAF Wing and Squadron records. In addition, primary evidence has been taken from personal testimonies and secondary evidence from the following publications.

Dorr, Robert F & Chris Bishop: *Vietnam Air Warfare*; Greenwich Editions 2002

Dorr, Robert F: *McDonnell F-101 Voodoo*; Osprey Publishing

Drendel, Lou & Paul Stevens: *McDonnell Douglas F-101*(Modern Military Aircraft) January 1986; Squadron/Signal Publications.

Fowler, Will: *The Vietnam Story*; Winchmore Publishing Services

Greenhalgh, William H: *The RF-101 Voodoo, 1961-1970*; Office of Air Force History, 1979

McIntyre, Robert: *CF-101 Voodoo - Canadian Profile*; SMS Publishing

Nalty, Bernard C: *Air War Over South Vietnam*; Air Force History and Museums Program

Pace, Steve: *McDonnell XF-88 Voodoo*; Air Force Legends

Schlight, John: *A War Too Long*; Air Force History and Museums Program

Thompson, Wayne: *To Hanoi and Back*; Air Force History and Museums Program 1996

Additional Sources

Aces & Aerial Victories: The USAF in South East Asia 1965-1973; Office of Air Force History

Airforce: The Magazine of Canada's Air Force Heritage

Air Power History: Voodoo Reconnaissance in the Vietnam War; John 'Bull' Stirling

Airpower: A Sentry Magazine: McDonnell's F-101 Voodoo (Vol 10 No 3, May 1980)

Flight Manual: RF-101 Voodoo

Famous Aeroplanes of the World No 59 - McDonnell Douglas F-101 Voodoo: March 1975

FlyPast: 66th Tactical Reconnaissance Wing; Doug Gordon

Recce Readers: The Official Publication of the TAC Recce Reunion Association

Warpaint No.47: McDonnell F-101 Voodoo; Kev Darling

INDEX

McDONNELL VOODOO

COLOUR PROFILES

created by Dave Windle

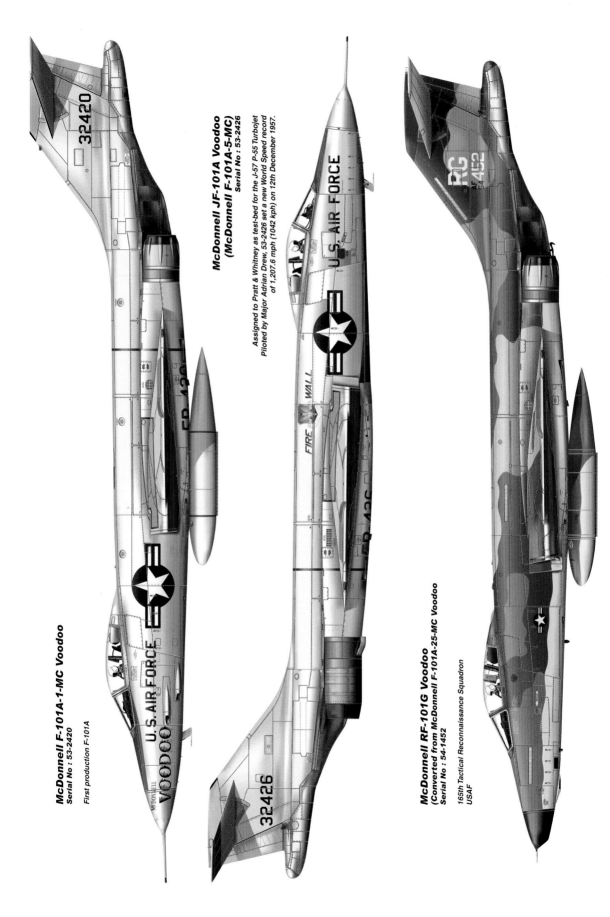

McDonnell F-101A-1-MC Voodoo
Serial No : 53-2420

First production F-101A

McDonnell JF-101A Voodoo
(McDonnell F-101A-5-MC)
Serial No : 53-2426

Assigned to Pratt & Whitney as test-bed for the J-57 P-55 Turbojet
Piloted by Major Adrian Drew, 53-2426 set a new World Speed record
of 1,207.6 mph (1042 kph) on 12th December 1957.

McDonnell RF-101G Voodoo
(Converted from McDonnell F-101A-25-MC Voodoo
Serial No : 54-1452

165th Tactical Reconnaissance Squadron
USAF

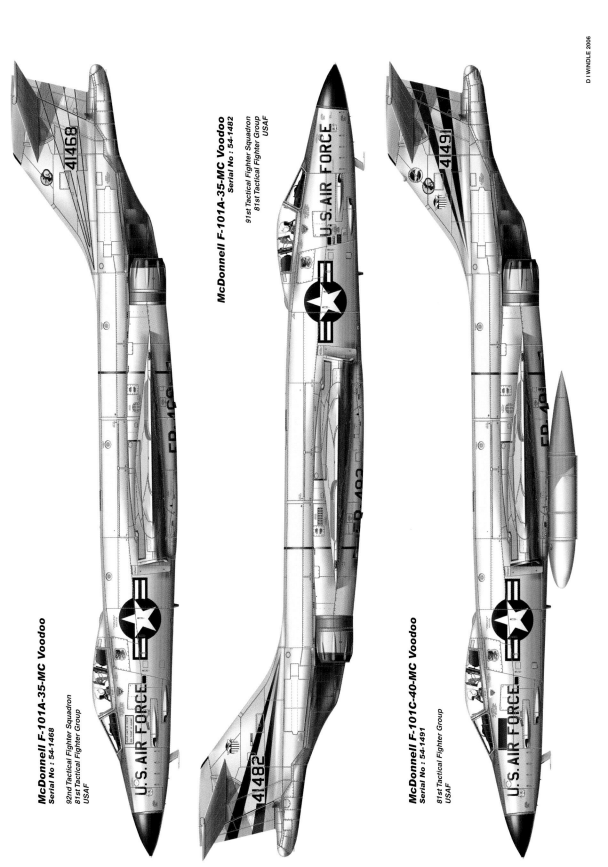

McDonnell F-101A-35-MC Voodoo
Serial No : 54-1468

92nd Tactical Fighter Squadron
81st Tactical Fighter Group
USAF

McDonnell F-101A-35-MC Voodoo
Serial No : 54-1482

91st Tactical Fighter Squadron
81st Tactical Fighter Group
USAF

McDonnell F-101C-40-MC Voodoo
Serial No : 54-1491

81st Tactical Fighter Group
USAF

D I WINDLE 2006

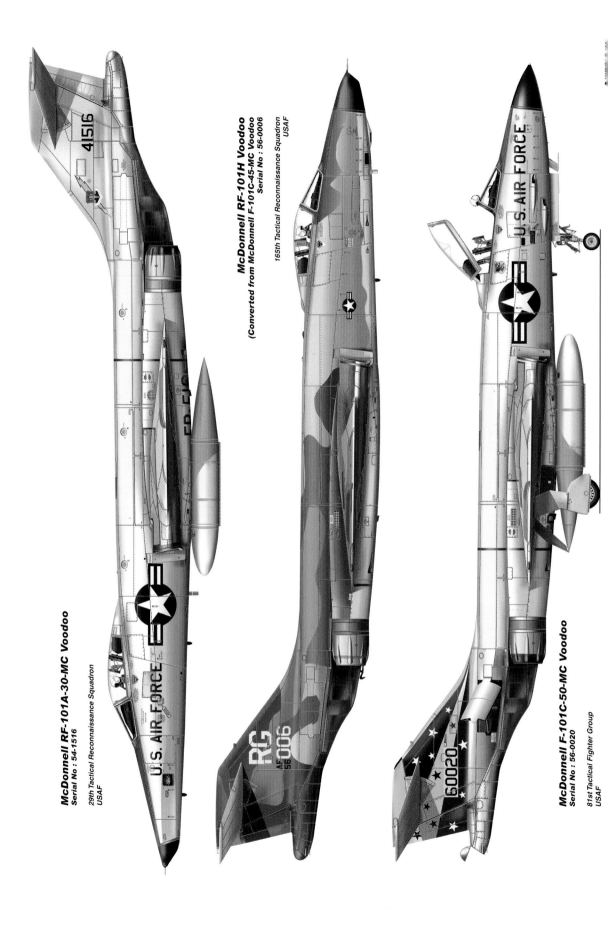

McDonnell RF-101A-30-MC Voodoo
Serial No : 54-1516

29th Tactical Reconnaissance Squadron
USAF

McDonnell RF-101H Voodoo
(Converted from McDonnell F-101C-45-MC Voodoo
Serial No : 56-0006

165th Tactical Reconnaissance Squadron
USAF

McDonnell F-101C-50-MC Voodoo
Serial No : 56-0020

81st Tactical Fighter Group
USAF

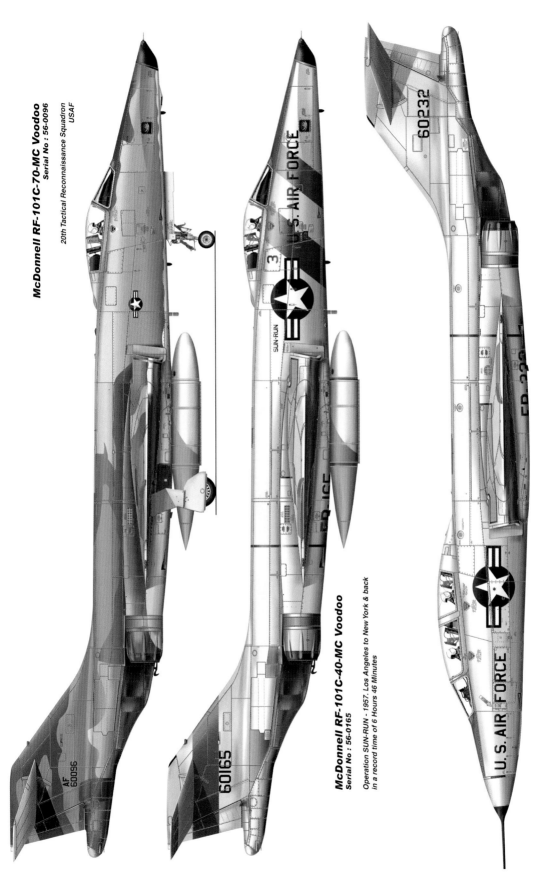

McDonnell RF-101C-70-MC Voodoo
Serial No : 56-0096

20th Tactical Reconnaissance Squadron
USAF

McDonnell RF-101C-40-MC Voodoo
Serial No : 56-0165

Operation SUN-RUN - 1957. Los Angeles to New York & back
in a record time of 6 Hours 46 Minutes

McDonnell NF-101B Voodoo Prototype
(McDonnell F-101B-30-MC)
Serial No : 56-0232

D I WINDLE 2006

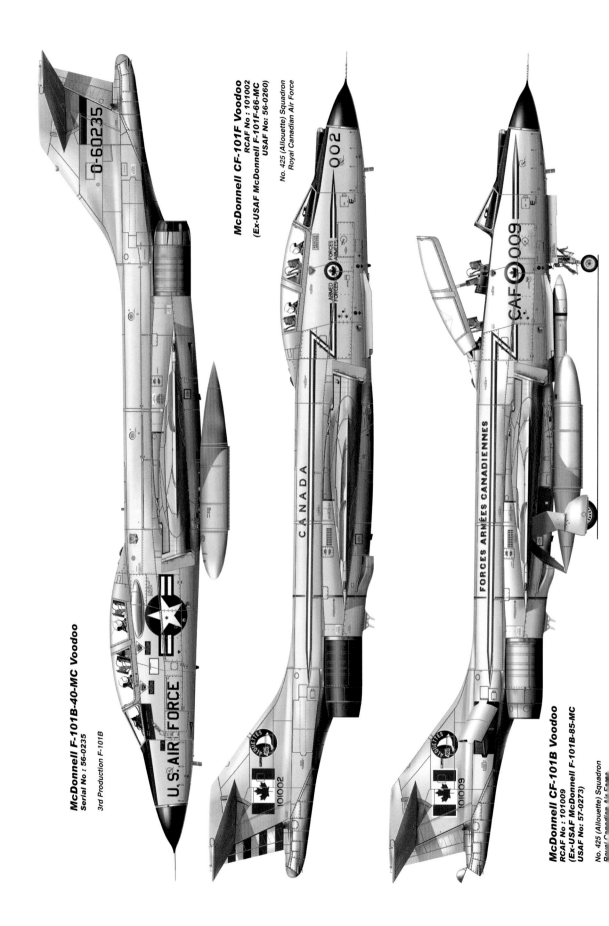

McDonnell F-101B-40-MC Voodoo
Serial No : 56-0235

3rd Production F-101B

McDonnell CF-101F Voodoo
RCAF No : 101002
(Ex-USAF McDonnell F-101F-66-MC
USAF No: 56-0260)

No. 425 (Allouette) Squadron
Royal Canadian Air Force

McDonnell CF-101B Voodoo
RCAF No : 101009
(Ex-USAF McDonnell F-101B-85-MC
USAF No: 57-0273)

No. 425 (Allouette) Squadron
Royal Canadian Air Force

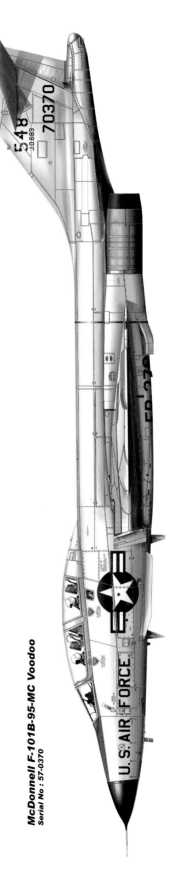

McDonnell CF-101B Voodoo
RCAF No : 101030
(Ex-USAF McDonnell F-101B-90-MC
USAF No: 57-0354)

No. 409 (Nighthawk) Squadron
Royal Canadian Air Force

McDonnell F-101B-95-MC Voodoo
Serial No : 57-0370

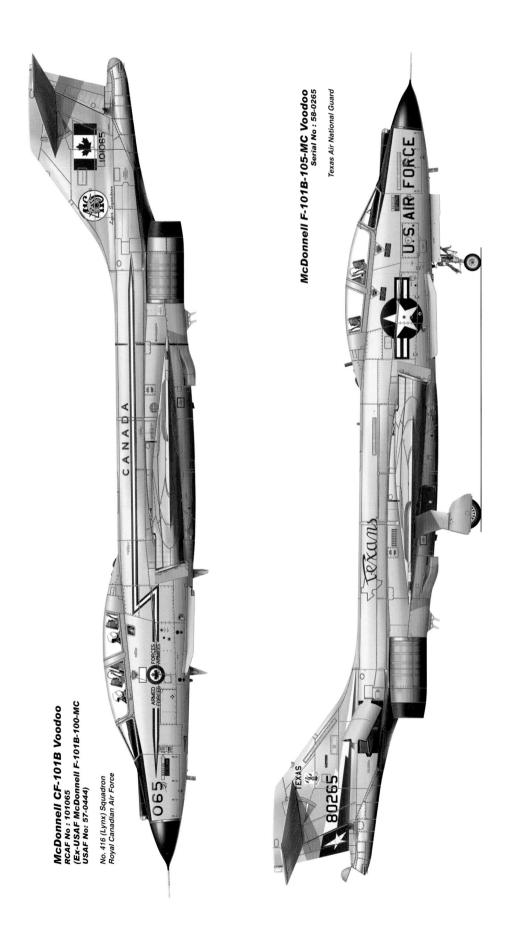

McDonnell CF-101B Voodoo
RCAF No : 101065
(Ex-USAF McDonnell F-101B-100-MC
USAF No: 57-0444)

No. 416 (Lynx) Squadron
Royal Canadian Air Force

McDonnell F-101B-105-MC Voodoo
Serial No : 58-0265

Texas Air National Guard

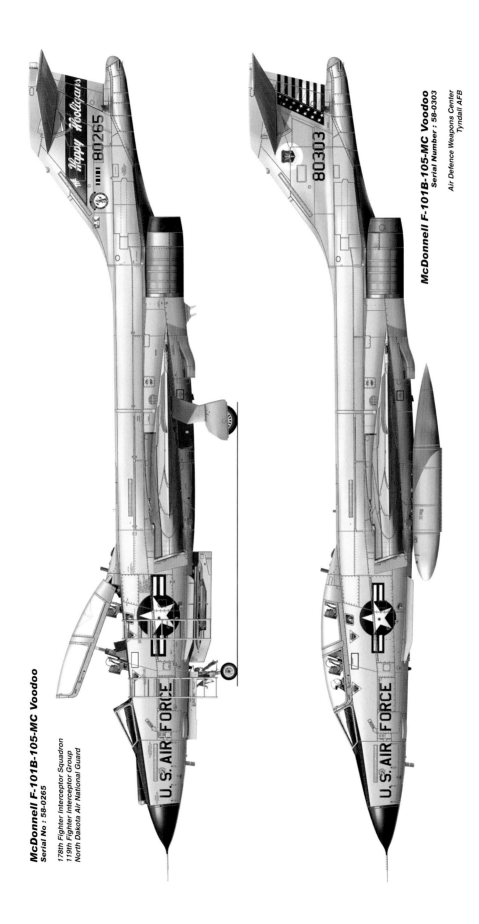

McDonnell F-101B-105-MC Voodoo
Serial No : 58-0265

178th Fighter Interceptor Squadron
119th Fighter Interceptor Group
North Dakota Air National Guard

McDonnell F-101B-105-MC Voodoo
Serial Number : 58-0303

Air Defence Weapons Center
Tyndall AFB

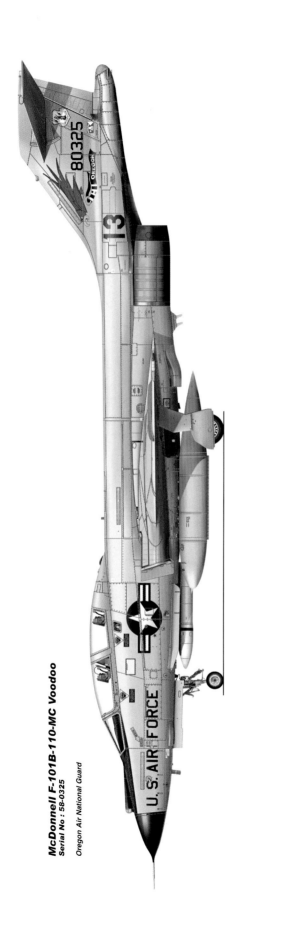

McDonnell F-101B-110-MC Voodoo
Serial No : 58-0325

Oregon Air National Guard

McDonnell RF-101B Voodoo
(USAF McDonnell F-101B-115-MC
Serial No : 59-397.
Transfered to RCAF as CF-101B
Serial No : 17397.
Back to USAF and converted
to RF-101B.

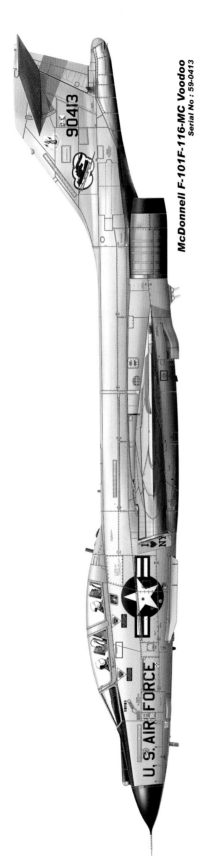

McDonnell F-101F-116-MC Voodoo
Serial No : 59-0413

136th Fighter Interceptor Squadron, 107th Fighter Interceptor Group, New York Air National Guard.

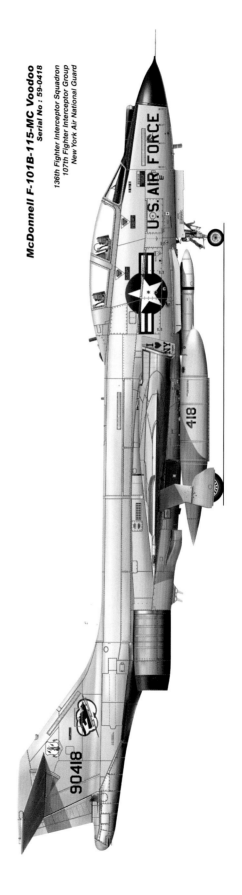

McDonnell F-101B-115-MC Voodoo
Serial No : 59-0418

136th Fighter Interceptor Squadron
107th Fighter Interceptor Group
New York Air National Guard

McDonnell CF-101B Voodoo
RCAF No : 17447
(Ex-USAF McDonnell F-101B-120-MC
USAF No: 59-0447)

No. 425 (Allouette) Squadron
Royal Canadian Air Force

ROYAL CANADIAN AIR FORCE

447O

17447

McDonnell CF-101B Voodoo
RCAF No : 17459
(Ex-USAF McDonnell F-101B-120-MC
USAF No: 59-0459)

No. 416 (Lynx) Squadron
Royal Canadian Air Force

ROYAL CANADIAN AIR FORCE

459O

17459

D I WINDLE 2006